DRAMA AT THE COURTS OF QUEEN HENRIETTA MARIA

Drama at the Courts of Queen Henrietta Maria considers Queen Henrietta Maria's patronage of drama in England in the light of her French heritage. Karen Britland challenges the common view of Henrietta Maria as a meddlesome and frivolous woman whose actions contributed to the outbreak of the English civil wars by showing how she was consistent in her allegiances to her family and friends, and how her cultural and political positions were reflected in the plays and court masques she sponsored. Unlike previous studies, this book considers the queen's upbringing at the French court and her later exile in France during the English civil wars, and is therefore able to challenge received notions about her activities in England during the 1630s. Karen Britland employs innovative research by combining discussions of literary texts with historical and archival research and discussions of art, architecture and music.

KAREN BRITLAND is a lecturer in Renaissance literature at Keele University. On the basis of the interdisciplinary and French-inflected nature of her work, she has been chosen by Gary Taylor as one of the six most exciting scholars working in the field of Renaissance drama. She is also an associate editor on *The Cambridge Edition of the Works of Ben Jonson.*

Figures

Acknowledgements

This book has been a very long time in the making and has amassed large debts along the way. Firstly, I owe a tremendous and unrepayable debt of gratitude to Martin Butler who saw me through my doctoral thesis on Henrietta Maria with much good humour, tolerance and sage advice. I am particularly grateful to him for his generosity in sharing his own ideas and work, and for his continued support over the years. I am also very grateful to my former colleagues at the University of Leeds, particularly to David Lindley and other regular participants in the Renaissance seminar: my work would be much the poorer without them. Julie Sanders and James Knowles have been pillars of sanity and guidance, particularly as this book was nearing completion. Both have been tremendously generous with their time and their own work. I hope I will have a chance to repay them.

I was fortunate to receive a Leverhulme Study-Abroad Studentship in 1998–9 which allowed me to undertake research in Paris. Many thanks go to the Leverhulme Trust, particularly to Jean Cater whose good humour and efficiency will go down in legend. Many thanks, too, to Professor Bernard Cottret for his warm welcome in France and for allowing me to attend his seminars at the Sorbonne.

My new colleagues at Keele have been tremendously welcoming and tolerant of a madwoman tearing her hair out over publishers' deadlines. Lucy Munro, especially, has been a source of inspiration and good practice, and Ann Hughes probably doesn't realise how helpful she was when I was tussling with chapter 6. I would also like to thank, in no particular order: Diane Purkiss, David Bevington, Ian Donaldson, Gary Taylor, Sophie Tomlinson, Clare McManus, Ian Atherton, Sarah Poynting, Marie-Claude Canova-Green, Lukas Erne, Tim Amos, Adam Smyth, Jerome de Groot, David Como, Katharine Craik, Orietta Da Rold, Sarah Graham, Eugene Giddens, Sarah Stanton and Caroline Bundy. Caroline Hibbard read several early drafts of my work and made invaluable comments. I also owe particular thanks to Victoria Cooper at Cambridge University Press who has been amazingly forbearing as I've been finishing this book.

This project would not have been completed without the support of my family. I would like to thank Ian, Sarah and Morgan for putting up with me without too many complaints. Most of all, though, I want to thank my parents, without whom I would never have been daft enough to do this in the first place. This book is dedicated to them.

Note on procedures

DATING

There were two calendars in use during the seventeenth century. Continental Europe used the Gregorian, or new style, system, while England maintained the Julian, or old style, and was thus ten days behind the rest of Europe. I have used Julian dating for English events, and, where necessary, have indicated both dates when discussing continental affairs. I have also taken January, rather than March, to be the beginning of the calendar year. Thus, for example, the performance of *Tempe Restored* is given as February 1632, rather than 1631/2.

EDITIONS

I have quoted Ben Jonson from Herford and Simpson's edition of his works (1925–52), and have preferred to quote Townshend, along with Davenant, from Orgel and Strong's convenient, *Inigo Jones: The Theatre of the Stuart Court* (1973).

Introduction

> No ambassador ever seemed to grasp the fact that Henrietta, who saw everything in terms of personalities, was simply not interested in affairs of state unless, of course, one of her friends happened to be involved.
>
> (Alison Plowden, *Henrietta Maria*, 2001)

The common perception of Henrietta Maria is one of an ignorant, political meddler, whose love of Catholic spectacle helped to provoke England to rise against its king. In Samuel R. Gardiner's massive *History of England*, for example, she is described as a woman who 'had nothing of statesmanship in her', and who wanted only 'to live the life of a gay butterfly passing lightly from flower to flower'.[1] Gardiner denigrates her political actions through his use of the loaded terms 'intrigues', 'contrivance' and 'feminine allurements', and remarks that the outbreak of the civil wars was 'so incomprehensible to her, that she was roused to mischievous activity by the extremity of her annoyance'.[2] His representation of Henrietta Maria effectively excludes her from serious politics because of her gender, and marks her as a frivolous woman whose nationality, religion and love of pleasure contributed to the downfall of the English king.

This view is not simply to be found in works from the nineteenth century. Alison Plowden's recent biography promotes a similar image of the queen consort, describing her as 'governed principally by her emotions' and 'heedless of the great political issues of the day'.[3] Citing selectively from the Venetian state papers, she builds up a picture of Henrietta Maria as politically ineffectual, manipulated by male advisers and controlled by her affections. Her book takes little notice of the notion of courtly faction, nor does it recognise the important role that noblewomen played in patronage and preferment at the early modern courts. Finally, her comment that 'no ambassador ever seemed to grasp the fact that Henrietta . . . was simply not interested in affairs of state' exposes a problem intrinsic to her interpretation – if ambassadors continuously expected the queen to involve herself in political affairs, is it then not possible that, to some extent, she did?[4]

By investigating the environment within which Henrietta Maria was raised and by detailing the cultural and political activities of her friends and family, most notably those of Marie de Médicis, her Florentine mother, I seek to counteract this image of the queen. In her world, ostentatious display was intricately bound up with political expression and she promoted a social fashion that drew on her French heritage and religion, maintaining throughout her life a lively interest in the affairs of her native country. Far from being a frivolous social butterfly, she corresponded with many of the major European statesmen of her age and was later to take up a position of adviser and financier to her husband in his efforts during the English civil wars.

This book takes a roughly chronological look at the entertainments associated with Henrietta Maria at the French, English and exiled royalist courts in order to plot the changes and development of her political activity and allegiances. I am particularly concerned to investigate how her productions reflected events on the continent, introducing a European dimension into discussions of the politics of court masque. Martin Butler has noted that Charles I's masques of the 1630s 'had very little to say about continental affairs'.[5] In contrast, I argue not only that the queen consort's personal iconography was strongly influenced by her earlier experiences at the Bourbon court, but that her English entertainments actively engaged with events in Europe. This work does not seek to offer a comprehensive historical analysis of Henrietta Maria's life as England's queen. Instead, it considers her court productions, suggesting that they should, at least in part, be read in the light of her national and familial concerns.

HENRIETTA MARIA'S CULTURAL HERITAGE

Born in 1609, Henrietta Maria was the youngest of the five surviving, legitimate children of Henri IV of France. She was sister to the future Louis XIII, who succeeded to the throne in 1610; to Elizabeth, who married the future Philip IV of Spain; to Christine, later duchess of Savoy; and to Gaston, duc d'Orléans. Her mother, Marie, was the daughter of Francesco de Médicis, late Grand Duke of Tuscany, and had married Henri IV after the 1599 annulment of his marriage to the childless Marguerite de Valois. Henrietta Maria maintained strong ties with her mother and Christine throughout her life, and was also closely associated with her brother Gaston.[6] Indeed, during her exile in France in the 1640s and 50s, she hoped to marry his daughter to her eldest son. Her links with her sister Elizabeth were less close, yet they wrote to each other occasionally, and, on at least one occasion, Henrietta Maria recommended a lady-in-waiting to her sister's court.[7]

The proliferation of common cultural images among the European courts was therefore not just the result of the mining of classical texts, nor of the foreign journeys undertaken by craftsmen such as Inigo Jones; it was aided by the marital exchange of royal women and by those women's continued patronage of the men and motifs familiar to them. For example, Marie de Médicis promoted ballets and plays at her court, calling a succession of Italian actors and artists to Paris, and, in 1609, collaborating in *Les Félicités de l'Age doré*, an entertainment to inaugurate the *salle de la fête* at the palais de l'Arsenal.[8] She also encouraged cultural interests in her offspring – all the royal children took part in French *ballet de cour*, and, in 1611, Princess Elizabeth was encouraged to stage a production of Robert Garnier's play, *Bradamante*. This interest in theatre was not deemed to be improper, nor was it inimical to devout feminine behaviour. Indeed, as Wendy Gibson has noted, the queen mother's 'enthusiasm for ballets was such that in 1612 she commanded the lords of her court to provide her with one every Sunday'.[9] As I will discuss, Marie's personal iconography, which specifically promoted women as peaceweavers as they moved between courts, made a virtue out of the itinerancy that was the royal woman's lot, situating the queen mother as central to a peaceful Europe and stressing her overwhelming importance as a mediator between monarchs who were also her relations.

Quite understandably, notable connections can be established between the artists employed by Marie de Médicis and those commissioned by Henrietta Maria. For example, in 1626, Orazio Gentileschi, the Tuscan painter, arrived in England with Marie's blessing.[10] Although he was in King Charles's pay, he was at first closely associated with the duke of Buckingham, and then, after Buckingham's death, was predominantly active for Henrietta Maria.[11] In the 1630s, the queen consort made a concerted effort to collect his paintings, particularly those with Biblical associations. She also gave him his largest commission in England when she engaged him to paint the ceiling of the Great Hall at her house in Greenwich.

Gentileschi's canvases for Greenwich House were completed by the time of his death in 1639 and figured an *Allegory of Peace and the Arts.*

Gabriele Finaldi has observed that all of the twenty-six figures represented on the ceiling were female, and remarks:

> This assemblage of iconographies suggests (I put it no more strongly) that the Great Hall may have been intended by the Queen as a sort of realm of womanly virtue at the heart of her 'House of Delight'.[12]

By creating a palace full of female-centred imagery, Henrietta Maria followed a tradition evoked by her mother at the palais de Luxembourg whose decorative themes also glorified women. For example, a series of eight sculptures of women were commissioned to adorn the Luxembourg's dome, while the walls and ceiling of Marie's bedchamber were decorated with a profusion of female allegorical figures that celebrated her success as a monarch.[13] In the case of both mother and daughter, the promotion of such imagery installed women as central to the nation's peace and prosperity, advocating feminine virtue as essential to the balanced governance of the realm.

Just as Marie de Médicis used designs that brought to mind her Florentine heritage, so Henrietta Maria surrounded herself with familiar motifs. Unlike James I's queen, Anna, whose upbringing in the cosmopolitan Danish court had exposed her to a variety of influences, Henrietta Maria actively sponsored art which emphasised her French background. This was not just an exercise in nostalgia, but a deliberate act of appropriation that distinguished her identity from that of her English husband. Henrietta Maria's evocations of her native land emphasised her status as the daughter of an important and civilised nation, demonstrating that England had much to gain from an appreciation of French design and behaviour.[14] In addition, her cultural patronage enabled her to maintain close links with her family, who supplied her with commodities from petticoats to fruit trees.

The exchange of artists and craftsmen between France and England was, of course, not a new phenomenon. At least seven French musicians were maintained in Anna of Denmark's household, playing at the late queen's funeral in 1619 before being granted passes to return to France. French dancing masters were also in demand at the Jacobean court: Jacques Cordier (known as Bocan), a celebrated dancer and violinist, was a member of Prince Henry's household in 1608 and appears to have remained in England until 1614 when his name disappears from exemption lists.[15] Peter Walls has noted that he was living in Paris between 1622 and 1625 when three of his children were baptised.[16] What Walls does not mention is that, at precisely this time, Bocan was listed as 'maistre de dance' in the household lists of Henrietta Maria.[17] In 1625, he returned to England, probably as a member of the queen consort's wedding party, and received a gift of £500, procured for him by the duke of Buckingham. He seems to have been in England periodically throughout the 1630s, receiving a payment of £60 from Henrietta Maria in 1630 and two from Charles in 1633 and 1634 respectively.[18] While his activity at the Caroline court cannot be attributed especially to the influence of the queen consort, it demonstrates a receptivity to French fashion that her presence helped to facilitate and which she was concerned to promote. It also indicates that, on the level of dancing at least, Charles and Henrietta Maria shared a common training and a common repertoire.

Sebastian La Pierre, another French dancing master, was also employed in England, starting his career in 1611 as the instructor of Charles, Prince of Wales, before, in 1625, transferring to the household of Henrietta Maria. A Guillaume La Pierre, possibly his son, was later employed as dancing instructor to the royal children, Charles and Mary, demonstrating the court's continued preference for French fashions in dancing.[19] The Frenchmen Bartholomew Montagu and Nicolas Picard were also members of Henrietta Maria's early entourage and were named in her household lists as dancers. Montagu danced in an anti-masque entry in *Luminalia*, the queen's masque of 1638, while Picard seems to have had the specific charge of training Henrietta Maria's maids of honour.[20] These French influences had a palpable effect upon the Caroline masque form which, under Henrietta Maria's patronage, saw a marked movement towards the style of French *ballet de cour*.[21]

Henrietta Maria's preference for French cultural forms also extended to her taste in music. She arrived in England accompanied by about a dozen French musicians, many of whom had previously served Anna of Denmark. These men's expertise, like that of the dancing masters, was inevitably employed in the service of Caroline court masques. Louis Richard, her master of music and one of Anna's former servants, composed the music for *Britannia Triumphans* (1638) and *Salmacida Spolia* (1640), while the talents of her harpist, La Flelle, were used in *The Temple of Love* (1635).[22] In addition, 'the more to please her M[ajest]ty', four of the queen consort's French musicians were invited to play in the Inns of Court masque, *The Triumph of Peace* (1634).[23] Indeed, nowhere is the queen consort's preference for French music more apparent than in an anecdote recounted by Bulstrode Whitelock, one of *The Triumph of Peace*'s organisers. After showing Henrietta Maria a coranto he had composed, Whitelock reported that she expressed surprise that it had been written by an Englishman 'bicause she said it was fuller of life and spirit than the English aiers use to be'.[24] Her patronage of French musicians can, therefore, be attributed to conscious choice and aesthetic preference, rather than to a bland mimicry of French fashion.

Interestingly, Henrietta Maria did not only patronise male musicians. Payments were made from 1637 onwards to a Margaret Prevost, the widow of Camille Prevost, one of the French musicians inherited by Henrietta Maria from Anna of Denmark. It is possible that this amounted to nothing more than a widow's pension, yet, during the interregnum, a specific payment of £10 was made from the queen consort's coffers to 'Margaret Provoe, servant to the late Queen in the Musick', indicating that she probably had a musical function in her own right.[25] However, Henrietta Maria's most notable contribution to musical patronage must be her promotion of female singers in the court masque. As I will discuss in chapter 5, it was in her production of *Tempe Restored* that Madame Coniack and Mistress Shepherd became the first named women to sing upon the English court stage. Even more notably, Henrietta Maria, herself, became the first recorded English queen to take a speaking and singing role in a dramatic production.

CATHOLICISM, NEO-PLATONISM AND PRÉCIOSITÉ

The preferred form of Catholicism practised at Marie de Médicis's court was pioneered by prelates such as St François de Sales, Pierre de Bérulle and Jacques-Davy du Perron. Marie patronised the Carmelite order of nuns introduced into France by Bérulle in 1602, and also supported the congregation of the Oratory that he founded in 1611. Significantly, when Henrietta Maria left for England in 1625, she was accompanied not only by a complement of Oratorian priests who were intended to serve in her chapel, but by Bérulle himself, who had been involved in the marriage negotiations and was to serve as her confessor. She was also presented with a farewell letter written by her mother and expanded by Bérulle which set out the behaviour expected of her as the Catholic wife of an apostate king. The message of this letter, together with the imagery deployed during her Parisian wedding, foreground the issues that would preoccupy her married life and consequently deserve investigation.

The letter exists in two versions, the shorter of which might well have been entirely written by Marie de Médicis and which is preserved in a manuscript draft under the title 'Instruction de la Reine Marie de medicis – a la Reine dangleterre sa fille marie-anriette de France 15 juin 1625'.[26]

The longer version, entitled, 'Instructions données par Marie de Médicis à sa fille Henriette de France, Reyne d'Angleterre', was transcribed in 1694 by Charles Cotolendi with the significant observation that the original was held in Henrietta Maria's convent at Chaillot (founded in 1651).[27] That the letter remained in the queen consort's care for more than twenty-five years emphasises the importance she placed upon it and perhaps supports the contention that it was strongly associated with her mother.

The shorter version is affectionate and declares itself to be written by Marie de Médicis in her own hand 'affin qu'il vous soit plus cher' [so that it will be dearer to you].[28] It reminds the new queen to be grateful for the privileges given to her by God and tells her to remember that she has been placed on earth for the sake of heaven. While exhorting Henrietta Maria to be diligent in her faith and not to shirk her religious observances, it does not overtly encourage her to proselytise. However, the longer version, which opens in an exact duplication of the former, continues in a more didactic strain. Henrietta Maria is urged to remain faithful to her religion and is exhorted to protect the English Catholics. Indeed, she is named their Esther 'qui eut cette grace de Dieu d'estre la déffense et la délivrance de son peuple' [who had this grace from God to be the defender and deliverer of her people].[29] Furthermore, although she is enjoined to be obedient to her husband, she is also encouraged to pray for him to be drawn to the true faith, and is exhorted to be charitable towards Protestants so that, by her example, she may lead them to convert.[30] In other words, while it is an overtly religious document, the letter also functions as a conduct manual, emphasising the behaviour appropriate for a Catholic queen. It gives Henrietta Maria a socio-religious role at the English court, encouraging her to lead by her good example in order to draw her subjects back to the old faith.

The expectation that she would take an active role at court was therefore incumbent upon the new English queen consort from the start. It is not enough, then, to mine her dramatic productions for signs of some sort of emergent female agency, or for a proto-feminist engagement with the issue of female voice. As Alison Shell has noted, the imagery of 'feminised religious love' found in the queen consort's entertainments 'is consistent with St Paul's injunction that wives professing the true faith and married to unbelieving husbands should use indirect means to convert them'.[31] 'To call this feminist is misleading', she says, although it does count 'among the incentives that prompted early modern women towards finding a voice'.[32] If Henrietta Maria's iconography was femino-centric, it was less because she was fighting the good fight for her sisters than because she was actively promoting her role as an exemplary Catholic princess in an apostate land.

Henrietta Maria was, furthermore, descended from a number of former queens consort and queens regent, numbering among her ancestors not only the powerful women of the Médicis family, but also her father's famous relatives, Jeanne d'Albret and Marguerite de Navarre. Although the example she set at the English court might well have inspired other less privileged women towards cultural creativity, she can hardly be deemed to have been struggling for role models herself. Indeed, her French wedding entertainments made a point of drawing analogies with other French princesses who had become queens of England, providing her with examples of active, effective and pious women and thus situating expectations about her own activities within a framework of previous female action.[33]

For example, in Amiens, on her way to the coast, Henrietta Maria was presented with a series of pageants, composed, as the French newsbook, the *Mercure François*, reported, in seven pieces like the seven wonders of the world.[34] The seventh and last pageant depicted five French princesses who had become queens of England, and who were each supposed to be the incarnation of a particular virtue. The first – Adilberge, who had converted her husband, King Ethelbert of Kent – represented Faith and Religion. She carried a sun in her hand, and declared to Henrietta Maria:

> J'estois fille de France espouse d'un grand Roy
> A qui j'ay fait cognoistre un seul Dieu qu'on adore:
> Je n'ay que commencé faisant comme l'Aurore
> Qui vous ay attiré vray Soleil de la Foy.[35]
>
> [I was a daughter of France and the wife of a great king
> To whom I made known a single God who is adored:
> I only began, acting like the Dawn,
> Which has drawn you, true Sun of the Faith.]

It is significant that the first queen to speak expressed a proselytising agenda. Her verses drew together a series of solar references from the previous six pageants, making the whole entertainment redolent of a conversionary programme that would see England returned to the true faith through the ministrations of its new queen. The imagery of light, so prevalent in English and French encomia to Henrietta Maria and so compatible with the tenets of neo-Platonism, was given a specifically Catholic gloss that was subsequently compounded by the virtues of Clemency, Humility, Prudence and Constancy incarnated in the other four queens.[36] These commendable Christian virtues were thus offered to Henrietta Maria as examples of the conduct that would draw the English nation back to Rome.

The letters and entertainments impressed upon her on her way to England therefore emphasised the importance of her conversionary mission, informing her that her marriage had been ordained by God to bring relief to suffering English Catholics and to save Protestant heretics by showing them the way to the true faith. They are significant for they are early manifestations of a vocabulary that can be identified throughout the queen consort's entertainments of the 1630s and beyond. Henrietta Maria arrived in England already associated with beauty, love and light, attributes that would be exploited in the development of her so-called neo-Platonic love cult. Most importantly, the image of light was glossed in the Amiens entries as the light of faith, locating Henrietta Maria as the purveyor of religious illumination in Britain. Erica Veevers does not make this connection in her work until she discusses the queen consort's 1638 production of *Luminalia*, yet the idea of Henrietta Maria as the divinely ordained saviour of Catholicism is explicit in French texts from the mid 1620s, and, as I will discuss, can even be perceived in *Artenice*, her first dramatic production on the English court stage.[37]

*

Veevers's study of Henrietta Maria's neo-Platonism and its resonances with Catholicism is superb. She argues that the queen consort's masques may have been an opportunity to show 'that she was active in the interests of Catholicism, and that her sponsorship of Platonic love was a means by which her religion was made acceptable at court', and, through readings of *The Temple of Love* (1635) and *Luminalia* (1638), makes a convincing case for the 'Catholic slant' of the queen's masques.[38] What arises from her study is the suggestion that these masques could be used to promote an agenda that differed, at least on the subject of religion, from that of the king. She also successfully renovates the older idea that Henrietta Maria's masques and their neo-Platonism were frivolous and facile.

To contextualise this neo-Platonic fashion, Veevers discusses the social trends and religious enthusiasms of the France of Henrietta Maria's youth, and summarises modern critical attitudes towards her drama. 'Most critics', she says, 'have distinguished different degrees of seriousness with which the fashion for Platonic love was taken at the English court, but they have not agreed about the seriousness with which it was taken by the

Queen.'[39] These differences of opinion, she notes, 'have arisen partly through the failure to distinguish between different phases of *préciosité* in France, and to determine exactly which phase was adopted by the Queen at the time when she came to have a decisive influence at court'.[40] Henrietta Maria's neo-Platonism, she suggests, was influenced by *honnêteté*, a standard of virtuous yet civilised behaviour advocated in France for both men and women.[41] Such *honnêteté* was in turn derived from the 'Devout Humanism' taught by St François de Sales and promoted in texts such as Honoré d'Urfé's *L'Astrée* which 'drew on the attractions of the romance to help popularise the ideals of religion'.[42]

Her analysis of St François de Sales's theology and of the development of *honnêteté* is subtle and thorough, and provides a firm basis for her discussion of the queen consort's theatrical productions. Nonetheless, it introduces a false distinction into her portrayal of Caroline neo-Platonism because of its use of problematic descriptive categories. The queen, Veevers asserts, was not 'a typically sophisticated *précieuse* of the Parisian *salons*' and favoured 'a side of the fashion that had more in common with the concept of *honnêteté* than with the exaggerated woman-worship of the romances'.[43] However, she suggests (paraphrasing J. B. Fletcher) that Lady Carlisle, one of Henrietta Maria's early English companions, was 'the typical "salon" *précieuse*: the beauty who dispenses her beneficent influence to a *coterie* of admirers, who in turn immortalize her in verse'.[44]

Veevers is correct to note that Caroline neo-Platonism was not a static phenomenon and her analysis of the queen consort's fashion is well developed. However, the distinction she makes between this and Lady Carlisle's activities is open to reinterpretation. Firstly, although she acknowledges that 'the term *préciosité* and its derivatives did not come into use . . . until about the middle of the seventeenth century', she projects it unproblematically on to the 1620s and 30s, asserting that 'the word will be used without the value judgments (of affectation, over-refinement of manners and language, or even of "advanced" views on morals) which have been imposed on it by its development later in the century'.[45] Nevertheless, Domna Stanton has shown that the concept of *préciosité* was conceived initially as a derogatory term for women by men. 'The only reality that can be claimed for the *précieuse*,' Stanton says, 'is her representation in a body of mid-seventeenth century texts which are designed to chastize her pervasive faults.'[46] Stanton characterises the *précieuse* as the negative pole of the *honnête* woman who, instead of helping society by promoting politeness and chaste conversation, transgresses social norms through her ambition and pride.[47] Veevers's portrait of Lady Carlisle participates in this notion despite her avowal that the term will be used without 'value judgments', and replicates the distinction between the *honnête femme* (Henrietta Maria) and the *précieuse* (Carlisle). Furthermore, her analysis reproduces stereotypical ideas about the queen consort and the countess in a manner that takes into account neither social status nor historical bias.

According to Veevers, Henrietta Maria lacked 'the sophistication that could turn love into a game' and was 'far more affectionate and demonstrative than the cold-hearted shepherdesses of the romances'.[48] Carlisle, on the other hand, took 'an intellectual rather than an emotional attitude towards love' and 'was constantly at the centre of intrigue'.[49] Henrietta Maria has gone down in history as an under-educated and frivolous woman governed by her emotions, while Lady Carlisle has been castigated as a woman whose 'wanton fascination and heartless treachery wrought evil widely'.[50] Veevers's analysis of their two characters is infected by these stereotypes and has led to a distinction between types of Caroline neo-Platonism that is problematic, but which has been accepted and perpetuated.[51]

Veevers concludes her argument for Carlisle's *préciosité* by commenting that 'after the Civil War when both Lady Carlisle and the Queen were in France, Lady Carlisle became a member of the fashionable Parisian *salons* ... whereas Henrietta ... founded a convent'.[52] Her evidence for this is Carolyn Lougee's work which, drawing on Antoine Baudeau de Somaize's *Grand Dictionnaire des pretieuses*, catalogues the *précieuses* in the Parisian *salons* and identifies a certain 'Madame de Carly' as 'Lucy Percy, married in 1617 to James Hay I, Earl of Carlisle'.[53] Veevers seems to have extrapolated from this that Lucy Hay was resident in France during the Stuart exile and that she attended the Parisian *salons*. However, Somaize's *Dictionnaire* terms 'Madame de Carly' an 'ancienne pretieuse, qui fleurissoit du temps de Valère'.[54] Valère is the *Dictionnaire*'s name for Vincent Voiture, a poet associated with Madame de Rambouillet's *salon* in the 1630s. Voiture died in 1648, at a time when it is easy to prove that Lucy Hay was still resident in England for she was involved in the abortive royalist plot of that year and was committed briefly to the Tower in March 1649. I therefore believe that Lucy Hay owes her inclusion in the *Dictionnaire* to the fact that she was admired by Voiture when he visited England in November 1633: she was never associated with the poet in Paris, nor did she have anything more than a tangential connection with the Parisian *salons*.[55]

In contrast, Henrietta Maria certainly had *salon* contacts, and, as I will discuss in my concluding chapter, attended her niece Mademoiselle de Montpensier's famous gatherings during the 1650s. Veevers creates a false notion of the Parisian *salons* which denies the variety and versatility of these fashionable centres and is hampered by a need to categorise their culture as 'sophisticated' and 'intellectual', in opposition to the more spiritual *honnête préciosité* she says was favoured by the queen consort. A glance at Somaize's *Dictionnaire*, though, reveals that religious devotion and *salon* life were not mutually exclusive.

The *Dictionnaire* contains several references to nuns or former nuns who were also *salon* members, generally terming such women 'prestresse[s] de Diane' or 'vestales'.[56] On some occasions, as was the case with a certain Mademoiselle La Chesnais and her sister, the *Dictionnaire* describes women forsaking their convents to enter 'le grand monde'.[57] Other women, though, appear to have been able to combine a *salon* life with that of the convent; for example, the *Dictionnaire* describes the convent of the 'prestresse' 'Dinocris' as one of the most frequented places in its area because of its mistress's 'feu', 'esprit' and 'conversation'.[58] Mary M. Rowan has remarked that the relations between *salon* and convent have never been studied by critics and begins to address the problem through her work on the Benedictine abbess Marie-Eléonore de Rohan.[59] Her investigation into Rohan's life shows that religious devotion and *salon* conversation were not inimical, and also makes clear that there was a certain crossover between so-called 'aristocratic' and 'bourgeois' *salon* gatherings.[60] Veevers's formulation of Henrietta Maria's neo-Platonic fashion, while accurate in its assertion that it was influenced more by Marie de Médicis's religious enthusiasms than by the concerns of Madame de Rambouillet's *salon*, is therefore a little too black and white.

In addition, studies of Madame de Rambouillet's *chambre bleue salon* have sparked an unhelpful critical trend that represents Parisian *salon* culture in opposition to the court. Rambouillet, it is argued, rejected the coarse pastimes of hunting and feasting favoured by Henri IV, preferring instead to promote refinement and civil conversation at her Parisian home. Although this might be an accurate representation of Rambouillet's own motives, it by no means covers the whole range of *salon* behaviours in the early 1600s, nor does it take into account the way personnel moved between different social locations.[61] It is also not an entirely accurate representation of the Rambouillet *salon* itself which, for example, was visited by Gaston d'Orléans, as well as by the duke of Buckingham. Julie Lucie d'Angennes, Rambouillet's daughter, became one of the French Queen Anne's *dames d'honneur* and danced at court in the poet Boisrobert's *Nymphes Bocagères de la Forêt Sacrée* (1627) and in Mademoiselle de Montpensier's *Le Triomphe de Beauté* at Saint Germain.[62] Boisrobert himself, as I will discuss, attended evenings at the *chambre bleue*, but was also patronised by Marie de Médicis, the duchess of Chevreuse and Richelieu. Therefore, although Rambouillet's own preferences can perhaps be distinguished from the devout neo-Platonism practised by Henrietta Maria and her mother, it must be remembered that poets, and even Rambouillet's daughter and Marie de Médicis's son, moved between the *salon* and the court in a manner that precipitated the cross-fertilisation of imagery and ideas.

Instead of following Veevers and identifying Lady Carlisle as a 'typical "salon" *précieuse*', I would therefore like to suggest that she differed from Henrietta Maria in social rank, religion and nationality, and that the tone of the work addressed to her takes this into account. Fashionable *salon* ideas obviously influenced the behaviour of both women but, while it is unthinkable that a poet would praise the queen consort in the *risqué* terms used sometimes of Carlisle, this is not necessarily an indication of the countess's more worldly or intellectual values. Rather, it is a symptom of her lower status at court and the fact that she was an easier target for prurient speculation. The countess certainly did have a circle of gallant admirers, but then so did the queen, whose predilection for male company was noted as early as 1628, and whose preference for young gallants directly influenced George Conn's appointment as papal legate.[63] There is a strong crossover in the imagery and vocabulary used of the two women, both of whose social positions led to the fusing of *salon* ideas with an extant English tradition. To conclude, I would like to stress that the anachronistic terms *préciosité* and *précieuse* will not be found in my account of Henrietta Maria's fashion because they carry with them unhelpful associations that it is this study's intention to call into question.

*

As the daughter of a French queen regent and as the wife and sister of monarchs, Henrietta Maria had an important role to play in both European culture and politics. The initial chapters of this book trace the imagery associated with her in France, showing how it influenced her early theatrical productions at the Caroline court. In addition, plotting the queen consort's problematic relationship with Buckingham, they also discuss how members of her French entourage nevertheless reached an accommodation with him that would affect her political affiliations throughout the 1630s. Chapters 4, 5 and 6 investigate the early years of that decade, demonstrating how Henrietta Maria's court entertainments shadowed continental current affairs and discussing her involvement in an international plot that sought to overthrow the chief ministers of both France and England. The later chapters investigate her position after the collapse of this plot, focusing on the ways in which her Catholicism was reflected in her court productions and discussing her continuing role as a mediator between her mother and Richelieu. Finally, chapter 10 investigates the queen consort's position during the civil wars, showing how she continued to exploit theatrical display for political ends and discussing how royalist identities were constructed out of earlier Caroline texts and influences.

Woven throughout this book is a consideration of Henrietta Maria's influence on female cultural production, interpreted not as a proto-feminist struggle for the rights of female public speech, but as an aspect of the queen consort's religious and social project. This said, her vocal participation in court theatricals has been largely credited as paving the way for the appearance of actresses at the Restoration and her neo-Platonic fashion certainly had a palpable effect upon popular and closet drama in the 1630s.[64]

Popular history might conceive of Henrietta Maria's theatrical interests as frivolous and facile, yet her productions should not be looked upon as the pale reflections of the monarch's will. They deployed an idiom that emphasised her status as a queen of England and a princess of France, synthesising English and French imagery into an iconography that was all her own. When she returned to her homeland during the English civil wars, she was returning to the land that had nursed her taste for theatre. Nonetheless, it was a place that encapsulated all her enemies hated about her: she was French, she was Catholic and she was a woman who acted in irrelevant plays. The image we have of her is one that has largely been influenced by this view and ultimately it is the victor's vision. In what follows, I hope somewhat to redress the balance.

CHAPTER I

Sex and dancing: Henrietta Maria's wedding ballets

On the first evening that Henrietta Maria spent with her new husband in Dover, the court entertained itself with dancing. Writing to Louis XIII about this event, George Villiers, the duke of Buckingham, explained candidly that 'le Roy s'est fort bien acquitté, com*me* ne [*sic*] Ie ne doubte pas qu'il n'aye faict la nuict passée' [The king acquitted himself well, as I don't doubt he did last night].[1] The new queen consort, though, did not dance, but was later seen by the king 'par vn pertuit' [through a hole], dancing a *sarabande* in her chamber 'et faisant en secret ce qu'elle n'a pas voulu en public' [and doing in secret what she did not want to do in public].[2] Buckingham presents her activity to Louis XIII as an illustration of her continuing good health, concluding the first draft of his letter with an oblique promise that the French king will soon hear good results of the marriage.

This letter opens up several important issues. The first is an equation between the physical activity of dancing and that of health, particularly sexual health. John Drakakis has explored the significance of dancing in early modern plays and has remarked that it carried an erotic freight that caused concern to antitheatricalists.[3] In the case of Buckingham's letter, the king's facility in dancing is an indication of his eagerness and virility as a husband and bodes well for the generation of royal offspring. Rather than being a problematic display of sexuality, it is entirely appropriate to his duties as a husband and a monarch. The new queen consort's reluctance to join her husband in the dance is therefore significant. In the first draft of his letter, written before Henrietta Maria had been observed secretly dancing in her room, Buckingham attributed this reluctance to a slight malaise, noting, though, that her complexion was as good as ever, 'qui me fait esperer qu'elle s'en portera mieux'.[4] In the second draft of this paragraph, written after Charles had spied on her, the duke noted instead that she was not ill and attributed her reluctance to a desire not to dance in public. In both cases, his language is neutral and does not indicate any positive displeasure with the queen. However, it is perhaps noteworthy that his second draft concludes with the phrase: 'I'espere que Votre Maiestie ne trouuera mauuaises les nouuelles que cy apres luy en mandera' [I hope your majesty will not find the news that will be sent to him hereafter unpleasant]. On one level, this is no more than a rather coy promise to Louis XIII of an imminent pregnancy. However, taken as a literal statement rather than as an example of courtly circumlocution, it also indicates anxiety, and perhaps a warning, about the queen consort's behaviour. Although the first of these interpretations might have been more properly meant, the second, it would turn out, was more prophetic. Within days, serious disagreements would break out between the new queen's household and the king's, leading to many letters of complaint and bad news crossing the Channel.

Buckingham's letter also draws attention to an important aspect of courtly dancing when it notes that Henrietta Maria performed 'en secret' what she did not want to do 'en public'. Although the occasion of the 'petit balet' was intimate, the duke still regards it as a public event, and Henrietta Maria, in refusing to participate, makes an equally public statement. A distinction certainly needs to be drawn between an elaborately public court masque held in the Banqueting House at Whitehall and an impromptu evening dance witnessed only by the monarch's immediate household. However, both can have equally forceful implications, and both can be disseminated to a much wider audience than the original spectators.[5] Indeed, Joan Landes has suggested, drawing on the work of Jürgen Habermas, that an early modern monarch could only ever perform in public. As God's anointed he showed himself constantly to be the embodiment of an ever-present divine power; his actions and the actions of his nobles were publicly available to, and had public consequences for, the entire nation.[6] Henrietta Maria's decision to participate in a 'secret' dance in her chamber shows her reluctance to take part in the performative display of Charles's court, immediately setting her and her French attendants apart from the English.[7] That Buckingham chooses to term this event secret rather than private is revealing, indicating as it does not an excess of modesty on the part of the new queen, but an act of deliberate concealment.

However, Buckingham's letter reappropriates this dance for the king's pleasure in a voyeuristic manner that resounds with previous historical events. In 1623, on his way to Spain to woo the Spanish infanta, Charles, incognito in a large periwig, attended a rehearsal for Anne of Austria's *Grand Ballet de la reyne représentant les Festes de Junon la nopcière* and watched Henrietta Maria perform the role of Iris. As I have discussed elsewhere, this event was seized on by panegyrists who maintained that the Spanish match had broken down because Charles became infatuated after seeing Henrietta Maria dance.[8] In 1625, he was again placed in a voyeuristic position, secretly watching his new wife's display of dancing.[9] Both Buckingham's letter and the panegyrists' verses reinforce the seductive nature of dance, particularly when it is observed without the participants' knowledge. In her refusal to dance, Henrietta Maria not only denied the court the pleasure of assessing her physical attributes, but effectively refused to accept her symbolic place within the court's sexual economy. Buckingham's letter makes a definite equation between dancing and procreation, and shows that the king nevertheless succeeded in being entertained, and even titillated, by his new wife.

The prevalence of moments like this in records from the period demonstrates the significance of dancing and theatre to the early modern courts. Rather than being an ephemeral form, court entertainments could serve a useful political function, not only as a means of promoting a particular royal agenda, but as a way of signalling the existence of a faction or of criticising the monarch's policies. Martin Butler, for example, has discussed how the presence at the Jacobean court of 'royal powerbrokers' such as Queen Anna or Prince Henry,

> meant that James's authority was never an uncontested monopoly but was constantly in balance, constantly being renegotiated with figures who had their own advisors, clients and followers, and who exerted significant sovereign pressures of their own.[10]

If the Stuart court is imagined to be an arena in which, in Butler's words, 'powerful individuals contended for prestige and influence', then the court entertainment can legitimately be seen to have performed functions 'such as negotiating or mediating between different interest groups . . . or of promoting the rival views on policy which were constantly in competition'.[11] This notion of factional politics allows for fluidity of debate within an establishment that tolerated a range of political positions, and complicates the idea that the Caroline court was entirely narcissistic and inward-looking. Such productions could be used not only for casual entertainment, but also to promote a particular political agenda and, as such, were an indispensable part of court life right across Europe.

The new queen consort's refusal to dance with the English on her arrival in her new country must therefore be interpreted as an act of deliberate resistance that would be echoed in the following months by further refusals to participate in significant moments of Caroline display. Interestingly, Clare McManus has documented similar instances of resistance in the behaviour of Charles I's mother, Anna of Denmark, who, like Henrietta Maria, did not fully participate in the rituals of her husband's Protestant coronation. McManus notes, particularly, that Anna's refusal to take the sacrament 'was above all a display of her difference from the English'.[12] This, I would argue, is precisely the interpretation that should be applied to Henrietta Maria's self-imposed exclusion from the court's dancing at Dover, an interpretation compounded by her subsequent 'secret' dance with her French attendants.

The *sarabande* has been described by Skiles Howard as a dance that 'confirmed a preoccupation with foreign exoticism and strange encounters'.[13] Supposedly invented by the Saracens, it was a 'sinuous, gliding dance accompanied by guitar and castanets' that was so in vogue on both sides of the Channel that 'even little children ... knew it'.[14] Henrietta Maria's performance of this dance with her French attendants, to the exclusion of the English, literally stamped her mark upon English soil. Rather than taking up a deferential position in a dance with Englishmen and therefore becoming the marker of an exotic import ripe for appropriation, she maintained the imperial position marked out in her French wedding ballets. Instead of taking up the feminised position of a land that should be conquered, she danced her own experience of an encounter with foreign exoticism.[15]

It cannot be argued that the new queen consort was so young at the time of her marriage that she was incapable of making politically motivated decisions. As I have discussed, her mission in England was forcefully impressed upon her before her departure from France and she cannot have failed to have understood the significance of her position. Furthermore, she was accompanied by trusted attendants, many of whom had been in her service for some years. Just as her new husband made decisions about protocol only after consultation with his advisers, so, it must be assumed, did Henrietta Maria. Her refusal to dance must therefore be seen as a calculated decision taken by the new queen consort in conjunction with her officials. It demonstrates that moments of cultural exchange between the two courts could be exploited for political ends, and shows the importance for court culture of noblewomen's acquiescence in such accepted forms of public display. Indeed, McManus has noted that,

The necessary presence of royal and aristocratic women in court performance allowed the space for the self-representation of that elite community to be questioned through, among other tactics, the public refusal to perform as one should or . . . the refusal to perform at all.[16]

Henrietta Maria's refusal to dance with the English demonstrated her reluctance to move from the performative economy of the French court into that of the English, and allowed her to maintain an identity distinct from that of her new husband; that is, as a Frenchwoman, a Catholic and a chaste princess.

These aspects of her identity had been at the forefront of the elaborate celebrations performed in France both before and after the wedding. In what follows, I will briefly describe the likely chronology of these French entertainments which were interrupted by the unexpected demise of James I. Then, by comparing them with similar English productions, I will attempt to shed light on Henrietta Maria's early reluctance to participate in public Caroline displays.

BALLET FRAGMENTS

The Anglo-French marriage treaty was signed in Paris in November 1624, and celebrated a few days later with fireworks and ballets at the Louvre. The next month, it was ratified in London by the English parliament although the festivities prepared for this occasion were cancelled because of King James's ill health. Most notably, as Marie-Claude Canova-Green has pointed out, Buckingham commissioned a masque from Sir John Beaumont, entitled *The Theater of Apollo*, which was intended to present an image of James I raised on a throne above his children Charles and Elizabeth, themselves seated in chariots drawn by Fame and Peace.[17] In the following year, on both sides of the sea, court entertainments were performed in anticipation of the marriage. Prince Charles's Jonsonian masque, *The Fortunate Isles and Their Union*, took place at Whitehall on 9 January, and would later be drawn upon by French commentators who exploited its imagery to represent the English.[18] In France, Louis XIII performed in the *Ballet des Fées des Forêts de Saint-Germain*, which Canova-Green has suggested was also part of the marriage festivities.[19] Certainly, the English wooing ambassadors, Henry Rich (now earl of Holland) and James Hay, earl of Carlisle, remained in France at this time and are likely to have been present at the performance.

The official wedding ceremony took place at Notre Dame on 1/11 May, and was supposed to be followed by a ballet danced by the French queen which appears to have been in preparation at least from the previous December.[20] However, out of respect for the death of James I, this and other entertainments were cancelled.[21] After the arrival of Buckingham on 14/24 May, though, festivities were renewed and a spectacular collation and firework display was provided for him at the palais de Luxembourg. Although Cardinal Richelieu linked his name to this event, it is probable that the French queen mother was its chief patron for it took place at her main Parisian residence.[22] Indeed, Deborah Marrow has noted that Marie was eager for Rubens's great commission of paintings depicting her life to be installed in the palace before the wedding, so it is more than likely that she played a role in hosting the celebration which took place under her roof.[23]

The texts of both Jonson's *The Fortunate Isles* and Beaumont's *Theater of Apollo* are extant, as are the French verses for the *Ballet des Fées des Forêts de Saint-Germain.* However, we do not have a printed text of the November 1624 betrothal ballets, nor of Anne of Austria's unperformed wedding entertainment. Canova-Green has, nevertheless, pointed out that fragments remain of two celebrations written for the Anglo-French marriage, one of which seems to have been entitled *Les Dieux descendus en France* (or *en Terre*), and the other the *Ballet de la Reyne d'Angleterre.* She associates the first ballet with the celebrations that took place after the signing of the wedding treaty in November 1624, and the second with the cancelled production prepared by Queen Anne. These were certainly occasions on which ballets were intended to take place, yet I am not at all certain, particularly in the case of *Les Dieux descendus,* that the textual fragments that remain can be unproblematically associated with them.

The *Ballet de la Reyne d'Angleterre* is undoubtedly the more significant of these two productions because, for the first time ever in a French court entertainment, Henrietta Maria was intended to take the principal role. The extant verses were written by François le Metel, sieur de Boisrobert, and by Claude Malleville, both of whom were well-known poets. Boisrobert had originally been in the service of Marie de Médicis, and was also favoured by Richelieu. In 1623, he was commissioned by Louis XIII to compose the *Ballet des Bacchanales* in collaboration with several other writers, and, in the same year, he joined with René Bordier, already an established ballet poet, to compose *Le Grand Ballet de la Reyne représentant les Festes de Junon la nopcière* which was danced by Anne of Austria. In 1624, he achieved great favour with Richelieu, and also courted the patronage of the duchesse de Chevreuse, a friend of the French queen's and the widow of Louis XIII's late favourite, the duc de Luynes.

Boisrobert was subsequently selected to travel to England with Henrietta Maria in the entourage of the duchesse and her second husband, Claude de Lorraine, duc de Chevreuse.[24] He was four years older than Malleville, one of the maréchal de Bassompierre's secretaries, known for his elegant verses and romances. Malleville, like Boisrobert, had access to all the Parisian *salons* and, in 1634, again like Boisrobert, would become a founder member of the Académie française. Both writers had, moreover, worked together before when they contributed verses to the *Ballet des Voleurs*, Louis XIII's shrovetide entertainment of February 1624.

Emile Magne, Boisrobert's twentieth-century biographer, has contended that the *Ballet de la Reyne d'Angleterre* was not performed in France at all, but was danced by Henrietta Maria in front of the English nobility.[25] As I will discuss, the new queen consort did sponsor a ballet very soon after her arrival in England. However, internal evidence in Malleville's verses for the *Ballet de la Reyne d'Angleterre* indicates that this production took place before she arrived in her new country. Most significantly, the goddess Diana is given lines whose future tenses indicate that the sea crossing to England has yet to take place: 'Ie veux l'accompagner en cet heureux passage' [I wish to accompany her on this happy crossing], Diana says, 'Et faire que l'orage / Respecte ses Vaisseaux' [And ensure that the storm / Respects her ships].[26] Furthermore, unlike Boisrobert, Malleville did not travel with Henrietta Maria to England, making it more likely that his verses were a contribution to a production intended for France.[27]

Boisrobert's extant contribution to the *Ballet de la Reyne d'Angleterre* comprises three sets of verses, two of which were intended to accompany Henrietta Maria's entry. These were the stanzas 'Pour la Reine d'Angleterre, representant Junon. Au Roy', 'Pour la Reine d'Angleterre, representant Junon qui meine les Nymphes de l'aire. A la Reine sa Mere' and the 'Recit de Galathee au balet de la Reyne d'Angleterre'. Malleville's single extant contribution is the long poem, 'Vers presentez par Diane a la Reyne Mere du Roy, pour le Balet de la Reyne d'Angleterre'. From these it may be deduced that the production was intended to be performed before both Louis XIII and the queen mother, and presented Henrietta Maria in the principal role of Juno. It is also likely, given the ballet's title, that it was scheduled for performance after the marriage ceremony.

In Boisrobert's 1623 ballet for Queen Anne, Henrietta Maria's sister-in-law took the principal role of Juno, while Henrietta Maria herself danced as Iris. Two years later in a maturation of the imagery associated with her, the former princess, now newly married by proxy to the King of England, was intended to undertake the role of Juno. If Anne was also to perform in this production, it is difficult to imagine what form she might be expected to take. Given this difficulty, I think it is only possible tentatively to suggest with Canova-Green that these verses formed part of the ballet that the queen regnant intended to perform for the wedding.[28] Nevertheless, this ballet is somewhat similar to Anne's 1624 *Ballet de la reine, dansé par les nymphes des jardins*, not least in its presentation of Henrietta Maria who was supposed to enter leading 'les Nymphes de l'air'. On balance, it is certainly possible to associate the *Ballet de la Reyne d'Angleterre* with the entertainment prepared by Anne that was cancelled because of the death of James I. However, until further evidence comes to light, this association must remain tentative and I would prefer to think of it as a different production.

Canova-Green has suggested that the second fragmentary ballet, *Les Dieux descendus en France*, should be associated with the completion of the negotiations for the marriage treaty in November 1624. However, I think that it is more likely that this production took place after the wedding, but again before Henrietta Maria's departure for England. With the duke of Buckingham's arrival in Paris to hasten the bride's departure, celebrations began again in earnest. Indeed, the *Mercure François* reported:

> Durant les sept jours que le Duc de Bucquingham fut à Paris pour accelerer le partement de ladite Royne, les festins et les resiouyssances se renouvellerent, et sembloient mesmes estre augmentez, car on n'entendoit les nuicts que des canonnades, que coups de boëttes, et le matin que le recit des festins magnifiques, entre lesquels nul n'esgalla celuy qui fit le Cardinal de Richelieu.[29]
>
> [During the seven days that the duke of Buckingham was in Paris to speed up the departure of the said queen, the festivals and rejoicings were renewed, and even seemed to be augmented, because in the night only cannon shot and pistols were heard, and in the morning only tales of magnificent feasts, among which none equalled that put on by Cardinal Richelieu.]

It is evident from this that official mourning for James I did not entirely disrupt the wedding celebrations and that many of the proposed entertainments went ahead. I would like to suggest, therefore, that *Les Dieux descendus* might actually have taken place, and that it was performed after the wedding.

One of the verses for this production is to be found in a seventeenth-century manuscript collection, the 'Recueil des plus beaux vers', and is attributed by Canova-Green to Germain Habert.[30] Others, written by the lawyer Antoine-André Mareschal, are, like Boisrobert's verses for the

Ballet de la Reyne d'Angleterre, contained in the 1627 edition of the *Recueil des plus beaux vers*.[31] According to Canova-Green, his contribution to the ballet was the sonnet 'Le Soleil au Roy, luy presentant les Dieux descendus en France, pour honorer la feste de l'Alliance d'Angleterre', and also perhaps the two poems, 'Junon, accompagnée de Henry le Grand, à la Reine Mere' and 'Venus à Madame la Duchesse de Chevreuse'.[32] In addition to these, I would like to suggest that his verses, 'A Monsieur le Duc de Cheureuse, sur son voyage d'Angleterre', were also written for this ballet. The poem's second stanza begins with the lines:

> Grand Duc, tous ces Dieux que voicy
> Mis à l'ombre de ton courage
> Sont exprès descendus icy
> Pour te ceder leur avantage.[33]

> [Great Duke, all the gods who are here
> Put in the shade by your courage
> Are deliberately descended here
> To give their superiority up to you.]

Like the other three poems linked to this entertainment by Canova-Green, the stanzas to the duc de Chevreuse invoke the image of gods descending from heaven. In May 1625, Chevreuse had not only stood proxy for Charles I at the wedding ceremony, but was about to embark on a journey to England with his wife and the new queen consort. It seems unlikely that a ballet performed for the betrothal ceremonies six months earlier would have fêted the Chevreuse couple to this extent. Instead, I would like to suggest that it took place just before they left Paris and that it was performed before the court, Louis XIII, the queen mother and perhaps the duke of Buckingham.

In a manner similar to Buckingham's unperformed *Theater of Apollo*, in which the likenesses of King James, Prince Charles and Princess Elizabeth were represented on the stage, *Les Dieux descendus* provided an image of the late Henri IV who, Mareschal's verses imply, entered on stage in the company of Juno. Interestingly, in 1626, Buckingham presented a masque to the maréchal de Bassompierre, the departing French extraordinary ambassador, in which the figures of Marie de Médicis and the monarchs of France, Spain and Piedmont were similarly presented.[34] One might speculate that these three entertainments were connected, and that *Les Dieux descendus* was deliberately conceived to present a conceit to Buckingham that he had failed to realise in England because of the demise of his king. In this scenario, particularly in the light of Buckingham's later masque, *Les Dieux descendus* becomes a prime candidate for a ballet that was actually performed. The most likely occasion for this must surely be the feast that took place in his honour at the palais de Luxembourg.

A study of the imagery contained in the fragments of these two ballets throws light not only on the iconography associated with Henrietta Maria before her arrival in England, but also on the conflicts that arose between her entourage and members of her husband's court. Canova-Green has noted that, in early seventeenth-century Europe, France's cultural and political supremacy was disputed, in the main, by Italy and Spain. When the English were invoked in court entertainments they were presented either as inoffensive, comic figures, or as a neutral or submissive race.[35] The notion of France as a supreme imperial power is pervasive in the 1625 wedding entertainments, and is counterbalanced by a representation of England as the grateful recipient of France's benevolence. For example, in Mareschal's verses for *Les Dieux descendus*, the Sun addresses the French King, presenting to him all the gods who have descended from heaven to worship him. Louis is hailed as 'Grand Roy, Prince fameux, fils aisné de la Terre' [Great king, famous prince, eldest son of Earth], and is described as subduing all the gods beneath his feet. Moreover, not only does the Sun emphasise Louis's victory over the heavens, but continues:

> Le renom de ce jour, où l'on voit l'Angleterre
> Son bon-heur en celuy de la France emprunter,
> N'est pas ce qui nous peut icy bas arrester,
> C'est ta seule Grandeur qui les nostre atterre.[36]

> [The renown of this day, in which England is seen
> To borrow her happiness from that of France,
> Is not what makes us linger here below,
> It's your greatness alone that draws us down to earth.]

The language of the verses is triumphant, representing England as a dependant who borrows her happiness from France and positioning Louis as an imperial monarch capable of subduing both divine and mortal kingdoms. Imagery invoked for Louis XIII's own wedding in 1615 was intended, in Canova-Green's words, to consecrate 'la suprématie de la France en Europe et, imaginairement, dans le monde' [the supremacy of France in Europe and, in imagination, in the world].[37] Unsurprisingly, this agenda was carried unchanged into the celebrations for the Anglo-French alliance. While ostensibly praising England, Mareschal's verses in fact position the country as inferior to France.

Similarly, Boisrobert's verses for the *Ballet de la Reyne d'Angleterre* invoke an image of Charles's subjection. Galatea is given lines which, at first glance, are highly complimentary to the new English king: 'Charles que i'ose bien nommer / Le plus puissant des Dieux qui regnent sur la mer' [Charles, who I dare to name / The most powerful of the gods who reign over the sea], she says, playing on the notion of England as a powerful maritime nation that had already been invoked in Jonson's *The Fortunate Isles and Their Union*.[38] However, she continues with an image of Charles submitting his sceptre and power to a great beauty who already commands in the air, but who will now 'gouuerner . . . sur les flots de Neptune' [rule . . . over Neptune's waves]. The entertainment's conceit of Juno (represented by Henrietta Maria) leading the nymphs of the air does not seem simply to have been chosen because of its resonance with Anne's 1624 ballet of the nymphs of the garden. It responds competitively to the maritime imagery associated with England in that only the winds and the storm might be said to be able to triumph over Charles's watery domain.[39] Furthermore, it accords Henrietta Maria a principal role in spreading the fame and empire of her royal brother.

In verses attributed to Juno/Henrietta Maria and directed to Louis XIII, we are told that she has 'laissé courir les vents de toutes parts . . . Enfler sur la terre & sur l'onde / Vos voiles & vos estandars' [allowed the winds to run everywhere . . . To swell your sails and standards across the earth and waves].[40] In other words, Charles has subjected himself to this nymph, but her main allegiance remains to the French king whose dominion is spreading across the face of the earth. Charles becomes a tributary king, co-opted into France's policy of world domination: 'S'il reste encore quelque Rois / Qui n'ayent pas sousmis leur orgueil à vos loix' [If there still remain any kings / Who have not submitted their pride to your laws], run Galatea's verses to the queen mother, 'Vos fils mettront bien-tost ardans à la conqueste / Le ioug dessus leur teste' [Your sons, fervent for battle, will soon put / The yoke over their heads].[41] The ballet erases all national, international and religious differences between Marie's sons and sons-in-law, assuring itself of a concord at home that will facilitate the conquest of foreign kings. Charles's submission to Marie's domination is taken for granted because he has already submitted to that of her daughter, described by Galatea as the living image of Marie's virtues, 'O celeste beauté, / Qui nous avez donné ceste diuinité / Qu'on void de vos vertus estre la vive image'.[42] Although Henrietta Maria is described by Galatea at the start of the poem as a great and commanding beauty, by the end of the verse her mother's beauty has emerged as the all-commanding and all-triumphant force that governs the world. In addition, of course, the poem carries a submerged threat: if Charles does not join with Marie's sons in their imperial expansion, he will be forced to submit to the yoke by their superior power.

The wedding ballets praise Marie in terms of the imagery she promoted of herself: as the mother of kings; as a peaceweaver between nations; and as the chaste widow of a great monarch.[43] Her peaceful influence is shown to be so fecund that Malleville's Diana promises in the *Ballet de la Reyne d'Angleterre* that she will repopulate Louis's caves and woods with beasts, and that her stags will give themselves up willingly to his snares.[44] Philippa Berry has undertaken a detailed investigation into the relationship between divine-right monarchy and figurations of nature, observing that 'as proof of [the] sacred character of their rule', Renaissance monarchs 'were asserted to wield an especial authority over the natural world'.[45] The *Ballet de la Reyne d'Angleterre* reflects this impulse, representing Louis XIII as a victorious Mars whose reign, following that of his parents, will be ordered and fruitful. Furthermore, Berry notes that 'the ruler's metamorphosis from ordinary man into a demi-god . . . was often implicitly attributed in French Renaissance literature and art to the transforming powers of a Diana-like beloved'.[46] The figure of Diana in the entertainment is therefore closely bound to the kingship of the young Louis, endowing him with a mystical control over his realm. Nevertheless, as a powerful goddess, Diana is also an incarnation of effective female rule in a manner that serves to compliment the queen regent.

The martial goddess encodes an ambivalence about gender, located precisely in her reputation for chastity. Indeed, Stephen Orgel has noted that both François I and Henri II depicted themselves as Diana, with the cross-dressed image of François accompanied by the motto: 'the king is a Mars in war, a Minerva or Diana in peace'.[47] Diana could become synonymous with balanced and harmonious rule, tempering a monarch's warlike tendencies with feminine softness and with the promise of such peacetime pursuits as hunting. The power of such a figure, as Marjorie Garber's work shows, inheres in her blurred gender, in the fact that she is not a man or a woman.[48] While a very feminine deity like Venus might serve to essentialise the notion of gender, taking the goddess's sex as a ground upon which to construct a binary relationship of the masculine and feminine, a goddess like Diana can often occupy an ambiguously gendered space. As such, her image can be appropriated by both men and women as a powerful enabling fantasy. In the case of François I, the figure of Diana subtends the king's image as an omnipotent god: he is a powerful being existing beyond the realm of mortal gender, combining the characteristics not only of Jove, but also of the goddess. In the case of a female ruler, the figure of Diana or Minerva can stand for the appropriation of a non-passive identity. She can be used to figure the rule of a woman like Marie de Médicis, combining feminine softness with the strength of a virgin Amazon. This is precisely the image conveyed in the series of huge canvases that Rubens had just finished for Marie's palais de Luxembourg which culminated in the representation of her as Minerva Victrix.

The memoirs of the comte de Tillières, former French ambassador to England and Henrietta Maria's 'Grand Chambellan' in 1625, make evident Marie's interest in promoting her daughter's match, as do the letters written home to England by Charles's ambassadors.[49] The imagery of the ballet fragments reinforces this sense of her involvement – her presence is strongly felt in a manner which signals her importance both as the mother of the bride and as the nation's former queen. An encomiastic precedent for this is set in Anne of Austria's ballets: for example, in the *Ballet de la Reine représentant les Festes de Junon la nopcière*, the French Queen gives up her role as Juno to the queen mother with the words: 'Vous m'ostez ma gloire et mon nom, / Grande et favorable Junon, / Qui presidez au mariage' [Great and kindly Juno who presides over marriage, you take from me my glory and my name].[50] Similarly, in the *Ballet de la Reyne d'Angleterre*, Juno/Henrietta Maria acknowledges her mother's influence with the words: 'tout l'empire de Iunon / Auiourd'huy n'est plein que du nom / Et des loüanges de Marie' [Today, all of Juno's empire / Is full only of the name / And praises of Marie], while in *Les Dieux descendus*, Juno (enacted by an unnamed performer) again gives her titles to the queen regent.[51] In both sets of fragments for the 1625 wedding ballets Marie de Médicis's presence and influence is acknowledged at length, indicating not only the primacy of her role as mother of the bride, but also, perhaps, her status in relation to the ballets' sponsors. The likely patron of *Les Dieux descendus* might well, therefore, be Cardinal Richelieu, or, indeed, Marie herself.

COMPETITIVE DANCING

As I discussed above, the French hoped that Henrietta Maria's marriage would lead to the conversion of Charles and his nation, and, furthermore, that this conversion would draw English Catholics into an alliance with France to the detriment of Spain and Spanish Catholicism.[52] In addition, it was hoped that the new queen consort would be in a position to prevent the English from offering assistance to French Huguenots.[53] By absorbing Charles into the imperialist agenda of Louis's France, the wedding ballets live out this fantasy by insisting that the English king will dance to the tune of his new brother-in-law. However, English hopes for the wedding were very different, and, as Buckingham's unperformed *Theater of Apollo* demonstrates, insisted upon an offensive and defensive league with France for the restoration and protection of the Palatinate. Canova-Green has suggested that Buckingham's masque, in its presentation of Elizabeth of Bohemia and the little Palatine princes, was a Protestant recuperation of French imperialist imagery at the same time as it disavowed James I's pacific politics and his reluctance to get involved in European conflict.[54] The masque certainly promises a martial future to the Palatine princes, asserting that 'their births soe blest by starres, / Doe fore-tell triumphant warrs'.[55] It also draws on the imagery of light so closely associated with French imperialism when it characterises James as the sun god Apollo, and Charles as his 'high heire'.[56] In this production, unlike the French ballets, Henrietta Maria, not Charles, is conceived as a tributary prince: she is 'borne to inrich this Shore', and 'must . . . ioyne her flames, vnto Apolloes fires'.[57]

Ben Jonson's *The Fortunate Isles and Their Union* presents a similarly imperialistic vision of England in its depiction of Neptune's fleet 'ready to goe or come / Or fetch the riches of the *Ocean* home, / So to secure him, both in peace, and warres'.[58] James, as Neptune, is presented as a powerful force for peace, the masque concluding with the lines:

> And may thy subiects hearts be all one flame,
> Whilst thou dost keepe the earth in firme estate,
> And'mongst the winds, do'st suffer no debate,
> But both at Sea, and Land, our powers increase,
> With health, and all the golden gifts of Peace. (lines 643–7)

Canova-Green sees in this masque an expression of the kingdom's nationalistic arrogance and an emphasis on its proud separation from the rest of the world.[59] However, to me, the masque presents a tension between the pacific policies advocated by James and the more interventionist policy promoted by Charles and Buckingham after their return from Spain in 1623. Rather than being perceived as a failure, the breakdown of the Spanish match was joyfully celebrated in England and has been interpreted by Tom Cogswell as a personal triumph for Charles.[60] The prince was subsequently able to associate himself with an active pro-Palatinate policy that differed from that of his father, and to entertain the possibility that war might be considered with Spain. It was in this climate of renewed hope that events were set in motion for a French match, not least because France would be an invaluable ally in an Anglo-Spanish war.[61] Jonson's *Fortunate Isles*, then, presents an image of Neptune's land as fecund and peaceful, much in the way that the *Ballet de la Reyne d'Angleterre* represented France. Moreover, again like the *Ballet de la Reyne d'Angleterre*, its vision of peace is predicated upon its ruler's powerful mastery over the earth in a manner that resounds more with Charles and Buckingham's desires for a Spanish war than with James's pacific policies.

As I noted above, Jonson's masque was drawn upon by French commentators who exploited its imagery to represent the English. For example, Jean Puget de la Serre's *roman-à-clef*, *Les Amours du Roy et de la Reine*, which describes Louis XIII's marriage to Anne of Austria in allegorical and mythological terms, ends with a description of the arrival of the English ambassadors to solicit Henrietta Maria's hand in marriage:

> Le Dieu des Iles fortunées fist demander en Mariage la chaste Diane, à Jupiter son frere, enuoyant exprès à sa Court le Dieu de la Courtoisie et le Dieu des Gentils, en qualité d'Ambassadeurs extraordinaires, pour faire réussir ses desseins.[62]

> [The god of the Fortunate Isles asked his brother Jupiter for the chaste Diana's hand in marriage, deliberately sending the god of Courtesy and the god of Pleasance to his court, in the quality of extraordinary ambassadors, to make his projects succeed.]

It is noteworthy, if not surprising, that Louis XIII is represented throughout this text as Jupiter, or 'le maistre des Dieux', and ranks higher than Charles, 'le Dieu des Iles Fortunées'. By adopting Ben Jonson's conceit of the Fortunate Isles, Puget de la Serre at once respectfully reflects Charles's own iconography back to him, but is able also to maintain his master's superiority by locating Louis as chief of all the gods. The god of the Fortunate Isles is termed Jupiter's brother, and thus ranks alongside the text's figurations of Neptune and Pluto, glossed as Monsieur and Monsieur le duc d'Orléans: he is aligned with powerful figures who nonetheless owe allegiance to the chief of the gods. Puget de la Serre's text tries to appropriate English imagery, making it tributary to French culture, just as it represents Charles as tributary to Louis. However, it cannot help but underline the alien nature of the Fortunate Isles conceit; the god of the Fortunate Isles is the master of an island, by its very nature not connected with, nor owing tribute to, anything beyond itself.

The tension that was manifest in the diplomatic negotiations for the wedding was, therefore, unsurprisingly evident in the imagery deployed in the English and French entertainments. Both countries hoped to achieve political advantage from the alliance, and both were determined to maintain their sense of national superiority, not least in the realm of culture. For example, in the *Ballet de la Reyne d'Angleterre*, Henrietta Maria is described as a woman who must without delay 'Rendre les bords de la Tamise / Des tresors de l'Inde embellis' [Embellish the banks of the Thames with the treasures of India].[63] Even more explicitly, in another contemporary Boisrobert poem, she is exhorted, ostensibly by her bridegroom, to 'Amenez dans une autre Cour / Les Ris, les Graces, et l'Amour / Dont vous estes accompagnée' [Bring the laughter, graces and love that accompany you to another court].[64] At once a stock image of royal politeness and an allusion to the queen's French household, this figure represents Henrietta Maria as a woman closely involved with festival and the arts, and shows her to be maturely embedded in the culture of her homeland. There is more than a hint of French cultural supremacy in these two poems for not only is Charles himself absorbed into their particular visions, he is also, particularly in the latter, shown to want to import French culture into his own kingdom. In this context, Henrietta Maria's refusal in Dover to dance with her husband has forceful political resonance, intimating that she would prefer to remain within the parameters of her own country and household.

In the next chapter, I will discuss the performance of the French pastoral play *Artenice*, usually acknowledged as the queen consort's first theatrical production in England. As I will show, this play can be seen as an early example of the French dramatic style she would go on to promote at her new court. It was not, however, the very first production she sponsored in England. In conclusion, here, I wish to draw attention to a previously unknown entertainment performed by Henrietta Maria's French attendants shortly after their arrival in London. This production pre-dates *Artenice*, and again demonstrates the manner in which, even from the very start, the new queen consort promoted herself through theatre and dancing.

SEX AND DANCING

On 7 December 1625, the noblewoman Katherine Gorges wrote a letter to her brother-in-law, Sir Hugh Smyth, describing a visit she had paid to court in the company of her kinswoman, Susan, Lady Denbigh.[65] This latter was Buckingham's sister and was soon to be installed as mistress of Henrietta Maria's wardrobe. Gorges remarked:

I receaued a great grace from the Queen, for shee kissed me, and that she doeth not useually doe to any, nor scarce speake to any Lady that speakes french to hir unless they be Papists. the Lady Denbeigh and the Lady Carlile was commanded by the King to waight on the Queen; but she will by noe meanes as yet admitt any Protastines to any place about hir. soe all the English Ladies are gon from hir Court, except the Cowntes of Arrundell who is the greatest with the Queen of all english Ladies.[66]

The strategies Gorges describes here are resonant of those employed by the queen consort that first night in Dover. Henrietta Maria expresses her position through resistance, a resistance figured as a refusal to participate in the giving of physical favours (the welcoming kiss) or through a refusal to speak. Gorges's letter implies that the queen consort will not converse in English, and she will not talk in French to anyone outside the community of her own faith. There is a definite attempt both by her French attendants, and by the queen consort herself, to maintain her religious and national integrity, and this is achieved through a policy of non-participation.

One of the most important aspects of the religious instruction received by Henrietta Maria at her mother's court was that a noblewoman could be pious and chaste and yet fully undertake the public duties that her position in the world demanded of her. Her policing of her environment here is directly bound up with the teachings of her Catholic prelates and her mother. For example, St François de Sales's *Introduction à la vie dévote* advised its readership to avoid immodest people, warning:

Ne hantez nullement les personnes impudiques, principalement si elles sont encore impudentes . . . car, commes les boucs touchant de la langue les amandiers doux les font devenir amers, ainsi ces âmes puantes et coeurs infects ne parlent guère à personne . . . qu'elles ne le fassent aucunement déchoir de la pudicité.[67]

[Do not ever associate with immodest people, especially if they are not ashamed of vice . . . because just as goats licking sweet almonds make them bitter, so these stinking souls and infected hearts rarely speak to anyone . . . unless it is in some way to make them fall from modesty.]

Henrietta Maria's control of her London environment, in the face of increasingly desperate incursions on the part of the English, was derived from the same religious source. As her confessor, Pierre de Bérulle, reminded her, hers was a perilous position in a land lacking in God's grace and full of iniquity. To counteract this iniquity she was to undertake the solitary study of edifying religious material in order to fortify herself and keep alight the flame of faith within her soul.[68] However, this did not mean that she needed to remove herself entirely from public view. Indeed, Gorges's letter indicates that Henrietta Maria actively sought to publicise her French household before the English court.

On Sunday 20 November 1625, the new queen was the patron of an entertainment that was danced at court by her French attendants. Gorges writes:

> my Lady Denbeigh my old acquaintance and kinswoman dyninge at Langford, would needs haue me promise hir that I would goe to see the Queen and the Masque, on Sunday night was fortnight, where I saw the Masque acted by the Queens seruants all french, but it was disliked of all the English for it was neither masque nor play, but a french antique; and for the french ladies the elder sorte that are neerest hir Ma^{ie}: are something like to Nurce Ball only Nurce is a litle hansomer, but whether it was the sight of the Masque, or the old french Ladies I know not, but I cam home the next day soe sicke that I kept my Chamber 3: or 4: dayes after, and soe weared with the Court, that for ought I know Ile' neuer desire to be Courtiar more.[69]

This entertainment took place on the day after Charles's birthday and might be said to be both a contribution and a response to the court's celebrations at this time. The queen consort herself does not appear to have performed, but the production certainly foregrounded her national identity as a Frenchwoman. Gorges's letter makes clear that the entertainment was unfamiliar to English observers for it did not fit into expected categories of theatrical display, being a French 'antique', rather than a masque or play. The *OED* defines 'antique' or 'antic' as a 'grotesque pageant or theatrical representation' (*OED* 'antic' 4), but presumably the production was similar to the French court's *ballet à entrées.* That is, it would not have followed the Jonsonian pattern of a formal masquing dance preceded by a grotesque anti-masque, but would have consisted of a series of disparate entries danced in different costumes.

Margaret McGowan has noted that, between around 1620–36, a burlesque form of ballet became popular at Louis XIII's court. Seriously reducing the mythological or romanesque elements of previous *ballets de cour,* it took its inspiration from day-to-day life, satirising social mores and exaggerating character-types into caricature.[70] Ridiculous costumes were a pre-requisite of this genre, which emphasised dance (performed in keeping with the burlesque character portrayed) over music and poetry. It was suited to relatively informal performance, perhaps in the private apartments of the monarch or a nobleman, and was also, as McGowan notes, adopted and promoted by bourgeois French society, becoming a fashionable pastime for lawyers and local officials.[71]

It is this kind of performance that Henrietta Maria seems to have sponsored in London, introducing what, to English eyes, was a confusing mishmash of antic dances. As I will discuss in subsequent chapters, elements from French *ballets de cour* were later to be specifically promoted in Henrietta Maria's English entertainments: for example, her masque *Chloridia* (1631) contains a series of anti-masque dances based on French *ballets à entrées*. In 1625, however, an English noblewoman like Katherine Gorges was bewildered by this foreign cultural form which, as the tone of her letter implies, she perceived as wearisome and undignified.

It is difficult to ascertain from her letter whether the entertainment included Henrietta Maria's more mature female attendants, or whether they too were spectators. On balance, and taking into account the queen's later predilection for staging relatively informal dances with her maids, I suggest that 'the old french Ladies' did take an active part.[72] Gorges's response to them is therefore very interesting, especially since hers was not the only derogatory opinion of these women.

In June 1625, John Chamberlain, the veteran letter writer and social commentator, wrote about Henrietta Maria's arrival in England to his friend Dudley Carleton, noting:

> The queen hath brought, they say, such a poor, pitiful sort of women, that there is not one worth the looking after, saving herself and the Duchess of Chevreuse, who, though she be fair, yet paints foully.[73]

This is an intensely nationalistic response to the arrival of the Frenchwomen, who are implicitly dismissed as inferior to their English counterparts. The phrase 'not one worth the looking after' implies at once that they are not worth looking *at*, and also that they are not worth *caring for* – that is, they were not worth contemplating as prospective mates. Henrietta Maria of course, as the new young queen consort upon whom hopes for the continuation of the Stuart dynasty were resting, is exempt from this criticism, as is Madame de Chevreuse, who, notably, was about seven months pregnant at the time.

Taken together, these two English letters combine to present an unflattering image of Henrietta Maria's attendants that is based, not simply on national prejudice, but on age and sexual potential. It is important to remember that there had been no queen's court in England since the death of Anna of Denmark in 1619 and that Henrietta Maria's arrival gave rise to new possibilities for social and political advancement.[74] Such hopes, though, were frustrated by the closed nature of her circle and by the unavailability (both romantically and otherwise) of her most influential female attendants.[75] It is no wonder therefore that the English desired to get rid of many of the French for this would open up channels of patronage and preferment closed by the new queen's position at the centre of a group of foreigners.[76] The problem in the royal marriage at the start of the Caroline reign was therefore, in part, one of cultural, as well as political, competition – a firm belief on both sides that theirs was a superior race and religion. It is, therefore, perhaps not surprising that the event described by commentators as the catalyst for Charles's expulsion of his wife's French attendants was one that involved dancing.

On Saturday 1 July 1626, John Pory wrote from London to the Reverend Joseph Mead with the news,

> On Monday, about three in the afternoon, the king, passing into the queen's side [of Whitehall palace], and finding some Frenchmen, her servants, unreverently dancing and curvetting in her presence, took her by the hand, and led her into his lodgings, locking the door after him, and shutting out all . . . presently, upon this my Lord Conway called forth the French bishop and other of the clergy into St James's Park, where he told them, the king's pleasure was, all her majesty's servants of that nation, men and women, young and old, should depart the kingdom.[77]

It was not, of course, the sole fact of 'unreverent' dancing that precipitated the departure of the queen consort's attendants. However, that this should be selected by Pory as the trigger of the king's displeasure is significant. It marks a cultural competition that was played out in the entertainments conceived for the Anglo-French wedding, and which was manifested for the first time on English soil when, in Dover, the queen refused to dance. The Frenchmen's behaviour before the queen is represented as inappropriate and, because the king comes upon it unexpectedly, unauthorised. Furthermore, it is again conceived along sexualised lines. Charles's actions in removing his wife and locking her in his own chamber underline his possession of her and his desire to eliminate the contaminating presence of her 'curvetting' countrymen whose dancing is implicitly dangerous to both the dignity of her rank and her reputation.

Pory's letter provides an appropriate conclusion to a history of secret dancing that began with Charles's presence as an unrecognised spectator at the French Queen Anne's ballet rehearsal in 1623. By June 1626, it would appear, the pleasure and the power of voyeurism had worn off and Henrietta Maria was now expected fully to take up her place within the public display of the Caroline court.

CHAPTER 2

Artenice: a new French fashion at the English court

In February 1626, four months before Charles would become incensed by the 'unreverent' dancing of the French and pack them out of England, Henrietta Maria and her ladies introduced an innovation into the Caroline court when they performed speaking parts in a French play. This chapter will consider the production, locating it first within the context of Henrietta Maria's troublesome household, before considering its cultural and social implications. Like the 1625 'antique' production, the entertainment was enacted solely by Henrietta Maria's French attendants and can be seen as showcasing a French cultural artefact on the English stage. Nevertheless, sanctioned by the king and worked on by trusted servants such as Inigo Jones, it marks the beginning of Henrietta Maria's co-operation with, and co-option into, the performative display of the Caroline court.

The play chosen for the queen consort's performance was identified in 1937 by Louis Arnould as *Les Bergeries*, a pastoral romance by Honorat de Bueil, seigneur de Racan.[1] As I will show, it provides early evidence of the predilection for romantic drama that would strongly influence Henrietta Maria's theatrical patronage throughout the next decade. Known at the English court by the title *Artenice*, it has received surprisingly little attention from modern drama critics despite its profound importance as the first production in England that saw a queen and her women perform as actors on the stage. Indeed, if it is discussed at all, it is invariably dismissed by critics as a frivolous imitation of French fashion that imported 'an affected platonism' into England.[2] Even Erica Veevers, whose work on Henrietta Maria's later productions is insightful and informative, has represented *Artenice* as a straightforward attempt to re-present the behaviours of the Parisian *salons*, commenting:

> When [the queen] first arrived in England, in June 1625, she undoubtedly brought with her a taste for romantic ideas fostered by *L'Astrée*, and for the kind

> of activities that formed the pastimes of the Hôtel de Rambouillet and the French court . . . she played the leading role in Racan's *Artenice* in 1626 . . . and when in 1627 most of her French retinue was dismissed, she took refuge in the activities she knew best – dancing, singing, and play-acting – to attract to her a group who could share her tastes and interests.[3]

Veevers's study does not accommodate a discussion of Racan's pastoral because it is seen as replicating Parisian fashion and as a way for Henrietta Maria to amuse herself with her maids.[4] Only after the dismissal of the queen consort's French attendants does Veevers attribute a strategic social intention to her performances: they are to attract like-minded courtiers to her side to fill the void left by the departed French.

In contrast to Veevers, rather than considering the production of *Artenice* simply as a French import, I will discuss what the pastoral's performance reveals about Henrietta Maria's situation at the English court. It was enacted during a time of conflict, not only between the king and queen's households, but between the English and French nations, and may be seen as Henrietta Maria's attempt to assert a cultural presence that would permit her to comment upon social and political events. At the same time, the play reflected the ideals of Madame de Rambouillet's *salon*, ideals that were compatible with the chaste social behaviour advocated, in particular, by St François de Sales. As such, *Artenice* became a manifesto that sought to redefine women's roles both at court and in the community at large. Enacting both male and female characters in the play, Henrietta Maria and her ladies exerted temporary control over the constructions of both masculinity and femininity, promoting a new kind of social relation at the Caroline court that was grounded in the queen consort's religious beliefs.

*

As I discussed in chapter 1, access to the queen consort's inner circle was a contentious issue between the English and the French. Her entourage was distrusted by Charles's courtiers, with several foreign observers remarking that the marriage had caused more bad feeling between France and England than it had resolved.[5] Blainville, the French extraordinary ambassador, was a particularly problematic figure and was thought deliberately to be stirring up trouble between Charles and his new wife. In February 1626, for example, Sir Nathaniel Bacon wrote home from court with the news:

Ther hath bin some distaste betweene the King & Queene by meanes of the French embassador, who left the court in a pett and departed for France, but was enforced to retourne, Mr Mountague being sent in his stead.[6]

Sir John Finet, master of ceremonies, also remarked upon Blainville's disruptive influence, noting that his precipitous departure from the court was prompted by a message which informed him that 'it was his Majesties pleasure that he should forbeare further accesse to the Kings or Queens Presence'.[7]

Blainville had played a role in a conflict over Henrietta Maria's coronation which had resulted in stalemate, and had left the queen uncrowned. Her Catholic bishop had demanded to officiate at the ceremony because he refused to recognise the authority of the Church of England. However, the archbishop of Canterbury would not entertain the idea, and Henrietta Maria was left to watch from a distance with Blainville while her husband was crowned alone.[8] At the opening of parliament a week later, Henrietta Maria (again, it was believed, at Blainville's urging) directly flouted Charles's instructions and refused to watch the procession from the place appointed her. As Alison Shell has noted, this 'may have been an act of dissociation from the proceedings of a Protestant nation, rather than the fit of adolescent pique as which it has usually been seen'.[9] This is a pertinent remark, suggesting that, although Henrietta Maria took advice from her attendants, she was also willingly complicit in matters that concerned her religion and native country.

The pastoral not only took place at a time of strained relations between the English and Henrietta Maria's French attendants, but also when feelings in England were running high about France's treatment of its Huguenot population. For example, in January 1626, the Venetian ambassador in London reported home:

The mission which the French ambassador was to have done was performed by the queen, who sent one of her gentlemen with letters in her own hand to her mother, begging her to interpose with her son for moderation towards la Rochelle, and expressing her anguish at being involved in the quarrels between her brother and husband.[10]

Even during the early months of her marriage, Henrietta Maria attempted to assert a political presence, taking upon herself the duties of an ambassador in the international dispute that was dividing her loyalties between her husband and brother. Her pastoral can be seen to intervene in this difficult situation, replicating, and perhaps attempting to reinforce, images of harmonious union that were put forward at the time of her wedding.

In a way, because it was worked on by many of the king's artists and craftsmen, the production necessarily promoted collaboration and harmony. It was, though, an unusual event, access to which was carefully controlled by the royal administrative machine. Amerigo Salvetti, the Tuscan Resident at the English court, observed of the occasion:

On Shrove Tuesday, which in their usage here was last Tuesday, her Majesty acted her beautiful pastoral, accompanied by twelve of her French ladies, whom she had rehearsed since last Christmas. Everything went off very well, the decoration and the changing of the scene as well as the gestures and the elocution of the ladies, among whom the queen outdid all the rest. All this was done at Denmark House as privately as possible, because it is no normal thing here to see the queen acting on a stage. And therefore, aside from a certain limited number of the principal nobility, others were not allowed to enter.[11]

Coming from a culture that tolerated actresses, Salvetti is more concerned to report on the production than to criticise the queen consort's behaviour. Indeed, his letter somewhat inevitably compliments her virtuosity in acting, and represents the king's desire for privacy as a curiosity. However, the observation that the pastoral was performed 'privately' is important, and demonstrates that the king recognised the novelty of his wife's activity and strove to limit any possible criticism.

The queen consort's production also furnished an expression of national difference, locating her within the performative culture of another, potentially aggressive, European monarchy. On one hand, therefore, it was assimilated into the court's shrovetide festivities. On the other, it presented her household as a distinct group, conversing in French from behind a proscenium arch in a manner that could certainly, if not deliberately, provoke disapproval and add fuel to the discontent about the French that was already rumbling at the English court.

*

Racan's pastoral was first performed in 1619 on the public stage of the Hôtel de Bourgogne in Paris. Its author was a member of Henri IV's bedchamber and also attended evenings at the famous Rambouillet *salon*, to which he had been introduced by François de Malherbe, one of Marie de Médicis's favourite poets.[12] The production was eagerly attended by the nobility, in part because it was a novelty to see a play on the public stage written by a member of the court. *Les Bergeries* was tremendously well received, and was applauded by the Rambouillet faithful for the nobility of its language. It drew its influences from Italian and Spanish romances such as Guarini's *Il Pastor Fido* and Montemayor's *Diana*, as well as containing echoes of Virgil's *Eclogues*. Most of all, though, it owed a debt to Honoré d'Urfé's *L'Astrée*, the first volume of which appeared when Racan was a page at court.

Both d'Urfé's romance and Racan's pastoral put forward spiritualised notions of social relations that echo St François de Sales's theological ideas. D'Urfé and François de Sales were acquainted and, together with Jean-Pierre Camus and Antoine Favre, participated in gatherings that, in the winter of 1606–7, came to be known as the Académie florimontane.[13] *L'Astrée* propounds a philosophy of love that privileges fidelity, discretion, marriage and control over the passions. It offers a way of living in the world without being corrupted by worldly vanity, and thus shares in the concerns of Sales's *Introduction à la vie dévote*, the first version of which was printed in Lyon in 1609. The *Introduction* was conceived as a handbook for those people, particularly women, who desired to live devoutly in the world, and took the form of an address to a female figure named Philothée – a name signifying 'one who loves God, or at least desires to do so'.[14] Through the example of her spiritual conversation, a noblewoman was encouraged to have an ameliorative influence on her companions, making her cultural activity indispensable to the health of good society.

Racan's play marked its debt to the *Introduction* through the significantly named vestal, Philothée, an acolyte at the temple of the Bonne Déesse. It drew upon Sales's theology to create a world in which slander and wrongdoing were overcome by chastity and fidelity, arming its characters with steadfast love. It was also embedded in the culture of the Rambouillet *salon*, and was reputed to shadow the romance between the marquis de Termes and Catherine de Chabot, his wife. Early in his career, Racan had looked upon Catherine Chabot as a muse and, together with Malherbe, whose own inspiration was drawn from the figure of Catherine, marquise de Rambouillet, he invented several anagrams of his beloved's name. Although the name Artenice was later to become synonymous with Rambouillet herself, at its inception it designated Chabot.[15] Part of the pastoral's early popularity, therefore, came from the coded references it made to the Parisian *beau monde*. *Les Bergeries*'s civilised society was a partial allegory of the play's own environment, and was, in its turn, taken up and used at the Rambouillet *salon* as a model for chaste social relations.

The play that Henrietta Maria imported into England in 1626, therefore, carried with it the traces of *salon* culture, Catholicism and the French court. It came from a society that privileged certain women as arbiters of taste, positing a form of social relations based upon politeness and chivalry. Furthermore, it had recently been licensed for printing in France, and was again the subject of public interest.[16] Whether a member of Henrietta Maria's entourage acquired a copy of the play before leaving for England is a matter only for speculation. What is certain is that Henrietta Maria was reported to be rehearsing a pastoral with her ladies as early as December 1625.[17]

In the 1950s, a copy of *Les Bergeries*, entitled *Artenice*, was acquired by the Houghton Library at Harvard. The scholars Jean Parrish and William A. Jackson subsequently suggested that it had been printed in England and had been prepared for performance at the English court. By cataloguing typographical errors, they showed that it was typeset from the 1625 French edition and that it came from Edward Allde's London printing house.[18] The first owner of the volume is unknown, but Parrish and Jackson surmised that it was produced for the use of the actors.[19] It is inscribed in a 'not very clear' French hand with various changes of scene, and with lighting and sound effects, giving weight to the theory that it was a performance text.[20] In addition, and again indicating that it was prepared for performance, this version has lost all of its dedicatory and commendatory verses, and 11 per cent of its lines (about 135 lines of dialogue, together with the verses of the chorus which concluded each act).

Although, from its first performance in Paris, Racan's play was known as *Arthénice, ou les bergeries*, the title page of the first French edition named it simply *Les Bergeries*. This title signalled that the play was an example of a fashionable pastoral genre, along the same lines as other bucolic romances such as *Il Pastor Fido*. However, by choosing to differ from the 1625 edition and to identify the play by the personal name, *Artenice*, the producers of the English version instigated a different set of significations. First, and most importantly, Artenice is the play's principal female character. Although the pastoral opens with a long soliloquy performed by the shepherd, Alcidor, the change of title makes Artenice the central focus of the production. Instead of being a play about a pastoral community, the production becomes a play about one woman. This change of focus reflects particularly upon Henrietta Maria, the actress who played Artenice. Not only does she become the play's most important figure (compatible with her status as queen), but she is also the focus of an innovative type of performance: one that permitted women to be actresses as well as dancers, and which demonstrated new scenic techniques on the English stage.

The new queen's play certainly did not go unnoticed in France, and was the subject of an anonymous poem entitled, 'Sur les figures, et changemens de Théatre lors que la Reyne d'Angleterre joüa la pastorelle de Mr de Racan, sous le personnage d'Artenice'.[21] This poem demonstrates that an interest was taken in the activities of the expatriated French princess, not only – as might be expected – at the French court, but by the Rambouillet *salon* whose affairs were allegorised in Racan's pastoral. Contained in a miscellany that belonged to Julie-Lucie d'Angennes, daughter of the marquise de Rambouillet and co-hostess of her famous *salon*, it also gives rise to the intriguing possibility that one of her acquaintances witnessed the production.

Representing the pastoral's changes of scene in elaborate terms, the poem reveals a lively interest in the technicalities of the play's production, and is conceived in the ornate language of a poet like Boisrobert. Indeed, it is feasible that 'Sur les figures' is his work: it is possible that he remained in England until August 1626, in which case he would have been in London at the time of the pastoral, and he certainly was acquainted with Julie-Lucie.[22] If he did witness the production, it would have provided him with invaluable experience of English staging practices when he came to write his own pastoral for the queen consort in 1635.

Henrietta Maria's production fell into two parts; the play, followed by a dance. Inigo Jones was employed to construct a 'lardge Theatre at the upper end of the hall', and to make 'a Tabernacle of Tymber for the Queene standing uppon viij pilleres with Architrave ffreeze, and Cornish'.[23] Only one design by Inigo Jones for the staging of the pastoral has definitely been identified.[24] It is inscribed in the top right-hand corner with the words 'pastoral sceane/Som: House/1625' and depicts a village street in which thatched country cottages jostle alongside a colonnaded building that might be a temple.[25] Orgel and Strong note that this setting is a composite one that combines elements from all three of Serlio's scenic types (the tragic, satiric and comic).[26] They also observe that no play in England had ever before been presented on this sort of stage and assert that the 'impulse to produce *Artenice* with illusionistic settings almost certainly derived. . .from a royal command'.[27]

John Peacock takes this idea further, arguing that the queen consort must have ordered Jones to follow French scenic conventions.[28] He therefore attributes the blend of Serlian styles directly to her influence, noting that she was used to the 'old-fashioned simultaneous settings' of the Hôtel de Bourgogne.[29] This demand for a specific type of setting, he says, forced Jones 'to regress to a convention he had originally turned his back on', surmising that the architect cannot have felt comfortable with this commission.[30] Nonetheless, Peacock's suggestion that Henrietta Maria (or one of her servants) exerted an influence over Jones's designs is significant and consistent with subsequent dramatic presentations sponsored by the queen.

John Orrell has noted that, during Henrietta Maria's residency at Somerset House, the hall there became 'the chief London centre for the production of the scenic drama until 1640'.[31] A special theatre was constructed in the Paved Court for a production of Walter Montagu's *The Shepherds' Paradise* in 1633; Fletcher's *The Faithful Shepherdess* was performed there in 1634; there were two performances of Heywood's *Love's Mistress* the same year; a play was put on by a visiting French troupe in 1635; the French pastoral, *Florimène*, was acted there by the queen's French ladies; and a performance of Lodowick Carlell's *The Passionate Lovers* took place there in 1638.[32] Whether Henrietta Maria had a direct influence over the way these plays were staged is impossible to prove. What is certain, though, is that Jones developed a style for her in England that drew on French precedents and promoted her national identity.[33]

The nature of this collaboration exemplifies one of the likely purposes of the production of *Artenice*. Funded and attended by the king and worked on by his servants, the whole process of mounting, rehearsing and performing the play helped to incorporate Henrietta Maria's household into the economy of Stuart court theatre while permitting her to retain a sense of her own culture and origins.[34] This process was nowhere more evident than in the concluding moments of the production when, after the queen and her ladies had descended from the stage to dance among the English, Jones's masterfully designed shutters closed to display a painted image of Somerset House and the Thames, ending the play with an image of the queen's new residence in London.[35]

Orrell describes this moment as 'a fine conceit', which brought the philosophical pretensions of the pastoral to focus on Henrietta Maria's court, 'as if the real world might be tuned with the harmony of what went before'.[36] The painted images do, I believe, tie together the performance, the descent of the masquers from the stage and the dance. However, they also connect Somerset House and the Thames to the play's setting near the rivers of the Seine and the Marne. The conclusion of the performance certainly focused attention on the queen's court, yet it was a court that had undergone a journey, moving from a representation of France to its present location at the feet of the English king. The movement from the stage to the dance floor is a movement from a French-dominated space into the world of London and the English court, and is one that symbolically connects the two locations. The queen's descent thus acquires specific connotations in this production, becoming a reconciliatory or largely inclusive gesture that signals the possibility of harmony between her household and her husband's entourage.

The decision to perform a version of *Les Bergeries* in England was not a random one, nor did it simply imitate a fashion imported from France. Although it was part of the court's shrovetide celebrations, it was also an assertion of the queen's identity, of her position within her own household and of her status as a princess of France. It therefore did not just provide an example of French court and *salon* culture on the Caroline stage, but facilitated that culture's translation into England.

CHASTE DESIRES: THE SALONS AND SOCIAL BEHAVIOUR

The pastoral can be seen as a manifesto of the kind of social behaviour favoured by Henrietta Maria. The most significant premise of French social manuals such as St François de Sales's *Introduction* was that a woman could govern her own chastity and could thus indulge in civil conversation with men, free from the taint of slander.[37] Discussing the subject of reputation, for example, Sales made the point that 'a good name is not particularly desirable in itself', and continued:

La réputation n'est que comme une enseigne qui fait connaître où la vertu loge; la vertu doit donc être en tout et partout préférée. C'est pourquoi, si l'on dit: vous êtes un hypocrite [ou] si l'on vous tient pour homme de bas courage . . . moquez-vous de tout cela. Car, . . . tels jugements se font par des niaises et sottes gens.[38]

[Reputation is merely a notice board on the door of virtue; it is the virtue that really matters; so if you are called a hypocrite . . . or a coward . . . it is no more than a laughing matter, for such statements are made only by foolish and empty-headed people.][39]

Sales represents human society as vain and malicious, proposing, in effect, that virtue is its own reward. In *Les Bergeries*, a similar comment is made upon restrictive mores that nonetheless reinforces the notion that a woman could govern her own chastity. Artenice's first speech, which begins the third scene and parallels her lover Alcidor's opening lament, rails against the injunction that prevents her, as a woman, from acknowledging her love:

> Ce fust toy [Honneur], qui premier fit glisser en nostre ame
> Ces foles visions de la honte et du blasme:
> Qui premier nous apprint à taire nos desirs,
> Qui premier nous apprint à cacher nos plaisirs,
> Et dont la tyrannie, aux amants trop cruelle,
> S'opposa la premiere à la loy naturelle.[40]

[It was you [Honour] who first made these mad illusions of shame and blame slip into our soul, who first taught us to silence our desires, who first taught us to hide our pleasures, and whose tyranny, too cruel to lovers, first opposed itself to the natural law.]

Feeling herself to be shackled by the constraints of human custom, Artenice compares her situation to that of wild creatures who can sing freely about their loves, and rejects 'honour' as a cruel tyrant imposed unnaturally upon the world.[41] However, even though her words have a touch of the *libertin* about them, her subsequent behaviour proves that she will abide by the edicts set out for her community by its governing deity.

As Sales's *Introduction* made clear, divine injunctions to maintain honour are very different from the dictates of human custom. 'Chastity', Sales remarked, 'is synonymous with honour and makes us honourable.'[42] Furthermore, we are exhorted to 'read the Scriptures for the word of God is chaste and purifies those who delight in it'.[43] Unlike debased human language which operates through the arbitrary association of sign and referent, God's Word *is* the thing it represents and has a material effect upon those who contemplate it. Chastity and honour matter as spiritual essences, not as cultural conventions, and belong to a prior reality held within the mind and Word of God.

Artenice's lament draws attention to women's difficult position in Renaissance society, revealing the double standard that proposed that women should be courted, but should not court in their turn.[44] When these words were uttered on stage by a woman, they constituted a direct challenge to the Biblical injunction that required them to remain silent and obedient. However, backed by Sales's new theological proposals, they were also, paradoxically, a declaration of religious devotion. This has a particular significance upon the stage in England for it demonstrates the French household's adherence to the Salesian mode of social interaction: Henrietta Maria and her ladies are seen devoutly to obey the injunctions of God, and to divorce themselves from the vanities of corrupt society. This gestures towards a new type of social organisation which privileges women as the arbiters of taste and delicacy, and which gives them a social role in the promotion of civility and polite behaviour. The queen's pastoral thus indicates that a space might be opened within the Stuart court from which a commentary could be made about social, religious and political affairs. Acted by women on the English stage, *Artenice* is a play which gives women the right to act.[45]

Charles's attempts to represent the pastoral as a private, domestic production make it likely that its provocative potential was recognised. Nonetheless, although a princess might be allowed to produce a play for private recreation at a residence away from the centre of power – as Henrietta Maria's sister did when she performed in *Bradamante* – a production by a queen at her main London residence must inevitably be open to scrutiny. Opinions about the pastoral quickly circulated beyond the court to London and the provinces, demonstrating that this was a cultural event that excited public opinion. By 4 March, the Reverend Joseph Mead in Cambridge was able to report that 'on Tuesday, February 21st, the queen and her ladies acted a pastoral before the King, wherein herself had the greatest part, and repeated, it is said, 600 French verses by heart'.[46] Other English commentators, though, were not so objective in their analyses: following the precedent set by Anna of Denmark's forays on to the stage, moderate disapproval of Henrietta Maria's production was not long in coming.

Henry Manners wrote home after the event that he heard 'not much honour of the Queen's mask, for if they were not all, some were in men's apparell', while John Chamberlain reported to Dudley Carleton that:

> On Shrovetuisday the Quene and her women had a maske or pastorall play at Somerset House, wherein herself acted a part, and some of the rest were disguised like men with beards. I have knowne the time when this wold have semed a straunge sight, to see a Quene act in a play but *tempora mutantur et nos.*[47]

Chamberlain's air of journalistic detachment leaves one in no doubt that he views the queen consort's activities with wry amusement. More significantly though, he also recognises a shift in fashion pioneered by Henrietta Maria when he comments that times change and that previously unusual sights have a habit of becoming commonplace. The urbane persona he adopts gives the impression that he takes this development in his stride. However, not all of the English apparently found it so easy to approve of the queen's acting, criticising her both for taking a vocal role in the production and for her ladies' cross-dressing.[48]

Stephen Orgel has investigated why, while apparently being banned in England, women were tolerated as actors upon the public stages of Italy,

France and even Spain. Although he notes that, in England, women on display became increasingly associated with foreignness and Catholicism, he marshals convincing – and surprising – evidence that they did, on occasion, perform as actors, noting that 'for those [in England] to whom theatre was not itself problematical, there was no stigma whatever attached to women performing in plays, so long as they did not do it as a profession'.[49] Might it be, therefore, that the objections raised against Henrietta Maria in 1626 were more concerned with the impropriety of a *queen* taking to the stage than with the fact that she was a woman? Certainly, the criticisms levelled at Queen Anna took account of her royal status, Ralph Winwood famously observing that the diaphanous costumes chosen for her *Masque of Blackness*, were 'too light and Curtizan-like for such great ones'.[50] Furthermore, similar criticism was soon to be levelled at the duke of Buckingham when he took a role 'which many thought too histrionical to become him' and acted as a fencing master in an antimasque before the king and departing French extraordinary ambassador.[51]

Such criticism supports the idea that courtly entertainments were politically significant, reinforcing the status and power of the nobility both to itself and, by report, to the nation. To take a role that undermined the seriousness of this display, while it might be fun, was nonetheless also to undercut the entertainment's purpose as a statement of royal power. In light of this, the decision to send Henrietta Maria's ladies on to the court stage wearing false beards is intriguingly provocative and marks the queen consort's household as fundamentally different from those of Queen Anna and King Charles, setting out the ways in which she and her attendants wished to be perceived.

Will Fisher has provided convincing evidence that the beard was fundamentally important in the construction of early modern gender identity. He argues that 'facial hair often conferred masculinity', and demonstrates how early modern portraiture, theatre and medical tracts all helped to fashion an 'historically specific vision of what it meant to be a man by fashioning an historically specific ideal of the male body'.[52] *Artenice*'s female actors appropriated this sign of masculinity, making the group on the stage into a demonstrably self-sufficient community. By enacting a love story in which all the parts were taken by women, the queen's household set itself apart from the English noblemen in the audience, at once displaying itself performatively, and yet remaining somehow self-sustaining and inward-looking.[53]

I want to digress a moment to illustrate this point. In the previous chapter I noted that John Chamberlain remarked of the new queen's attendants in 1625 that they were 'poor, pitiful sort of women . . . not one worth the looking after', observing that this was an intensely nationalistic response to the arrival of the Frenchwomen, who were implicitly dismissed as inferior to their English counterparts.[54] The phrase 'not one worth the looking after', I suggested, implies that they were not worth looking *at* and not worth *caring for* as prospective mates. What happens on stage in the production of *Artenice* is very similar: Henrietta Maria's French entourage enact their own men, because English men don't measure up. In effect, they construct images of men who adhere to the polite rules of the *salon* world, who are *honnête* and socially acceptable to them. The cross-dressed French actress fashions an alternative kind of masculinity, in contrast, perhaps, to that available at the English court. In order to do so, she playfully travesties the signs of masculinity promoted by European culture, laying claim to the beard, but also, and simultaneously, attempting to influence social relations at the Stuart court itself.

Joan Landes has profitably explored the changing social roles of élite women in France during the seventeenth and eighteenth centuries. Starting her analysis with a critique of Jürgen Habermas's theory of the development of a bourgeois public sphere, she has shown how noblewomen occupied a far more privileged social position under the *ancien régime* than they did later when their social roles became increasingly defined as domestic. 'The French court,' Landes argues, 'always accorded royal women positions of leadership in taste and pleasure', but these were gradually extended into the world of the *salons*.[55] In such genteel urban assemblies, invariably hosted by a woman, 'men of the aristocracy mingled with writers, artists, scholars, merchants, lawyers, and office-holders' in a manner that encouraged the integration of new individuals into the élite.[56] 'Noble values,' Landes pertinently observes, 'became dissociated from birth and attached to behaviour', while the women who presided over these groupings 'functioned not only as consumers but as purveyors of culture'.[57]

While Landes's work is primarily concerned with the Parisian *salons* of the 1650s, her ideas are nonetheless useful to a discussion of Henrietta Maria's early activities at the English court. Although Henrietta Maria's royal status necessarily placed her in a position from which she could affect fashion, her performance of a *salon*-influenced romance nevertheless imported into England traces of this new type of social organisation in which polite behaviour and a chaste relationship between the sexes was ostensibly privileged over noble birth. In the light of this, I now want to investigate the question of Henrietta Maria's marriage to demonstrate how the choice of this play raised questions about chastity and fidelity pertinent to the Caroline couple's situation in 1626.

LOVE AND MARRIAGE AS A SPIRITUAL VOCATION

Racan's play negotiates the problems of infidelity and previous betrothals in a manner that is entirely appropriate to Henrietta Maria's early marital situation. In the pastoral, Artenice's parents have arranged her marriage to the shepherd Lucidas because he is both wealthy and local. Exhorting his daughter to accept this match, her father declares that the only thing he desires before his death is a grandchild, and explains that he has chosen Lucidas as Artenice's mate because 'La fortune luy rit, tout luy vient à souhait' [Fortune smiles on him, everything he desires comes to him].[58] Economic and dynastic necessity drive Artenice's father, in contrast to the shepherdess's own romantic desires for Alcidor. Promised by her parents to one man, Artenice has already lost her heart to another.

Although the gender roles are reversed, this is precisely the romantic fiction that was deployed to explain Charles's marriage to Henrietta Maria after his attempts to woo the Spanish infanta. In this romantic story, Charles was imagined to have undertaken the journey to Spain because of familial and dynastic pressure. Falling in love with Henrietta Maria before meeting the infanta, he was emotionally committed prior to his ill-fated sojourn at the Spanish court, broke no vows and never professed love to anyone but the French princess. Just like the story of Artenice's marriage, the Anglo-French union is represented as the result of a single, true love: an idea of particular importance to Caroline iconography that would resonate throughout the court drama of the period.

Racan's pastoral was therefore an appropriate vessel through which to showcase questions of love and fidelity, and was entirely compatible with this developing Caroline fashion. In the play, the turning point for Artenice comes when Alcidor is brought half-drowned to Philothée's temple. Realising the strength of her love, Artenice declares that she will die alongside him because their souls are intertwined.[59] This romantic conceit of two souls existing in complete accord has obvious neo-Platonic connotations and came to serve as a keystone of Caroline monarchical iconography: Artenice's words in the pastoral resonate with the image of the 'Mary-Charles' of *Albion's Triumph*, and the 'Carlomaria' of *Coelum Britannicum*, representing the harmonious compatibility of the two lovers.

The shepherds' relationship also demonstrates a certain sexual equality and, more importantly, permits Artenice to undergo spiritual amelioration through her love. When she declares that her own death will follow closely upon Alcidor's, she demonstrates a degree of love that transcends the purely physical and selfish. The lovers' relationship contains an element of spirituality that raises them above the mundane and sets them on the road to an understanding of divine love. Their union becomes a spiritual vocation, providing an anchor of faith in a mutable world.

Henrietta Maria, too, was encouraged by her mother to cultivate this sort of spiritual relationship with her husband, loving him in a manner only exceeded by her love for God.[60] The distinction made here by Marie de Médicis is important and introduces the theme of Henrietta Maria and Charles's different religions. Because Charles was a heretic in the eyes of the Roman Church, permission for the marriage had to be sought from the pope. Its eventual solemnisation led to the hope that Charles might be turned back to the Catholic faith, thus returning his whole country to the true Church. In Racan's pastoral, the resolution of the shepherds' romantic problems therefore has particular significance. The implicit association of Charles with the character of Alcidor – who is at first thought to be a stranger but who is ultimately discovered to be a native of Artenice's community – gives rise to the possibility that the pastoral figures the fantasy of the king's return to 'la vérité de la Religion'.[61]

Gisèle Mathieu-Castellani has described how the limits of Racan's pastoral world are defined by the fields where the river Marne crossed the Seine.[62] The main obstacle in the play, she asserts, is the river itself, because Artenice, born by the side of it, is forbidden by the community's goddess to marry a foreigner. *Les Bergeries*'s eventual revelation that Alcidor is a native of Artenice's region unites the lovers under the blessing of their parents and the 'Bonne Déesse', and allows Alcidor to be accepted into the community because he is implicitly subject to the same laws as the woman he loves.

In a similar way, Marie de Médicis's farewell letter to her daughter evoked Charles and Henrietta Maria's common roots, exhorting the new queen to pray for her husband's return to the truth of the religion 'en laquelle et pour laquelle même est morte sa grande mère' [in which and even for which his grandmother died].[63] Mary Stuart, Charles's grandmother, was not only a Catholic, but a queen of France. The implication here is that Henrietta Maria and Charles actually have the same religious and national heritage. Significantly, if the equation between Charles and

Alcidor is maintained, the French position is privileged for, like Alcidor, it is Charles who shares Henrietta Maria's roots, not she who is discovered to be English: like Alcidor, Charles should embrace his heritage and submit to the edicts of his beloved's God.

Acted in England, Racan's pastoral therefore accumulated new meanings, and can also be seen to have had a proselytising purpose. Furthermore, it introduced a strain of imagery on to the Caroline court stage that would be seen again in the queen consort's other dramatic productions, *The Shepherds' Paradise* and *Florimène*. In despair because Lucidas has led her to believe that Alcidor is unfaithful, Artenice renounces the mundane world, and laments:

> Quant à moy desormais le seul bien que j'espere,
> Est de passer ma vie au fond d'un Monastere,
> Où sage à mes despends, ie veux à l'aduenir
> Au seul amour des Dieux mes volontez vnir.[64]
>
> [As for me, from now on, the only good I wish for,
> Is to pass my life in the depths of a monastery,
> Where, wise to my expenditure, I want in the future
> To unite my wishes to the sole love of the Gods.]

Later editions of *Les Bergeries* replaced the phrases 'au fond d'un monastère' and 'des Dieux' with 'un desert austere' and 'du Ciel' respectively.[65] The text of *Artenice* follows that of the 1625 original, and thus makes a specific equation between the fictional space of the temple into which Artenice desires to retreat and a monastery. The religious significance is obvious and is further underlined by Artenice's subsequent *adieu* to the world: she renounces its physical pleasures for the austere life of the cloister with the words, 'Je prends congé du monde et de ses vanitez' [I take leave of the world and of its vanities].[66] Drawing upon Ecclesiastes 1.2 ('vanity of vanities; all is vanity') and 1 John 2.15 ('Love not the world, neither the things that are in the world'), this passage has an obvious religious significance.

The play's specifically religious message is repeated in Act three and gains a Catholic gloss when Artenice declares her intention to join Philothée's religious community. The convent scene prominently starts the central act of the play, and marks a turning point in Artenice's spiritual life as she recognises the follies of the world and fixes her faith on the stability of eternity, evoking the mundane world as a vale of shadows and smoke:

La gloire des mortels n'est qu'ombre et que fumée,
C'est vne flame étainte aussi tost qu'allumée.
Dessillez-vous les yeux, vous dont la vanité
Prefere ceste vie à l'immortalité.[67]

[Mortals' glory is only shadow and smoke,
It is a flame extinguished as soon as [it is] lit.
Clear your eyes, you whose vanity
Prefers this life to immortality.]

Artenice's words here represent the mortal world as a mere reflection of a greater truth. However, Philothée's reply to Artenice makes evident an aspect of the pastoral's message that, by the end of the production, will be of great importance. Privileging the world of the cloister as the most certain way of attaining eternal peace, Philothée nonetheless remarks:

Ma soeur ne plaignez point ceux que le sort conuie
A passer loing de nous la course de leur vie,
Parmy les vanitez qui ne sont point icy,
Où le combat est grand, la gloire l'est aussi.[68]

[My sister do not pity those who fate urges
To pass their lives far from us,
Among the vanities which are not [present] here,
Where the fight is great, so is the glory.]

Racan's Philothée teaches Artenice that it is possible to live virtuously in a corrupt world. Sales's preface to his *Introduction* declared that his intention was to instruct those who lived in towns, in households, at the court, and those who, because of their condition, were obliged to live with others in the world.[69] Racan's Philothée expresses similar sentiments and, moreover, makes it clear that glory is to be won by living 'where the fight is great': one can have a spiritual vocation and yet, because of unavoidable obligations, one can remain in the world.

Artenice is subsequently manoeuvred into precisely this situation and leaves the convent to be married to Alcidor. This marriage serves two strategies in the text, one secular and one religious: it mystifies the dynastic necessity which insists that, as her father's only child, Artenice must renounce the virginal life and produce an heir; and it underlines the impression that her fate is divinely ordained. The Bonne Déesse's edict, by forbidding Artenice to marry a foreigner, is nonetheless indicative of the fact that Artenice is expected to marry. The shepherdess is made aware that she belongs in the world and her marriage to Alcidor becomes her spiritual vocation.

There is a very evident parallel to be drawn between Artenice's fate and that of Henrietta Maria. As a French princess, Henrietta Maria's role was to marry a foreign prince: she could not choose a cloistered life because marriage was always her destiny. Indeed, Marie de Médicis's parting letter to her made it clear that she was to believe that her marriage was divinely ordained:

C'est un des desseins de Dieu sur vous, qui vous veut faire en nos jours une autre Berthe, fille de France comme vous, et reyne d'Angleterre comme vous laquelle obtint par sa saincte vie et par ses prières le don de foi à sa mari et à cette Isle en laquelle vous allez entrer.[70]

[It's one of God's plans for you. [He] wants to make you another Bertha in our time. [She was] a daughter of France like you, and queen of England like you, and through her holy life and her prayers, obtained the gift of faith for her husband and for this Island into which you are about to enter.]

According to the letter, Henrietta Maria was to follow the example of Bertha in attempting to convert her husband and to return his country to the Catholic faith. Indeed, she was to enter into the bonds of marriage in the same way that others entered into religion.[71] Artenice's situation in *Les Bergeries* was therefore particularly resonant when performed on the English stage by the queen and her ladies, presenting before the Caroline court the figure of a woman who turned from a cloistered life to follow her vocation in the world.

Henrietta Maria's pastoral production was not, therefore, simply a facile reproduction of *salon* culture as so many critics have believed; it was a cultural manifesto that enabled her to assert her position as the new wife of Charles I. Produced at a time when diplomatic relations with France were increasingly strained, it was a bridging exercise between French and English courtiers and foregrounded issues of love and commitment that would echo throughout the Caroline reign. Nevertheless, it was also a noteworthy declaration of the queen's very particular arrival on the English court stage.

CHAPTER 3

Foreign bodies: conflict and co-operation in the early masques

The years between the performance of *Artenice* and that of Henrietta Maria's 1631 masque, *Chloridia*, have largely been ignored by critics of the queen's dramatic productions. This can largely be put down to a paucity of evidence, yet, like the 1625 wedding ballets, what remains of these sorely neglected entertainments provides invaluable information about Henrietta Maria's early iconography. Indeed, by the end of the decade, a comparison of the queen consort's cultural activities with those of her new husband reveals an interesting difference. The king's productions gradually renovate his new wife's foreignness until, by 1632, she comes to stand for the goddess of England itself. Nevertheless, her own entertainments continue to emphasise her status as a princess of France through their promotion of French authors and of symbols such as the fleur-de-lis.

This chapter will examine what little can be gleaned about the queen consort's early entertainments. It will also investigate in more detail the nexus of relations surrounding her during her early years at the Caroline court in an attempt to shed light on the people and policies that influenced her actions. Previously, I noted that several of her prominent advisers (most notably Blainville, the French ambassador) succeeded in antagonising Charles and his ministers by advising her publicly to demonstrate her religious allegiances. Here, I want to investigate the new relationships she fostered after the expulsion of her French attendants, and to examine her apparent rivalry with the duke of Buckingham.

*

Many of the tensions between Henrietta Maria's French household and the English court sprang from events in France during the negotiation of the marriage treaty. Not only had there been much wrangling over the wording of the treaty itself, but, after his arrival in Paris to hasten Henrietta Maria's departure to England, Buckingham had managed personally to antagonise Louis XIII and Richelieu, not least through his very obvious admiration for, and solicitation of, the French Queen Anne.[1] Alison Plowden describes this interlude as the duke's 'flirtation with . . . Louis's pretty but neglected wife'.[2] However, this romantic interpretation obscures the political advantage to be gained from the favour of the French queen.

In 1625, Anne represented a possible focus for opposition against Richelieu within the French establishment. She had already formed the close tie with Marie de Chevreuse that, as I will show in later chapters, subtended much of the political resistance to the cardinal throughout the 1630s. As such, she represented a very valuable asset to Richelieu's opponents. Indeed, such was the seriousness with which the friendship with Buckingham was regarded at the French court that several members of Anne's household were subsequently dismissed by Louis XIII for their encouragement of it. At least one of these, the chevalier de Jars, would later be implicated in further intrigues against Richelieu in a factional alliance that saw collaboration between, among others, Anne of Austria, Marie de Chevreuse and Buckingham's former client, the earl of Holland.[3] In 1625, Buckingham's 'flirtation' with the French queen was, therefore, more likely to have had a strategic, rather than a romantic, purpose, tapping into an anti-Richelieu opposition that would raise its head on several occasions throughout the next decade.[4]

Henrietta Maria's allegiances at this time lay with her mother and the French king, her brother, and so were largely opposed to those of Buckingham and his adherents. Indeed, there is early evidence of her personal awareness of and participation in courtly intriguing. For example, in the summer of 1626, she attempted to take steps against the duke, informing her lord chamberlain, Tillières, that,

Le duc et sa soeur en sont en grande jalousye et je croyt que sette jalousie me servira. Croyés que je ne me feray pas aller ny tromper, et que je fais tout cela pour mieux couvrir mon deseing. Montrés sette lettre à la royne et puis la brulés. Je diray à M. de Bassompierre plus de particularités. En atandant, je vous ay voulu mander sesy. Faites que je puise voir la royne ma mere, vous m'obligerés tout ce que l'on peut.[5]

[The duke and his sister are in great fit of jealousy about it and I believe that that jealousy will serve. Believe that I won't be misled by it, and that I do all this to fulfill my design the better. Show this letter to the queen and then burn it. I will tell Monsieur de Bassompierre in more detail. Meanwhile, I've wanted to ask you this. See to it that I am able to see the queen my mother; I'll owe you all that can be [owed].]

This intention to play on the duke and his sister's jealousies demonstrates both Henrietta Maria's understanding of court politics and her willingness to resort to subterfuge to facilitate her projects. It also bears witness to her almost objective detachment from Buckingham and his relations: there is no sense in her letter that she will ever need to welcome them into her circle or cultivate a friendship. In contrast, the letter underlines her reliance on her mother, demonstrating an affection for and allegiance to Marie de Médicis's cause that would continue throughout her life.

Henrietta Maria's entourage seems, nevertheless, to have contained both servants of the French crown loyal to the queen mother and to Richelieu, and those, like Marie de Chevreuse and de Jars, who could be persuaded to support Buckingham. The duke's opposition to the new queen's French household has often been attributed to his desire to find places near her for his own relations and thus to consolidate his influence with Charles I. However, this can be interpreted not so much as a personal conflict between Henrietta Maria and the old favourite for influence over the king, but as a more extended tussle for international political influence that saw Buckingham winning a point in the game against Richelieu.

Caroline Hibbard has noted that rather more of the French household remained in England after August 1626 than has otherwise been thought, observing that there were around twenty French men and women in chamber offices, as well as musicians, cooks, dressmakers and others 'below stairs'.[6] The documentation for the household in the late 1620s is incomplete, but it is possible to ascertain that certain of Henrietta Maria's ladies remained with her after the expulsion of the rest of her attendants. Three women in particular stand out in the records for their close relationship with her from her arrival in England to her exile in France in the 1650s and 60s, and all three can be shown to have been more the clients of Buckingham than of Richelieu. These were the ladies Garnier, Coignet and Vantelet.

Françoise de Monbodeac, Madame Garnier, is named as 'première femme de chambre' in the 1622–5 French records of Henrietta Maria's household. She appears to have travelled to England with Henrietta Maria in the role of her nurse and was one of the few women permitted to remain when the rest of the attendants were dismissed. Indeed, the comtesse de Tillières, wife of Henrietta Maria's lord chamberlain and herself a woman of the bedchamber, bitterly reported to her husband in August 1626 that Garnier had been recalled to the queen consort's side, adding: 'elle est plus pour ses alliés que pour sa maîtresse, encore qu'elle n'en fasse pas de semblant' [she is more for her allies than for her mistress, although she gives no sign of it].[7] Madame Tillières even went so far as to say that all the reappointments to the queen consort's household were 'les effets de la cabale de la nourrice' [the effects of the nurse's cabal], implying that Madame Garnier was working in close collaboration with Buckingham.[8] This opinion is corroborated by Madame de Saint Georges, Henrietta Maria's close friend and companion, who noted in the summer of 1626 that the queen's household 'n'est composée que des parents du duc ou de ses valets' [is composed only of the duke's relations or servants].[9] In other words, it was not just the duke's kinsfolk who were given positions in the rearranged household, but also those members of the former French entourage who had shown sympathy towards him.

Among those reinstated were two more women who remained by Henrietta Maria's side throughout their lives and who may also have been among those who performed in her early entertainments. Elizabeth Coignet, Garnier's daughter, travelled to England in the company of her husband Jacques, one of the queen's gentlemen ushers and daily waiters. She was enrolled in the queen's establishment lists as a 'chamberer' and held a position of some responsibility in the household during the 1630s, receiving money for the queen's progresses in 1635 and 1636, and accompanying the Palatine princes during their visit to the north of England during the summer of 1636.[10]

In addition, a certain Mademoiselle Vantelet, also a 'chamberer', was permitted to remain with the queen. She was married to Jacques de Lux, a gentleman usher of Henrietta Maria's privy chamber, and had a daughter to whom Henrietta Maria later stood as godmother.[11] In 1626, Père Sancy, an Oratorian priest and one of Richelieu's adherents, wrote to his master to assert that, although she was intelligent and faithful, Vantelet was being maintained by Buckingham and would probably end up of his party.[12] Sure enough (and despite Buckingham's death), by 1634, Richelieu had conceived a fierce distrust of her and tried to get her dismissed from the queen's service, suspecting her of being involved in the Châteauneuf plot that sought to depose him.[13]

It is possible to surmise, then, that many of the French who remained alongside Henrietta Maria had demonstrated their willingness to compromise with Buckingham. Nevertheless, this does not mean that they were his dupes. It is, therefore, interesting to consider the entertainment for the maréchal de Bassompierre put on in November 1626 by Henrietta Maria and her household after the former's extraordinary embassy to smooth over the early troubles of the Anglo-French alliance. It was the first time that English and French courtiers performed together, and was markedly different from the 'antique' entertainment performed by Henrietta Maria's French attendants in 1625. Indeed, to a greater extent even than *Artenice*, it constituted a display of the queen's household's readiness to participate in the ceremonial display of the Caroline court.

*

Martin Butler has suggested that both Buckingham's and Henrietta Maria's masques for Bassompierre dramatised a similar agenda; that is, a 'constructive interdependence between royal affinities' facilitated by the new queen consort's ties to her European family.[14] He also notes that Bassompierre had cultivated Buckingham assiduously during his time in England, presenting him with a letter from Marie de Médicis that pleaded for unity and that played on fears of English isolation.[15] Buckingham's masque, which reflected these French arguments, was performed at York House on 5 November 1626, and was, to Bassompierre's mind, 'le plus superbe festin que je vis de ma vie' [the most magnificent feast that I saw in my life].[16] Replicating imagery from the French wedding entertainments which praised Marie de Médicis as a peaceweaver between nations, it presented the queen mother encouraging her various offspring and their royal partners 'to come and join themselves with her among the gods, and there to put an end to all the discords of Christianity'.[17] In contrast to Buckingham's unperformed *Theater of Apollo* – which, in its presentation of Elizabeth of Bohemia and the little Palatine princes, recuperated French imperialist imagery for the Protestant cause – the November 1626 masque unashamedly flattered the national vanity of the French in a manner that indicated the English would honour the terms of the marriage treaty, newly renegotiated by the ambassador.[18]

Henrietta Maria's entertainment, performed at Somerset House eleven days later, also had a French theme, taking its inspiration from Rabelais's *Gargantua*. It was a significant production, not only because it was the first occasion in which English and French courtiers performed together, but because, for the first time ever, one of the king's leading counsellors took part in a queen's masque.[19] The production's ostensible purpose was, like Buckingham's, almost certainly to demonstrate reconciliation between the English and the French, and between the duke and Henrietta Maria, showing the ambassador the fruit of his labours and promising a continuing *entente*.

Bassompierre certainly regarded Henrietta Maria as the driving force behind the entertainment, noting in a letter of 12 November that she had delayed his planned departure 'pour une feste qu'elle fait Jeudy prochain en son palais de Sommerset à ma consideration, & à l'imitation de celle que fit dimanche passé le Duc de Boukinquam' [for a feast that she holds for me next Thursday at Somerset House in imitation of the duke of Buckingham's last Sunday].[20] This statement might be read as signifying the emergence of a new voice at the Caroline court and a new centre of cultural production to rival those of Whitehall and York House. However, this interpretation should be tempered. Just as Buckingham's production flattered the French through its reflection of Marie de Médicis's iconography, so Henrietta Maria's entertainment, despite its French theme, gave a privileged role to Buckingham and the English. Moreover, as John Holles attested in a letter to Doctor Williams, bishop of Lincoln, the masque was mounted 'at the Kings charge' in a manner that saw the two royal courts working together to produce a cultural event.[21]

The night of the performance was described by one of the Reverend Joseph Mead's correspondents in the following terms:

> His grace [the duke of Buckingham] took a shape upon the other (Thursday) night, which many thought too histrionical to become him; when in the presence of king, queen, ambassadors, and the flower of the court, he acted a master of defence, to teach the great porter to skirmish, as my Lord of Holland, a privy counsellor, also taught him the mathematics, and Sir George Goring to dance. For in the great masque on Thursday was sennight that overgrown Janitor, hight Gargantua, son and heir to Pantagruel, after whose decease Gargamella his master, desirous to breed up the young gentleman in virtuous qualities, recommended the care of his youth to those three grave tutors, whereof though the third might be excused, yet never before then did any privy counsellor appear in a masque.[22]

Although it describes a queen's production, this letter is principally concerned to advertise the roles undertaken by the male courtiers, lingering in residual Jacobean style on the significations of the duke's physical display. Criticising Buckingham for enacting a histrionical role, it nevertheless disregards Henrietta Maria entirely, leaving one with the impression that the duke was the prime mover in the entertainment.

This impression is compounded by the structure of the production which was evidently very different from the 1625 'antique' masque. It seems to have been organised along the lines of a traditional Stuart masque, with a series of light-hearted anti-masque entries, followed by a main masque of ladies wearing plumes of coloured feathers and carrying black fans.[23] Indeed, it is interesting to speculate whether Ben Jonson, the pioneer of this form, might have collaborated in the entertainment, employed, for the first time, to work on a production with the new queen. As Anne Lake Prescott has suggested, Rabelaisian themes were not new to him for he appears to have incorporated such motifs into several of his earlier masques.[24] Given the masque's structure, that the king financed the production and that Buckingham danced in it, I think it is not unlikely that Jonson was involved. Certainly, it was the first of Henrietta Maria's entertainments obviously to adopt the English masque form, blending this with a series of anti-masque entries like those from a *ballet burlesque*. It thus bears witness to the new levels of co-operation between her reduced French household and the wider Caroline court.

Nevertheless, there is a strong possibility that the entertainment was not performed in English and that it took its inspiration from a recent French production. John Holles called it a 'frenche maske' and it is notable that Buckingham, Holland and Sir George Goring, the courtiers who danced in the anti-masque, were all French speakers, making it possible that the entertainment was, indeed, performed in the queen's native language.[25] An entertainment similar to hers, the *Balet de la naissance de Pantagruel*, had been enacted in Blois during shrovetide 1626 and certainly seems to have provided inspiration for the English production for it, too, included the figures of a schoolmaster, a dancing master and a fencing master, as well as Pantagruel's nurse.[26] Some of the verses for this production were contributed by the poet Antoine Girard, sieur de Saint-Amant, who was to visit England in 1631 in what Françoise Gourier has suggested was a mission on behalf of Bassompierre.[27] While it is not impossible that he was a member of Bassompierre's train in 1626, it is more likely that his close friend Malleville, Bassompierre's secretary, was called on to contribute to the new entertainment, perhaps in collaboration with Jones and Jonson. As I noted in chapter 1, Malleville had already collaborated with Boisrobert to create the 1625 *Ballet de la Reyne d'Angleterre*. He was almost certainly in England in the autumn of 1626, and is very likely to have made use of his friend's recent work.

Saint-Amant's entertainment in Blois took the form of a series of entries performed by 'Monsieur dEsclimont', the son of the comte de Cheverny, and 'autres gentishommes', depicting the youth and education of Pantagruel.[28] The verses, particularly those attributed to Pantagruel's teachers, describe the young men's amorous attachments in an appropriately Rabelaisian manner with barely disguised innuendo. For example, the dancing master explains how, every night when his beloved 'Phylis' is asleep, he makes such a sweet noise that he awakens her with the sound of his instrument, the rhyme word 'instrument' carrying an obvious *double entendre*.[29] Similarly, the fencing master observes that, although other instructors are more competent, everyone attends his fencing school to uncover a secret known only to himself and his mistress.[30] The tone of the ballet is playful and, indeed, smutty. If the verses were carried over wholesale into Henrietta Maria's entertainment, then Mead's correspondent was probably right to suggest that Buckingham and his companions were acting undignified parts. However, the *Balet de la naissance de Pantagruel* is no more smutty and undignified than, for example, Jonson's *Gypsies Metamorphosed*, commissioned and performed by Buckingham for James I in 1621. Moreover, transformed into an entertainment at the English court, it would have seen this risqué anti-masque superseded by the arrival of Henrietta Maria and the main masquers to calm and reform the Rabelaisian excesses.

I strongly suspect that the queen's masque for Bassompierre was a highly collaborative project designed to show that she was willing to cooperate with her husband and his advisers. It emphasised her French origins through its Rabelaisian theme – and, perhaps, through its choice of language – and helped to establish her London residence as a new centre of cultural production. Nevertheless, unlike her 1625 'antique' entertainment, it demonstrated that her household had finally been infiltrated by the English. It also, importantly, marked the beginning of the development of Henrietta Maria's personal iconography as a Stuart queen, synthesising English masque forms with motifs that emphasised her French heritage.

*

The following 14 January, Henrietta Maria and fourteen of her ladies took part in an expensive masque that was described as 'tres beau' by Monsieur du Moulin, the secretary to the French embassy in England.[31] It was performed on a Sunday and a certain Mr Chalmer was alleged to have provided 1,000 yards of taffeta and satin for it.[32] Very little else is known about this production, but, more than any other, it marked the queen consort's assumption of a central place within Caroline theatrical display because it was performed prominently at Whitehall, rather than at Somerset House.

The masque also marked the start of Charles I's policy of privatising court entertainments, in part to avoid the perennial disputes about precedence among foreign ambassadors. Before the performance, John Finet received instructions from the king's lord chamberlain that the

Venetian and States ambassadors were to be welcomed, but that 'his Majesty was resolved never more to admit any Ambassadors resident to sit next his person under the State'.[33] By the time of *Love's Triumph* (1631), ambassadors were being encouraged to attend masques in a private, not a public, capacity: a decision that prevented such occasions being represented as expressions of royal favour and foreign policy. In 1631, as I will discuss, Henrietta Maria could still show her appreciation of the French ambassador by facilitating his attendance at her husband's masque. However, unlike Queen Anna, she was never able publicly to invite foreign emissaries to her theatrical productions.

Despite this injunction, such events provided ample opportunity for demonstrations of domestic favour. For example, after the 1627 masque, the Reverend Joseph Mead was informed by a correspondent that the 'king took much pains in placing the ladies' gentlewomen with his own hand', and that he had subsequently led the queen and the other masquers in a dance.[34] In other words, the occasion constituted a quasi-public display of courtly unity, with the king demonstrating his domestic harmony by dancing with his wife, and by showing his approval of the women who attended on her.

Four days after the masque, Elizabeth, countess of Huntingdon, wrote home to her husband, the fifth earl, noting:

> I was twice at Court to see the Queen practise, and stayed the play, supped with my Lady Denby then, and the masque night also, being earnestly invited, so in all I was thrice at Court, but went not till 4 or 5 o'clock. The Queen kissed me and asked if I could speak French. I denied it because I could not speak well.[35]

This letter provides interesting information about the masque, rehearsals for which began about four or five o'clock and could be attended by invitation. It also demonstrates how such royal events could have a political resonance for Caroline courtiers beyond any intentions encoded in the masque itself.

As a young woman, Huntingdon had performed in Queen Anna's *Masque of Queens* (1609) and might, therefore, be deemed to have an interest in Henrietta Maria's first major masquing event. Nevertheless, as Gordon McMullan has observed, both the countess and her husband, despite being important literary patrons, were largely averse to the court, preferring instead the 'honest delights' of a 'Cuntrie life'.[36] The winter of 1626/7, though, saw the earl beleaguered on all sides: he was reluctant to subscribe to the Forced Loan, pleading an inability to pay, at the same time as an inquiry was being called into his financial dealings as lord lieutenant of Leicestershire.[37] To guide him in this crisis, he dispatched his wife to Whitehall, where, as Tom Cogswell has noted, she was received graciously by the royal couple, most particularly by the king.[38]

Her presence at the masque in the company of Lady Denbigh must surely be seen as an aspect of her activity on behalf of her husband, not least because the Villiers family, of which Denbigh was a daughter, were large landowners in Leicestershire. Indeed, as James Knowles has noted, during the 1630s, Lady Huntingdon engaged in an extensive lobbying campaign in support of her husband, re-establishing the family's links with Whitehall.[39] Although her strongly Protestant outlook made it unlikely that she would ever become a confidante of the new queen, her attendance shows how important such cultural events were for the propagation of ties of clientage and friendship.

Huntingdon's letter, like that of Katherine Gorges in 1625, demonstrates that access to the masque was facilitated by Lady Denbigh. As first lady of the bedchamber and mistress of the queen's wardrobe, Denbigh had daily contact with Henrietta Maria and held a hugely responsible position with a large amount of control over expenditure. Her signature appears consistently in the queen's account books, and she was also responsible for overseeing the accounting for all the queen's masques and entertainments. In February 1627, for example, just after the Whitehall masque, she passed on a bill to the queen's treasurer for £83.16s.9d for lace, while in 1633 she was responsible for a bill worth over £1,000 payable to 'dyvers Creditors of London . . . for her Maties Pastorall'.[40] The state papers are full of warrants granting her funds, most particularly for the queen's progresses and lyings in, and also contain letters in which she sought patronage from the king and from the duke of Buckingham for various family servants.[41] It is beyond the remit of this study fully to explore the undoubted significance of her activities at the Caroline court. Nevertheless, she was obviously engaged in introducing important clients into the queen consort's circle, and was courted for her influence by significant noblemen and women.

Henrietta Maria's reaction to this is interesting. As I discussed in chapter 1, on her arrival in England, she sometimes adopted a policy of non-participation, refusing to speak in English or to converse with non-Catholics. Although Huntingdon's letter indicates a softening of this earlier position, similar strategies are invoked in welcoming a stranger into her sphere as she marks out a favoured circle through her preference for the French language. However 'earnestly invited' the countess might have been by Lady Denbigh, her unwillingness to converse in French separated her from the queen and, despite Cogswell's assertion that Henrietta Maria was 'gracious' to her, there is no evidence that she received any direct benefits from her introduction.

*

Throughout the early months of 1627, and despite the Whitehall masque's manifestation of unity, the queen consort seems to have continued her opposition to Buckingham by neglecting his associates and befriending those he had offended. That spring, du Moulin noted that she was ostentatiously favouring Lucy Hay, wife of the earl of Carlisle, by inviting her to suppers with the countesses of Exeter, Oxford and Berkshire without including either Lady Denbigh or Buckingham's wife.[42] In late 1626, the earl of Carlisle, who coveted the post of the king's lord chamberlain, had fallen out with Buckingham whose preferred client was the eventually successful earl of Montgomery.[43] In 1627, moreover, Carlisle was more favourably disposed towards Louis XIII than the duke who was soon to take England into a war with France. Henrietta Maria's position at this time is consistent with her previous familial and political allegiances in that she continued to favour her mother and brother's cause and chose her friends accordingly.

During the early part of 1627, du Moulin's dispatches indicate that Henrietta Maria and Charles were becoming increasingly attached to one another. In April, he noted that the king (who, he said, now loved his wife extremely) had presented her with a beautiful diamond and that she appeared very happy.[44] Nevertheless, encoded parts of the letter remark that she was very short of money and had been forced to borrow from the London financier Burlamachi.[45] Moreover, despite her gradual acceptance of some English ladies, Henrietta Maria still clung to her countrymen and women in a manner that became increasingly problematic as England drew closer to war with France.

Du Moulin himself got into trouble in late April for attempting to send letters out of England with some of the queen consort's musicians, in a manner that indicates that, even if she was not directly involved, the regular concourse between Henrietta Maria's entourage and their native country could pose a problem for the English crown.[46] Indeed, the queen's innocence in this attempt to transmit information is not entirely convincing. Soon after the discovery of his activities, du Moulin wrote again to Richelieu to say that, despite her initial resolution to do so, Henrietta Maria had decided against writing to her mother with important information, explaining that the king had forbidden her to communicate with France and that she was afraid that the rest of her French household would be dismissed if she did.[47] This complicates the idea that the queen was simply not interested in politics, demonstrating that, from May 1627 when Buckingham sailed for La Rochelle, her international correspondence was curtailed both by the war and by fear of reprisal.

Malcolm Smuts has suggested that, by 1628, Henrietta Maria had 'learned to avoid politics' and had 'settled into a gay, harmless life in the company of a few English ladies'.[48] That year certainly saw a continuing interest in court theatre, although it is possible that this was less the sign of the queen's 'harmless' life than a displaced means of registering a political opinion. At shrovetide, Charles disbursed substantial sums towards a 'new Maske intended to haue bynne performed', although, as Butler notes, there are no eyewitness accounts of the performance so it is impossible to say with certainty that it took place or whether it was intended for the king or the queen.[49] Nevertheless, the same year, Henrietta Maria was painted by Gerrit van Honthorst as an Arcadian shepherdess in what might have been masque costume and, on 12 August, she apparently intended to perform in a masque with her ladies during her progress to Wellingborough.[50] In the context of Smuts's comment, this masque and the progress itself are interesting for what they suggest about Henrietta Maria's attitude towards the Anglo-French war being pursued by her husband. Although she was not in a position to intervene politically in the conflict, she could certainly allude to it culturally.

OPPOSING CAMPS

At the end of July 1628, while her husband travelled south to Portsmouth to ready his fleet against the French, Henrietta Maria departed on progress to Wellingborough. John H. Astington has noted that the queen commissioned a set of blue calico tents for her progresses in 1627–8, decorated with gold fleur-de-lis, pyramids and stars. Between 1628 and 1630, a mock castle was created for her in cloth with 'ffower Turrets' and 'A lardge ffower square wall of Canvas embattayled and painted like a Stonewall with battlements and peeces of Ordenaunce'.[51] Astington notes that these tents were used at Wellingborough, Holdenby, Tunbridge Wells and Oatlands, observing that this 'playful conceit was nothing more than a large piece of theatrical scenery set *en plein air*, a mocking invasion of the English landscape by a French conqueror'.[52] In the light of Charles and Buckingham's war against the French, this 'invasion' is perhaps not only what Astington terms a 'testimony to [the queen's] sense of humour', but also her response to English relations with France.[53] Erected around Wellingborough, the tents make no bones about the French princess's nationality, recreating a French military camp that is set up *inside* the bounds of England.

Notably, the 1628 progress was also to include an entertainment for which Hugh Pope, a servant in the office of the Robes, made '13 Capes [caps] of tinnsell and tafitie in the fation of hellmittes' as well as '4 wooden swords with sheathes'.[54] Although this production does not seem to have taken place, the martial nature of the props participates in the redefinition both of the land and of Henrietta Maria's place within it.[55] Camping at Wellingborough, Henrietta Maria enacted a fantasy of military action, both by inhabiting a theatricalised martial space and through her intention to mount an Amazonian entertainment. Indeed, in her appropriation of martial imagery, the queen invoked the iconography that had marked her wedding and accompanied her to England. As I discussed in chapter 1, Marie de Médicis celebrated the Anglo-French marriage with the unveiling of a series of paintings by Rubens, the last of which depicted her as Minerva Victrix surrounded by the trappings of good government, victory and immortality. Henrietta Maria was later to mirror this imagery in *Salmacida Spolia*, her masque of 1640, appearing before her mother in Amazonian dress.[56] In 1628, while her husband was inhabiting the very real military camp at Portsmouth prior to sending his ships against the French, Henrietta Maria lived out a fantasy which, paradoxically, saw England already occupied by a French force.

Although the queen's household was now tamed by the infiltration of the English and by the removal of Richelieu's strongest supporters, its foreign presence at the heart of the nation could still be an issue, even if only symbolically. During the late 1620s, Henrietta Maria's familial and political allegiances remained with her mother, and with her mother's Catholic cause. Indeed, Alison Shell has noted that the queen's faith and her duty as her country's representative would have made it impossible for her always 'to sustain a perfect [wifely] submissiveness'.[57] Sometimes this meant demonstrating her willingness to compromise with the English; at other times, it meant filling the English landscape with reminders of her national identity.

Henrietta Maria was, like her husband, surrounded by advisers, and worked within a framework of duty and responsibility. It is therefore sometimes difficult to separate out her personal preferences from the obligations imposed on her by her role. Her entertainments during the late 1620s show her progressive incorporation into the economy of Stuart theatrical display, moving from a Rabelaisian masque that blended a Jonsonian structure with aspects of *ballet burlesque* to an expensive production performed at Whitehall in the midst of the Forced Loan crisis. At the same time, however, her wider social behaviour demonstrated her antipathy towards Buckingham and his adherents, and a desire strongly to promote her religious and dynastic affiliations.

*

As I noted at the start of this chapter, an interesting difference had developed between the king and queen's theatrical iconographies by the end of the 1620s. Where Henrietta Maria's entertainments emphasised her status as a princess of France, Charles's productions absorbed her into a fantasy of virile masculine heroism. To conclude, then, I wish to consider the first two extant king's masques of the Caroline reign, Jonson and Jones's *Love's Triumph* (1631) and Aurelian Townshend and Jones's *Albion's Triumph* (1632), to explore the ways in which Henrietta Maria was represented in her husband's productions.

Writing of early Greek culture, Page duBois has noted that, as 'the objects of the culture-founding act of exchange', women inhabited a contradictory position. They were excluded from the city, yet necessary for its reproduction and 'came to represent a potentially dangerous, even poisonous force which was both within the city and outside it'.[58] This is an interesting concept when applied to Henrietta Maria's position in England. Exchanged in marriage to cement links between powerful European nations, she also represented the reproductive hopes of the Stuart dynasty. Nevertheless, she was a foreign body at the heart of the nation and a potential threat to national security. In what follows, I will explore the ways in which Charles's iconography sought to minimise this threatening possibility.

Love's Triumph Through Callipolis was written by Ben Jonson and performed by the king at Whitehall on 9 January 1631. The following year, after Jonson's fall from grace, Charles took to the stage again in Inigo Jones and Aurelian Townshend's *Albion's Triumph*, performed on 8 January 1632. Butler has noted that 'the implied motif underlying the anti-masque' of *Love's Triumph* was Theseus and the minotaur, a 'myth of kingly virility and heroic eroticism directly cognate with the St George and the dragon fable that was a favourite with Charles'.[59] Despite the masque's neo-Platonic theme, he asserts, Charles was not represented 'solely as a spiritualized being', but instead as 'an able and physically active lover, whose qualifications for empire were inextricably mixed with the sexual satisfaction the royal couple enjoyed'.[60] Just as Buckingham's 1625 letter from Dover equated the monarch's facility in dancing with his eagerness and virility as a husband, so Charles's first masque after the birth of a living heir evoked his credentials as the father and guardian of the nation.

Love's Triumph's opening argument, declaimed by Euphemus ('a Person, *boni ominis*, of a good Character'), describes how the suburbs of Callipolis, city of beauty or goodness, have been penetrated by depraved lovers.[61] On one level, this textual anxiety about the permeability of the city's margins reflects an historical reality: in 1626, 1627 and 1632, Charles published proclamations exhorting the nobility to return to their estates in the country in an attempt to reinvigorate traditional modes of government and to reduce disorder in the city. The masque registers an anxiety about malign influences existing at the edges of the city but, by a clever manipulation of circular motifs, imagines itself, and, by extension, the state, to become impermeable through a process of binding and purification. *Love's Triumph* invokes images of civil disorder only to contain and reform them by the example of the purity of the Caroline royal union.

Significantly, such disorder is shown by the text to have arrived from elsewhere. The depraved lovers are represented in the masque as 'expressing their confus'd affections in the Scenicall persons, and habits, of the foure prime *European* Nations' (lines 32–3), thus indicating that the problems afflicting Callipolis are not domestic, but the result of external penetration.[62] The fiction of the city's coherence is maintained – to reassert order it is only necessary to police Callipolis's borders, closing them off from the influences of outside. Nevertheless, the European antimasque figures are essential to the integrity of the masque, providing an image of discord against which harmony can be measured. In other words, European disorderliness is a necessary adjunct to the masque's representation of peace. This evocation of European disorder, moreover, has a direct bearing upon the figure of Henrietta Maria, the masque's principal observer, who is addressed by Euphemus as 'The center of proportion' (line 130). As the 'obiect, of Heroique *Loue*' (line 128), she completes a circuit that is begun in Charles for, in the Chorus's words, '*Loue*, without his obiect soon is gone: / *Loue* must haue answering loue, to looke vpon' (lines 121–2).[63] The harmony of the royal marriage is expressed in the reciprocity of Charles and Henrietta Maria's gazes which reflect each other and unite the king and queen consort in an orderly, chaste whole.

By incorporating Henrietta Maria into the masque's fiction in this way, *Love's Triumph* claims her for itself and for Callipolis. Its imagery renders the royal union whole and solid: the couple's reciprocal gazes, providing a pattern of unity for the nation, are circular and unbroken. As the European disorders are expelled beyond the boundaries of Callipolis, so the alien queen consort is recast as a national treasure and the borders of the country closed up. *Love's Triumph* not only imagines the expulsion of foreign disorders from Callipolis, but purifies Henrietta Maria, locking her identity to a circle of impenetrable reciprocity with Charles.

The masque's conclusion reinforces this sense of reciprocity in its image of a palm tree 'with an imperiall crowne on the top, from the root whereof, Lillies and Roses twining together, and imbracing the stem, flourish through the crowne' (lines 206–8). Echoing the floral imagery of the 1625 wedding celebrations, *Love's Triumph* ends with an image of mutual dependency couched in the terms of natural abundance. The masque's gesture to the national flower of France serves less to invoke images of difference, than to prefigure the image of assimilation proposed by the masque's closing lines:

> Who this King, and Queene would well historify
> Need onely speake their names: Those them will glorify.
> MARY, and CHARLES, CHARLES, with his MARY named are,
> And all the rest of *Loues*, or *Princes* famed are. (lines 218–21)

Love's Triumph sets up an image of the fertile royal union that would echo through the masques of the next ten years. Charles and Henrietta Maria are inseparably joined together: they are the 'Mary-Charles' of *Albion's Triumph* (1632) and the 'Carlomaria' of *Coelum Britannicum* (1634).

The importance of this reciprocal image is nowhere more apparent than in an innovative portrait of the king and queen by Anthony Van Dyck. Painted in 1634, Van Dyck's portrait shows Charles presenting Henrietta Maria with an olive branch, while she, in turn, gives her husband a laurel crown. Charles's gaze rests upon Henrietta Maria, while hers spreads the couple's influence beyond the frame to those who observe the image. The portrait provides an emblem of the process of Jonson's masque, demonstrating the fecund possibilities of complementary gift giving. It evokes the harmony of the royal union and, by using the curve of the queen's arm to emphasise her pregnant figure, shows this union to be productive, not sterile.

Figure 3.1. Daniel Mytens, with additions by Van Dyck, *Charles I and Henrietta Maria*, 1630–2.

Van Dyck's portrait reworked and superseded a picture by Mytens that had been produced around 1630 for Somerset House.[64] A comparison of Mytens's portrait with that of Van Dyck shows the latter's increased emphasis on reciprocity, as well as its reference to the fecundity of the royal couple. The Mytens portrait gestures to reciprocal gift giving only through an ambiguity: a laurel crown is passed between the royal couple, but it is difficult to work out just who is passing it to whom (figure 3.1). The Van Dyck image is far more specific, making it obvious that its gift-giving gesture involves an *exchange* of icons (figure 3.2). Furthermore, in contrast to the Mytens's blank background, a rural vista opens up behind Van Dyck's royal couple, extending the iconic exchange of gifts out to the country. The laurel crown (compatible with the masques' representation of Charles's heroism) and the olive branch (expressive of the Caroline peace) spread their combined virtues both into the background countryside, and out to the picture's observers, caught in Henrietta Maria's gaze. Although the couple's hands at the centre of the picture complete the circle of the gift, the queen's gaze crosses that circle. The king looks at the

Figure 3.2. Robert van Voerst after Van Dyck, *Charles I and Henrietta Maria*, 1634.

pregnant queen and the queen looks at the nation. Van Dyck's portrait shows the royal couple to spread their beneficent influence beyond themselves; through their union, Charles and Henrietta Maria promulgate both the royal peace and the royal line.

Townshend's *Albion's Triumph* followed *Love's Triumph* in its valorisation of Henrietta Maria's beauty, imagining her in an indissoluble pairing with her heroic husband. The printed text declares that the masque's subject is a triumph in Albipolis, the chief city of Albion.[65] The idea of the triumph has an obvious connection with *Love's Triumph*, continuing themes of imperial rule compatible with the king's iconography of Roman heroism. It invokes the old name of Albion, 'Albion being (as it once was) taken for England' (lines 7–8), locating its action in a legendary past governed by the Roman gods. Charles (who as a young prince had been duke of Albany) is represented by the figure of Albanactus, '*quasi in Albania natus*, born in Scotland' (lines 8–9), while Henrietta Maria, seated in the audience, is shadowed in the goddess Alba.[66]

In an opening similar to that of *Love's Triumph*, *Albion's Triumph* begins with the descent of Mercury, Jove's messenger, who informs Alba that Jove has decreed a triumph. His opening song emphasises the virtues of vision, as each of its three stanzas begins respectively with the exhortations: 'Behold', 'Observe' and 'Admire'. Kevin Sharpe has said of *Albion's Triumph* that it depends 'upon poetry and prose rather than spectacle', yet Mercury's opening verses explicitly introduce the theme of sight.[67] In the ensuing anti-masque, this theme is explored further as the characters of Publicus and Platonicus indulge in a debate which sets physical appearance against intellectual apprehension. As Sharpe comments, their exchange becomes a philosophical dialogue, much like those of Plato from whom Platonicus takes his name.[68] Publicus describes the physical nature of the triumph he has just observed in the street. Platonicus, too, declares that he saw the triumph, although, unlike Publicus, he states that he remained at home. He comments that, with his eyes of understanding, he witnessed the moral virtues of Albanactus Caesar in contrast to Publicus who only perceived a superficial, physical show. Graham Parry has noted that this 'engaging interlude' presented the idea that the true triumph 'was not the external display of greatness but the triumph of the moral virtues that may be apprehended only by the philosophic mind'.[69] However, although this is certainly part of the masque's message, a reading which unproblematically privileges Platonicus's intellectual position does not do justice to the full implications of the anti-masque. It is the combination of Platonicus with Publicus, of mind and matter, which underlies the masque's meanings and which, moreover, has a particular effect upon the character of Alba.

After the anti-masque, the triumph of Albanactus ensues, introducing the king and his fellow masquers on to the stage near a temple sacred to Jove. Cupid and Diana descend to subdue Albanactus to love and chastity, after which they present him to Alba who makes him 'co-partner of her deity' (line 21). The masque ends with a representation of Whitehall and London, and with the appearance of Peace and her companions who, Astraea-like, herald the return of a new golden age. The closing song of the masque celebrates the united figure of the Mary-Charles in a manner which corresponds to, and effectively synthesises, the Platonicus/Publicus debate, praising the perfect intellectual and physical symbiosis of the royal couple, 'whose minds within / And bodies make but Hymen's twin' (lines 445–6). Like *Love's Triumph*, the masque concerns itself with England's peace, linking Alba to Albanactus in a pairing that is the foundation of Charles's ideology of government. Indeed, *Albion's Triumph* has two things to say about Alba: she is the goddess of Albion and she stands for the queen, 'whose native beauties have a great affinity with all purity and whiteness' (lines 10–11). Just as *Love's Triumph* transformed the figure of the queen into a symbol of domestic harmony, so *Albion's Triumph* naturalises Henrietta Maria, making her a native of Albion and the true partner of Albanactus. Her foreign origins are expunged and she comes to signify everything that is pure and white as she is incorporated into the nationalistic economy of the masque.

She also becomes irreducibly associated with the maternal. The love celebrated in *Albion's Triumph* is, in Sharpe's words, both 'pure *and* fertile: it procreates virtues which attract the blessings of concord, peace and justice to the king, the queen and the realm'.[70] Indeed, *Albion's Triumph*'s sixth song wishes that the couple 'may perpetuate themselves by a royal posterity' (lines 365–6) and contains the invocation:

> May your virtuous minds beget
> Issue that never shall decay,
> And so be fruitful every way. (lines 372–4)

Following the body/mind dualism of the masque, the song conceives of the royal couple's posterity as spiritual, as an immortal issue that will spread pleasure and peace. However, precisely *because* of the masque's body/mind dualism, this very metaphysical posterity works in a binaristic combination with some entirely physical matters. Once again (and unsurprisingly), it is upon the figure of Alba that this imagery turns. Alba is invoked in a manner that appropriates her generative capabilities for Albanactus, leaving him the sole author of himself and his posterity, both physical and metaphysical.

The masque's argument describes Albanactus as born in Scotland (see above), while Alba is goddess of the island of Albion. Alba is the spirit of the isle, Albanactus's motherland; in effect, Alba *is* Albion, the matter/*mater* from which *Alba*-nactus was born. The king (described as 'seeking that happy union which was preordained by the greatest of the gods' (lines 12–13)), therefore undertakes a journey which seeks to return him to his origins, his final union with Alba standing for his return to the place from which he was derived. It is a redemptive return to paradisal unity where he may exist 'breast to breast' with his lost (m)other/wife. The notion of matter is displaced on to the feminine half of the Alba/Albanactus equation, leaving Albanactus free to inhabit the realms of rational self-identity. Although the masque ends with the apparently equal image of the Mary-Charles, maintaining the mind/body dualism in perfect and productive balance, it is Alba who has been absorbed into the economy of the self-identical masculine Same, giving rise to a 'royal posterity' that will secure Albion's identity and its peace. In other words, just like the Theseus imagery that subtends *Love's Triumph*, *Albion's Triumph* proposes a version of heroic masculinity predicated upon the monarch's virile conquest of territories conceived as feminine.

Charles's early masques, then, defuse the threat posed by his foreign wife, absorbing her into his personal iconography and Anglicising her name to 'Mary'. Notably, although an early Caroline proclamation decreed she was to be known as 'Queen Mary', Henrietta Maria consistently favoured the French version of her name, signing herself in her letters as 'Henriette R'.[71] In the light of this bid to conserve her French name and identity, the next two chapters will discuss her own early productions, asking whether, through them, she was able to assert a cultural and political presence independent of that of her husband.

CHAPTER 4

Family affairs: Henrietta Maria and continental politics in 1631

Chloridia, the queen consort's masque of 1631, gave rise to Ben Jonson's notorious and definitive rupture with Inigo Jones, ostensibly because Jones objected to his name appearing second on the title page of the printed text.[1] However, as the last collaborative project between the two men, the masque is also fascinating in its own right. Danced on 22 February 1631, together with *Love's Triumph Through Callipolis* (performed by King Charles on 9 January), it is one of the first two Caroline masques whose texts have survived and, as David Lindley has remarked, it 'indicate[s] clearly the new direction and new thematic preoccupations of the masques of the period, with their celebration and idealization of the royal marriage'.[2] *Chloridia* provides a striking example of the emergent royal iconography that presented Charles and Henrietta Maria's union as chaste, fecund and beneficial for the nation. In addition, I would argue, in contrast to Charles's own masques, it also makes a surprising engagement with continental politics.

Martin Butler has observed of the king's masques of the 1630s that they 'had very little to say about continental affairs'.[3] He continues:

> The 1630s masques concentrate almost exclusively on domestic politics, and if Europe appears at all it is always in tropes elaborating on the contrast between shipwreck abroad and peace at home.[4]

This is certainly true of a masque such as *Love's Triumph* in which riotous European turbulence is returned to a decent order by the presence of Charles. However, Jonson's *Chloridia*, written for the queen, can be shown actively to engage with both European politics and culture. Henrietta Maria's productions, while they often formed complementary pairs with Charles's entertainments, did not simply echo those entertainments' domestic concerns. Unlike Anna of Denmark's productions, they deployed an idiom that emphasised Henrietta Maria's national origins, constructing her identity as both a queen of England and a princess of

France. Furthermore, they could sometimes also express political ideas that did not find a counterpart in the king's productions. In the first part of this chapter, I will therefore investigate the ways in which Jonson's masque for the queen developed an iconography that was compatible with Charles's domestic concerns, providing appropriate images of chaste love and fecundity that would echo throughout the subsequent masques of the reign. However, in the second part I will demonstrate how, unlike *Love's Triumph*, *Chloridia* engaged with French current affairs, bearing witness to Henrietta Maria's anxieties about events in her native France.

*

The printed text of *Chloridia* establishes that the masque is to be coupled with *Love's Triumph* through the assertion:

> The King and Queenes Maiesty, hauing giuen their command for the Inuention of a new argument . . . wherein her Maiesty, with the like number of her Ladies, purposed a presentation to the King. It was agreed, it should be the celebration of some Rites, done to the Goddesse Chloris, who in a generall counsell of the Gods, was proclaim'd Goddesse of the flowers . . . And was to be stellified on Earth, by an absolut decree from Iupiter, who would haue the Earth to be adorn'd with starres, as well as the Heauen.[5]

The number of lady masquers in *Chloridia* will mirror the number of masquers who danced in the king's production, structurally reinforcing the idea that *Chloridia* is the second half of a pair. Moreover, just as Charles ordered *Love's Triumph* to be produced for his 'vnmatchable Lady, and Spouse', so *Chloridia* will operate as a compliment to Charles.[6] However, while the queen consort was simply the recipient of the earlier masque, the king is shown to take an active role in commanding 'the Inuention of [the] new argument' (line 2); it is the king *and* the queen who have decided upon the new production, not the queen alone. Such a sense of paternalistic control is reinforced within the structure of the masque itself when Jupiter is invoked as the prime mover of the plot: it is he who has issued the 'absolut decree' (line 10) which leads to the transformation of Chloris into Flora; the figure of Chloris is under his control.

Criticism of this masque quite rightly connects it to *Love's Triumph.* Orgel and Strong emphasise that '*Chloridia* opens where *Love's Triumph* had ended, in a garden',[7] while the figure of Chloris, dressed in white, is proleptic of *Albion's Triumph*'s vision of the pure Alba. Henrietta Maria's masque participates in and contributes to the iconographical vocabulary of the Caroline reign, locating the queen consort as a divine beauty and the king as the incarnation of heroic virtue. Indeed, as Erica Veevers has perceptively commented, *Chloridia* is 'built on a structure of complementary opposites personifying the masculine and feminine principles of the universe'.[8] Within these opposites (of Heaven and Earth, Zephyr and Spring, king and queen), the masculine is 'the dominant and commanding power', but, as Veevers observes, 'the feminine brings to it the beauty and variety which belong to the universal order, as ineluctably as the beauty and variety of the seasons and elements belong to the natural order'.[9] In other words, within *Chloridia*, just as in the king's masques, the masculine principle is to be associated with Law, with an 'absolut decree' (line 10), with *mind*, while the feminine principle chastely inhabits the realm of nature and generation.

The opening scene of *Chloridia* emphasises this conceit of chaste fecundity when the figure of Zephyr descends to tell Spring that Chloris is to be stellified on earth as the goddess Flora. The masque immediately effects a purification of its source in Ovid's *Fasti*, which had characterised Zephyr as the violator and then husband of Chloris.[10] In *Chloridia*, Zephyr is described as a 'plumpe Boy' (lines 30–1); his potentially violent sexuality is erased, and his youth is appropriate to the masque's conceit of spring. Indeed, *Chloridia* is full of the images of children, befitting the queen consort's status as a new mother (the future Charles II had been born the previous May). The production's proscenium arch is 'enterwouen with all sorts of flowers; and naked children, playing, and climbing among the branches' (lines 15–17), while the main plot involves the disobedience of 'the Boy', Cupid (line 110). The figure of Chloris is therefore surrounded in the masque with images of fecundity in a manner that befits Henrietta Maria's position as a young wife and the mother of the Stuart heir. Her masque operates in a close pairing with the king's *Love's Triumph* and deploys imagery that would be picked up again in her next masque, Townshend's *Tempe Restored* (1632). Indeed, Veevers remarks that *Tempe Restored* 'begins in a sense where *Chloridia* left off', opening with a garden, 'in which the Naiades and Dryads, the good powers of nature, are the companions of Circe, as before they were of Chloris'.[11]

The mythological and horticultural imagery used in *Chloridia* adopts the queen consort for England by drawing upon ideas that had already found expression in Elizabethan and Jacobean entertainments. The idea of Cupid-the-runaway appeared in the third book of Spenser's *The Faerie Queene* to explain how Venus came to adopt Britomart's twin,

Belphoebe.[12] Jonson's *Haddington Masque* (1608), composed for the marriage of Viscount Haddington and Lady Elizabeth Ratcliffe, was a dramatisation of a poem by Moschus, which was known to the Renaissance as *Amor Fugitivus* and which also figured Venus asking for help in finding her runaway son.[13] As in the case of the *Haddington Masque*, images of floral abundance and the associations of spring, love and birth were often also used as motifs to celebrate marriages. The image of Zephyr and Flora appeared in *The Lord Hay's Masque* of 1607 in celebration of the marriage of James Hay, James I's favourite, while the gentlemen of Gray's Inn produced an elaborate *Masque of Flowers* in 1614 for the marriage of Robert Carr and Lady Frances Howard. The conceit of *Chloridia* is, therefore, appropriate for a masque which celebrates the Caroline couple, particularly after the recent birth of their first son.

Jonson's masque for the queen consort, therefore, seems to replicate the ideas put forward in *Love's Triumph*, linking her to the king in a nationalistic manner that propounds an agenda of royal fecundity and pastoral bliss. Nonetheless, the production also draws upon continental sources, both co-opting them to the service of the Caroline iconography and promoting an image of Henrietta Maria that was compatible with her identity as a foreign princess. Veevers has suggested that Jonson's main source for *Chloridia* was *La Flora*, a Florentine entertainment performed in 1628 at the marriage of Odoardo Farnese and Margherita de Médicis.[14] Margherita, the daughter of Grand Duke Cosimo II, was Henrietta Maria's second cousin on her mother's side, and it is a measure of Jonson's sensitivity to his patron that he should choose to base his masque on such a recent and genealogically significant production.

La Flora was a five-act opera composed by Andrea Salvadori, Marco da Gagliano and Jacopo Peri, with scenery designed by Alfonso Parigi.[15] Its opening conceit saw Hermes appearing as the messenger of Jupiter to announce 'to the Great Mother, goddess of fertility and mistress of nature, that the father of the gods had decided to endow the earth with a counterpart to the stars – that is, flowers'.[16] Jonson's masque adapts this motif, presenting Zephyrus as the messenger of the gods, exhorting the Spring to 'carry the glad newes, I bring, / To Earth, our common mother' (lines 45–6). Zephyrus then explains that, 'Ioue will have Earth to haue her starres, / And lights, no lesse then Heauen', and Spring replies, 'It is alreadie done, in flowers' (lines 54–6). The similarities with the Florentine production are striking, and are continued as Cupid descends to Hell to seek infernal assistance for his troublemaking. However, in the earlier entertainment, Cupid's machinations resulted in angering Zephyrus who called up the winds and brought a great storm down on the countryside. In Jonson's masque, a spectacular storm scene also takes place, but at Cupid's instigation, and in the typical manner of a French *ballet à entrées.* This is an intriguing development, and one which, I think, connects *Chloridia* not only with *La Flora,* but with entertainments performed during Henrietta Maria's childhood at the Bourbon court.

Prior to her marriage, Henrietta Maria danced in the *Grand Ballet de la Reyne representant le Soleil* (1621), the *Grand Ballet de la Reyne representant les Festes de Junon la Nopcière* (1623) and the *Ballet de la reine, dansé par les nymphes des jardins* (1624), taking the roles of Aurora, Iris and a Sunflower respectively. It is the 1621 ballet whose imagery is most compatible with that of *Chloridia* and which deserves to be investigated in some detail.

Like *Chloridia,* Anne of Austria's *Soleil* operated as a counterpart to a ballet performed by her husband. The ballet's printed text declared that, in the king's production, Louis XIII appeared as Apollo, while in the queen's ballet, he is to be understood as the Sun. Similarly, like *Chloridia* (whose women masquers equalled the number of noble dancers in *Love's Triumph*), there is an expressed intention in *Soleil* to create a structural parallel between the two French productions. In Louis's ballet 'les quatre professions firent les quatre scenes' [the four professions made up the four scenes], while in *Soleil* 'les quatre saisons en feroient autant, si l'Hyuer n'estoit chassé de la derniere' [the four seasons would have done as much, if Winter hadn't been chased from the last].[17] Complementing each other, each of the productions served as an elaborate compliment to the king.

Soleil opened with an image of Dawn chasing dreams and chimeras from the world in a manner that would later find an echo in Henrietta Maria's *Luminalia* (1638). The first scene of the ballet was dedicated to Spring and showed ice being transformed into fountains, the earth being overspread with flowers and Zephyr and Flora falling in love. It has an obvious resonance with the conceit of *Chloridia* and was significantly the scene with which Henrietta Maria, as Aurora, was the most involved. The imagery of rivers and fountains reappears in Jonson's masque, which also draws upon the figures of Zephyr, Spring and floral abundance. Later in *Soleil,* a dance representing a storm was followed by the appearance of a rainbow and Winter being chased from the stage by the Sun (played by Anne of Austria) and her attendant Hours. In *Chloridia,* great emphasis is placed upon the tempest Cupid raises from Hell, which Chloris calms while seated in a bower before the image of a rainbow (line 201). Upon her descent to the stage, she is welcomed by a song which lauds the preservative capabilities of the Hours, of Juno and of Iris (lines 215–28).

Significantly, *Chloridia*'s tempest is danced like a French *ballet à entrées* and comprises masquers who appear in themed groups and move in a manner appropriate to their theme. It differs markedly from the anti-masque of *Love's Triumph* which figured one large dance, and alerts one to the production's indebtedness to French ballet. Indeed, Marie-Claude Canova-Green has commented that this was the first time that the word 'entries' was applied to an English anti-masque.[18] She is not entirely correct in this; the word was used by Thomas Campion in *The Lords' Masque* (1613) and was employed for the first time by Ben Jonson in *Lovers Made Men* (1617).[19] Nevertheless, its use in *Chloridia* designates a typically French succession of comic dances and indicates the promotion of a relatively new dramatic structure on the English stage. Although its classical images were stock-in-trade for European entertainments, *Chloridia* is filled with the echoes of foreign productions, particularly Anne of Austria's *Soleil*.

Jonson's masque therefore achieves a very effective synthesis of continental and English cultural motifs upon the Whitehall stage by representing Henrietta Maria as Chloris in a manner compatible with her position as the English queen and at the same time providing her with an iconography that draws upon her familial heritage. In addition, I believe that it is possible to see in *Chloridia* traces of close collaboration between Jonson and the queen, or members of her household, over the structure and content of the masque. It has often been noted that Henrietta Maria exercised control over the designs of her masque costumes, with Inigo Jones providing several different sketches from which she would choose her favourite.[20] The echoes in *Chloridia* of French ballets, most notably the adoption of the *ballet-à-entrées* structure and the echoes of the scene from *Soleil* in which Henrietta Maria danced, seem to indicate a similar artistic collaboration, with the queen or one of her servants acting as a consultant during the masque's preparation. Furthermore, the queen's contribution to *Chloridia* might not have stopped at the choice of costume design or the suggestion of source material. The masque can be shown to have reflected obliquely upon continental current affairs, thus opening a space on the stage in which Henrietta Maria could express her own, very pressing, political concerns.

*

Orgel and Strong's discussion of *Chloridia* includes the intriguing observation that 'the masque is, curiously, more directly political than [*Love's Triumph*]' and notes that the figure of Juno is a vision of 'divine and providential power'.[21] Veevers's interpretation of the masque's politics goes a little further. She reads the production as 'a delicate compliment from the Queen to the King on their reconciliation after the early years of marriage, which were disturbed by Jealousy and Disdain'.[22] This is an appropriate reading, but it only considers the production as a commentary upon English domestic affairs. If one considers *Chloridia* in the light of Anglo-French relations and internal French politics, one reaches some very different conclusions about the masque's significations.

The performance of *Chloridia* came shortly after England had signed a treaty of peace with France at Susa, thus ending the war that had begun with the duke of Buckingham's support of the La Rochelle Huguenots in 1627.[23] If the masque can be interpreted as a compliment from the queen consort to the king after the turbulent early years of their marriage, it can also be read as a statement of reconciliation on a wider scale. *Chloridia*'s conceit, which establishes concord between the rival powers of heaven and earth through the medium of the nymph Chloris, has a strong resonance with contemporary political events which saw Henrietta Maria caught in a war between her brother and her husband. Zephyr's opening song is particularly relevant in this context. Descending to the stage, he sings:

> It is decreed, by all the Gods,
> The Heau'n, of Earth shall haue no oddes,
> But one shall loue another:
> Their glories they shall mutuall make,
> Earth looke on Heauen, for Heauens sake;
> Their honours shall bee euen:
> All æmulation cease, and iarres;
> Ioue will haue Earth to haue her starres,
> And lights, no lesse then Heauen. (lines 47–55)

Veevers is right in identifying a reconciliatory tone in this ballet. However, the image of two large powers (earth and heaven) coming to an harmonious agreement is more compatible with the Anglo-French peace accord than with the resolution of marital conflict. In fact, Zephyr's song calls to mind the imagery of some of Henrietta Maria's wedding entertainments, notably that of the *Ballet de la Reyne d'Angleterre*, which declared of Henrietta Maria:

> C'est elle qui doit sans remise
> Rendre les bords de la Tamise
> Des tresors de l'Inde embellis,
> Qui deux Sceptres unit, et comme en son visage

Va faire un mariage
De la rose et du lis.[24]

[It is she who must without delay
Make the banks of the Thames
Embellished with the treasures of India,
Who unites two sceptres, and, as in her face,
Is going to make a marriage
Of the rose and the lily.]

The wedding ballet positioned Henrietta Maria as a peaceweaver between England and France; her union with Charles was represented as joining the two countries together in harmonious accord. Coming after the conflict over the Ile de Rhé, *Chloridia*'s imagery draws again on the idea of harmonious union, positing a reconciliation between earth and heaven, symbolised by the deification of Chloris/Henrietta Maria. *Chloridia*, echoing the imagery of Henrietta Maria's wedding ballet, promotes the figure of the queen consort as a vehicle through which conflict is resolved; she is positioned as a mediating symbol between two significant European powers. The masque posits a resolution of conflict that not only looks back to the Caroline couple's previous domestic difficulties but to the recent international troubles between England and France.

However, while it may perhaps be seen to celebrate the peace of 1629, the masque took place at a time when Anglo-French relations were again troubled. Its opening song, therefore, is not only concerned with celebrating an achieved peace, it is concerned with maintaining it. In light of this, the song's future tenses – 'Ioue *will* haue Earth to haue her starres' (line 54; my italics) – and the fact that the masque opens *before* the gods' decree has been effected are very significant. They show that the peace between heaven and earth is not yet perfect and open up a space of danger within which the desired harmony can be disturbed. In good masquing tradition, this lack of closure permits the arrival on stage of a series of anti-masque dancers who figure disruption before being subdued by the appearance of Chloris and her attendants. If the masque is to be regarded as a partial commentary upon international affairs, then these anti-masque dancers must be looked at more closely, for they have a significant role to play in the masque's message of peace and reconciliation.

In 1631, the status of Henrietta Maria's relationship with her French family was complicated by a dispute that arose between Marie de Médicis and Cardinal Richelieu, Marie's erstwhile protégé and the former *surintendant* of her household. Louis XIII had given Richelieu a seat on his council in 1623 to show that an unfortunate quarrel between himself and his mother was at an end. In a letter to Marie, he declared: 'J'ai choisi un de vos serviteurs . . . pour montrer que notre réconciliation est réele et définitive' [I chose one of your servants . . . to show that our reconciliation is real and final].[25] Richelieu soon managed to gain the king's confidence and, by 1624, was exercising the powers of French Secretary of State. In 1627, he accompanied Louis to the war at La Rochelle and there consolidated his influence over the king. However, his ambition and his ascendancy brought him into conflict with Marie de Médicis. She stripped him of his position as *surintendant* of her household, and an animosity developed between the two which reached a head in November 1630.

In 1630, Madame de Fargis, one of the French Queen Anne's waiting women, was sent from court apparently for scandalous behaviour. However, it soon became known that she had revealed to the queen mother and Anne of Austria that Richelieu had been stirring up trouble between them. The two queens resolved their differences and Marie set out to destabilise Richelieu's position with the king.[26] By the autumn of 1630, she had succeeded in obtaining from Louis the vague promise that he would expel Richelieu from his council. On 10 November (French style), afterwards known as the Day of Dupes, Louis XIII agreed to a meeting with the queen mother at the palais de Luxembourg.[27] Richelieu was alerted to the conference and burst in unannounced. Marie was furious and, for a while, it looked as though the cardinal's humiliation at her hands would cause him to leave Paris. However, that same night he sought out the king at Versailles and persuaded him to take his part in the dispute. From that moment on, Marie de Médicis and Richelieu became locked in the struggle that would eventually result in the former's permanent exile from France.[28]

It did not take long for the news to reach England. On 9 November (English style), only nine days after the Day of Dupes, George Goring, Henrietta Maria's master of horse, wrote a letter of allegiance to Richelieu declaring that 'une fausse alarme avoit mis la glace au coeur de tous vos serviteurs' [a false alarm had struck ice into the hearts of all your servants] and stating that no man had ever honoured the cardinal with more reverence, or served with more devotion, than he.[29] Goring might well have been acting on his own initiative and for his own benefit in writing this letter, but it is possible that his words were intended to keep open a channel of negotiation with the cardinal for Henrietta Maria herself. However, whatever its motivations, it demonstrates the incredible speed with which news of the events in France crossed the English Channel and arrived at Henrietta Maria's court.

The queen's masque was composed by Jonson in the months that followed the Day of Dupes and, unsurprisingly, resonates with the events of November 1630. For example, in the masque's second song, the figure of Spring approaches the king and sings verses which explain the production's argument. Spring declares:

> Cupid hath ta'ne offence of late
> At all the Gods, that of the State,
> And in their Councell, he was so deserted,
> Not to be call'd into their Guild,
> But slightly pass'd by, as a child. (lines 94–8)

In *La Flora*, Jonson's probable source, Cupid's motivation for stirring up trouble was simple perversity; asked by his mother Venus to make Chloris fall in love with Zephyrus, he not only refused to shoot his golden arrow at the nymph, but swore he would set her heart against her admirer.[30] In contrast, Cupid's motivations in Jonson's masque are entirely political and have a strong resonance with the conflict unfolding at the French court. After Madame de Fargis's revelations, the powerful alliance between Marie de Médicis and Queen Anne had turned many people against Richelieu and was effectively eroding his power in the king's council. In *Chloridia*, echoes of Richelieu's position may be felt in the actions of Cupid, who is shown to have taken offence because his authority is not recognised in the council of the gods. Furthermore, the association of Cupid with Richelieu gains credence from the fact that Richelieu was Marie de Médicis's former servant, a position of dependence that can be equated with the masque's emphasis on Cupid as a child.

If Cupid's mother is to be partially identified with Marie de Médicis, then Spring's second stanza again has a strong resonance with French current affairs. Spring's verse continues with the lines:

> And though his Mother seek to season,
> And rectifie his rage with reason,
> By shewing he liues yet vnder her command,
> Rebellious he, doth disobey,
> And she hath forc'd his armes away. (lines 102–6)

In *Chloridia*, Cupid rebels against his mother's efforts to re-establish her authority over him, forcing her to confiscate his weapons. Similarly, in the autumn of 1630, Marie de Médicis tried to regain ascendancy over her servant, Richelieu. However, he resisted her attempts, which led to his humiliation and his flight from court on the Day of Dupes. Interestingly, in *Chloridia*, the balance of good opinion lies with Cupid's mother, who is shown to be acting reasonably, while Cupid is portrayed as a petulant child. As subsequent events would prove, Henrietta Maria's sympathies in the Marie de Médicis/Richelieu conflict lay firmly on the side of her mother. If an equation is to be made between French politics and *Chloridia*, then the representation of Cupid's mother as fair and reasonable leaves no doubt about the masque's bias.

The concluding stanza of Spring's song also contains echoes of internal French conflict as it describes how Cupid has gone to hell,

> There to excite, and stirre up Iealousy,
> To make a party 'gainst the Gods,
> And set Heauen, Earth and Hell at odds. (lines 112–14)

This movement echoes the departure from court of Richelieu on the Day of Dupes and carries resonances of the trouble that he subsequently stirred up at Versailles for Marie de Médicis and her associates. Furthermore, in the masque, Cupid later returns from hell and dances an anti-masque entry accompanied by the figures of Jealousy, Disdain, Fear and Dissimulation. As I remarked above, Veevers interprets Jealousy and Disdain as the vices which disturbed the early years of the Caroline marriage.[31] However, this reading cannot accommodate the ideas of Fear and Dissimulation which are too radical to be applied to a recently resolved marital conflict. Jealousy, Disdain, Fear and Dissimulation were, though, all attributes of the struggle that saw Richelieu turning a simulated departure from court into a political triumph. If *Chloridia* is to be read allegorically, it is necessary to locate the production within the context of Europe and European politics, rather than interpreting it simply as a commentary upon English domestic affairs.

Interestingly, for a reading that considers both the masque's internal dynamics and its political implications, Spring's song to the king in *Chloridia* never specifically names Cupid's mother as Venus. Indeed, the name 'Venus' appears nowhere in the entire text of the masque. This is a significant departure from *La Flora* in which Venus played a notable part in the action.[32] In contrast to the earlier entertainment, the real repository of power in *Chloridia*, as Suzanne Gossett observes, is Juno, who has the ability to stop the havoc caused by Cupid.[33] This peculiarity is significant for it means that Cupid, as the god of erotic love, and Juno, as the goddess of marriage, are in direct competition with each other for sovereignty over the realm of the affections. The harmonious influence exerted by Juno at the end of the production is, therefore, compatible with the masque's conceit of purity and chaste love in that it purges

Cupid's intemperate disorders. However, the effacement of Venus in the masque is also particularly relevant for a reading which locates *Chloridia* in the context of France. In French *ballet de cour*, the favoured identification for Marie de Médicis was with Juno. Thus, if *Chloridia* is to be read as a partial allusion to French politics, Juno is the figure who provides the strongest iconographical echo of the queen mother.

Gossett comments that *Chloridia*'s figure of Chloris is essentially decorative and observes that, by attributing power to Juno, the goddess of marriage, the masque emphasises that Henrietta Maria acquired her significance from her marriage to Charles.[34] *Chloridia*'s closing song, as Gossett remarks, does evoke Henrietta Maria/Chloris's relationship with Charles. However, the masque's attribution of power to Juno also follows in the tradition of ballets danced at the French court where a performance's internal dynamic was invariably ruptured by a gesture beyond itself to the queen mother seated in the audience. For example, in the *Grand Ballet de la Reyne representant les Festes de Junon la Nopcière*, in which Anne of Austria and Henrietta Maria danced Juno and Iris respectively, both Juno and Iris were given lines which deferred their power to the power of Marie de Médicis. Juno, in particular, stated to the queen mother that 'c'est de vos mains que je tiens mon espoux' [it's from your hands that I take my husband].[35] Furthermore, in a manner which resounds particularly with *Chloridia*, she gave up her name to Marie de Médicis with the words, 'Vous m'ostez ma gloire et mon nom, / Grande et favorable Junon, / Qui presidez au mariage' [Great and kindly Juno who presides over marriage, you take from me my glory and my name].[36] Authority in Queen Anne's *ballet* ultimately resides with Marie de Médicis, just as Juno is the real repository of power in *Chloridia*. Moreover, the French production's representation of Marie emphasised her role as a marriage broker in a manner compatible with *Chloridia*'s conceit of Chloris and the fecund spring. Juno's arrival in the Caroline masque presages the song which lauds Chloris as the 'top of Par-amours' (line 338), emphasising the nymph's relationship with the king and thus figuring Henrietta Maria's union with Charles. The figure of Juno presides over the royal union in *Chloridia* in a manner compatible with representations of Marie de Médicis in Anne of Austria's *ballet* and in Henrietta Maria's French wedding celebrations.

However, *Chloridia*'s representation of Juno's power is ambivalent. Juno and Iris's combined forces are described by the song of the Fountains to have quenched Love's rebellious war, yet the dialogue which ensues between Juno and Iris is inconclusive on the subject of an accommodation with Cupid. Iris's remark that 'Cupid sues' (line 263) is interrupted by Juno's presumptive question, 'For pardon. Do's hee?' (line 265), which leaves open the possibility that Cupid's intention is not to ask for forgiveness. Juno's subsequent benevolent assertion that 'Offences, made against the Deities / Are soone forgot' (lines 271–2) is qualified by Iris's codicil, '*If* who offends, be wise' (line 274; my italics). The resolution of Cupid's trespass (and its allegorical connection with Richelieu's disgrace and recuperation) renders *Chloridia*'s fantasy about the re-establishment of harmony uncomfortable by opening a space in which Cupid may reject a reconciliation. Indeed, this sense of discomfiture has an historical echo. An appearance of rapprochement between Marie and Richelieu occurred on Christmas Day 1630 when the queen mother was persuaded by her bishops that 'une princesse chrétienne se doit de pardonner les offenses' [a Christian princess must forgive transgressions]. Richelieu, confronted with this attempt at reconciliation, reputedly replied, 'Votre Majesté a bien dit qu'elle ou moi sortirions de la cour' [Your Majesty definitely said that she or I would leave the court].[37] While the masque locates the figure of Chloris as the vehicle through which peace is to be established, effectively setting her up as a mediator between Juno and Cupid, the closure proposed by the masque's final visions of peace and fame is disturbed by the inconclusive nature of the gods' reconciliation.

The uncertainties at the end of *Chloridia* were mirrored on the continent by contemporary historical events. In February 1631, the month in which *Chloridia* was to be performed, Marie de Médicis was exiled from Paris by Louis XIII and Richelieu. Interestingly, attempts were made in England to withhold this news from Henrietta Maria until after the performance of her masque. Salvetti, the Florentine agent, commented in a dispatch to his masters:

> The news that came from France the Sunday before this masque touching the troubles of the Queen Mother, the Duc d'Orleans and other great people of the realm, would greatly have disturbed the happiness of the queen had not the king given strict command that no-one should say a word about it to her until she had finished her masque.[38]

If one takes this information at face value, the suppression of the news must simply be acknowledged as an expression of the king's concern for his wife's well-being, tempered perhaps by concerns about wasted expense should the masque have to be cancelled. However, given *Chloridia*'s motifs of reconciliation and its possible echo of the Day of Dupes, Marie de Médicis's exile might also be said seriously to destabilise the masque's conciliatory agenda. If *Chloridia* was intended, in part, as a commentary upon French current affairs, offering up an image of harmonious resolution brought about by the mediating figure of Chloris/Henrietta Maria, then the queen mother's exile represents the failure of this project and, therefore, negates the masque's purpose.

In a letter of English court news addressed to Elizabeth of Bohemia, Sir John Ashburnham also commented upon Marie de Médicis's exile and Henrietta Maria's masque, writing:

> [Mr Maxfill] and my lord Treasurers sonnes came then to court full of the tourmoyles in France, which yett would not by the queen be beleeved, till her Maske was solemnis'd, bycause she had no particular advertisements of them.[39]

Here again, although Ashburnham's letter contradicts Salvetti's opinion that the queen consort was not alerted to her mother's disgrace, the news of Marie de Médicis's exile is suppressed in order to facilitate the performance of the masque. There is a sense in both these reports that the masque and events in France are connected by more than their immediate impact upon the English queen; in other words, the performance of *Chloridia* is somehow linked to France and French politics and cannot accommodate the queen mother's exile. This view can be supported by a consideration of Henrietta Maria's relationship with the French ambassador, François de Val, marquis de Fontenay-Mareuil, whose association with the queen consort usefully illuminates her attitude towards France in the early months of 1631.

Following a precedent set with *Love's Triumph*, none of the foreign ambassadors in London were invited to the performance of the queen's masque. However, as Salvetti reports, the French ambassador went privately to the production 'as a servant of the queen and not as an ambassador.'[40] Salvetti had previously commented upon the French ambassador's close relations with Henrietta Maria, remarking that he could have attended *Love's Triumph* 'very easily, by reason of the daily and very familiar access he has to the Court through the queen'.[41] If *Chloridia* has a message of reconciliation to offer to France, then Fontenay-Mareuil's presence at the production is of particular importance. Furthermore, the close ties between the queen and the ambassador, and the daily access he had to her court, show that she was in a position to assert an opinion about French affairs and could intervene as a mediator between her relatives in France.[42]

However, after her mother's disgrace, Henrietta Maria's relationship with the French ambassador rapidly soured and, by June 1631, she was actively taking sides against him. Fontenay-Mareuil became involved in a dispute with the chevalier de Jars, who had himself been exiled from France for intrigues against Richelieu. De Jars was supported in his complaints by the queen, so the French ambassador took his case to Charles who resolved events in his favour. Commenting upon the affair, John Finet, the Caroline master of ceremonies, observed that for 'a year and more after', the queen 'never assented him a gracious look' although 'shee fayled not to remember the kyng her brothers honor, in bestowing those respects, which she knew dewe in publick to his ambassador'.[43] While Finet puts all of Henrietta Maria's animosity down to Fontenay-Mareuil's dispute with de Jars, her support of the chevalier is indicative of a larger discontent with France. While she behaves with appropriate decorum towards her brother's representatives in public, this is simply diplomatic politeness. Henrietta Maria's attitude towards her native land had changed and in 1632 she would be involved in a notorious plot to topple Richelieu from power.[44]

Chloridia took place at a moment which marked a change in the queen's relationship with France and her French relations. While the production draws upon imagery that was prevalent in English courtly entertainments of the previous two reigns, and while it operates in a pair with Charles's *Love's Triumph*, it nonetheless contains echoes of continental politics. It demonstrates that a space could be opened upon the Caroline court stage in which Henrietta Maria could articulate her own concerns, inhabiting a political position that was potentially different from that of the king. In light of the pacific, nationalistic messages that Butler has identified in Charles's masques, *Chloridia*'s closing scene of Fame ascending to heaven, singing that 'The life of Fame is action' (line 287), has a peculiar resonance, intimating that the queen wished for a far more engaged political policy. In a way, I would argue, the masque itself becomes her means of political engagement in the crisis that would result in her mother's expulsion from France. The production's concluding moments present an encomium to the victorious triumvirate of Chloris, Iris and Juno, aligned against Cupid's accomplices, 'Iealousie and Hell' (line 300). Enshrined in culture, Juno/Marie's deeds will live to be vindicated by posterity, as the figures of Poesy, History, Architecture and Sculpture combine to make great actions 'last to memory' (line 305). In Henrietta Maria's masque at least, the women are, and will remain, triumphant.

The text of *Chloridia* also provides circumstantial evidence that Henrietta Maria or her advisers contributed ideas and motifs to Jonson and Jones during the preparation of the masque. It is even possible that this royal interference might have exacerbated the tensions between the two collaborators, leading to Jonson's frustrated declaration that 'Painting and carpentry [were] the soul of masque,' and that the 'tire-man' Jones had now become 'the music-master, fabler, too; / He is, or would be, main Dominius Do- / All in the work!'[45] Jones would go on to collaborate fruitfully with Henrietta Maria's household in all of her subsequent dramatic productions. Jonson's services would never be required again.

CHAPTER 5

Tempe Restored: *exile/dispossession/restitution*

In 1632, Ben Jonson was replaced as royal masque writer by the little-known Aurelian Townshend, who, to add insult to injury, was paid £10 more by the queen than was his predecessor.[1] Kevin Sharpe has suggested that Townshend attached himself to Henrietta Maria's circle in the late 1620s, and suggests that he might have been introduced to her by her close associate, the earl of Holland.[2] The poet was a gifted linguist and had spent a considerable time in France in the company of Sir Edward Herbert, the future Lord Herbert of Cherbury.[3] This places him at the side of an extremely cultured man who was respected by Henrietta Maria's French family: a fact that can only have helped to advance him with his new mistress.[4] That said, very little evidence remains of the literary grounds for his appointment, although Peter Beal has uncovered an earlier entertainment which provides evidence of his familiarity with the masque form.[5] I strongly suspect that it was because of his links with Holland that Townshend received his commission and suggest, furthermore, that *Tempe Restored* reflected the political concerns of the earl and his circle.

Before addressing the political and religious aspects of the masque, though, I wish to consider the notion of female voice. *Tempe Restored* has persistently been seen by critics as a statement of the queen consort's femino-centric court fashion, not least because it is deemed to have included the first two professional female singers to perform on the courtly masquing stage. The first part of this chapter will investigate the significance of these singers, suggesting that they have been misrepresented and that, therefore, the critical notion of the masque's proto-feminist agenda has been exaggerated. Alison Shell has cautioned that the 'historian sensitive to conscience ought never to assume that any individual in early modern Europe endorsed philosophical and theological systems for entirely self-interested reasons', adding, nonetheless, that those systems had incidental benefits in individual cases.[6] Taking this into account, the chapter will re-evaluate *Tempe Restored*'s meanings, investigating it first as a production that had to negotiate a tricky political moment, and then arguing, in accordance with Shell's observation about religious conscience, that its femino-centrism is linked more with the queen's religion than anything else.

*

The masque was performed in the Banqueting House at Whitehall on 14 February 1632, having been postponed from Twelfth Night because of Henrietta Maria's ill health. It took as its main source Baltasar de Beaujoyeulx's *Balet Comique de la Royne*, an entertainment performed in 1581 at the Valois court by the French queen, Louise de Vaudemont, for the wedding of her sister to the duc de Joyeuse.[7] *Tempe Restored* follows the opening of the French ballet very closely, figuring Thomas Killigrew, one of Charles's pages and the son of Henrietta Maria's vice chamberlain, as a Fugitive Favourite, fleeing from Circe's clutches. Circe, enacted by a certain 'Madame Coniack', has a strong vocal part in the masque, lamenting the loss of the young man and commanding a series of barbarous anti-masque dances, before being superseded on the stage by Harmony, played by 'Mistress Shepherd'. Harmony heralds the arrival of Henrietta Maria and her ladies, who, as Divine Beauty and her stars, reform Circe's excesses and to whom the sorceress finally voluntarily submits.

Sophie Tomlinson has noted of *Tempe Restored* that Circe's combination of 'musical and sexual allure' was 'especially associated with continental women' such as the French Madame Coniack.[8] Both she and Melinda Gough also draw attention to the *Balet Comique de la Royne*, observing that the role of Circe in the former production was played by a woman and noting that the casting of Madame Coniack in the English masque deliberately drew attention to the different codes governing female performance at the French and Italian courts.[9] James Knowles, taking this idea further, has suggested that Madame Coniack's casting as Circe was a deliberate response to criticism of Henrietta Maria's French-influenced theatrical endeavours and that it served 'to mount a defense against those who regarded female actors as "whorishly impudent"'.[10] He argues that Madame Coniack, as Circe, stood 'as the symbol of dangerous femininity, performance, and even Catholicism' in a manner that was 'almost directly a public gesture of defiance'.[11] All three critics base their observations on two assumptions: first, that the woman employed to play Circe was a French professional singer; and, second, that this was the first time an adult female singing voice had been heard in an English court masque. While I agree that the figure of Circe opens up some interesting questions about *Tempe Restored*'s presentation of female voice, I would like to add a note of caution, particularly about reading the production as a radical expression of 'defiance'.

The idea that Circe was performed by a French professional singer was put forward in 1997 by Roy Booth who suggested that Madame Coniack was the subject of Thomas Randolph's poem, 'Upon a very deformed Gentlewoman, but of a voice incomparably sweet' (alternatively titled in various locations as 'Upon the French Woman . . . that singes in Masques at Court', and 'On a ffrench woeman, one of the Queenes Chapple').[12] Booth recognises that the poem is 'a hyperbolically witty variant upon "Ugly Lady" poems' in which a lovely voice is set off against a foul appearance, but is nevertheless convinced that its subject is Madame Coniack and that she was a professional vocalist.[13] His work is persuasive, but it has led, I believe, to a misconception both about Henrietta Maria's household and about *Tempe Restored.* I have searched extensively but have found no other reference to professional female singers at the queen's court.[14] The variant title that Booth cites, which names the French singer as 'one of the Queenes Chapple', does not necessarily indicate the existence of a female choir, but simply those women who shared Henrietta Maria's religious beliefs and accompanied her to services. In sum, if Coniack was a professional singer, like the famous Angélique Paulet of the Parisian *salons,* then her name would surely be recorded in more places than the quarto of *Tempe Restored.*

Instead, I believe Madame Coniack was one of Henrietta Maria's ladies. Indeed, it seems reasonable to associate her with the Elizabeth Coignet who was a member of the new queen's household in 1625 and who is likely to have performed alongside her in the French pastoral, *Artenice.* She is also likely to have been one of the ladies who performed in the entertainment observed by Katherine Gorges on her visit to court in November 1625. As I discussed in chapter 1, this entertainment probably consisted of a series of disparate entries danced in different costumes, possibly with the inclusion of female song. Significantly, one of the alternative titles of Randolph's poem on the French female singer asserts that she performed in '*Masques* [plural] at court', so it is entirely likely that *Tempe Restored* was not the first entertainment in which this Frenchwoman's voice was heard.

If this is the case, the masque ceases to look like quite such a departure from earlier Caroline productions. Although it obviously engaged with the issues of female dramatic performance, juxtaposing Circe's vocal histrionics against Divine Beauty's silent dancing, it figured a woman who is likely to have been familiar to the court audience and who had already very probably taken a singing part on the stage. As a gentlewoman, not a noblewoman, her role in the anti-masque was similar to that of Thomas Killigrew, the royal page who played the part of the Fugitive Favourite. Indeed, on the level of class, rather than gender, her performance was perhaps less shocking than the duke of Buckingham's anti-masque impersonation of a fencing master in 1626.

Nevertheless, given Madame Coniack's likely history as an actor on the court stage, Circe's histrionics must certainly have reminded watchers of the kind of criticisms that were directed at court theatricals and Catholic women. Indeed, only the previous year, Nathaniel Richards's poem 'The Vicious Courtier' had condemned court 'Masques', 'Musicke' and 'Banquets' as activities which 'affright the blood of *Chastitie*' and 'Turne *Virgin Loue*, to hot Lust's Plurisie'.[15] The poem made evident that the theatrical display of female bodies led to degradation and sinfulness, and also registered an anxiety about Catholicism in its observation that 'Neuer was any great Arch-mischief done, / But by a Whore, or a Priest, first begun'.[16] In the light of Richards's verses, the Catholic Frenchwoman cast in the role of Circe might certainly have stood for some as 'the symbol of dangerous femininity, performance, and even Catholicism', although, as I will show, this representation is more satirical than defiant.

Gough has suggested that the casting of Mistress Shepherd as Harmony was a deliberate attempt to counteract the audience's recognition of 'the conjunction between Circe's gender and the gender of the singer-actress performing her'.[17] In other words, by including a female Harmony who sings a song that was 'not her own but the queen's', the masque posited that 'queenly voices [could] be lustful, as was Circe's, but also categorically ethereal and chaste, as is Divine Beauty's Harmony'.[18] As Gough astutely notes, the equation of female song with unrestrained passion is modified by Harmony's presence, disrupting the binarism that says women's continence and chastity can 'only be embodied in women's silence'.[19] Furthermore, the close association between the Frenchwoman playing Circe and the Frenchwoman who is Divine Beauty is somewhat weakened by the mediating force of the female Harmony (figure 5.1).

Harmony's place in the masque is certainly important for it marks the moment of transition from the disruptive anti-masque to the masque proper. However, again, I think her role has been misread because of the prevalent assumption that she was a professional singer, and because

Figure 5.1. Inigo Jones's sketch of 'Harmony' for *Tempe Restored* (1632).

Tempe Restored has been interpreted as a kind of female-centred renovation of previous Stuart masquing practice. Gough, noting that Harmony appears nowhere in *Tempe Restored*'s source, traces her to a 1589 Florentine *intermedii* in which Doric Harmony, sung by the professional vocalist Vittoria Archilei, performed a prologue 'from the Highest Spheres'.[20] Gough also notes that Harmony sang alongside Henrietta Maria in the 1623 ballet, *Les Festes de Junon la Nopcière* (although it is not certain whether this performance figured a male or female singer). *Tempe Restored*, she concludes, incorporated motifs from French productions with which Henrietta Maria was familiar and thus had an encomiastic function because it emphasised her royal status as a princess of France and an English queen.[21]

Mistress Shepherd's casting was certainly a departure from the norm at the Stuart court, although the figure of Harmony was not. She had appeared relatively recently alongside Apollo and 'the spirits of music' in Prince Charles's *Fortunate Isles and Their Union* (1625), and should have entered on stage in the company of Apollo, Mercury and the Muses in the unperformed *Neptune's Triumph* (1624). Nevertheless, there is no reason to believe that she was not intended to be played by a man in these productions. It certainly seems, therefore, that *Tempe Restored* deliberately promoted a female singer as Harmony, not least to counteract the disruptive elements of the Circean song and to stand as both the herald of, and voice for, Henrietta Maria as Divine Beauty. However, I suggest that, like Madame Coniack, Mistress Shepherd was not a professional singer and that a consideration of her possible identity links *Tempe Restored* to a tradition of Stuart masquing practice that complicates assumptions about the masque's presentation of female voice.

Harmony arrives on stage after the voluntary departure of the histrionic Circe and her nymphs. She is attended by a chorus of music and has '*under her conduct*' fourteen influences of the stars, played by noble children.[22] Tomlinson has noted that her singing part in the masque was as large as Circe's.[23] However, I would like to suggest that her solo responsibility was actually significantly shorter. Circe sings three solo quatrains punctuated by couplets sung by her nymphs, and then, at the end of the masque, performs nine lines in dialogue with Cupid, Pallas and Jove. Harmony sings a solo five-line stanza on her first entry, and then performs three solo lines in a song with the chorus of the spheres. Although she participates in other songs, it is always with the support of other voices. Circe therefore has thirteen more solo lines than Harmony, nearly double her part. On one level, this serves to emphasise

Circe's self-centred love passion by juxtaposing her single, imperious voice against Harmony's integration within a group. However, it might also indicate that Mistress Shepherd's voice could not sustain a substantial vocal part – in other words, it might suggest that she was not, after all, a professional adult. Indeed, I would like to suggest that she was not an adult at all, but a child.

At first glance, this seems a bit bizarre, but it is to be remembered that Harmony enters on the masquing stage in the company of the fourteen influences of the stars, played by noble children. Furthermore, she associates herself with these children through the very first words she sings:

> Not as myself, but as the brightest star
> That shines in heaven, come to reign this day;
> And these the beams and influences are
> Of constellations, whose planetic sway,
> Though some foresee, all must alike obey. (lines 155–9)

Harmony describes herself as the representative of Divine Beauty ('the brightest star'), introducing her young companions as the representatives of the other ladies who will descend with the queen. An analogy is therefore drawn between her position and that of the children who accompany her.

The children who played the influences were all born between 1619 and 1623 (giving an age range of about nine to thirteen years).[24] They included Lady Alice Egerton and her brother John, Lord Ellesmere, who, two years later at the ages of fifteen and eleven respectively were to undertake substantial dramatic parts in Milton's *Masque at Ludlow.* (Thomas, their nine-year-old brother, would also take part in this later entertainment as well as performing in King Charles's masque, *Coelum Britannicum,* in February 1634.) It is, therefore, not absolutely beyond the bounds of possibility that Harmony was played by a child, in which case the argument that *Tempe Restored* drew heavily on continental precedents needs to be re-examined.

I would like to suggest one candidate for the role of Harmony, primarily to interrogate the assumption that *Tempe Restored*'s singers were professional women. In the late 1630s, a certain Anne Sheppard was part of the circle of Philip Herbert, fourth earl of Pembroke and the king's lord chamberlain.[25] She was painted by Van Dyck around 1637 with Mary Villiers Herbert, daughter of the late duke of Buckingham and wife of Pembroke's eldest son.[26] Both Mary and Charles Herbert, who were married in 1635, performed as influences in *Tempe Restored* alongside

Harmony. They were about ten and thirteen years old respectively at the time. Their companion, Sheppard, was later married to Richard Gibson, the miniaturist, in the presence of Charles and Henrietta Maria at St Pancras, Soper Lane, on St Valentine's day 1641.[27] At the time of *Tempe Restored* she was around eleven or twelve years old. She was also a dwarf who never grew beyond 3 feet 10 inches tall.

There is, of course, a strong tradition of male dwarves performing in Stuart court masques. For example, the year before *Tempe Restored*, Jeffrey Hudson, Henrietta Maria's servant, had performed a large and histrionic part in *Chloridia* as a 'Dwarfe-Post from Hell'.[28] He was then about twelve years old and was evidently thought capable of delivering a long and complicated prose speech. In addition, as Lucy Munro and others have examined, the professional early modern English stage was no stranger to plays performed by boys aged as young as ten.[29] Performances by young women, though, were more unusual, although a precedent does exist.

In 1617, Lucy Harrington Russell, Anna of Denmark's most prominent female courtier, organised an entertainment for the queen at her court at Greenwich. This production, *Cupid's Banishment*, was undertaken by students from the Ladies Hall at Deptford and included a speech that appears to have been uttered by one 'Mistress Ann Watkins' who acted Fortune, as well as a song sung by eight wood nymphs, also female students at the school.[30] Other participants in the entertainment included the young Elizabeth Cranfield, daughter of Sir Lionel Cranfield, James I's lord treasurer, as well as the musician Charles Coleman, who later contributed to the children's masque at Richmond, presented by Prince Charles to Henrietta Maria in 1636. These figures not only provide a link between Jacobean and Caroline productions, but, in the case of Coleman, show a continued involvement in children's theatre. In addition, it is notable that two of Lucy Harrington's nieces, Anne and Mary Russell, took to the stage with Henrietta Maria in *Tempe Restored*.

Clare McManus points out that *Cupid's Banishment* pre-dated Madame Coniack and Mistress Shepherd's songs in *Tempe Restored* by fifteen years, and notes, moreover, that one later moment of comparison is to be found in Milton's *Masque at Ludlow*, which, she says, is 'remarkably similar' to *Cupid's Banishment* 'in terms of their performers' age'.[31] Indeed, she suggests:

> It is possible that the youthfulness of Ann Watkins and Alice Egerton granted a degree of impunity similar to that exploited by the earlier children's theatre companies, an impunity less available to those who no longer stood beneath the control of a father, a family or a school.[32]

In other words, the youth of the performers in both *Cupid's Banishment* and *Tempe Restored* secured the impression of their innocence, reducing the potentially transgressive nature of their performances. Moreover, their participation in the productions was validated as it was a means of both gaining and displaying social skills in dancing and singing, and bringing them to the attention of potential patrons, sponsors or marriage partners.

If *Tempe Restored*'s female singers were not professionals, but instead a gentlewoman and a child, then the masque may be seen to engage with the limits of *permitted* female performance. Although innovative, Mistress Shepherd's role was not particularly shocking, but was instead intricately linked to Henrietta Maria's status as the mother of the Stuart heirs. While Circe is characterised as an inconstant and overly passionate woman, Harmony and her companions demonstrate that the proper end of desire lies in marital alliance and the chaste generation of children. Therefore, rather than allowing Henrietta Maria to 'participate vicariously in the . . . vocal virtuosity of women singers', Shepherd stands more as the voice of the uncontaminated future promised by the Caroline royal union.[33]

Tempe Restored, then, certainly does privilege the role of women upon the stage, both through its presentation of female singers and through its celebration of the queen consort as Divine Beauty. Nevertheless, as Shell has cautioned, it should not be interpreted as a self-interested declaration of women's agency. Rather than being almost a gesture of defiance, the masque pushes at the limits of female performance already sanctioned at court. Like *Chloridia*, it locates Henrietta Maria as the mother of the Stuart line, uniting her influence with that of her husband. More significantly, although the queen consort here maintains a sense of her own national identity, the masque sees a movement from French-inflected imperialism (figured in Madame Coniack's Circe) to the queen consort's harmonious appearance on the stage surrounded by her new countrywomen and their offspring.

It is to these children that I now want to turn in a discussion of the masque's political implications, investigating the significance of the courtier families represented on the stage. Although, as Veevers has suggested, aspects of *Tempe Restored* have strong Catholic, and even Marian, undertones, a large number of those who took part in the entertainment came from families of a firmly Protestant persuasion.[34] In the light of this, I want to examine the masque's presentation of harmony in the context of its political milieu, before concluding with an exploration of how, nonetheless, *Tempe Restored* registered an indebtedness to Henrietta Maria's Catholic faith.

*

If *Chloridia* shadowed the events on the continent that led to Marie de Médicis's expulsion from France, then it seems likely that Henrietta Maria's next masque would again engage with European politics. In September 1631, Marie arrived in Antwerp in the Spanish Netherlands, while her son Gaston and his followers, who had supported Marie in her grievances, fled to Nancy in Lorraine where they were promised military aid by the duke. Louis and Richelieu proceeded to exact punitive measures against the rebellious noblemen, charging them with the crime of *lèse majesté* and confiscating their lands and titles.[35] By mid-winter 1631, under the severe threat of invasion from France, the duke of Lorraine was finally forced to expel Gaston from his lands, but not before the prince had strategically married his sister. Gaston travelled to Brussels to rejoin his mother in a move that was to realign Henrietta Maria's family allegiances, leading her, by the summer of 1632, to become involved in a cabal that sought to overthrow the chief ministers of both France and England.

Given the political upheaval within France in 1631/2, the choice of Beaujoyeulx's entertainment as the source for *Tempe Restored* is an interesting one. The production celebrated the union of Marguerite de Lorraine, sister of the Valois queen, to the duc de Joyeuse, the king's favourite, and its use emphasised the historical, dynastic links between France and the duchy now threatened by Richelieu. Furthermore, the *Balet Comique* text also foregrounded the notion of healing, drawing attention, in its dedicatory epistle to Henri III, to the wars that had wracked the Valois kingdom, and praising the monarch and Catherine de Médicis, his mother, for resolving them. As Thomas M. Greene has suggested, Beaujoyeulx obviously 'understood his fable to have a specific political application, and wanted the application to be recognised'.[36] The entertainment's printed text makes no bones about its status as a political allegory, locating Circe as a symbol of disorder vanquished by the virtuous French king.

In light of this, *Tempe Restored*'s opening scene, drawn almost directly from the *Balet Comique*, takes on additional resonance in its presentation of the Fugitive Favourite seeking sanctuary at Charles I's feet. I have argued that *Chloridia* promoted the queen consort as a vehicle through which conflict might be resolved, positioning her as a mediator between Richelieu and her mother. *Tempe Restored*'s impulse is very similar, seeing Circe's disorders reformed through the mediating presence of Charles and his wife who are preferred by the sorceress over Jove and Cupid. It would, perhaps, be pushing the analogy too far to see the French king and his chief minister reflected in the figures of these classical gods. Nevertheless, there is something problematic about the way in which Cupid and Jove attempt to coerce Circe into giving up her land and subjects.

Cupid was the main cause of disorder in *Chloridia* and, in a complete departure from the 1581 French source, performs the same function in *Tempe Restored*. Tomlinson has noted that the masque presents Circe as a 'lovelorn woman' as well as a 'seductress and female sovereign', and it is noticeable that the agent responsible for her distress is Cupid who, we are told by her nymphs, has stung her with his dart.[37] In effect, Cupid is the driving force of Circe's passion and is, therefore, largely responsible for the disorderly anti-masque. The end of the masque sees him reforming his dominions and joining with Jove to parcel out Circe's subjects and land. It is to this that Circe insolently objects, preferring instead voluntarily to submit to Divine Beauty and Heroic Virtue.[38]

Nevertheless, Cupid and Jove proceed to celebrate victory in a manner that is oddly troubling. 'She gives but what she cannot keep', crows Jove. 'Then was the wound I gave her deep', comes Cupid's reply, before both gods join in a concluding couplet that announces: ''Twas I, whose power none can withstand, / That opened both her heart and hand' (lines 292–5). Their macho posturing admits to a violence that has invaded and opened Circe's body in a manner that is both arrogant and disrespectful.[39] In the light of the *Balet Comique*'s association of Circe with a rebellious nation, it is hard not to read this moment as allusively political in a manner that locates Charles and Henrietta Maria as the true peacemakers in their factious relations' troubles, mediating between Lorraine, the exiled rebels and a sabre-rattling France.

The idea of England as a political mediator was not far from the truth in 1631/2. Françoise Gourier has suggested that the poet Antoine Girard, sieur de Saint-Amant, arrived in England in August 1631, in part to seek English aid for the maréchal de Bassompierre, imprisoned in the Bastille because of his support for Marie and Gaston.[40] Furthermore, several significant fugitives were angling for accommodation in England that winter. In November, César de Bourbon, the duc de Vendôme, Henrietta Maria's half-brother and kinsman by marriage to the duc de Lorraine, arrived in London 'to wear out some tyme of his commanded absence from the court of France'.[41] He was a veteran opponent of Richelieu, and although he had little love for the French queen mother, was an ally of Gaston. Moreover, he had travelled to England via Brussels and Antwerp, the new homes of the French exiles, so may well have been bringing more than felicitations to his half-sister. He was so welcome that he was permitted, 'wyth a French liberty', to attend on Henrietta Maria 'not ten hours' after she had given birth to her daughter Mary.[42] In addition, his son, the duc de Mercoeur, was promised a part in *Tempe Restored*, probably as one of the influences of the stars. As I will show, Mercoeur's inclusion in the masque, alongside the children of important Caroline noblemen, has significant political implications.

In the event, Vendôme and his entourage left London before the masque was realised, in John Pory's opinion because there was a rumour that Marie de Médicis was attempting to cross to England.[43] Negotiations for this were certainly going on at the time, with the *Gazette de France* reporting that Charles was considering sending an extraordinary ambassador to Louis on her behalf. Nevertheless, Marie's representative at the English court received small encouragement and departed in February 1632 with no more to recommend his efforts than a Jesuit and two priests, released from prison to accompany him.[44]

Tempe Restored, then, took place at a particularly significant moment in the life of Henrietta Maria's French family. Its strongly political source text and its figuration of the royal couple as the cause of Circe's voluntary reformation combine to suggest that it was designed obliquely to shadow affairs on the continent. Nevertheless, the masque is less obviously on the side of the French queen mother than was *Chloridia*, instead following the *Balet Comique* in its figuration of Circean political discord and showing that this may be resolved only through the virtuous mediation of the English king and queen. Notably, although no ambassadors were formally invited, the French ambassador, in the words of John Finet, 'came voluntarily' and was thus a witness to the masque's potentially reconciliatory message.[45]

Although, throughout her life, Henrietta Maria's affiliations remained largely with mother, from 1629 onwards, as Malcolm Smuts has observed, she began to associate with a group of Protestant peers, including the earls of Holland and Northumberland, whose interests were largely anti-Spanish and whose advocation of an aggressive foreign policy included a desire to see the restoration of the Palatinate to Charles I's brother-in-law.[46] This association, coupled with the queen consort's desire to help her mother, might explain the peculiar grouping of children who danced as influences in *Tempe Restored*.

Charles's *Albion's Triumph*, performed a month before the queen's masque, included among its masquers a notable contingent of Scotsmen (such as the lords Dunluce and Bruce), in a manner that can be explained by the king's expressed intention to undertake his Scottish coronation that summer.[47] The selection of masquers in court entertainments could obviously have a socio-political resonance: indeed, Erica Veevers has shown that Henrietta Maria regularly performed with Catholics or Catholic sympathisers.[48] *Tempe Restored*'s main masque is not unusual in this respect, involving such habitual participants as the countesses of Newport and Carnarvon, both of whom had strong Catholic predilections. However, the dance of children is interesting for it introduces a cross-section of moderate Protestant belief into the entertainment.

Obvious participants in the dance of the influences were the offspring of the Villiers and Feilding families, Buckingham's powerful relatives. In 1632, these families were the loyal servants of the crown and were nominally Protestant, although several of the women demonstrated strong Catholic tendencies.[49] The rest of the dancers, however, appear to have come from politically moderate, Protestant, backgrounds. On one level, they represent the apparent unity of a court that had survived early conflict and which, moreover, now had a settled succession. On another, they demonstrate the queen consort's connection to a section of the English nobility that Smuts has described as supporting moderate policies and, later, dividing their loyalties 'between the Crown and its parliamentarian and puritan enemies'.[50]

Principal among these was Henry Rich, earl of Holland, who, I suggest, was closely involved in the organisation of the masque. Barbara Donagan has described his political beliefs as largely pro-French and pro-Palatinate, noting that, in 1636, Charles Louis, the Prince Palatine, thought that the only courtiers in England who truly favoured his cause were Holland, the marquis of Hamilton and the earl of Pembroke.[51] Holland, together with his relatives, Essex and Northumberland, would eventually declare for parliament in 1642. However, in the early part of the reign, he was strongly in favour with the royal couple, especially with the queen, and, as I have suggested, might well have helped obtain the masque commission for Aurelian Townshend. Unsurprisingly, Holland's nephew, Richard, was included in the masque and, notably, danced alongside Pembroke's two sons, Charles and Philip Herbert.

Pembroke was a godly Protestant, who, despite sharing Charles I's artistic and architectural interests, was opposed to Laudianism and who does not appear to have pleased Henrietta Maria.[52] His career at court progressed rapidly through the 1620s and 30s: he became a privy councillor in 1624 and Charles's lord chamberlain in 1626. Roy Schreiber has noted that, as a member of Charles's foreign affairs committee in 1629, with, among others, Holland and the earl of Carlisle, he was inclined towards a French peace, providing a swing vote between Carlisle's pro-Spanish and Holland's anti-Spanish tendencies.[53] His religious sympathies also led him to favour peace with the Scots during Charles's campaigns of 1639–40, and, as David L. Smith has observed, he, together with Holland and the earl of Salisbury, urged the king to accept the Scots' terms in October 1640.[54] Becoming disillusioned with the court, he was dismissed as lord chamberlain on Henrietta Maria's recommendation in July 1641, and, like Holland, finally took up arms for parliament.

Given the queen consort's apparent antipathy towards him, the inclusion of his sons in *Tempe Restored* could be put down simply to social diplomacy were it not that they were accompanied on to the stage by other children from families of a similar political colouring. For example, Elizabeth Cecil, daughter of Pembroke's friend, Salisbury, also danced in the masque alongside her future husband, Charles Cavendish, son of the third earl of Devonshire. Like Pembroke, Salisbury was favoured by the new king in the early part of the reign, but inclined towards moderation at the outbreak of the civil wars, preferring a course of non-alignment to that of taking sides.[55] Nevertheless, not only his associate Pembroke, but also his friend and son-in-law Algernon Percy, tenth earl of Northumberland, declared for parliament in a manner that shows how much political opinion would polarise as the decade progressed.

In the early 1630s, as I have said, Northumberland was one of Henrietta Maria's staunch supporters, significantly aligned alongside Holland in his advocation of an anti-Spanish, pro-Palatinate policy. What the dance of the influences appears to show, then, is an assembly of children from a group of noble families who represented reasonably moderate religious and political views, and who were loosely associated with each other and with the queen consort. Indeed, this association can be further underlined by a brief consideration of two more of the families represented in the dance.

Barbara Ravelhofer has pointed out that, by 1649, Lord Thomas Grey of Stamford, one of the influences, had 'metamorphosed from "auspicious light" to regicide', signing his name on the death warrant of the king.[56] In 1631/2, however, he was aged only ten, and the son of Henry Grey, first earl of Stamford, and Anne Cecil, youngest daughter of the second earl of Exeter.[57] In the early 1630s, Stamford's standing at court was rising and his home in Leicestershire was favoured by a royal visit in August 1634. Nevertheless, he, like his son, became disillusioned with royal policy and took up arms for parliament in 1642. Unlike Thomas, though, he preferred a path of moderation and, along with his son-in-law,

Sir George Booth, husband of his daughter Elizabeth (who also danced in *Tempe Restored*), he declared for Charles II in August 1659.

Finally, the two Egerton children who danced in the queen's masque came from a devoutly Protestant background. John Egerton, first earl of Bridgewater, was greatly in favour with King Charles during the early years of the reign, gaining a seat on the privy council and becoming president of the council in the marches of Wales in the summer of 1631.[58] Like so many of the other noblemen whose offspring danced in the masque, he was no great supporter of Laud's ecclesiastical policy, and became progressively disillusioned with the court as the decade wore on. Although he joined Charles at Newcastle in 1639, he later withdrew to his lands which were subsequently sacked by royalist troops. Nevertheless, as Louis A. Knafla notes, there is no evidence that he assisted either side in the civil wars.[59] In other words, both the Greys and the Egertons also represented a moderate form of Protestantism that not only linked them to other families whose children performed in *Tempe Restored*, but was also somehow compatible with Henrietta Maria's position in 1631/2.

I suggest that *Tempe Restored* was conceived, in part, to reflect the desires of Henrietta Maria's associates, most notably the earl of Holland, for assistance towards the Palatinate and aggression against Spain. In 1631/2, with Gustavus Adolphus, the King of Sweden, gaining great victories for Protestantism in northern Europe, this active intervention looked ever more possible and attractive.[60] Holland had been sent as extraordinary ambassador to France in July 1631 and was temperamentally inclined to support a French alliance against the Spanish. Indeed, as Kevin Sharpe has noted, this was exactly what the marquis de St Chaumont, French extraordinary ambassador to London, was entrusted with promoting in May 1632.[61]

In 1631/2, Richelieu and Louis were keen to obtain English aid and were erring towards an alliance with Sweden against the Habsburgs.[62] Marie de Médicis, however, was stirring up trouble in the Spanish Netherlands and raising troops against France.[63] The French were so keen to stop this they offered to pay her the full value of her revenues (this being, in John Pory's words, 'not so little as £100,000 a year') if she agreed to live 'in any place out of the King of Spain's dominions'.[64] Charles and Henrietta Maria could accommodate this French desire by allowing Marie to travel to England. In addition, by acting to reconcile her factious relations, the queen consort would not only ameliorate her mother's situation, but would aid her Protestant adherents. When Harmony (who was very possibly a member of Pembroke's household) sang as the voice of the queen, her words, therefore, had a political colouring, associating Henrietta Maria with a coalition of Protestant peers who supported an alliance with France against Spain for the restitution of the Palatinate and for the cause of international Protestantism in general.

Like *Chloridia*, *Tempe Restored* advocates a far more engaged foreign policy than Charles was prepared to contemplate. Marking the point just before the queen's allegiances turned firmly away from her brother and his chief minister, it provides evidence both of her association with the earl of Holland, and of his important influence upon her political activities. By the end of 1632, as I will discuss, both he and his mistress had become involved in a complex international plot against Richelieu and Charles's lord treasurer Weston. Nevertheless, that February, *Tempe Restored* intervened in the international conflict to propose Charles and Henrietta Maria as the facilitators of harmony, both nationally and internationally.

The reality was, of course, very different. Although Holland seems to have exerted an important influence in temporarily reconciling the queen's agenda with those of moderate Protestants, Charles was unwilling to accommodate the queen mother in England and persistently refused to engage in European conflict. As a result of this intransigence, the political views of those who danced in the masque began widely to diverge as the decade progressed. *Tempe Restored*, through its figure of Harmony leading out the innocent offspring of the Caroline court, manages to maintain these tensions in balance, but only just. Indeed, the absence of the young duc de Mercoeur from the masque demonstrates the fragility of an alliance that relied as much on personal sentiment as it did on political expediency. Moreover, despite the religious views of many of its participants, the masque, as Veevers has suggested, has an allusively Catholic subtext.[65] It is to this that I now want to turn, asking how this aspect of the production can be reconciled with the Protestant beliefs of many of its participants, and addressing the question of what it is that the masque might seek to restore.

*

As I discussed earlier, Henrietta Maria arrived in England having received injunctions from her mother and the pope to work to return England to the true faith. In November 1631, the *Gazette de France* gleefully reported that Charles had had a blasphemer against the Virgin publicly flogged, and expressed the hope that England would soon revert to Rome.[66] In August 1632, the king gave Henrietta Maria £20,000 towards her Catholic chapel at Somerset House: a gift that was also enthusiastically reported in the *Gazette*.[67] Despite the religious beliefs of many of its personnel, *Tempe Restored* may be set between these events as an allusively Catholic production whose agenda was to promote the queen consort's faith at her husband's court. It places an unusual emphasis on visual display, progressing from the figure of Harmony to that of Divine Beauty, and transforming the music of the spheres into a visible manifestation of beauty on earth. In its movement from sound to sight, I suggest, it seems to want to draw observers to an ecstatic state compatible with the spiritual elevation advocated by the queen's former confessor, Pierre de Bérulle, in a manner that has a conversionary impetus.

Bérulle was closely associated with Marie de Médicis and had been instrumental in composing the queen mother's farewell letter to her daughter. He accompanied Henrietta Maria to England in 1625, but his stay was shortlived and he was dismissed along with the majority of the new queen's attendants the following summer. Returning to France, he published a devotional work entitled the *Elévation sur sainte Madeleine* which he dedicated to his mistress, explaining that he had written the text at her instigation. The *Elévation* is, therefore, a particular example of Henrietta Maria's literary patronage, and one that is intimately connected to her faith.

Bérulle was evidently appalled by the state of religion in England and disgusted by the treatment that he and his compatriots received at the hands of the English. In the dedication to the *Elévation*, he warns:

> Souvenez-vous, Madame, que les beautés que vous voyez sont périssables et que ce ne sont que des ombres de la beauté suprême et éternelle, et que tout ce qui frappe vos yeux, en cette Cour où vous êtes, est mort et infect devant Dieu.[68]

> [Remember, Madam, that the beauties you see are perishable and are nothing but the shadows of supreme and eternal beauty, and that all that meets your eyes in this court where you are, is dead and loathsome before God.]

In Bérulle's eyes, England was a poisoned land and an extreme example of the corruption of the fallen world. Turning its back on Catholicism, it had become a country filled not with roses, but with thorns, a sterile desert of heresy and venomous serpents.

Although, in *Tempe Restored*, Circe's garden is described as a '*delicious place*' (line 52), it nevertheless appears to be as spiritually sterile as Bérulle's England. Indeed, Circe herself indicates that she is aware of the imperfect nature of her material pleasures. Lamenting the escape of her Favourite, she calls to her attendant nymphs, and commands:

> Then take my keys! and show me all my wealth!
> Lead me abroad! Let me my subjects view!
> Bring me some physic! though that bring no health;
> And feign me pleasures, since I find none true. (lines 120–5)

The eclectic anti-masques of barbarians, hogs, apes and asses that ensue, reinforce the notion that Circe and her companions circulate and recirculate in a realm of base matter. The sensuous pleasures that she provides are shown to be no pleasures; her medicines cannot heal; her worldly riches have no true value. Everything adds up to indicate that a form of truth exists *beyond* her realm and we become aware that her physic will 'bring no health' because 'true' health is spiritual not physical. Similarly, her pleasures must be 'feigned' because 'true' pleasures do not exist in the material world.

While Circe and her companions are locked into an endless metamorphosis of one physical body into another, the impulse of the masque itself, by contrast, is one of refinement and spiritual amelioration. A comparison is consequently invited between the materialism of the Circean anti-masques whose magic is sterile and whose pleasures are feigned, and the representations of Divine Beauty and Heroic Virtue. The masque's printed allegory notes of the figure of Divine Beauty that:

> corporeal beauty, consisting in symmetry, colour, and certain unexpressable graces, shining in the Queen's majesty, may draw us to the contemplation of the beauty of the soul, unto which it hath analogy. (lines 361–4)

A connection is posited which at once reveals the inability of the physical world to represent the spiritual world of the soul, and which nonetheless plays upon the mystical nature of beauty, showing it to enable an observer to make a conceptual movement between, in this case, the realm of matter and the realm of the spirit. Thus, contemplation of Divine Beauty/Henrietta Maria carries an observer over into a contemplation of the soul. Importantly, *Tempe Restored*'s allegory describes Divine Beauty as containing 'unexpressable' graces: emptied of a language that provides an eternal reminder and replication of the error of the fall, the visual image breaks free to carry its observer up to a comprehension of beauty that transcends the merely physical. This movement, while profoundly neo-Platonic, accrues a specific proselytising impulse in the context of the queen's Catholicism. While the observation of Charles and Henrietta Maria's marital union is imagined in Caroline masques to project harmony out on to the world, the vision of Divine Beauty here draws observers to a state compatible with the spiritual ecstasy recommended in the *Elévation* by Bérulle.

Through the example of Mary Magdalen, Bérulle demonstrates that, by allowing the spirit to be moved by beauty, one can be inspired by the ideal of divine perfection to embrace virtue and to strive towards the good. The *Elévation* emphasises the overwhelming importance of the female saint and holds her up as an example to women everywhere. Discussing her fidelity and constancy by the Cross, he observes:

Jésus donc voit Madeleine à ses pieds et Madeleine contemple Jésus en sa croix. Ces regards sont mutuels et réciproque, et ces deux coeurs sont des miroirs qui, étant proches, se rapportent et se représentent l'un à l'autre. Qui verrait le coeur de Jésus, y verrait Madeleine empreinte. Qui verrait le coeur de Madeleine, y verrait Jésus, et Jésus souffrant, vivement imprimé. Que cette âme et l'amour de cette âme, et sa force et constance en amour, nous ravisse et nous étonne.[69]

[Jesus therefore sees Magdalen at his feet and Magdalen contemplates Jesus on his cross. These gazes are mutual and reciprocal, and these two hearts are mirrors which, being close, relate and recall one to the other. Who would see the heart of Jesus, would see Magdalen stamped there. Who would see the heart of Magdalen, would see Jesus, and Jesus suffering, deeply imprinted there. May this soul and the love of this soul, and its strength and constancy in love, enrapture and astonish us.]

Magdalen forms a complementary pairing with Jesus whose image is imprinted in her heart. On one level, therefore, the imagery in the *Elévation* is similar to that in Caroline masques which sees Henrietta Maria and Charles exchanging mutual gazes: the masques raise the royal couple to the status of gods and their love is fittingly represented in profoundly spiritual terms. However, on another level, the figure of Henrietta Maria takes on a particular significance.

Bérulle's Magdalen was specifically conceived to appeal to courtly women and to give them an important role model in the Christian story. She was, Bérulle says, favoured above the Apostles because she was chosen to inform them of Christ's resurrection and, thus, she demonstrates that women can be socially and spiritually revered.[70] Furthermore, at the end of his text, the prelate adds an essay entitled, 'Observations Sur le Texte de Saint Luc en Faveur de la Madeleine', in which he attempts to exculpate her from accusations that she was a reformed prostitute. Interestingly, he describes her as one of the most distinguished women of her province who was visited and honoured by the great men of Jerusalem.[71] In other words, she was a woman who had to lead a public life, not a woman who was public. She stands as an example of good conduct for noblewomen and, in effect, she validates women's positions as public figures in the courtly world.

In addition, the *Elévation* represents Magdalen as a vessel expressing the love of the divine. For example, Bérulle, addressing Christ, observes that 'vous deviez avoir un sépulcre vivant et un sépulcre d'amour, et vous choisissez maintenant le coeur de Madeleine' [you had to have a living tomb and a tomb of love, and you would now choose the heart of Magdalen].[72] Her spiritual union with Christ abolishes the mediation of language and renders Magdalen at once ignorant of herself and of the fact that she loves. She is invaded by the spirit of Christ, and her love, being stripped of intelligence, is filled with power.[73] All traces of self-love are erased; she is emptied out of herself, becoming an ecstatic figure, the contemplation of which can lead an observer into new states of spiritual understanding.[74] Bérulle's dedication to the *Elévation*, therefore, advises Henrietta Maria that the contemplation of the Magdalen will light a flame in her spirit, inspiring her devotions with heavenly fire.[75]

Tempe Restored's construction of Divine Beauty participates in this idea of contemplation leading to ecstasy in a manner which replicates the anti-intellectual impulse of Bérulle's discourse. This ecstasy, of course, is very different from the intellectual applications of reason preferred by Ben Jonson.[76] It also seems to contradict the Fugitive Favourite's assertion that he covets to be a 'man again / Governed by reason, and not ruled by sense' (lines 77–8). However, in the context of Henrietta Maria's religion, to be reasonable does not mean to exercise some sort of logical rationality, but to submit voluntarily to the sovereign grace of God.[77] Voluntary submission is one of the main themes of *Tempe Restored* which not only sees Circe's victims consenting to become perfect slaves, but which concludes with the nymph's resignation of her possessions to the royal couple by her own free will. The Fugitive Favourite's assertion that he covets to be 'Governed by reason' therefore fits quite comfortably with the impulse of the masque which demands that its audience reject sensual desire in favour of ecstatic obedience. The masque seems to demand a temporary renunciation of the self in the face of the blazing spectacle of Divine Beauty whose dance among her stars provides a powerful and supremely visual manifestation of cosmic harmony.

Tempe Restored therefore dramatises a movement from Circe's material pleasures to Divine Beauty's inspirational dance of the spheres. The production certainly makes a case for women's efficacy as the promoters of social harmony, reversing Nathaniel Richards's contention that masquing turned '*Virgin Love*, to hot Lust's Plurisie'. By replacing the vocal Circe with the vision of Divine Beauty, *Tempe Restored* satirised criticism of the queen's theatrical endeavours and responded with a demonstration of the social and dynastic benefits of masquing. Nevertheless, although the masque might be read as a bid for female vocality on the stage in the face of English traditions that had not kept pace with those on the continent, it seems to me that Henrietta Maria did not really need to challenge such masquing codes. After all, the injunction for the queen's silence upon the masquing stage applied equally well to her husband, who, unlike his wife, never took a speaking role in a court production. Instead, the masque privileges women as socially beneficial in a manner that has a particular resonance with the queen consort's religion.

As Shell has noted, the issue of religious conscience complicates any assumption that an individual might endorse a philosophical or theological system 'for entirely self-interested reasons'.[78] The privilege accorded to the female figure in *Tempe Restored* is therefore less a proto-feminist engagement with injunctions against female speech, than a means of promoting women as the instigators of social harmony conceived along Catholic lines. Just as Bérulle's Magdalen was to provide inspiration for courtly women everywhere, so Henrietta Maria's Divine Beauty was to show them how to lead their lovers towards goodness. It was no accident that the queen descended from *Tempe Restored*'s heavens in a 'sky color' gown that drew visual parallels with the figure of the Virgin Mary.[79] In a manner compatible with Bérulle's description of the corrupted garden of England, *Tempe Restored* wishes to restore the Vale of Tempe to the true (and implicitly Catholic) followers of the Muses.

Interestingly, Malcolm Smuts has suggested that Henrietta Maria gained more benefits for her religion from an alliance with Protestant courtiers than she did by working with officials sympathetic to Catholicism, largely because the English Catholics were both riven by internal disputes and afraid to reveal themselves.[80] *Tempe Restored* bears witness to a moment in the political history of the Caroline court that saw a group of Protestant peers advocating an alliance with Catholic France for their mutual benefits. It manages to hold in tension the highly allusive Catholic imagery associated with the queen consort and the political desires of her Protestant adherents. Nevertheless, even in 1632, this unity was, to an extent, fictitious. Many artists and courtiers found that the beliefs and allegiances they held in the early 1630s led them further and further from agreement with the king's policies by the end of the decade. It is therefore not surprising that the demanding spectacle of Divine Beauty was not, in the end, welcome music to everybody's eyes.

CHAPTER 6

'It is my voyce': the fashioning of a self in The Shepherds' Paradise

If *Tempe Restored* provides evidence of Henrietta Maria's involvement with a group of Protestant peers, then *The Shepherds' Paradise*, her second pastoral play, commissioned from the courtier Walter Montagu and performed twice in the Christmas season of 1632/3, demonstrates a continuing engagement with European current affairs. The queen consort's pastorals, unlike her court masques, were habitually performed, not in the Whitehall Banqueting House, but in the more intimate space of Somerset House.[1] As events that took place before a select audience, they were, I suggest, more radical, both politically and in what they could propose about women's social roles. This chapter will therefore investigate the pastoral genre preferred by Henrietta Maria, examining its particular benefits for women's entry on to the stage, before discussing the play's political allusions and its engagement with her religion.

*

The queen consort arrived in England already associated with pastoral imagery. In 1625, for example, Abraham Rémy, a romance writer, dedicated to her his *La Galatée et les adventures du Prince Astiagés*, which declared its allegorical intentions in its subtitle, *Histoire de notre temps, ou sous noms feints sont representez les amours du roy et de la reyne d'Angleterre* [History of our times, in which the loves of the king and queen of England are represented under assumed names]. I will investigate this text in more detail later in this chapter: here, it is only necessary to observe that *La Galatée*'s opening pages locate Galatée/Henrietta Maria as a nymph in a pastoral setting, and show Astiagés, her future husband, indulging in a love lament similar to Alcidor's in *Artenice*.[2] In other words, Rémy's *roman-à-clef* invokes the fashionable pastoral discourse of the Parisian *salons*, conceiving Henrietta Maria's betrothal in flatteringly romantic terms.[3] When she arrived in England, then, she already had direct experience of the pastoral form and of its allegorical applications.

French pastoral and romance plays, as I noted in chapter 2, often shadowed the people and events of the Parisian social world. In 1629, for example, Boisrobert published his *Histoire Indienne d'Anaxandre et Orazie*, an allegorical drama for Mademoiselle d'Effiat, daughter of the former French ambassador to England.[4] Indeed, the late 1620s and early 1630s in France saw a burgeoning of tragi-comic and romantic drama written by a new generation of poets, such as Boisrobert and Corneille, who took their inspiration more from prose romances and the social fashion for *honnêteté* than from the legacy of dramatists like Alexandre Hardy.[5] *The Shepherds' Paradise* has a great deal in common with such plays: indeed, as Sarah Poynting has noted, 'there are no shepherds and no sheep' in Montagu's pastoral which 'is peopled entirely by aristocratic characters'.[6] Despite its title, *The Shepherds' Paradise* is more a romance than a genuine pastoral, and reflects the values of the queen's circle in a manner that, in Poynting's words, leaves 'their view of life unchallenged'.[7]

As a product of the English court and an English writer, Montagu's play obviously belongs within a tradition different from Racan's *Les Bergeries* or Boisrobert's *Histoire Indienne*.[8] Nevertheless, English pastoral, like its French counterpart, developed a tradition of social and political commentary that, I argue, is intrinsic to an understanding of *The Shepherds' Paradise*. Lucy Munro has discussed the genre's connection with political and anti-courtly satire, showing, for example, how the poet Fulke Greville 'criticised King James's pacifism . . . and used the *Arcadia* as part of this project'.[9] Annabel Patterson, meanwhile, has proposed that Henrietta Maria's preference for pastoral led to a 'suppression' of all 'responses to [Virgil's] *Eclogues* that might have interrogated the [Caroline] myth of peace and prosperity'.[10] Remarking that 'the queen's fixation on pastoral drama was one of the factors that exacerbated class conflict', she asserts that this 'pastoral myth' was 'a proposition designed to ratify the behavior and circumstances of the ruling class'.[11] Henrietta Maria's play certainly does focus exclusively on noble characters and behaviour, yet, through the virtuous character of Fidamira, it also criticises courtly corruption and bad kingship.[12] In addition, as I will show, it draws on the opportunities for social and political commentary made available by the pastoral genre, interrogating Charles's policy of non-intervention in Europe and also proposing new ways of social interaction at the Caroline court.

As a dramatic event, not a danced spectacle, the play marked the queen consort's court as a site of innovation, at once within, and yet distinct from, established forms of Stuart monarchical display. Like *Artenice* and *Tempe Restored*, it pushed at the boundaries of female theatrical performance, proposing a new sort of social relationship based upon a woman's ability to govern her own chastity. Moreover, despite earlier anxieties about cross-dressing, it again courted controversy by featuring women in men's clothing: indeed Sophie Tomlinson has observed that, out of a total of fourteen roles in the play, ten were for masculine characters.[13] The virtuous character of Fidamira, played by Sophia Carew (a maid of honour to the queen before her marriage in December 1632), also spends much of the play blacked up as Gemella, a Moor, and thus echoes the racially cross-dressed figures that drew disapprobation upon Queen Anna and her ladies in the 1605 *Masque of Blackness*. Indeed, Gemella is, in part, a continuation of, or a response to, the ideas put forward in the *Masque of Blackness*, incarnating a spiritual virtue that makes a woman's body beautiful whatever its colour.

Famously, the phenomenon of the actress did not pass without comment in Caroline society. Shortly after the production of the queen consort's pastoral, William Prynne's polemical *Histriomastix* was published, famously terming 'Women-Actors', 'notorious whores'.[14] Nevertheless, *The Shepherds' Paradise* provoked surprisingly few other adverse comments. Indeed, several court dramatists went to lengths to distance themselves from Prynne's accusations and to validate female theatrical production. The dedication to the 1633 edition of James Shirley's play, *The Bird in a Cage*, satirically addressed Prynne, asserting that the original production's music and an interlude 'personated by Ladies' would have pleased him 'infinitely in the Presentment'.[15] Similarly, the printer's dedication to the 1633 collected works of John Marston addressed Lady Elizabeth Cary, herself a playwright and close friend of the queen consort, and exempted Marston's *oeuvre* from the 'Many opprobies and aspersions [that] have not long since been cast upon Playes in generall'.[16] These dedications are at once a defence of the dramatists' craft, yet they also demonstrate the queen consort's perceived importance as a patron of theatre, presenting women's interest in dramatic production as a welcome phenomenon. They raise the question of the noblewoman's power of patronage, complicating the increasingly untenable assumption that, in the seventeenth century, men had a privileged access to a culture that excluded women.

The Shepherds' Paradise has been castigated as 'one of the worst [plays] in the language' and as the turgidly moral product of a woman's household.[17] Nevertheless, it engages with questions of marriage, government and masculine constancy, interrogating notions of personal identity and promoting a role for women as the cornerstones of a virtuous society. As Sarah Poynting has shown, its playwright, a courtier, political negotiator and former protégé of the late duke of Buckingham, was intimately connected with Henrietta Maria's circle and was well known to the queen consort's family and friends on the continent.[18] His play certainly is, in Erica Veevers's words, 'a pattern for the kind of conduct acceptable amongst [the queen consort's] group at court', and an entertainment which set the tone for the neo-Platonic drama of the 1630s.[19]

SELF-DETERMINATION IN MONTAGU'S PASTORAL

In chapter 2, I noted that Racan's pastoral, *Artenice*, drawing on the modes of polite social interaction proposed by St François de Sales in his *Introduction à la vie dévote*, gave women the right to act by according them a social role in the promotion of civility and polite behaviour. The same is true of Montagu's play and it is this I now want to consider by investigating the ways in which it constructs both masculine and feminine identities.

Fidamira, despite (or perhaps because of) her cross-racial costume, is *The Shepherds' Paradise*'s virtuous lodestone, providing a clear example of self-knowledge and strength. At the start of the play, she is commended into the care of the King of Castile by Prince Basilino, her erstwhile lover. However, fearing courtly corruption, she begs to be allowed to remain at home, arguing that it would be 'a retreat out of [her] selfe to be any where but in [her] ffathers house' (1.7.625–6). In other words, she derives her sense of self more from her ability to police her own chastity than from her position as the king's subject, resisting his will by invoking the convention of filial obedience by which it is subtended, and presenting herself as a modest daughter in order to delay having to obey as a subject. Her duty to her own virtue, and her concomitant idea of herself, is shown to be solid and something that transcends even her obedience to the monarch.

Fidamira, then, is able to govern her own chastity just like the titular character of *Artenice*. In addition, an obvious analogy may be drawn between her potential disobedience as a subject and that of a Catholic wife who owed a duty to her husband in everything but religion. Indeed, Henrietta Maria herself was informed by her mother that her first duty was to the king, 'après Dieu et la Religion' [after God and religion].[20] Montagu's pastoral presents Fidamira as a woman whose virtue ensures her own safety, whether she remains in her father's house or travels abroad in Moorish disguise, but also condones passive disobedience if obedience compromises her virtuous position.

In contrast, Prince Basilino and Agenor, his companion, are incompletely aware of themselves at the start of the play. Both are inconstant in their loves and both deploy the hyperbolic language of extreme neo-Platonism.[21] Nevertheless, by the play's conclusion, their youthful excesses have been tempered by their experiences among the women of the Shepherds' Paradise. Their journey from the Castilian court, undertaken both in disguise and with assumed names, becomes a personal odyssey of self-discovery through which they explore new identities divorced from their previous social roles. Indeed, Basilino represents his assumption of the name 'Moromante' as a movement away from his former self, and, eventually, rather than reassuming his original name, asks his father if he may 'keepe this happy name, *Morom:*' (5.2.3,819). Although this refiguring of his identity needs to be validated by the law of his father, the pastoral nevertheless opens up a space in which personal identities may, in part, be self-constructed.

Agenor's movement towards self-knowledge is conceived slightly differently for it is completed by the discovery of his genealogy. In the 1659 printed text of *The Shepherds' Paradise* (although it is missing from the Tixall manuscript edited by Poynting), the revelation of his identity gives rise to an explanation of his unusual name. The opening Act of the pastoral informs us that, as a child, Agenor had been saved from slaughter by Basilino. Now we are told that a jewel he wears identifies him as Palante, son of the King of Navarre. Addressing Agenor, Basilino/Moromante observes:

> If this jewel be a certain mark of your birth, I can assure you that you were brought to me with it, and then I call'd you Agenor, a name fitted to the not-knowing who you were.[22]

In other words, the name Agenor is derived from *a-genus*, meaning 'without family'.[23]

While, as I say, this explanation is omitted from the Tixall manuscript, that text, too, makes a great deal out of the revelation that Agenor is the recovered son of 'the now blessed king of Navarr' (5.2.3,680–1). With his heritage revealed, Agenor is encouraged to 'put off that vnhappy name Genorio, / & call [him] selfe Prince Pallante' (5.2.3,679–80). The pastoral negotiates successfully between a manner of conceiving identity as something arising from within, imagining its characters in a development towards healthy self-knowledge, and as something that shows the social importance of kinship ties. In other words, it tempers notions of self-determination with an emphasis on blood relationships and human affection.

The notion of naming is not only of interest within the pastoral, but paradigmatic of the adoption of pastoral identities upon the stage by Henrietta Maria and her ladies. Diane Purkiss has proposed that a woman's fashioning of a stage self was an implicit resistance to the power of male protectors to shape her, and that women's control of aspects of cultural production led to fears that men would be blocked from achieving their desires.[24] Despite the fact that *The Shepherds' Paradise* was penned by a man, it nevertheless accorded its female participants the means of investigating alternative ways of expressing themselves, not least because they were members of a female acting troupe whose interaction upon the stage produced a specific cultural artefact. Rather than simply patronising works of masculine genius, the women collaborated with court artists to create a dramatic event for themselves. In sum, like *Artenice, The Shepherds' Paradise* demonstrates an awareness of the constructed nature of social identity and pushes the boundaries of permitted female behaviour at the Caroline court.

'IT IS MY VOYCE'

Concomitant with its investigation into the construction of personal identity, Montagu's pastoral provides an innovative commentary upon the subject of female speech, drawing attention, like Racan's play, to the gendered injustice that decreed a woman could not speak publicly about her affections. Entering the wood, 'loves Cabonett', to muse upon the subject of love, Bellessa declares she will speak her thoughts aloud because the plants will not be able to reiterate them (5.1.3,296–308). In this private space, she explores the idea of her affections, concerning herself with the notion of Moromante's constancy. However, not only does the presentation of this nominally private space allow the audience to imagine they are privy to the secrets of a woman's mind, but Bellessa's monologue becomes a dialogue when she is answered by Eccho, anomalously represented as a male 'Councellor' who is 'old & a litle deafe' (5.1.3,360–4).[25]

Bellessa's private musing at once allows the audience to trespass on the forbidden and also, in its performance, transgresses the social code that says a woman should not publicly debate such issues. Nevertheless, her discourse is validated by the masculine Eccho's encouragement despite the fact that she draws attention to his advantage in being invisible when she notes that, unlike hers, his speech is made possible because he always has 'a Curtaine drawne before [him]' (5.1.3,320–1). Eccho's subsequent advice to Bellessa is couched in the terms of an active verb: the princess has already been urged to 'Speake' and to '*Word Love*', now she is exhorted to '*Doe*'. On one level, as Sophie Tomlinson has noted, the transformation of Eccho into a male 'Councellor', 'doubly alienates Bellessa from her own voice'.[26] However, paradoxically, it also legitimates the princess's position, first by permitting the play to debate the problems of female speech and then by counselling action.

As Tomlinson has also observed, by transforming Echo into a masculine 'Councellor', Montagu 'avoids splitting the dramatic focus of the scene between two female characters'.[27] Instead, the male Eccho becomes the princess's adviser, just as Moromante was her tutor in love. Nevertheless, it might be said that Bellessa, who must manipulate Moromante's words of love to voice her own wishes, remains coloured by the figure of the original mythological nymph. Condemned only to be able to answer, the classical Echo's position is one of dependence upon another's speech: she cannot accede to full presence, and has no proper personal identity.[28] Indeed, Echo becomes a metaphor for early modern women's fragmented speech, echoing back another's discourse and standing for the violence that prevents them from publicly expressing their desires.

At a further remove from the play's narrative, Echo's position parallels that of the speaking courtly woman upon the stage, for she, like Echo, is condemned to ventriloquy, echoing back the words of the pastoral's male author. However, as Clare Nouvet has explored in relation to Ovid's version of the story, the nymph does not simply ventriloquise a prior discourse, for, in order to transform 'the repetition of "sounds" into "answers"', the Ovidian text grants her the privilege of imposing meaning on the words she echoes back, thus restoring Echo as 'a self, a speaking consciousness'.[29] In order to establish herself as a vocal presence upon the stage, the queen consort is reliant upon the good will and complicity of the king and of the poet whose words she speaks. However, by inhabiting the positions within the discourse written for her by a man, the courtly woman may transform his discourse by reading it against the grain, thus establishing a position from which she may speak of her own concerns.

This active appropriation of another's discourse is significant if one considers Henrietta Maria's position as the patron of the pastoral's author: it is not primarily the story of Echo as a pitiable and disembodied voice speaking unrequited love which concerns the pastoral's text, but the story of Echo punished by Juno for facilitating Jove's inconstancies. In the Ovidian narrative, garrulous Echo delayed the goddess with speech, while

Jove entertained himself with amorous nymphs. When Juno discovered Echo's deception she cursed the nymph with the ability only to reiterate what another had spoken. *The Shepherds' Paradise* allies the character of Bellessa more with the punishing Juno than with the punished nymph in a process which complicates the myth's gender binarism with notions of status.

When asked by Bellessa if Eccho dare promise Moromante's constancy, the answer that echoes back is the word 'constancy'. Bellessa, showing an awareness of the duplicitous nature of language and thus of Eccho's treacherous potential, swears she will be revenged on Eccho if Moromante should prove inconstant:

> And for you Eccho I will wth my reproaches force you to answer somuch, as it shall hoarce that litle voyce is left you; Nay I will search all the Earths concavityes, & fill them vp soe to choake you quite, There shalbe nothing left you hollow to reside in, but Moromante's Heart that I will leave you for a greater punishment, then death. (5.1.3,337–43)[30]

By threatening to stop Eccho's voice altogether, Bellessa will complete the punishment that Juno inaugurated in revenge for the infidelities of Jove. The parallel between Bellessa and Juno in the punishing of Eccho offers a paradigm of the relationship between a noble patron and a patronised poet: Henrietta Maria's patronage of Montagu's text allows Montagu a voice, but it is a voice that it is in the queen consort's power to deny or transform, and for which Montagu, like Jonson before him, may also be made vulnerable.[31]

The Shepherds' Paradise explicitly dramatises the relationship between a poet and his mistress when the overly neo-Platonic Martiro presents a poem to Bellessa. His representation of the queen conceives of her as an inexpressible 'impossibility', too refined and elevated from the world for worldly things to comprehend. Not surprisingly, the queen fails to understand the poem and does not recognise herself within it. 'Sure Martiro', she observes, 'they that could vnderstand your verses, might knowe your love, th' impossibilityes to me seeme equall' (4.4.2,782–4). Martiro's love is represented as a neo-Platonic abstraction that has no foundation either in the material world or in Bellessa herself. He explains to Moromante that his love is 'Angellicall, at first created infinite, without neede of propagation' (4.4.2,801–2). The queen is to him an impossible ideal, a goddess figure like the Alba of *Albion's Triumph*: her own desires and fantasies are erased as she becomes the means through which he constructs himself as a neo-Platonic philosopher and poet. Furthermore, his poem demonstrates that, to be comprehensible, words and ideas must circulate within a community that shares certain linguistic understandings. To function correctly, they must be received and interpreted in the manner in which they were intended.

In 'loves Cabonett', Eccho not only gains presence by returning Bellessa's voice, but is also the mediator between Bellessa's desires and Moromante. If Moromante doesn't hear Eccho (that is, if he takes up Narcissus's position as vainly self-regarding, or if he is inconstant) then Bellessa, like Martiro, speaks in a closed circuit: Eccho returns the queen's words only to herself. The reciprocal nature of the identities proposed within *The Shepherds' Paradise* is made evident in the text at this moment: self-knowledge is to be gained only through conversation and an awareness of one's effects upon other people. In addition, the mediating presence of the voice of Eccho between Bellessa's mind and the ears of Moromante underlines a disjunction in speech which occurs at the point where language becomes disconnected from the speaking body and which offers an opportunity for misreadings that endanger the position of the speaker/writer whose intentions may be misconstrued and punished.

The disjunction between the speaking body and the words that are spoken is exploited in the pastoral to investigate the production of, and constraints upon, women's speech. In response to Moromante, who has asked her whether she is in love, Bellessa positions her voice alongside that of the disembodied Eccho with the words:

> It is my voyce Moromante & I have lett it loose from mee: that it might not have somuch as modesty to hold it back, beleive it, for if you put me to take it into me againe, I have a virgin cold that will not let it speake soe cleere. (5.1.3,373–7)

By saying she has sent her voice out from her, Bellessa makes a parallel between her speaking position and that of the classical Echo (whose body, in some versions of the myth, became cold stone). This disconnection between her voice and her gendered body opens up a split between the notions of body and mind, freeing the queen's voice from sexual impediments. Bellessa's words in *The Shepherds' Paradise* gesture towards the possibility that a woman could speak with clarity if that clarity were not denied her by the masculinist construction of discourse which always reduces her to her biology and circumscribes her speech with notions of propriety. In other words, the pastoral makes evident a gendered prejudice within society which denies a woman the ability to express her love.

In its text, then, *The Shepherds' Paradise* proposes a form of self-determinism for both its male and female characters that divorces them from their relationships with their fathers and permits a certain resistance to authority. Like *Artenice* before it, it proposes a new type of relationship based upon social interaction and self-reflection which opens up a space within which social conventions and laws may be subject to debate. Similarly, in its production, *The Shepherds' Paradise* allowed its women to step outside their social roles as noblewomen, wives and mothers to perform as socially, racially and sexually different others. Although their acting was sanctioned by the Stuart administrative machine, and although the play also bore witness to their privileged status as cultural patrons, the space of the stage offered a place of resistance to a masquing discourse that habitually represented them as mute goddesses. In sum, it created a place from which the queen consort could articulate a position of both cultural and political difference: it is this that I will explore in the next section.

PASTORAL POLITICS

Despite its romantic tone, aspects of the queen consort's production, most notably the style of costume designed for the character of Fidamira, hint that the entertainment has an allegorical subtext.[32] Orgel and Strong note that the drawing of Fidamira is a copy of a portrait of an unknown Spanish infanta and that it is the only known instance of Inigo Jones copying a portrait for a costume.[33] Taking this supposition further, Erica Veevers has argued that the pastoral might be concerned allegorically with King Charles's two courtships, and has suggested that Fidamira's costume would have been picked out by the play's audience as a visual reference to the Spanish court and its infanta.[34] She associates Montagu's pastoral with the kind of romance being written at the time of the Anglo-French marriage, and draws a particular comparison with *La Galatée*.[35] Poynting, on the other hand, states that the play 'bears no resemblance at all' to *La Galatée*, although she does agree that its similarities with Charles's journey to Spain are 'blatant'.[36] In addition, she remarks that 'there was more than one Spanish princess with whom Fidamira might be identified', and concludes that her Spanish dress 'might simply have been intended to represent her as an aristocratic Spanish lady'.[37]

In contrast to Poynting, I am convinced that *La Galatée* made a contribution to *The Shepherds' Paradise*, and also believe that, on one level at least, the character of Fidamira shadowed the Spanish infanta, invoking the already romanticised events that surrounded the Anglo-French marriage.[38] However, I do not believe that Montagu's play should be read as a straight allegory of the affairs of 1623–5, and share Poynting's opinion that it is improbable that we are supposed to identify one character with one historical figure throughout the play.[39] Nevertheless, the play *is*, in part, a *roman-à-clef*, and also follows in the tradition of Buckingham's 1626 masque which figured a representation of Marie de Médicis waving together the monarchs of Europe. The play intervenes in international disharmony, proposing a form of peace based upon reciprocal love very similar to that pursued by the French queen mother during her Regency. Representations of this policy were prevalent in celebrations at the time of the Anglo-French wedding, and were evinced again in *Salmacida Spolia* (1640). Although Poynting is correct to interpret the pastoral in the light of Walter Montagu's position and politics, imagery peculiar to the queen consort and her family should certainly not be overlooked.

In this respect, the text of *La Galatée* bears further investigation. It is prefaced by a printer's note which declares: 'Voicy comme ie me persuade les noms des principaux personnages qui sont representez' [Here is how I interpret the names of the main characters who are represented].[40] The printer then identifies a selection of figures from the tale, naming Astiagés as 'Le Prince de Galles', Galatée as 'Madame Soeur du Roy' and, interestingly, Elpisas as *both* 'le Duc de Boucquingan' and 'le Comte de Carly'. Most significantly, the figure of 'Le Comte Agenoris' is recorded as being the allegorical shadow of 'Le comte Palatin Roy de Boheme'. If a comparison is to be made between *La Galatée* and *The Shepherds' Paradise*, then surely the similarity between the names of Comte Agenoris and Agenor, Basilino's faithful companion, must be taken into account. *La Galatée*'s association of Agenoris with the figure of the Elector Palatine, coupled with the revelation in *The Shepherds' Paradise* that Agenor is actually a prince with the resonant name of Palante, make it virtually impossible not to read Montagu's pastoral as somehow a commentary upon European political affairs.

The Shepherds' Paradise is a production which resonates particularly with its time of composition and which needs to be situated within the specific context of the early 1630s. It was written and performed in the aftermath of Marie de Médicis's exile, and in the context of Gaston d'Orléans's military mobilisation against Louis XIII. Set in a European frame, it makes reference to the kingdoms of Navarre, Castile, France and Albion, engaging with its political moment in complex ways. In a manner compatible with the queen consort's neo-Platonic masques, it offers a romantic solution to international discord, and yet it also foregrounds her household as a closely knit group with a particular investment in Europe. The pastoral was performed at a time when Henrietta Maria's involvement in international politics had just been revealed through the shattering of the Châteauneuf plot, and, as a product of her household, can be seen as a vehicle for her own political concerns, as well as for the concerns of its author.

By the middle of 1632, as I discussed in the previous chapter, Henrietta Maria's allegiances had swung away from Louis XIII's administration, and she became more politically aligned than ever with Cardinal Richelieu's opponents. Interestingly, this increased her connections with many of the late duke of Buckingham's followers, and implicated her in an international network with interests in Brussels, Lorraine, Savoy, France and Spain. In my discussion of *Tempe Restored*, I investigated the queen consort's associations with Protestants at the English court and showed how her interests coincided with the largely anti-Spanish, colonialist politics of nobles such as the earls of Holland and Northumberland.[41] At the risk of gross generalisation, what manifested itself in 1632/3 was an anti-Richelieu cabal, comprising, among others, Anne of Austria, Marie de Chevreuse and Henrietta Maria's servants, the earl of Holland, Walter Montagu and William Crofts.

After Marie de Médicis's exile from France, Marie de Chevreuse, together with Holland and the chevalier de Jars, began to plot once more against Richelieu. Charles de l'Aubépine, marquis de Châteauneuf, who had visited England in 1628 as Louis XIII's extraordinary ambassador and who was a close friend of the duchesse de Chevreuse, passed confidential council information to her and to Queen Anne who retransmitted it to their allies in London, Madrid, Brussels and Nancy.[42] At the same time, Marie de Chevreuse kept up a very public friendship with Henrietta Maria, sending her a present of a silver cabinet in April 1632 that was so significant it was reported in the *Gazette de France*.[43] On her side, the English queen consort supported the anti-Richelieu cause, and was also antagonistic to Weston, Charles's lord treasurer. Weston's programme of peace and non-parliamentary government did not serve the purposes of her associates, Holland and Northumberland, who were more inclined to an aggressive foreign policy, and Weston had also irritated her personally by attempting to trim expenditure in her household. Now he aligned himself with Fontenay-Mareuil, the French ambassador, who was known to be a *créature* of Richelieu.[44]

By the end of the year, and despite a severe illness which threatened his life, Richelieu had been made aware of the cabal against him. In February

1633, he struck against his enemies, exiling Châteauneuf to Angoulême and imprisoning Jars in the Bastille. The French had intercepted enough letters to implicate Henrietta Maria in the intrigue and to link her manoeuvres against Weston to the activities of a Protestant faction in England that included the earls of Warwick, Bedford and Holland. The international plot collapsed, leaving Henrietta Maria's political credit damaged.[45]

As one of Buckingham's clients, Walter Montagu had been employed in diplomatic missions across Europe and was known to all the major players in the conspiracy. In the mid 1630s, he was still carrying letters between Henrietta Maria, her sister, Christine, Anne of Austria and Marie de Chevreuse. His name occurs frequently in Henrietta Maria's correspondence with her sister, as does that of William Crofts, a page at court whose cousin, Cecilia, acted in *The Shepherds' Paradise*.[46] Moreover, in 1633, when Marie de Chevreuse had once again been expelled from France by Richelieu, both Montagu and Crofts carried letters to her from Queen Anne in Paris.[47] Montagu's identity as the author of Henrietta Maria's 1633 pastoral shows his close connection with her court at the time of the plot, and makes it entirely possible that the entertainment commented obliquely on international affairs.

Sarah Poynting has investigated the possible allegorical meanings of the pastoral's evocations of Navarre, France and Castile, drawing attention to Navarre's historical status as a territory contested by both France and Spain, and observing that although 'the equation between Princess Saphira of Navarre and Henrietta Maria might be a simple one', it is 'difficult to see any work involving relations between Spain, France and Navarre in the early 1630s in quite such an innocent light'.[48] No straight analogies can be drawn between the dynastic alignments dramatised in the pastoral and European factional politics, yet the resolutions of conflict proposed in *The Shepherds' Paradise* have a strong connection with Marie de Médicis's pacific iconography and can also be shown to comment obliquely upon the restoration of the Palatinate. Poynting has suggested that Montagu might have used Navarre's territorially contested position as a way of alluding to the dangers posed by Spain and France to the independent dukedoms of Savoy and Lorraine.[49] As he was closely allied with the rulers of these dukedoms and as it is possible that *Tempe Restored* had already made this allusion, the observation is extremely pertinent. Nevertheless, Poynting's model might be extended to include a consideration of the Palatinate, annexed by Spain at the expense of its prince, Charles I's brother-in-law.

In the virulently anti-Spanish *La Galatée*, Comte Agenoris, whose kingdom has been seized by the Syrians (Spain), is rescued from pirates and eventually taken home to 'Cilicie' (England) by Prince Astiagés. In *The Shepherds' Paradise*, Agenor, whose very name suggests his dispossession, is saved from slaughter by Basilino and is subsequently looked after by him as a brother. Agenor is later discovered to be Prince Palante and leaves the Shepherds' Paradise to be restored to his rightful place as heir of Navarre. This aspect of the pastoral resonates strongly with desires among the queen consort's adherents for a policy of active assistance towards the Palatinate, dramatising the fantasy that the support of a dispossessed prince would lead to his restoration. In the light of this, *The Shepherds' Paradise* can be seen as a forerunner of the later productions patronised by Henrietta Maria and performed for the entertainment of the visiting Palatine princes in 1635–6.[50]

Furthermore, through its representation of the realm of Albion, the pastoral also obliquely criticises the Caroline regime's non-interventionist foreign policy. Malcolm Smuts has argued that the pacific nature of the cult of the Caroline royal couple served to justify the crown's withdrawal from continental affairs through lack of finance.[51] *The Shepherds' Paradise* gestures to England's non-interventionist stance, modifying the official Caroline iconography of conjugal union in a manner which accords Henrietta Maria/Bellessa a role in international affairs. In the pastoral, Genorio, sent out of the Shepherds' Paradise by Moromante to discover the whereabouts of Saphira, princess of Navarre, returns with a story of her marriage and death:

> [Sir,] she dyed marryed to the king of Albion, whome her beauty (wch was only vndisguiz'd in her retreat into his Countrey, wch she chose for solitude) tooke, & rays'd her to the Publicke Eminence of Queene, wthout the helpe of any other quality; All wch vntill her death, they kept conceal'd. (3.7.2,133–8)

Genorio's tale is discovered to be a fantasy, conceived to permit him to return quickly to the Shepherds' Paradise and pursue his devotion to Bellessa (who is eventually revealed to be a very-much-alive Saphira in disguise).

The difference between the devotion Saphira's beauty inspires in the Shepherds' Paradise and that which she is conceived to have inspired in Genorio's fantasy, is one of action. Albion (whose association with Caroline England had recently been underlined by Charles's *Albion's Triumph*) is understood to have been chosen by Saphira for solitude, implicitly because of its lack of connection with the worlds of Castile and

Navarre. She is imagined to have lived there in relative obscurity, effectively dead to the world beyond its borders, until the news of her physical demise found its way to Genorio's ears. Albion erases Saphira's natal identity (just as *Albion's Triumph* incorporated the figure of Alba into its nationalistic economy). It is an internationally apolitical realm, abstracted from the conflicts of its neighbours, encouraging a peaceful philosophy of beauty which ultimately, and disturbingly, leads to its princess's complete disappearance in death. In contrast to the 'real' Saphira/Bellessa's active leadership and participation on the world stage, this Saphira's life has been sterile and her potential unrealised.

The Shepherds' Paradise, therefore, obliquely criticises both the idealised neo-Platonism propounded in masques like *Albion's Triumph* and the non-interventionist politics of the Caroline regime. While the solutions to discord it puts forward are based upon marriage and dynastic alliance, rather than the military intervention pushed for by Henrietta Maria and her adherents, it nevertheless proposes that women might have a role to play in the international arena. If it does nothing else, through its figuration of Bellessa as a queen, it dramatises female authority while, simultaneously, invoking an ideal of feminine behaviour similar to the chaste, but public, spirituality proposed by St François de Sales.

RELIGION AND FEMININITY

While the queen consort's politics in 1633 were, if not entirely anti-French, then certainly anti-Richelieu, her pastoral, like *Artenice* before it, still drew on French cultural and religious forms in order to maintain her specific iconography. *The Shepherds' Paradise* presented a vision of female responsibility compatible with the spiritualised neo-Platonism popular in devout circles in Paris, and drew upon religious imagery to underline Henrietta Maria's status as a Catholic princess of France. Veevers has commented that the rules which govern the community of the Shepherds' Paradise 'are those of a tightly organized group, not unlike those of a religious order', and that the activities of the society, 'with its vows, ceremonies, priests, altar, temple, and prayers', are carried out 'with a religious solemnity'.[52] Responding to such theories, Poynting has countered that 'the representation of a religious order as consisting of both men and women whose central concern is love owes as much to a hostile Protestant stereotype as to a Catholic model'. She observes that for Veevers to read *The Shepherds' Paradise* as consistent with Montagu's later spiritual essays constitutes a failure 'to recognise how much [he] changed in the intervening decade', and proposes that the pastoral's world is largely secular.[53]

While her arguments are persuasive, they are focused entirely upon the figure of Montagu as playwright, and do not take into consideration the pastoral's status as a production paid for and enacted by the queen consort. My own opinion is that the sanctuary of the Shepherds' Paradise does bear deliberate comparison with the institution of the convent, and that it also has connections with the neo-Platonic academies popular in Renaissance Italy and France. The pastoral's religious vision is certainly not consistent, but neither is its political allegory nor its philosophical position. Rather, it represents faith in an allusive way, compatible with that presented in *Artenice*, demonstrating that it is conducive to an harmonious social existence, but is not necessarily something that must dominate it. In addition, and again like *Artenice*, the pastoral's allusions to religious institutions provide a convenient framework through which to limit the subversive nature of female rule, circumscribing the bucolic community with gender-prescriptive laws that are seen as natural because they are apparently ordained by heaven.

The location of the Shepherds' Paradise was chosen, we are told, because it was 'secur'd by natures impregnablenes, as if it was meant for Chastity only to make a plantation here' (2.1.847–9). Chastity is naturalised by nature's provision of a space for its protection, creating the impression that the society is organised as a reflection of preordained, fixed, natural laws. The Shepherds' Paradise is as chaste as the human bodies it encloses for, 'at one passage only the Rockes seeme to open themselves, wch is mainteyn'd by a Garrison of the kings' (2.1.849–51). The chastity of the location is guarded by soldiers, just as the chastity of a nun is guarded by the Church, or the chastity of a wife by her husband. Nonetheless, the natural impregnability of the rocks defuses the implication of the soldiers' presence by constructing chastity as something provided for by nature, mystifying its benefits to society through the insistence that it is incontrovertibly 'natural'.

Similarly, the laws which govern the Shepherds' Paradise, strongly reminiscent of the rules set out for convents, operate within a conservative, heterosexual framework, even when they appear to be praising women's rational autonomy. Although the sanctuary of the Shepherds' Paradise is maintained for both men and women, it is governed by a queen annually elected by the female members of the group alone. The election is represented in the text through the eyes of Agenor and Basilino, disguised as Genorio and Moromante, who ask Votorio, the sanctuary's priest, to explain why the queen is chosen by an exclusively female electorate. Votorio replies that men are excluded because to include them would be to make them judges in their own causes:

> Since there is noe man but hath a particuler interest that doth prepossesse his choyce; whereas all women are rather Inquisitors, then Admirators one of another, & being voyd of passion noe freindshipp, can incline them to yeild priority in beauty: & so 'twas thought most probable, & where most of them agreed to yeild, the advantage must be vnquestionable. (2.1.874–9)

Votorio asserts that men were believed by the sanctuary's foundress to have a vested interest in the subject of female beauty. Masculine judgement is represented as polluted by desire, and thus as subjective and flawed. However, the standard against which female beauty is measured remains uncontested in the pastoral, and is undoubtedly conceived along heterosexual and patrilineal lines. The sanctuary's laws state that the queen must be aged less than thirty and that her beauty must be most considered in her election. Within the economy of neo-Platonism, physical beauty is the manifestation of inner virtue; through this extremely convenient conflation, the Shepherds' Paradise's queen is effectively chosen for her suitability as a chaste wife and mother. In addition, the reasons given for an exclusively female electorate represent women as intrinsically competitive, dividing them one from another in their vanity and their implicit competition for men. Although providing a very qualified image of masculine judgement and thus enabling women to assert themselves as the arbiters of aesthetic choice, the pastoral does not, in effect, escape from its grounding in a discourse of heterosexuality that equates femininity with chaste beauty and which maintains division between women.

However, the election of a woman by women does conjure up the notion of the Catholic convent, foregrounding a femino-centric organisation within which women govern themselves (albeit by monastic rules). Certain of the Paradise's laws deliberately evoke monastic vows, even down to the vocabulary they deploy. For example, the rules of the Visitandine nuns patronised by Henrietta Maria in the 1650s stated that a mother superior would be elected by the other sisters for a fixed term of three years, following 'la pluralité des voix'.[54] In *The Shepherds' Paradise*, the queen is elected for the fixed term of a year 'by the plurality of the sisters voyces' (2.1.731–3). Similarly, in a Visitandine convent, all goods are to be common, just as 'there is noe propriety of any thing among the Society' (2.1.750). Nevertheless, the Shepherds' Paradise's mixed-sex ethos and philosophy of love are not consistent with Catholic ideals and, as Poynting has observed, resemble hostile Protestant stereotypes as much as they do a Catholic model.[55] This does not necessarily mean, though, that *The Shepherds' Paradise* is an entirely secular pastoral whose Catholic allusions are used in a way that 'undermines [their] religious connotations'.[56] The allusions to faith provide a spiritual framework within which women's social conversation with men can be enacted. This certainly makes the Shepherds' Paradise more like a Parisian *salon* than a Catholic convent, but it does not negate the importance of faith as a way of conserving chastity within the secular sphere.

In its geography, its isolation and its binding rules, the Shepherds' Paradise also bears a passing resemblance to the community established by the King of Navarre in *Love's Labour's Lost*. This youthful idyll (itself reminiscent of the Fontainebleau academy patronised by the French king, François I) is subjected to gentle mockery in Shakespeare's play when the noblemen's vows of chastity are broken by the problematic arrival of the princess of France. What ensues is a series of linguistically playful courtships and the exposure of the pose of the languishing Petrarchan lover. *The Shepherds' Paradise*, too, punctures the pretensions of extreme neo-Platonism, and presents its rural retreat as a place of interaction between the sexes. The Paradise is a place where people talk and learn about love, much in the manner of the academies and *salons* of Florence and Paris. Indeed, this connection is underlined by the costume of Votorio, the Paradise's priest, which was copied by Inigo Jones from the figure of Plato in Raphael's *School of Athens*.[57] Poynting has described Votorio as acting 'more as a combination of vice-chamberlain and tour guide than as a priest'.[58] However, the image he presented in the pastoral's *production* was one that alluded to Platonism, to an academy and, because the fresco was painted for the Vatican, to the fact that they were sanctioned inside Catholicism.

The text of *The Shepherds' Paradise* might, on occasion, satirise Catholic ritual by deploying it in the service of love, yet this does not mean that the play necessarily had a secular impulse. While the figure of a convent-like retreat imbued with *salon* qualities was certainly satirised in Protestant texts, it also found expression in one particular French work whose influence was profoundly felt upon the Caroline court stage. Rabelais's *Gargantua* figures the mixed-sex retreat of the abbaye de Thélème, a community of *religieux* and *religieuses* whose lives are governed by the injunction 'FAIS CE QUE VOUDRAS' [do what you will]. This injunction is in place because:

les gens libres, bien nés, bien instruits, conversant en honnêtes compagnies, ont, par nature, un instinct et un stimulant qui les pousse toujours à accomplir de vertueuses actions et à s'éloigner du vice.[59]

[free people, well born, well educated, conversing in honest companies, have, by nature, an instinct and incentive which always pushes them to virtuous action and makes them distance themselves from vice.]

Thélème's noble and devout young people spend all their days in luxury, hawking, courting and knocking back wine in a manner that makes an obvious mockery both of the convent ideal and of the Catholic doctrine of free will. Their activities are, of course, represented as profoundly virtuous because they abide by a *salon*-inspired code of honour. Rabelais's text, therefore, satirises the institutions of both the convent and the *salon* at the same time as it appears to approve of the abbaye's ethos. Most significantly, and in a way that is important for an understanding of *The Shepherds' Paradise*, it was a popular hit in France: French society knew how to laugh at itself.

One of Thélème's very interesting conventions is its stance on marriage. The community's statutes decree that, if a young gallant decides to leave the abbaye, he can take with him one of the ladies, to whom he must then get married.[60] This injunction prefigures the Paradise's law that:

every yeare at the Election of the Queene, what brother or sister shall desire to retire out of the Order, vpon designe of marriage, shall then (vpon their demaund) be lycenc'd. (2.1.739–41)

Echoes of Rabelais's text fill *The Shepherds' Paradise*, demonstrating that the pastoral did not just have to draw upon a serious French Catholic model like d'Urfé's *L'Astrée*, but that an alternative, and humorous, precedent was also available that might well have been more acceptable to the Protestant English court.

Sarah Poynting has identified several moments of somewhat coarse humour within Montagu's play, remarking that these 'may have been slipped in by Montagu to amuse himself or his friends'.[61] When she later remarks that a sexual pun uttered by the cross-dressed actress playing Moromante 'was presumably productive of amusement or pleasure (of a different kind) for some spectators', we realise that the 'friends' she intends are implicitly male.[62] The play's humour is attributed to masculine genius, conceived for the amusement of a male audience. Henrietta Maria's participation in this playfulness is, if not denied, then certainly not explicitly included. However, as I will discuss in the next chapter, *The Temple of Love*, her masque of 1635, also contains sly allusions both to the queen consort's household and to its sexual misconduct. (Interestingly, the masque also includes a character named Thelema, or Free Will.) Henrietta Maria cannot be considered to have been either entirely innocent or devoid of humour, and had already taken part in at least one production that invoked Rabelaisian burlesque.[63] I find it impossible to accept that she could have sponsored two major theatrical productions by two separate authors in relatively quick succession without being aware of their irreverent stance towards neo-Platonism. The common denominator between these productions is not masculine scepticism, but the queen herself, giving rise to an image of Henrietta Maria as a critic of her own fashion and not as a woman who unthinkingly replicated French court and *salon* culture.

The production of *The Shepherds' Paradise* was a collaborative effort that involved both the king's administrators and the queen consort's household. Written by Montagu, it intervened in international politics as well as commenting obliquely upon the problematic relationship between a poet and his patron. The sort of neo-Platonism it presented was not the supremely metaphysical ideal of the Florentine academies, but a tempered philosophy informed by theologians such as St François de Sales. It evoked the Catholic convent in a playful and humorous manner that called to mind the mixed-sex groupings of the *salons*, and did not shirk from gently mocking its own pretensions. It is at once sadly ironic and inevitable that, historically, it has suffered the same fate as the poem of 'impossibility' penned by the hyperbolic Martiro. Condemned by its critics as impossible to understand, it has, until recently, been almost universally ignored. Nevertheless, for a history of female acting, it was a particularly significant theatrical moment, and one in which, for the first time, a queen was heard speaking and singing in English on the court stage.

CHAPTER 7

'Fate hath made thy reign her choice': The Temple of Love *(1635)*

Despite the gains made for women's acting in *The Shepherds' Paradise*, it is notable that Henrietta Maria did not perform in another major court production until she took to the stage as the beautiful and silent Queen Indamora in the 1635 court masque, *The Temple of Love*. Indeed, she never again performed as an actress, a fact that Kenneth Richards has linked to William Prynne's strictures against female publicity and performance.[1] Martin Butler has astutely pointed out that Prynne 'was condemned less for having attacked the stage than for his scandalously extravagant and inflammatory language against virtually the entire social order', noting that 'his judges specifically disavowed that it was "the meaning of any of their [lordships], to apollogize for stage playes"'.[2] Nevertheless, in France particularly, the overwhelming understanding of the affair was that Prynne had attacked female acting, with the *Gazette de France* reporting that he was condemned for having printed a book 'dans lequel il soustenoit putains toutes les femmes qui assistoient au bal, balet & comédie' [in which he said that all women who went to dances, masques and plays were whores].[3]

Although the queen consort's French maids continued the tradition begun by their mistress and performed in a pastoral play, the years around the publication of *Histriomastix* show a distinct attempt by the Caroline administrative machine to clean up the image of court theatre. This chapter, therefore, will briefly investigate the royal patronage of professional drama in the important seasons of 1633–4 and 1634–5, before considering the queen's production of *The Temple of Love*, performed in February 1635 after the arrival in England of Gregorio Panzani, the papal envoy. Through a consideration of the dramatic productions sponsored at this time, I will show how the royal couple promoted a united front in support of the theatre and how they were complicit in a project of social and moral reform.

*

Richard Dutton has described the period between November 1632 and January 1634 as a 'particularly fraught' one for Henry Herbert, master of the revels, suggesting that the limits of his authority were tested both by the acting companies and by the intervention of William Laud who, as bishop of London, 'oversaw the whole process of licensing for print'.[4] He argues convincingly that Jonson's play *The Magnetic Lady*, William Prynne's polemical *Histriomastix* and a revival of John Fletcher's *The Woman's Prize* were censured during this time because of their potentially subversive religious content, and notes that Herbert's 'policing of "oaths" and "prophaness" . . . primarily [spoke] to the heightened religious tensions around the court'.[5] David Como, who has more widely investigated Caroline religious censorship, similarly suggests that the early 1630s saw Laud deliberately attempting to 'shut down Calvinist discourse in the capital', noting, especially, that he took a hard line on the issue of predestination.[6]

As I will show, the notions of free will and predestination are of particular importance to a discussion of *The Temple of Love*. More immediately, though, I am concerned to investigate what seems to be an undeniable example of the queen's patronage of a professional company – the Twelfth Night (1634) performance at Somerset House of Fletcher's *The Faithful Shepherdess* by the King's Company – as well as her promotion at court of Thomas Heywood's *Love's Mistress*, performed the following November by her own actors. The first of these events has been interpreted by Meg Powers Livingston as part of Henrietta Maria's attempt to 'create a cult of platonic love that would foster an idealized view of women'.[7] However, by looking at other plays put on at court around that time and by investigating the wider social and religious context of its performance, I hope to complicate this view of the production.

On 16 November 1633, the court watched Shakespeare's *Richard III*, performed by the King's Company in celebration of Henrietta Maria's twenty-fourth birthday. Three nights later, the Queen's Company performed Shirley's *The Young Admiral* for the king (who was thirty-three). Both productions took place in the intimate setting of St James's and, perhaps significantly, they were the first of only two occasions when the couple's birthday celebrations were mentioned across the Channel in the *Gazette de France*.[8] As with the mutual shrovetide masques that took place in 1631 and 1632, Henrietta Maria and Charles seem to have provided reciprocal entertainments on these anniversaries. However, this time, rather than employing members of their own households, they employed their respective acting companies.

The King's Company's *Richard III* seems an anachronistic choice for a birthday celebration and it becomes even more odd when one considers Henrietta Maria's taste for pastorals and tragi-comedies in which refined manners and language were combined with plots about constant love. In 1633, Joseph Taylor, the leading actor with the King's Company, had been employed to coach the queen and her ladies in *The Shepherds' Paradise*, a production conceived in part, according to John Pory, to help the queen practise her English.[9] It is tempting to see a similar kind of didacticism at work in the production of *Richard III*: on Henrietta Maria's birthday, she was encouraged to increase her knowledge of her adopted country by watching a popular play about English history.[10]

More importantly, though, I think this performance had a political agenda, much as Prince Charles's 1625 promotion of *1Henry IV* was probably intended to imply that he, like Hal, prince of Wales, would soon emerge as England's martial saviour.[11] As I have discussed, the early months of 1633 had seen the uncovering of the infamous Châteauneuf plot which implicated Henrietta Maria in international intrigue and which was reputed to have aspired so far as to set Gaston d'Orléans on his brother's throne. *Richard III* famously dramatises the results of a usurping brother's tyranny and might well have served as a warning to the English queen not to become embroiled in her family's problems.

In October 1633, Henrietta Maria had given birth to a new prince, an occasion seized upon by her exiled brother and mother who both sent envoys to London, ostensibly to congratulate her. That autumn, Vincent de Voiture, renowned poet and member of Gaston d'Orléans's household, also turned up in London on his way back to Brussels from Spain. He appears to have spent some time courting the favours of Lucy Hay, countess of Carlisle, whose husband, unlike the queen consort, was beginning to lean more towards a pro-French policy of help for the Palatinate.[12] Voiture was introduced into Lucy's circle by a certain 'Monsieur Gourdon', probably a relation of the elderly George Gordon, first marquis of Huntly, who, five years previously, had been involved in secret negotiations with Richelieu intended, in part, to foster a military alliance between France and Scottish Catholic peers.[13]

Indeed, in the early spring of 1633, the *Gazette de France* reported that the 'Marquis de Gourdon Prince de la maison d'Escosse' was awaiting the arrival in London of a troop of Scottish horse that he intended to conduct into Picardy for Louis XIII.[14] Voiture's association with Gaston d'Orléans and his solicitation of the countess of Carlisle, taken in conjunction with the latter's apparent association with 'Monsieur Gourdon' and her husband's inclinations towards the French, make it unlikely that the poet's presence in London was politically innocent. He returned to the side of his master in December 1633, probably having tried to muster support for him among those whose eyes were turning towards Richelieu.[15]

Whatever his mission in London, his presence alone makes it clear that the Châteauneuf conspiracy was still having repercussions that could damage the English queen. I suggest, therefore, that the November 1633 performance of *Richard III* spoke directly to Henrietta Maria about her factious family: not only does the play foreground the political instability caused by Machiavellian intriguing, it also demonstrates that the position of women in such circumstances is particularly invidious. Queen Margaret especially (like Henrietta Maria, a Frenchwoman who was also an English queen) bears witness to the dispossession that can result from a woman's active political involvement. The only properly political role a woman can take up, the play seems to conclude, is as a peaceweaver, cementing alliances between opposing parties, and bearing the promise of generation.

Three days after this production, the Queen's Company responded with a performance of Shirley's *The Young Admiral* for the king's birthday.[16] Rebecca Bailey has suggested that the play, written by a man she believes to have been Catholic, 'powerfully displays . . . the real pain inflicted on the recusant community by the Oaths of Allegiance and Supremacy'.[17] Arguing that in Vittori, the play's titular character, King Charles would see played out before him 'the agony of a subject whose innate loyalty is complicated by state intervention', she also suggests that *The Young Admiral* 'urges the Queen Consort of England to fulfil her own proselytising mission'.[18] Indeed, it is possible that Shirley's play was chosen for performance on Charles's birthday because of its oblique dramatisation of politico-religious concerns.

The Young Admiral's plot, which bears some initial flattering resemblance to that of *The Shepherds' Paradise*, centres around two women: the court lady Cassandra (beloved of both Cesario, prince of Naples, and Vittori, a Neapolitan admiral); and Rosinda, princess of Sicily (Cesario's betrothed). However, where *The Shepherds' Paradise* saw the lovers' discords removed from the city and resolved in a pastoral sanctuary, *The Young Admiral* sees them played out in the political realm in a war fought between Naples and the scorned state of Sicily. Indeed, the play, like *The Shepherds' Paradise*, dramatises a society in which even the rulers find it difficult to govern their passions, so it is to the female characters and to Vittori that one looks to find temperance and virtue. However, in *The Young Admiral*, unlike Montagu's play, constant love is not a panacea for the state's problems – indeed, there are indications that it is a potentially destabilising force.

Captured by the Sicilian army, Vittori is offered a choice – to fight against his native land, or to be the cause of his beloved Cassandra's death. In a truly neo-Platonic manner, Cassandra declares to the Sicilian king that she loves Vittori so much 'we are one soule, life cannot be / So precious as our loves'.[19] Vittori, though, knows that his public duty far outweighs his private desires: 'It was / Articled in the creation of my soule / I should obey,' he says, 'and serve my Country with it / Above my selfe' (F1r). In other words, the play initially represents men as intrinsically and selflessly linked to the state, while women define themselves through love. Nevertheless, in a rapid three and a half lines, after nearly 110 lines of moralistic debate, Vittori suddenly changes his mind and resolves to 'bring [his] honour to the grave' to save Cassandra's life (F2r).

Bailey notes of Vittori's faithful soul that it provides an 'image of an inextricable union between religion and state allegiance', and comments of this moment of crisis that it dramatises 'the over-riding fear of Protestant England', that of an English Catholic who finally decides to 'take arms' against the state.[20] She reads the play's love discourse as an allegory of a subject's religious commitment that calls into question his allegiance to his nation. Nevertheless, as she points out, 'Vittori is finally saved from betraying his country through the salvatory figure of Rosinda, daughter of the King of Sicily' who 'dissolves the inextricable tensions surrounding the issues of treason and allegiance'.[21] She concludes that the play 'surely recalls the adumbration within Roman Catholic Europe of Queen Henrietta Maria as a second "Esther", whose vocation was to re-convert England to the "old faith"'.[22]

Her argument reinforces Veevers's contention that Henrietta Maria's neo-Platonic love fashion provided a fitting discourse through which to manifest her Catholicism. The choice of this suggestively allusive play for the king's birthday certainly does not seem arbitrary and speaks to the king's position as much as *Richard III* reflected on that of the queen. Nevertheless, while its text might well have dramatised the conflicts experienced by a Catholic subject torn by his allegiances to his king and faith, *The Young Admiral*'s performance also expressed the royal couple's mutuality, showing them to be united in promoting civil manners and language through their patronage of public cultural forms. Indeed, one might be inclined to suggest that the play had an ecumenical impulse, showing how disparate faiths could be drawn together for the benefit of the health of the nation.

Ira Clark has suggested that the court production came about through the involvement of Henry Herbert, master of the revels, who so appreciated the play, he included a rare approbation of it in his office book, noting:

The comedy called *The Yonge Admirall*, being free from oaths, prophaness, or obsceanes, hath given mee much delight and satisfaction in the readinge, and may serve for a patterne to other poetts, not only for the bettring of maners and language, but for the improvement of the quality, which hath received some brushings of late.[23]

N. W. Bawcutt interprets Herbert's obscure phrase, 'some brushings', as a reference to Prynne's *Histriomastix*.[24] Dutton, however, believes it might refer to the master of the revels's own previous objections to Shirley's *The Ball* (acted in costumes that mocked 'real' courtiers) and to the 'intervention of the High Commission over *The Magnetic Lady*'.[25] Invoking the common view that Herbert was a pious and fastidious man, Dutton notes, nevertheless, that the early 1630s saw him evincing an '*intensified* concern' about 'oaths' and 'prophaness' in plays, and links this to a religious sensitivity about Calvinism among the new Arminian Church hierarchy.[26] In other words, Herbert, like Laud, sought to reduce the scope for the public discussion of Calvinism, at the same time as he limited the 'relatively casual anti-Catholicism' of older, Jacobean plays.[27]

The Young Admiral was probably put on at court on the important occasion of the king's birthday, because either Dorset, the queen's lord chamberlain, or Pembroke, the king's, had been made aware of its exemplary nature.[28] Performed at St James's by the Queen's Company, it was both a birthday present to Charles from his wife and a declaration of her household's complicity in his reformatory projects, demonstrating the cultural and religious values he wished to promote at court and throughout his country. Indeed, given that Charles allegedly took it upon himself to suggest the plot of *The Gamester* to the playwright, it is entirely possible that Shirley's plays were more appreciated by the king than they were by his wife.[29]

The same, I suggest, might well be true of Fletcher's plays, the 1630s' revivals of which should not necessarily be attributed to the influence of Henrietta Maria. Fletcher's work certainly did provide models of virtuous femininity, but his plays were being performed in significant numbers at court prior to the queen consort's arrival in the country. For example, *A King and No King* was acted at Whitehall by King James's Men at Christmas 1611, and a performance of *The Coxcomb* was sponsored by Prince Charles in the winter of 1612/13. Indeed, during that season, Fletcher's plays were put on at court at least seven times, three times under Charles's sponsorship.[30] From 1621 to Henrietta Maria's arrival in London in 1625, records show that fourteen Fletcher plays were acted at court. In the same period, three plays apiece are recorded for Middleton and Shakespeare, two each for Jonson and Massinger, and one for Dekker.[31] Admittedly, this is hardly a comprehensive list as many of the plays performed were not named or noted down. However, the number of Fletcher productions is significant and indicates that the Stuart court, and perhaps Charles himself, was already predisposed towards such drama. It is impossible, therefore, to say that the Caroline court performances of Fletcher's plays served an agenda that was exclusively the queen's. Instead, as I have argued, they seem to be part of a reformatory project, presenting a new moral standard for both dramatic productions and courtly behaviour, advocated, significantly, by both the king and queen's households.[32]

In this context, the production of *The Faithful Shepherdess* on Twelfth Night 1634 takes on a slightly different appearance. Rather than being part of a project to 'create a cult of platonic love that would foster an idealized view of women', it seems to be a moment in a broader courtly campaign to promote a certain type of exemplary drama.[33] The performance took place in the Presence Chamber at Somerset House and was acted by the King's Company in costumes donated to them from *The Shepherds' Paradise*. Both the donation and the decision to call the King's Men to perform a play at the queen's residence were acts of patronage that neglected the company that bore Henrietta Maria's name, so it might be argued that she had established a relationship with Joseph Taylor and his company during the rehearsals for Montagu's pastoral and that this event was a continuation of that connection. However, I would like to suggest that the performance of *The Faithful Shepherdess* was conceived with the king's particular tastes in mind, and was presented to him as a quasi-public declaration of the queen's household's complicity in his project of moral reform.

The Faithful Shepherdess had not been a success on the Jacobean stage. In his preface to the printed text (published in 1610), Fletcher explained that the audience 'having ever had a singuler gift in defining, concluded [it] to be a play of country hired Shepheards . . . And missing whitsun ales, creame, wassel and morris-dances, began to be angry.'[34] This uncontrolled Jacobean anger makes the play especially fitting for production at the reformed Caroline court, contrasting an earlier uneducated misrecognition with a new Caroline sensibility. The play promotes the spiritual over the physical, self-denial over personal pleasure and defines heroism as an interior virtue that is achieved through the renunciation of lust and appetite. However, *The Faithful Shepherdess* does present a complimentary view of women, compatible with that promoted in *The Shepherds' Paradise*, and it is for this reason, I think, that it was selected for this particular performance. Cécile Istria has suggested that it was a play conceived by Fletcher as a Protestant response to the reformation of drama on the continent, and it certainly does bear comparison to plays such as Racan's *Les Bergeries*.[35] As such, it was a very appropriate vehicle for Henrietta Maria's type of neo-Platonism, at the same time as it unproblematically flattered the tastes of the king.

It opens, unusually for a play conceived for the public stage, with a woman's speech. 'Haile holy earth', the shepherdess Clorin laments over the grave of her dead love,

> thus do I pay
> My early vowes and tribute of mine eies,
> To thy still loved ashes: thus I free
> My selfe from all ensuing heates and fires
> Of love, all sports, delights and games,
> That Shepheards hold full deare. (1.1.4–9)

Clorin is the play's virtuous heart and promotes the value of chaste women within a community. Dedicated to tending the grave of her lost love, she rejects the advances of further suitors and serves as a regenerative force, healing the physical and spiritual wounds of the less virtuous characters. Indeed, like the figure of Divine Beauty in *Tempe Restored*, her virtue extends even to the transformation of wild beasts – her most faithful servant in the play is a satyr, traditionally a figure of lust and disorder, but here seconded to her by his master Pan and ultimately dedicated devoutly to her service.

In keeping with its origins on the Jacobean stage, *The Faithful Shepherdess*'s governing deity is Pan – much as Pan was the chief figure of authority in *Pan's Anniversary* (a masque danced before King James in 1621 which Martin Butler has shown played on the idea of the king as a benevolent yet potent ruler).[36] However, the 1634 performance was prefaced by a dialogue written by William Davenant which shifted Pan's authority to Henrietta Maria with words placed in the mouth of a priest. Appearing on stage in the company of a nymph, the priest declared:

> A Broyling Lambe on *Pans* chiefe Altar lies
> My Wreath, my Censor, Virge, and Incense by:
> But I delay'd the pretious Sacrifice,
> To shew thee here, a gentler Deity
> . . .
> Blesse then that Queene, that doth his [the King's] eyes envite
> And eares, t'obey her Scepter, halfe this night.[37]

In this new Caroline context, Henrietta Maria takes over from Pan as the play's presiding deity – her gentle rule supersedes his reign, and she is hailed as 'Welcome as Peace' (line 13). In their reference to the sacrificial altar, abandoned by the priest in favour of this new deity, Davenant's verses also shadow the reformation of the Old Testament God of Abraham and Isaac by the New Testament's merciful Christ. In like manner, *The Faithful Shepherdess* itself is transformed from its paternalistic Jacobean origins into a Caroline production which refines and redefines heroism, not as martial valour, but as self-abnegating devotion, and which validates spiritually strong women as the caretakers of a community's moral health.

The Faithful Shepherdess, then, when performed by the King's Company in 1634, was transformed into a spectacle that suited the queen's neo-Platonic agenda, providing an image of a strong heroine whose presence purified a community of lust and disruption, and whose actions were always at the service of others not herself. It would have been possible to sponsor a production of one of Shirley's plays that night, but instead Henrietta Maria and her advisers chose to rehabilitate an old play in a manner that drew a direct comparison between the apparent lack of discernment of a former age and a new Caroline sensibility that located women as the gatekeepers of an honourable society. Furthermore, the use of the King's Company rather than her own demonstrated again the royal couple's close and mutual relationship and the integration of their dramatic interests, particularly in the wake of the prosecution of William Prynne.

*

On several occasions from May 1634 onwards, after the completion of Prynne's trial and punishment, Henrietta Maria attended the public playhouses, reinforcing the Star Chamber judgement that playgoing was a lawful activity.[38] She went with Charles to see her own comedians perform Heywood's *Love's Mistress* at the Phoenix, and subsequently sponsored two court performances of the play, again legitimating the public theatre by her overt approval of its product.[39] In addition, she seems personally to have had a profound influence on the ways that court plays were staged, pioneering the use of masque-like effects and scenery for dramatic productions.

As I noted earlier, John Orrell has suggested that Somerset House was 'the chief London centre for the production of the scenic drama until 1640'.[40] Indeed, nowhere is the queen consort's influence more pervasive than in the court productions of *Love's Mistress*, the preface to whose printed text describes how '*M*r. Inego Jones . . . *to every Act, nay almost to every Sceane, by his excellent Inventions, gave such an extraordinary Luster; upon every occasion changing the stage, to the admiration of all the Spectators*'.[41] Significantly subtitled *The Queenes* <u>*Masque*</u> (my emphasis) after its two court performances, the play illustrates how, by 1634, dramatic productions, particularly at the queen's court, were being infiltrated by masque elements to the point of generic confusion.

No easily identifiable stage designs remain for *Love's Mistress*, but I would like tentatively to suggest that Inigo Jones's drawing of the 'Temple of Apollo' constituted its opening scene and was the location in which Phoebus uttered his prophecy about Psiche's fate.[42] Similarly, it seems likely that the drawing of 'Cupid's Palace' belongs to this occasion rather than, as Orgel and Strong suggest, to lost productions of 1619 or 1621.[43] These possible attributions aside, the play was certainly accompanied by plentiful and splendid decorations, helping to install Somerset House as the leading location for elaborate scenic drama in London. Furthermore, the performances of *Love's Mistress* also show how influences from court masque were deployed to heighten the moral and spiritual significances of a play first performed on the public stage.

The play is notable, for example, for its employment of music to create atmospheric and mystical effects: the scene at Apollo's temple is accompanied by the soft music of recorders to signal the supernatural solemnity of the moment; Psiche's welcome into Cupid's Palace sees her ears enchanted with 'ravishing tones' (sig. C1v); and '*Hiddeous Musicke*' concludes her later sojourn in Hell (sig. H4v). The play itself, very much like a court masque, ended with a dance of the gods and goddesses, with Cupid encouraging the audience to 'view . . . how our joy appeares, / Dancing to the sweet musick of the spheares' (sig. I4r). In other words, the production's tone was heightened throughout by the use of musical effects, and it concluded, like a masque, with a gesture to the cosmic harmonies incarnated in music and dance.

At the end of each act, *Love's Mistress* also drew on the masque tradition, presenting an *intermedii*-type dance or display, followed by a quasi-choric commentary that explained the play's allegorical meanings. As such, it was similar to the performance of *Florimène* by the queen's French ladies later in 1635, which was also punctuated by short displays only tangentially related to the main plot. These interludes (which, in *Love's Mistress*, included a burlesque dance of asses, a pastiche of the Helen of Troy story and the 'Pastorall mirth' of country wenches) demonstrate the influence of masque and anti-masque on popular theatre, and also show how Henrietta Maria's French-influenced tastes were permeating English dramatic culture. In 1625, Katherine Gorges was at a loss to understand the 'antique' dances performed by the new queen's servants. By 1634, a popular playwright like Heywood was incorporating such moments into a play for the public stage and receiving royal approbation.

The court productions of *Love's Mistress* were, therefore, highly decorated, decorous and, if not overtly Catholic in nature, then allegorically religious, representing Psiche as 'Anima' or 'the Soule' whose yearning for heavenly immortality was corrupted by Venus or 'untemperate lust' (sig. C3v–4r). Like *Tempe Restored*, the play shows the human soul confronted by a 'Desire' that can be used for either good or ill (sig. C4r) and, furthermore, suggests that true repentance can be achieved only with the help of 'Heavens providence' (H2v). Figuring a strong heroine, Heywood's play was compatible with the kind of drama favoured by Henrietta Maria; it also fulfilled the purposes of the new, moralised tone of Charles's court, presenting a quasi-religious message within a framework of scenic and musical decorum that heightened the play's mystical and inspirational effects.

*

I want to turn now to the production of the queen's masque, *The Temple of Love*, performed on 10, 11 and 12 February 1635, to investigate its role and significance in the 1634–5 court season.[44] The masque was written by William Davenant, the playwright who had penned the theatrical preface to the court production of *The Faithful Shepherdess*. Like Townshend before him, Davenant was paid £50 for writing the masque, a sum collected for him by Henry Jermyn, one of the queen consort's favourites.[45] Davenant was probably introduced into Henrietta Maria's circle in the early 1630s by his friend Endymion Porter, and seems also to have been closely associated with Jermyn. Indeed, as I will discuss, *The Temple of Love* contains sly allusions to courtly misdemeanours that shadowed Jermyn's position in 1635. If it does nothing else, Davenant's selection as masque writer at this time provides strong evidence of Henrietta Maria's burgeoning cultural influence: he would go on to write all the remaining masques of the Caroline reign, including the king's *Britannia Triumphans* (1638); would regularly proffer poetic New Year gifts to the queen; and would eventually join her in her French exile, significantly lodging with Jermyn at the Louvre.[46]

The Temple of Love was written, therefore, by a man who was closely connected with the queen's circle. It also, notably, participates in Charles's project of social reform. Despite its strong thematic interest in the ideal of chaste love, Kevin Sharpe has proposed that the masque demonstrates an ambivalence about Henrietta Maria's neo-Platonism through the images of sterility that it uses to evoke the chastity of Queen Indamora's followers.[47] Similarly, Kathleen McLuskie has commented that the production's anti-masque magicians provide 'an all too coherent attack on the affectation of platonic lovers who "practise generation not / Of Bodies but of Soules"'.[48] However, read in the context of Charles's domestic reforms, *The Temple of Love* is a festive occasion which, through the use of mild satire, softens the severity of the monarch's policies and showcases a standard of moderate behaviour more acceptable in its courtly audience.

Describing the chaste innovations brought to the world by Indamora, one of *The Temple of Love*'s anti-masque magicians explains:

> Certain young lords at first disliked the philosophy,
> As most uncomfortable, sad, and new,
> But soon inclined to a superior vote,
> And are grown as good Platonical lovers
> As are to be found in an hermitage. (lines 223–7)

This reference to the disaffected young lords folds out from the masque into the historical reality of Charles's court. For example, in 1627, Jacques Gaultier, one of the queen's French musicians, was arrested and tried for allegedly assaulting the daughter of the earl of Carlisle. In 1632, assisted by the earl of Holland, Doncaster, Carlisle's son, married Margaret Russell, daughter of the earl of Bedford, without his father's knowledge or consent. In 1633, Holland was placed under house arrest for challenging Jerome Weston to a duel, and, at the end of the same year,

Eleanor Villiers, one of Henrietta Maria's ladies-in-waiting, gave birth to the illegitimate child of Henry Jermyn.[49] Jermyn's case, in particular, is apposite in the context of *The Temple of Love* for it is closely associated with ideas of chastity and marriage. Moreover, Davenant notably dedicated his satirical play, *The Platonic Lovers*, to the courtier, thus associating him again with a tongue-in-cheek production compatible with the masque's mockery of neo-Platonic love.

Having been committed to the Tower and threatened with banishment from court, Jermyn steadfastly refused to wed Eleanor, and eventually reappeared, unmarried, his credit with the queen apparently intact. *The Temple of Love*'s representation of the young lords' youthful misdemeanours occurs, therefore, at the expense of Jermyn and others like him. However, it also implies their complicity in the joke and therefore their presence at the masque: indeed, both Doncaster, Carlisle's son, and Thomas, the brother of Jerome Weston, danced as noble Persian youths in the production. By satirising the excesses of neo-Platonism, *The Temple of Love* softened the seriousness of the young lords' previous misdemeanours. In addition, establishing a thematic parallel between its fiction and historical reality, the masque constructed a boundary and invoked a spirit of community in its audience.

Jermyn's banishment to the Tower and the threat of his perpetual exclusion from the court served precisely to define its parameters. For a time, he existed in a liminal state beyond a court circumscribed by its standards of chastity and marriage. In making him the butt of a joke, *The Temple of Love* not only recuperated him, giving him back his privileged position *inside* the court's boundaries, but also generated a sense of community among the members of the audience who understood the allusion. The masque's assertion that the young lords have fallen in line with neo-Platonic chastity therefore not only demonstrates the unified nature of Indamora's train, but, through a humorous moment of festive satire which extends the masque fiction out to the audience, demonstrates the boundaries of, and the unity within, Charles's establishment.

If the young lords' misdemeanours are partly an allusion to the disgraces of Jermyn and Doncaster, it is also significant that they are invoked in a queen's masque. Jermyn was one of Henrietta Maria's favourites, while Doncaster's marriage was facilitated by Holland, her close associate. If one adds to this the rape trial of Jacques Gaultier, one of her musicians, then the masque serves as an apology for incontinent behaviour within Henrietta Maria's own household and as a promise that it won't be repeated. In effect, it connects that household with the standards of moral chastity promoted and policed at court by the king. Rather than registering ambivalence about Henrietta Maria's neo-Platonic affectations, the masque, like *The Shepherds' Paradise* before it, presented a tempered version of the fashion that advocated virtuous chastity rather than hyperbolic extremes.

Martin Butler has suggested that the masque's multiple performances 'reflect the importance it held for the queen who was emerging from a period of eclipse after the collapse of her intrigues against Weston in 1633'.[50] Weston had died in January 1635, just after the arrival in London of Gregorio Panzani, an Oratorian priest and the first accredited representative from the pope. The masque was performed, therefore, at a time when Henrietta Maria's promotion of her religion was becoming more pronounced and before her gradual swing back towards a pro-French political policy. Indeed, both Veevers and Bailey have read *The Temple of Love* as an entertainment strongly linked to the queen's Catholicism.

For Veevers, the 'Indian' side of the masque, ruled over by Indamora, represents England, and the 'Persian' side, those who have arrived on the English shore. The anti-masque's usurping magicians are, for her, 'perhaps a reference to Jesuit priests who were suspected of harming Panzani's mission', while 'the arrival of "Orpheus" would have been appropriate as a reference to Panzani, who was a priest of the Oratory, an order noted for its music'.[51] While allowing that Catholics and non-Catholics would have different opinions of the masque's significations, Veevers nonetheless imagines that the production's message was the same for both parties. In 'Catholic eyes' Charles's approval of the masque, and, more importantly, of the nearly completed Somerset House chapel, was a 'crowning triumph', while 'non-Catholics' might have cause to fear that the conversions to chaste love staged in the masque would be mirrored in the world by conversions to the queen's religion.[52] Bailey concurs and suggests that the 'gay Altar' erected by malign magicians in the antimasque 'could refer to Laudian reforms which were perceived as impinging on Roman Catholic territory', adding that the true Temple is deemed always to have existed on the masque's island: like English Catholicism, it has just been hidden.[53]

The Temple of Love certainly seems to allude strongly to the possibility of the restoration of the Catholic Church in England. In 1625, French representations of Henrietta Maria's nuptial voyage across the Channel suggested that her marriage had been ordained by God to return England to the true faith.[54] A similar divine grammar may be perceived behind *The Temple of Love* which significantly identifies Henrietta Maria/Indamora as 'the delight of destiny', and which declares to Charles, seated under the State, that 'Fate hath made thy reign her choice'.[55] The Argument of the masque also declares that it is Fate who has engaged Divine Poesy in the cause of the Temple of Chaste Love (line 2), and it is Fate's divinely sanctioned intervention that is shown to be the cause of 'Love's blessings', usually translated by masque critics as the princely offspring of the royal union (line 123). In other words, the masque dramatises the purification of the world through the influence of chaste love, manifested in the pattern of the royal marriage. However, it also links Love's blessings irrevocably to the restoration of the true Temple, thus implicitly connecting the royal couple's perfect unity to the unity of one Church and one divine law.

In this, it echoes the sentiments of an anonymous French commentary upon the construction of Henrietta Maria's chapel at Somerset House which expressed the hope that it would draw Charles and his people back to the Catholic faith, joining England to France in a league that would subject the whole world to one religion.[56] Similar sentiments were also expressed by Cardinal Barberini, Panzani's immediate superior in his mission to England. For example, in October 1635, Barberini commented that 'It is well known that his holiness has an uncommon affection for that prince [Charles I]; and his conversion is the only thing he aims at', while, two months later, he observed to Panzani: 'St Urban desired nothing more of St Cecily than the conversion of Valerian her husband. This is all the present pope expects from her Britannic majesty.'[57]

Interestingly, in the light of this, the queen's choice of colour for her masquing costume gains in significance. When she and her ladies descended to the stage in *The Temple of Love*, they did so in habits of Isabella colour. This is the yellow of soiled calico and derives its name from strange tales attached to both Isabel of Austria and Isabel of Castile. Isabel of Austria, daughter of Philip II, vowed not to change her linen at the siege of Ostend until the place was taken, while Isabel of Castile made a similar vow to the Virgin not to change her linen until Granada fell into her hands.[58] Both Isabels, therefore, demonstrated a somewhat bizarre level of constancy and faith in their own causes. Henrietta Maria's choice of colour may have been meant to reflect her religious constancy; indeed, her appearance on the masquing stage, in a scallop-shell chariot which Veevers has related to emblematic settings for the Virgin, connects neatly both to her Catholicism and to the idea of the restoration of the true Church in England.[59]

Nevertheless, while *The Temple of Love* certainly does have a strong Catholic subtext and, in its multiple performances, seems to have had a particular significance for the queen consort, it was still performed with Charles's sanction and, like *Tempe Restored*, manages to demonstrate the compatibility of the royal couple's imagery. Although Bailey makes a connection between Laudian reform and the 'gay Altar' erected by the masque's magicians, I think *The Temple of Love* sets out to demonstrate that the distance between the king and queen's faiths is not that great. Sharpe and Bailey have both suggested that Davenant's writings for the queen in the mid to late 1630s encouraged her to pursue a moderate path in the face of her own increasing religious militancy and her husband's political intransigence; *The Temple of Love* seems to advocate a similar path, acting as a showcase for the queen's religion, but also, I would argue, demonstrating its similarities with Charles's social and religious reforms.[60]

In 1634, for example, the king's masque, *Coelum Britannicum*, had dramatised the renovation of the ancient heavens after the model of the Caroline union, and was part of a wider and well-documented programme of reform at the Caroline court which sought to eliminate impiety and all forms of excess. Indeed, Elias Ashmole, the Caroline historian of the Order of the Garter, observed that 'King Charles I designed and endeavoured the most complete and absolute reformation of any of his predecessors.'[61] Roy Strong notes that the Caroline Garter Festival on St George's Day became less a public spectacle and more a pattern 'of the High Church Ceremonial so loathed by the Puritans', observing that Charles changed the Garter badge to enhance its religious imagery by adding 'a huge aureola of silver rays . . . in emulation of the French order of the holy spirit'.[62] This adaptation demonstrates the manner in which French religious imagery could be recycled in a Protestant context, and has a pertinent connection with *The Temple of Love* for it shows that spiritualised imagery in a queen's masque does not necessarily have to have Catholic connotations, complicating Veevers's suggestion that the masque's meanings were the same for both Catholics and non-Catholics.

In a manner compatible with Strong's reading of the Garter Festival, John Adamson has described how *Coelum Britannicum* operated as an allegory of the king's repudiation of old-fashioned knighthood, replacing this with 'a new, purified, order of . . . men distinguished by moral virtues'.[63] Indeed, in a song by its chorus to the queen, *Coelum Britannicum* privileged Love and Beauty as the goals of a virtuous journey, explaining how, 'thus the darlings of the gods / From Honour's temple, to the shrine / Of Beauty and these sweet abodes / Of Love we guide'.[64] This image is entirely compatible with the appearance of the Temple of Chaste Love in the queen's masque and demonstrates how love and virtue were accorded precedence within the Caroline couple's iconography. Rather than being an unqualified commentary upon the queen's religion, *The Temple of Love* replicates both the iconography of *Coelum Britannicum* and that subtending the Order of the Garter, participating in the impulse of moral reform prevalent at the Caroline court.

Most significantly, for a consideration of ecumenicalism and religious tensions in 1635, Davenant's masque ends with the appearance of the allegorical figures of Sunesis, 'Understanding', and Thelema, 'Free Will', who combine to generate Amianteros, or 'Chaste Love'. Noting that 'masculine understanding is stronger than feminine affectivity', Alison Shell points out that the masque nevertheless sees the masculine Sunesis yielding to the feminine Thelema.[65] She reads this as a 'possible model of how Charles might succumb to the wishes of his wife', concluding that 'Henrietta Maria's ecumenical programme co-existed with a sturdy maintenance of the Catholic faith, and would not have eschewed this type of light-handed encouragement towards Catholicism'.[66] In other words, the queen's masque, like her pastorals, shows women guiding men towards chastity, spiritual understanding and, ultimately, Catholicism. Indeed, Davenant's masque might be seen as a very particular declaration of the queen consort's religious position, not least because, as Veevers has noted, the allegorical figures of Sunesis and Thelema were deployed by St François de Sales throughout his *Traité de l'amour de Dieu* to argue that Amianteros, or Chaste Love, was the result of the union of Free Will and Understanding.[67]

This said, the notion of ecumenicalism is pertinent here and connects to the wider Laudian campaign to limit dissent about religious reform that was being played out in the censorship of plays, sermons and other printed tracts. Orgel and Strong have noted that Inigo Jones's early sketches for Will reveal that the figure was originally intended as 'Gnomê' or 'Divine Will', rather than 'Free Will'.[68] In the light of Caroline Arminianism, this is a particularly resonant change, offering a challenge to the Calvinist repudiation of free will in favour of divine predestination. W. B. Patterson has noted that James I was a moderate Calvinist who believed in 'the loss of free-will by Adam's fall'.[69] Early in his reign, however, Charles I issued three declarations banning debate of contentious religious issues, culminating, in 1629, in a proclamation that specifically prohibited the discussion of predestination.[70] Indeed, as Como has demonstrated, during the 1630s the very subject of predestination was associated in the minds of Arminian reformers like William Laud with 'moral chaos', because it disrupted social hierarchies and introduced 'all manner of profaneness into the world'.[71]

The Temple of Love's anti-masque clearly associates Calvinist Protestantism with chaos and disruption. Invoking a dance of elemental spirits in an attempt, significantly, to 'try / If we have powers to hinder destiny' (lines 258–9), a group of disruptive magicians call upon 'a sect of modern devils . . . that claim / Chambers and tenements in heaven as they / Had purchased there' (lines 273–7). In a neo-Platonic context, the dance of spirits alludes to the elemental chaos described in Plato's *Timaeus* and demonstrates that the magicians' influences on Indamora's island have been so perverting that the land has reverted to primordial disorder. More importantly, the devils' Calvinistic arrogance, which has led them to think they are of the Elect, is shown to be an error and the source of extreme disruption. By figuring this disruption in the anti-masque and by demonstrating that it has not hindered the rediscovery of the true Temple of Love, the masque both satirises Calvinist commentators like William Prynne and promotes an idea of religion compatible both with Henrietta Maria's Catholicism and with Charles and Laud's Arminian reforms. In effect, the masque shows how Laudian Arminianism and the type of Salesian Catholicism practised by Henrietta Maria were not irreconcilably opposed.

Interestingly, *The Temple of Love*, in its emphasis on the role of fate, resounds with the assertion in *Love's Mistress* that true repentance can be achieved only with the help of heaven's providence. It thus bears witness to a doctrinal consistency in the drama sponsored prominently at the Caroline court that eschewed extreme predestinarianism in favour of what Como terms the 'stock Arminian claim that Christ had died for all'.[72] *The Temple of Love* might, therefore, be seen as trying to bridge the gap between Caroline and Romish beliefs by locating radical Calvinism as the source of chaos, and (like Bailey's reading of *The Young Admiral*) by rendering English Catholics less threatening by showcasing their virtues and doctrinal similarities.

In reality, though, this *rapprochement* was never going to happen, nor were doctrinal differences so easily reconciled: Henrietta Maria and Laud were notorious rivals and each was ultimately determined to protect and promote their own faith.[73] In 1637, for example, and in a manner that bears witness to his commitment to Protestantism, Laud violently suppressed an English translation of Sales's *Introduction à la vie dévote* because it contained 'unorthodox passages'.[74] Similarly, as I have discussed, Henrietta Maria was exhorted throughout her life to avoid heretics and to be firm in the practice of her religion. Dutton is, therefore, entirely correct to describe this period for the master of the revels as a 'particularly fraught' one. Caught between the queen's increasingly militant Catholicism, Laud's crackdown against Calvinism, and Puritan polemicists, his was a very difficult position indeed.

CHAPTER 8

Florimène: the author and the occasion

At the end of the year that saw the multiple performances of *The Temple of Love*, Henrietta Maria sponsored *Florimène*, her third pastoral in England. The play was performed at Whitehall on 21 December 1635, but its text has been lost, leaving us only with Henry Herbert's English summary of what was a French-language production. Significantly, neither this summary, nor contemporary comments upon the pastoral, have provided an indication of the play's author, yet *Florimène* has always excited the interest of theatre historians, primarily because a complete set of Inigo Jones's drawings has survived to illustrate the manner in which the production was staged. Attention has thus focused on *Florimène*'s contribution to understandings of seventeenth-century practicalities, while the cultural and political significances of the pastoral have been overlooked.[1]

This significant imbalance in critical discussions of *Florimène* must be attributed to two things. Firstly, as I have noted, Henrietta Maria's theatrical productions and the neo-Platonic sentiments they express have historically been viewed as apolitical, intellectually facile and, therefore, frivolous and ephemeral. Under this interpretation, the play is simply yet another manifestation of the queen consort's taste for interminable romances. Secondly, it is not a coincidence that modern discussions of *Florimène* approach the play through the figure of Inigo Jones, attempting to contextualise the production by recourse to external biographical details and an existing corpus of architectural work. Even Veevers uses *Florimène* to expound a theory about Catholicised stage design and does not really engage with its significance as a theatrical event.[2] In the absence of an authorial figure to give coherence to the pastoral's meanings, she categorises the text by referring it to another critic's authority, stating that *Florimène* 'seems to conform to the [pastoral] type described by H. C. Lancaster . . . in which shepherds and shepherdesses pursue each other offering unrequited love'.[3] There is a profound reluctance to deal with the pastoral's internal dynamic without recourse to some form of external guarantee. Indeed, such was Alfred Harbage's need to give the pastoral coherence by attributing to it an author that he went so far as to suggest that Henrietta Maria wrote the play herself.[4]

To redress the critical imbalance surrounding *Florimène*, this chapter begins by discussing some of the more significant cultural aspects of the production. I will then propose a political reading of the pastoral based on information from a French source about its author's identity. Finally I will discuss a series of anti-masques by Aurelian Townshend (identified by Stephen Orgel as connected with this production), showing how these, too, might be linked to the pastoral and to the queen's promotion of her religion.[5]

*

The English summary of *Florimène*, prepared by Henry Herbert, master of the revels, represented the play's basic plot as follows: Filène, a shepherd of Arcadia, goes to visit his friend Damon's native Delos and there falls in love with Florimène, a shepherdess. Florelle, Damon's sister, disguises Filène as a woman and introduces him to Florimène, calling him by the feigned name of Dorine. Aristée, Florimène's brother, falls in love with the visitor, and eventually dresses up in Florimène's clothes in order to 'sound the thoughts of Dorine'.[6] Meanwhile, Lycoris, a shepherdess from Arcadia, arrives in the disguise of a man, searching for Filène whom she loves. Much confusion reigns until the goddess Diana descends to tell Lycoris that Filène is her brother, and to sort out the love tangles of the other characters.

This plot, in its interweaving of multiple assumed identities and its concluding revelation of genealogical origins, is very similar in type to that of *Artenice* and *The Shepherds' Paradise*. However, its most innovative aspect, in the context of its performance on the English stage, is the fact that it dramatises cross-gendered disguise. Both *Artenice* and *The Shepherds' Paradise* were performed by ladies who cross-dressed as shepherds, yet, within the economies of the productions, masculine disguises were only adopted by masculine characters, and feminine by feminine: for example, Basilino became Moromante; Fidamira became Gemella. In *Florimène*, for the first time in one of Henrietta Maria's productions, a cross-dressed actress assumed a cross-gendered identity. This is a daring innovation and gives rise to several moments of quite dubious propriety in which a woman playing a shepherd disguised as a shepherdess is wooed by a shepherd acted by another woman. These multiple disguises and gender confusions are obviously intended to be amusing, both within the context of the play, and, more importantly, in the context of a female-only theatrical production. As with *The Shepherds' Paradise*, they demonstrate that the queen's pastorals were not didactically serious, but were intended to entertain.

Herbert's summary makes evident a neo-Platonic framework behind *Florimène*, particularly in its report of a discussion about love that occurs between Florimène and the disguised Filène. Like Bellessa before her, Florimène is innocent in the ways of love, but astonishes Damon and Filène by broaching the subject. Damon marvels to hear her speak of it, and she answers that she finds it 'a trouble to the thoughts, and a depriving of liberty'.[7] Filène answers, in true neo-Platonic style, that all things created have 'their being, and their contentments from love' in a way that reflects Bellessa and Moromante's discussions in *The Shepherds' Paradise* and locates Filène, like Moromante, as his beloved's teacher.[8] However, the situation is made all the more ambiguous in the French pastoral because Filène is wearing the clothes of a woman.

The pastoral's audience is placed in the position of having to decipher all the different possibilities in the scene, savouring the dramatic irony of Florimène unwittingly discussing love with a suitor, and recognising the titillating possibility of two women wooing each other. In addition, by allowing Filène to speak of love while dressed as Dorine, the pastoral dramatises the possibility of a woman speaking authoritatively about her emotions. In *The Shepherds' Paradise*, Bellessa hinted that she would give voice to her feelings if she were not constrained by the gendered proprieties attached to her body. In *Florimène*, this possibility is raised again, challenging the social convention that forbids forthright speech to women. It raises the suggestion that a woman might have the ability to choose her lover, rather than be chosen by him, and transforms the female body from a mirror of masculine desire into a forceful and decisive presence. In addition, again like *The Shepherds' Paradise* whose character Camena represented marriage as a burden for women, *Florimène* gives voice to sentiments which represent married life as curtailing women's liberties.

This pastoral, more than any other, allows its actresses to experiment and play with their gendered identities, and also raises the question of how women look at other women. Suzanne Trill has commented that the pleasure of looking for a woman comes from an interplay between identification and desire, and not from a purely erotic or objectifying stance.[9] Henrietta Maria herself took a seat in the audience of *Florimène* because of her advanced state of pregnancy, occupying a position from which she could both identify with, and desire to be, one of the actresses. In this context, to be on stage as the object of the gaze is empowering; it gives the actress the ability to perform herself before the admiring and envious gazes of other women.

Facilitated by their disguises which allow them to adopt different subject positions, Florimène's characters are led towards greater self-awareness. For example, Aristée, discovering his beloved Dorine to be a man, repents of the way he had previously treated Lucinde, his own admirer, 'and goes away with a resolution to seeke her out'.[10] Nevertheless, while opening up the possibility of a new form of social relations based upon responsibility towards others, the pastoral, like *The Shepherds' Paradise*, concludes with a series of revelations about its characters' paternal origins. Lycoris is revealed to be Filène's sister, with Herbert's summary of the narrative conserving a relation of the whole of her genealogy:

> Diana . . . tels Lycoris, that Filène is her owne brother, and that Montan is not her father, as she hath ever beleeved, but that he tooke her from Orcan, which had saved her from the cruelty of a Satyre, which stole her from her Father Tityre in Arcadia.[11]

The forms of identity posited at the conclusions of *The Shepherds' Paradise* and *Florimène* are grounded in a notion of patrilinearity which insists upon knowledge of one's father. Lycoris gains understanding and self-awareness through the revelation of her origin, and this revelation contributes meaning and closure to the pastoral's narrative. Gender roles are reaffirmed by Diana as she pairs off the characters, thus stamping heterosexual marriage with the authority of a divine injunction.

The pastoral's use of the discourse of love permits its characters and its actresses to explore alternative notions of identity, yet the production concludes by locking its meanings down to conservative formulations and ultimately by having recourse to the law of the father. The fact that this law is revealed by Diana just underlines the pastoral's gendered stereotypes, putting authority in the hands of a female deity only to see that authority subtending masculinist and heterosexual conceptions of society. However, even in Herbert's summary of the production, it is impossible not to notice that the figure of Diana in the play is endowed with a profoundly spiritual significance that has a strong connection with the queen consort's religion.

In 1633, Henrietta Maria was painted by Van Dyck in a blue hunting costume with Jeffrey Hudson, her dwarf, and a monkey called Pug (figure 8.1). The painting's perspective places an observer in a position subservient to the queen: one almost feels as though one is kneeling, looking up at Henrietta Maria and at the orange tree over her right shoulder. Iconographically, the orange tree is the tree of the Virgin Mary, its fruit symbolic of her chastity, and its position in this picture, level with the queen's eyes and therefore close to the focal point of the painting, gives it great significance.[12] Henrietta Maria lays her hand on Pug who, in his turn, sits on Hudson's shoulder. Symbolically, monkeys are representative of vice and the erotic passions, while in Pierre Dinet's *Cinq livres des hieroglyphiques*, published in Paris in 1614, dwarves symbolise the voluptuousness that must be overcome by a virtuous man.[13] Van Dyck's painting therefore has a definite allegorical subtext strongly compatible with the neo-Platonic imagery of, for example, *Tempe Restored*, representing the virtuous queen gently but firmly suppressing sensuality and vice. Furthermore, as well as invoking the image of Diana, chaste goddess of hunting, Henrietta Maria's blue costume calls to mind depictions of the Virgin, an association reinforced by the presence of the orange tree.[14] The young queen stands in the painting as the object of quasi-religious adoration and as the representative and reminder of that other Mary with whom she shared a name.[15]

In the year she acted in *The Shepherds' Paradise*, then, Henrietta Maria was painted by Van Dyck in a costume that evoked both the goddess Diana and the Virgin Mary. Indeed, this connection between the classical goddess and the Virgin can be traced in all of the queen's pastorals. Montagu's play opened with the masque-like appearance of Diana, who in the course of a conversation with Apollo, demonstrated that she guaranteed the production's propriety with her reputation for chastity. In *Artenice*, perhaps more obviously, the figure of Diana came to stand, not only for chastity, but for a female-centred religion that had a strong connection with Catholicism. Indeed, in France, where *Artenice* was first performed by professional actors, the third act of the play came to be known as the act of the convent because it figured its heroine's retreat among the 'filles voüées à Diane', a community of women organised under monastic rules who worshipped the virgin huntress. When Henrietta Maria imported this pastoral into a Protestant court, the resonances between Diana and the Virgin inevitably took on an even greater force. In the queen's pastorals, therefore, Diana is the focus of women's veneration, just as the Virgin was conceived to merit adoration because of her

Figure 8.1. Anthony Van Dyck, *Queen Henrietta Maria with Sir Jeffrey Hudson* (1633).

purity and her ability to intercede with God on behalf of the Catholic faithful.

Florimène begins with a procession of 'the Priests of *Diana*, with the Arch Flamine and Sacrificers' who approach the temple of Diana singing an encomiastic song. In a manner similar to *The Shepherds' Paradise*, it is at this solemn ceremony that Filène is struck by the beauty of Florimène and which therefore initiates the series of events that incorporate him into the shepherdess's community. Overt spiritual display is shown to lead to virtuous thoughts and a desire to unite oneself with purity. The end of the play returns to the temple of Diana where three marriages are contracted which cement the society's bonds and which, like Artenice's marriage to Alcidor in Henrietta Maria's first pastoral, endow marriage with the sense of a spiritual vocation. Furthermore, and again like Racan's pastoral, there is a sense that, by the end of the play, all the characters are united by the same faith. This is particularly obvious in the case of Lycoris who, like Alcidor before her, discovers her true family. After a lifetime of believing herself the daughter of one father, she discovers she was stolen away by 'the cruelty of a Satyre', and that her real identity lies elsewhere. The religious significance of this moment, revealed to Lycoris by the goddess Diana in the quasi-Catholic setting of a temple, cannot have been lost on the pastoral's audience.[16]

THE AUTHOR AND THE OCCASION

Florimène was performed on St Thomas's Day (St Thomas fittingly being the patron saint of architects) before King Charles, Prince Charles, the visiting Prince Palatine and the Caroline court, and was mentioned briefly in the dispatches of Amerigo Salvetti and Anzolo Correr, the Tuscan and Venetian ambassadors. Salvetti remarked before the event that the king and Prince Palatine were to attend 'a French comedy with scenery which the queen intends to present . . . by the French court ladies', while Correr reported after the performance that the queen had presented 'a most beautiful pastoral to her maids in French'.[17] The production was also remarked upon outside England in a source that has been overlooked in English-language discussions of the entertainment and which not only provides important information about the pastoral, but casts light upon the play's political implications.[18] Under the heading 'De Londres, le 9 janvier 1636', the *Gazette de France* observed:

Le dernier du passé, les filles d'honneur de la Reine d'Angleterre representerent à Withal la Florimene, pastorele Françoise du sieur de Boisrobert devant leurs

Majestez Britanniques: où l'elegance des vers fit un agreable parallelle avec la gentillesse des actrices: entre lesquelles les Damoiselles de Ventelet, Cataut et la Difficile, firent voir que ce n'est pas sans sujet qu'elles ont merité les faveurs de leur Maistresse. Le Prince Palatin y estoit et toutes les Dames de la Cour avantageusement parées: le theatre paroissant changé a chacun acte: à la fin desquels il y eut balet.[19]

[At Whitehall, on the last day of last month, the Queen of England's ladies of honour presented Florimène, a French pastoral by Boisrobert, before their Britannic Majesties: where the elegance of the verses made a pleasant parallel with the sweetness of the actresses: among whom the ladies Ventelet, Cataut and la Difficile, showed that it was not without reason that they merited the favours of their mistress. The Prince Palatine was there and all the ladies of the court flatteringly adorned: the stage appearing changed at each act: at the end of which there was a ballet.]

This report not only provides us with the name of *Florimène*'s author but with the names of three of the actresses. The mademoiselle 'Ventelet' in question was Christian, Henrietta Maria's god-daughter, soon to marry William Shelley, son of Sir John Shelley.[20] She would subsequently take up a position as a 'chamberer' alongside her mother in the queen consort's household and would accompany them both to France in exile from the English civil wars. Both women are mentioned in documents associated with Henrietta Maria's convent at Chaillot, founded outside Paris in 1651, and were thus among the very privileged few who attended the queen in her religious retreats.[21] The 'Cataut' mentioned by the *Gazette* was Catowe Garnier, daughter of Henrietta Maria's nurse and sister of the Madame Coignet who is likely to have sung in *Tempe Restored*. She was married to Thomas Arpe around the same time that Christian Vantelet married Shelley, and, like her, subsequently became a 'chamberer' to the queen.[22] The identity of the woman the *Gazette* terms 'la Difficile' remains, unsurprisingly, a mystery, but she, too, is likely to have been a member of the younger generation of the queen's French servants.

The most significant aspect of the *Gazette*'s report is its indication of the pastoral's author. As I discussed in chapter 1, François le Metel, sieur de Boisrobert, was a well-known French court poet. He had entered the service of Marie de Médicis around 1616, wrote several ballets for the Bourbon court and was responsible for at least some of the verses in the *Ballet de la Reyne d'Angleterre*, Henrietta Maria's own entertainment for her wedding.[23] He cultivated a connection with the duchesse de Chevreuse in the early 1620s and secured a place in her entourage when she and her husband accompanied Henrietta Maria to London in the summer of 1625. Once in England, Madame de Chevreuse delighted in stirring up animosity between Boisrobert and the earl of Holland, showing Holland a controversial elegy the poet had written about England's 'climat barbare' over which the two men fiercely quarrelled. Boisrobert fell ill at Windsor, and later wrote a letter to the earl of Carlisle in which he thanked him for lodging and caring for him during his sickness. Of particular interest in this letter is Boisrobert's comment that Carlisle had wanted to make the poet known to the English king ('vous avez voulu que j'eusse l'honneur d'estre cogneu de vostre Roy' [You wanted me to have the honour of being known by your king]).[24] Indeed, during his stay in England, Boisrobert received a cash payment from Charles I. He also wrote a sonnet in which he thanked Henrietta Maria for her favours, although, as Jean Jacquot has warned, this might be a reference to a gratification for verses the poet contributed to the marriage celebrations held in Paris.[25] This problem aside, it can be asserted that, by the start of 1626, Boisrobert was not only a major contributor to French court entertainments, but had also been introduced to the English court and its king.

Though he had the appropriate experience and connections to be the author of *Florimène*, the fact that Boisrobert composed this work for the queen consort in 1635 implicates it in the vexed political relationships between England and France. After his return to Paris in August 1626, the poet strengthened his connection with Richelieu, becoming the cardinal's 'secrétaire litteraire'.[26] At first, he maintained his links with Henrietta Maria's female relatives at the French court, undertaking a paraphrase of *Les Sept Pseames de la Penitance de David* for the queen mother in 1627, and writing the verses of Anne of Austria's ballet, *Les Nymphes Bocagères de la Forêt Sacrée*, danced in the Louvre the same year. However, in November 1630, Marie de Médicis and Richelieu became involved in the power struggle that would result in the queen mother's permanent exile from France. Thus, from July 1631 when Marie de Médicis fled to the Spanish Netherlands, Boisrobert's connection with her was severed. Moreover, as I have noted, the circumstances leading to Marie de Médicis's exile swung Henrietta Maria's loyalties firmly away from Richelieu and his adherents. Despite Boisrobert's early connection with Henrietta Maria, it does, therefore, seem strange that in the mid 1630s the English queen should have sponsored a pastoral by a poet whose master she seriously disliked, particularly considering that this pastoral was prominently staged at Whitehall. However, the significance of *Florimène*'s production in 1635 can be clarified by reference to the change in Henrietta Maria's political position that year, and also by casting a glance at cultural developments occurring in Paris around the figure of Richelieu.

After her mother's exile in 1631, Henrietta Maria was known to be discontented with Richelieu and, as I have discussed, was implicated in the Châteauneuf conspiracy. However, in 1635, Richelieu began to seek to repair his quarrel with her in the hope of enlisting English aid in his recently declared war with Spain. A new French ambassador, Henri de Senneterre, was dispatched to London, arriving in March 1635. Malcolm Smuts has commented upon Senneterre's arrival and on Henrietta Maria's reaction to it that, 'always susceptible to gallantry and the influence of people she liked, the queen was soon "showing all affection for France" and beginning once more to meddle in politics'.[27] Smuts's evidence for the change in Henrietta Maria's position is convincing, and is borne out by Sharpe's more detailed investigation into the summer of 1635.[28] However, instead of being an irrational about-turn manipulated by the French ambassador, the queen consort's change of position in 1635 can be shown to be consistent with her previous political, or rather familial, associations.

In a letter to her sister Christine, duchess of Savoy, written in October or November 1635, Henrietta Maria showed her awareness of Senneterre's agenda:

> Osytost que l'ambassadeur de France à estté arivé ysy, je vous en ay voulu donner avis pour . . . vous faire entendre que il me recherche extrèmemant de la part du cardinal de Richelieu. Mais croyés que se que j'aycouteray sera seulemant pour vostre considération pour tâcher par sela à vous randre quelque servise.[29]
>
> [As soon as the French ambassador had arrived here, I wanted to let you know of it so I could make you understand that he is soliciting me heavily on the part of Cardinal Richelieu. But believe that what I will listen to will be only out of consideration for you, to seek in this way to render you some service.]

In 1634, Savoy had dispatched an ambassador extraordinary to England to seek English recognition of the duke of Savoy's claims to the throne of Cyprus, recognition already refused by France and Spain.[30] This ambassador, Gianfrancesco San Martino, marquis of San Germano, received particular expressions of friendship from Henrietta Maria who was reported by John Finet to be casting her favours upon the Savoyard 'for the sake of her syster the Duchess'.[31] In June 1635, Benedetto de Cize, count of Pezze, arrived in London as the Savoy agent, again to ask for English validation of the 'royal' title, and to seek supplies for protection against the French. Henrietta Maria's letters to her sister at this time are full of promises that she will assist Christine, this assistance, as the letter above reveals, involving negotiation on Savoy's behalf with the newly arrived French ambassador. In addition, Charles was on the point of sending an ambassador extraordinary to Paris, in part to negotiate the queen mother's return to France. The Venetian ambassador, trying to divine the agenda behind the embassy, commented that 'this opinion [about negotiations on behalf of Marie de Médicis] fits in very well, because the queen here is very desirous of seeing her [mother] settled'.[32]

Thus, while Smuts has shown how *rapprochement* with France suited Henrietta Maria's anti-Spanish courtiers and was compatible with the cause of the visiting Palatine Prince, an English–French alliance could also be offered to Henrietta Maria as a means of aiding her sister and ameliorating the position of her mother: Senneterre could solicit the queen's support by addressing the situation that had caused Henrietta Maria's split with Richelieu in the first place.[33] It was to the queen's advantage to listen to the French ambassador's overtures, and it would appear from Finet's comments upon Senneterre's arrival that Henrietta Maria was readily disposed to entertain the ambassador from the moment he appeared in London.[34]

In this political context, *Florimène*, rather than being regarded as an expression of Henrietta Maria's love of elaborate spectacle, must be treated with the same critical attention as the other theatrical events sponsored by the queen in 1635–6, notably Davenant's *Triumphs of the Prince d'Amour* and Prince Charles's entertainment at Richmond.[35] The production of the pastoral might be construed as an expression of the queen's willingness to be wooed by Richelieu and a demonstration before the English court of her swing towards a more pro-French policy. Written by a *créature* of the cardinal, and reported in the *Gazette de France* (a paper authorised and supported by Richelieu and recognised to be part of his personal propaganda machine), *Florimène* might well have been a gift from him to Henrietta Maria for political purposes. The pastoral does not appear in any twentieth-century lists of Boisrobert's plays, nor have I been able to trace any of the French songs whose first lines were conserved in Henry Herbert's English summary of the production. Had this pastoral been performed in France, one would expect to find some other contemporary comment upon it, beyond that already cited. This leads me to believe that the pastoral was especially commissioned from Boisrobert by Richelieu and sent to Henrietta Maria at the English court.

The cardinal's attitude towards theatre at this time deserves consideration for it has a direct bearing upon the queen's production of *Florimène* and shows the pastoral to be compatible with Richelieu's cultural programme. In the mid 1630s, Richelieu discovered the political value of culture and began to surround himself with poets and playwrights. His connection with Boisrobert was well established and he had started to regard theatre as a political tool for the glorification of the state.[36] The cardinal's active interest in the arts has been precisely dated to the year 1635, notably by Georges Couton who stated that, prior to 1634, only a few traces of Richelieu's interest in theatre were discernible, while, at the end of 1634 and in 1635 'tout change: les événements se précipitent et il apparaît clairement que le Cardinal s'est décidé à avoir une politique culturelle et spécifiquement une politique théâtrale' [everything changed: events rushed forward and it clearly appeared that the cardinal had decided to espouse a cultural policy and specifically a policy for the theatre].[37] Richelieu's sponsorship of the arts in 1635 involved the financial patronage of the two Parisian theatre troupes (the Hôtel de Bourgogne and the théâtre du Marais), the defence of theatre as a legitimate pursuit (as opposed to an invitation to venery and disorder) and his association with the emergent Académie française.[38]

In the context of *Florimène*, it is Richelieu's involvement in the birth of the Académie française which is of particular significance. In 1634, Boisrobert was instrumental in attracting Richelieu's interest and patronage to the group of *sçavants* who met at Valentin Conrart's house in the rue Saint-Martin. In March of that year, having received the cardinal's approbation for their activities, the nascent Académie composed its statutes and prefaced these with a 'Projet de l'Académie', written by Nicolas Faret. This 'Projet' laid out the *sçavants*' designs, significantly stating that, under Richelieu's protection, the French language was to be retrieved from among other barbarous tongues, and was to succeed Latin, as Latin had succeeded Greek. In a disquieting moment of cultural imperialism, the 'Projet' asserted that the French language would be that which 'tous nos voisins parleroient bien-tost, si nos conquestes continuoient comme elles avoient commencé' [that which all our neighbours will soon speak, if our conquests continue as they have started].[39] This assertion has a resonance with the performance of *Florimène* upon the English court stage and adds a new dimension to the *Gazette de France*'s praise of the pastoral's elegant verse. The elegant verse becomes a manifestation of France's cultural superiority, and a constitutive element of the 'gentillesse' displayed by the play's French actresses. The *Gazette*'s report reappropriates Henrietta Maria's ladies for France as symbols of French civilisation. In contrast, the English court ladies are simply nicely dressed ('avantageusement parées'): they are all decorative show and no substance.

In his sponsorship of such popular vehicles as Renaudot's *Gazette*, and in his association with the Académie française, Richelieu's cultural project was supported upon the twin pillars of public propaganda and intellectual respectability. The poets of the Académie could be called upon to produce laudatory literary works, and the *Gazette* was only too happy to promote the cardinal's cultural enterprise.[40] In addition, and importantly with regard to *Florimène*, he appears to have collaborated with Académie poets and playwrights in the production of theatrical spectacle.

In 1634–5, Boisrobert was involved in the production of *La Comédie des Tuileries*, a tragi-comedy staged before the French queen in March 1635 and again before Louis XIII, his queen and the duc d'Orléans in April of the same year. The events surrounding the composition of this play are significant and have been explored at length by Georges Couton. In letters to Boisrobert dated between November 1634 and January 1635, Jean Chapelin described how he received a prose narrative from Richelieu with the instruction to make it into a play in verse and to conceal the cardinal's artistic contribution. Having done what he was instructed (in collaboration with Boisrobert and three others), Chapelin wrote to Boisrobert with the request that Richelieu should be asked for his corrections.[41] Richelieu's involvement in the play was thus manifest at all stages of its production, although the cardinal suppressed public knowledge of his personal contribution.

Therefore, although the *Gazette de France* named Boisrobert as the author of *Florimène*, it is intriguing to speculate whether Richelieu himself was instrumental in the composition of the pastoral. What is certain, setting aside the question of his active role as a contributor, is that the play demonstrates signs of his influence. Part of Richelieu's project for the renovation of French theatre involved an adherence to classical forms, especially to the unities of time, manner and place. *Florimène* is exemplary in this regard, its action taking place on the island of Delos and appearing to unfold within one day. Moreover, the pastoral both opens and closes with images of the temple of Diana, neatly concluding events on the same spot in which the action began.[42] In addition, *Florimène*'s five acts are interspersed with four *intermedii* representing winter, spring, summer and autumn. This seasonal conceit is compatible with, indeed a marker of, the play's adherence to the three unities, providing a balanced, harmonious image of time. A comparison may be drawn here with the printed text of *Mirame*, a tragi-comedy commissioned by Richelieu in 1641 to inaugurate his new theatre in the Palais Cardinal. The text of *Mirame* appeared in a luxurious quarto edition with plates by the Florentine Della Bella. Each act was illustrated with an image of a different time of day (moonrise, dawn, etc.), the sequence of drawings concluding with the representation of noon.[43] The edition thus demonstrated a clear respect for the unities of time and place and was yet another public manifestation of Richelieu's project to glorify the state through culture.

Florimène, while appealing to Henrietta Maria's taste for pastoral romances, was therefore fully compatible with the cultural tradition that Richelieu was sponsoring in France. However, it must be acknowledged that the play was also embedded within the tradition of anglicised French culture sponsored by Henrietta Maria at the English court. As such, the production was an integral part of Caroline monarchical spectacle and had a nationalistic agenda that was in direct competition with Richelieu's cultural imperialism. John Peacock has shown how Inigo Jones drew on predominantly French sources to develop an architectural idiom suitable for Henrietta Maria's theatrical productions.[44] Financed by the queen, the production of *Florimène* became an instance of French dramatic culture mediated through English expertise. While the pastoral might well have been written by Boisrobert for Richelieu as a gift for Henrietta Maria, its performance (albeit by the queen's French ladies) was nonetheless a product of the English court. Furthermore, although demonstrating her willingness to entertain the idea of *rapprochement* with France, the pastoral production was coloured by the fact that Richelieu's gift to the queen was transformed, in performance, into a gift from her to her husband. At once suggesting Henrietta Maria's willingness to intercede with Charles on France's behalf, this transformation paradoxically excludes France through the insertion of the pastoral into the economy of English court spectacle.

A critical interpretation of *Florimène* based on the authorial guarantee of Boisrobert is therefore problematic, not only because it is complicated by Richelieu's possible involvement, but also because the production was authorised by the English queen and took place within a tradition of Caroline court theatre. However, the new information provided by the *Gazette de France* which links *Florimène* to Boisrobert, and therefore to Richelieu, does mean that the production should be considered in the light of Anglo-French relations. In addition, it demonstrates that Henrietta Maria was as consistent in her theatrical patronage as she was in her politics, continuing to support a poet whose work she had experienced at the French court and who had written a *ballet* for her wedding. Lastly, the production also provides an indication of Henrietta Maria's significance on the international scene, gesturing towards the important part she could play in political negotiations between the Bourbon and Caroline courts.

MAKING CONNECTIONS: TOWNSHEND, 'FLORIMÈNE' AND MARRIAGE

In 1632, as I have discussed, Aurelian Townshend, who was probably introduced into Henrietta Maria's circle by the earl of Holland, superseded Jonson as the court's masque writer. Although subsequently overlooked in favour of Davenant for major masque commissions, he went on to contribute a song to a production performed before the king and queen at the court revival of Cartwright's *The Royal Slave* in 1636, and also penned a poetic fragment that Stephen Orgel has associated with *Florimène*. This fragment, which exists in an apparently unique printed pamphlet in the Huntington Library, was first identified by Veevers who, like Orgel, thinks it post-dates *Tempe Restored*.[45] It is undated, has no proper title, but is inscribed with Townshend's name. Orgel remarks that the succession of entries it describes formed an anti-masque that was danced as a 'comic eclogue' at the end of the queen's pastoral.[46] Cedric Brown, though, argues that the whole fragment represents a 'short masque to follow the play', with the first verses belonging to a series of comic anti-masques, followed by a 'Subject of the Masque' which introduces and explains the masque figure.[47] The *Gazette de France*'s fascinating report that *Florimène* concluded with a ballet seems to corroborate both critics' suspicions, with Brown's suggestion that the fragment represents an anti-masque followed by a main masque seeming the most likely scenario.[48]

Townshend's anti-masque entries see the successive arrivals on stage of 'A Man of Canada', '2. AEgyptians', '3. Pantaloones' and '4. Spaniards'.[49] These are followed by a song to 'the Moone' whose 'sweet Influence' is felt by the masque's singers in a manner that evokes both *Florimène*'s Diana in her incarnation as Cynthia and, of course, Henrietta Maria herself. The following 'Subiect of the Masque' describes how a group of shepherds have been drawn to woo four shepherdesses, explaining how, after the men have been purified, a deity will assign at least one of them a bride. The fragment then concludes with a rather risqué speech by 'A Pigmee' and an address to the king and queen.

The first anti-masque entry in the undated pamphlet is significant. While feathered Indians had already made an appearance upon the English masquing stage, notably in Chapman's *Memorable Masque* of 1613 and in Townshend's own *Tempe Restored*, this figure, as a Canadian, stands out as an innovation.[50] What is more, in the light of Anglo-French negotiations over the ownership of Canada, the verses he recites are significant. He declares:

> From Canada, both rough and rude,
> Come I, with bare and nimble feet;
> Those Amazonian Maides to greet,
> Which Conquer'd them that us subdu'd:
> Love is so Just,
> Our Victors must
> Weare Chaines, as heavy as ours bee:
> Fetters of Gold make no Man free.[51]

Brown has noted that the word 'Amazonian' in the Huntington Library pamphlet is underlined and glossed in the margin with the words 'faire Franc', probably meaning France.[52] This is consistent with the idea that the entertainment was performed by a group of Henrietta Maria's French ladies, who become synonymous with the production's 'Amazonian Maides'. If Brown is to be believed, and the entertainment also involved a group of Englishmen who danced with the French ladies, then the 'Victors' who subdued the Canadians must be the English. The Man of Canada's stanza therefore represents Englishmen as the conquerors of Canada, but allows those Englishmen, in their turn, to become the subjects of the Amazonian (or rather the French) maids. In the spring of 1632, Sir Isaac Wake, the English ambassador to France, signed a treaty at Saint-Germain which passed all English colonial interests in Canada over to the French. In Townshend's anti-masque, the Canadian's subjection to the French is romanticised and becomes a celebration of chaste love rather than a reminder of France's diplomatic victory over the English.[53]

The Man of Canada's stanza also makes a tongue-in-cheek reference to 'Fetters of Gold' which make 'no Man free'. Linked with the subsequent verses which note that 'the Deity that doth reside / In yonder Grove, shall point One out a Bride', it becomes possible to see this entertainment as part of a wedding, or betrothal, celebration, rather than as directly connected with the plot of *Florimène*.[54] Gently mocking the institution of marriage in its anti-masques, the entertainment is later concerned to point out a bride to *one* specific bridegroom. Indeed, the risqué speech uttered by the 'Pigmee' towards the end of the production seems compatible with the kind of exhortations that accompanied a bride and bridegroom to bed on their wedding night.

For example, *The Lord Hay's Masque* (1607), performed at the wedding of James Hay and Honora Denny, saw Night informing the revellers that 'Hymen long since the bridal bed hath dressed, / And longs to bring the turtles to their nest'.[55] Here, the Pigmy announces impertinently:

> The Night is shorter now than I;
> Loose it not all, too mannerly;
> Rest would doe well, If ye can get it;
> Beshrew their fingers would permit it,
> Untill the Morning Clocke strike Ten;
> Speake out like Clerks, and cry Amen.[56]

This would seem an inappropriate conclusion to a production that saw male lovers purified until they were able 'in white paper' to write their 'Virgins name'.[57] However, in the context of a wedding celebration, it might seem less an invitation to venery, than a recognition of the physical pleasures attendant on the married state.

Significantly, Henrietta Maria's household accounts for 1636 contain evidence of two marriages, both of them for French ladies who acted in *Florimène*. In February that year, 'Catowe Garnier', daughter of her majesty's nurse, and 'Christian Vantlett her Ma*jes*t*ie*s Goddaughter' received wedding gifts of money from the queen consort.[58] Mademoiselle Vantelet's marriage was the more prestigious of the two for she married a nobleman, 'Will*ia*m Shelly Sonne to S*ir* John Shelly', while Garnier married into the gentry.[59] It seems likely, therefore, that Townshend's verses referred to Vantelet's wedding and that they either constituted the 'ballet' that followed *Florimène*, or were produced for a slightly later occasion, but looked back to the pastoral.[60] In the light of this, both the production of *Florimène* itself and Townshend's related anti-masques take on a slightly different colouring.

As I discussed in chapter 7, December 1634 saw the arrival in England of Gregorio Panzani, the first accredited representative of the pope, who was charged with negotiating the formal exchange of agents between the English court and Rome. As Veevers has noted, *The Temple of Love* was the first court function after his arrival, and was 'an appropriate occasion for the Queen to impress on him the part she was playing in advancing her religion'.[61] Boisrobert's pastoral for the queen consort did not, therefore, just demonstrate her importance on the stage of international politics, it also provided her with another appropriate vehicle to showcase her religion. Indeed, it went further than this: it actively demonstrated her French household's integration with English Catholics.

The Shelleys were an old Catholic family, distantly related to Edward Sackville, earl of Dorset and the queen's lord chamberlain.[62] William Shelley's marriage to the queen consort's god-daughter showed, at last, that meaningful connections were being established between members of her French household and English Catholics. Rebecca Bailey has skilfully demonstrated how the Salesian Catholicism practised by Henrietta Maria was not the same as the Catholicism practised in an England that had seen years of religious oppression. She notes that there was a dissonance between the queen's 'passive approach' to her religion, characterised by a belief that beauty could inspire one to spirituality, and an 'active zeal' that was being urged on the queen from English recusant circles.[63] This characterisation is, perhaps, a little stark, yet the point is valid. Although as early as 1626 Henrietta Maria's entertainments demonstrated her Catholic allegiances, she was, as Malcolm Smuts has demonstrated, as much inclined to build alliances with English Protestants as with Catholics.[64] However, the years 1635–8 marked, in Veevers's words, 'a period of optimism for the Catholic party at court', with several public conversions and the open practice of their religion by 'others who had been Catholic before'.[65] The marriage of the queen's god-daughter into a noble family of English Catholics seems to be part of this religious resurgence. Like the early entertainments performed by the queen and her own generation of French waiting women, *Florimène* and its attendant masque foregrounded the talents and eligibility of the Frenchwomen in Henrietta Maria's entourage, at once showcasing the queen consort's importance on the European political stage and celebrating her household's connections with the English recusant community.

CHAPTER 9

Marie de Médicis and the last masques

In a manner compatible with my reading of *Florimène*, Erica Veevers has argued that, after 1635, the religious aspects of the queen consort's neo-Platonic imagery became more pronounced.[1] Through a consideration of *Luminalia* (1638) and *Salmacida Spolia* (1640), I will explore how this religious emphasis was connected, not only with the arrivals of Panzani and George Conn, the papal legate, but also with Henrietta Maria's family and their political situation.

The last great masques of the Caroline reign have traditionally been read as ephemeral productions that symbolise the decadence of a court teetering on the brink of extinction. Thus, for Graham Parry, *Luminalia* 'dramatises the divine power of majesty at a time when the King needed every assurance of his infallible rule', while Gerald Eades Bentley terms *Salmacida Spolia* 'the swan song of the Caroline court'.[2] Although I do not doubt that, for example, *Salmacida Spolia* can be read as a response to the Scottish rebellion or to Charles's recall of parliament after eleven years of personal rule, I am very resistant to criticism which reads the masque retrospectively in the light of the civil wars. Furthermore, *Luminalia* and *Salmacida Spolia* were both masques which involved the participation of the queen, and yet they have been interpreted as demonstrations of the *king's* will.[3] While I am by no means suggesting that these productions did not register domestic concerns, I think that they should both be opened up to readings which draw specific attention to the position of Henrietta Maria.

*

Luminalia, according to its printed text, was conceived and put together 'in shorter time than anything here hath been done in this kind'.[4] Performed in 1638 on Shrove Tuesday night in the temporary masquing room constructed to prevent damage to the new Banqueting House ceiling, it followed the king's *Britannia Triumphans*, beginning at the point where the former broke off. Charles's masque ended with a Valediction, bidding the lords and ladies 'To bed, to bed', and informing them that 'Wise Nature' had prepared the dew of sleep, to 'intermit our joys and ease our cares'.[5] *Luminalia* begins with Night arriving in her chariot 'to give repose to the labours of mortals', and reinforces the connection with *Britannia Triumphans* through a verbal parallel when Night declares she will 'intermit' the sins of toiling statesmen whose days are measured not by hours, but by 'cares'.[6]

Nonetheless, as Veevers has admirably shown, this does not mean that *Luminalia* blithely reiterated the sentiments and politics of Charles's masque. Arguing that *Luminalia* took place during a period of optimism for the Catholic party at court, she demonstrates convincingly that it encoded Marian references both in its central motif of light and in its imagery of priest-like flamens and arch-flamens. 'The masque celebrates', she suggests, 'the triumph of spiritual illumination over the forces of darkness and superstition', concluding:

> *Luminalia* . . . which in terms of poetry and literary ideas is the most incoherent and meaningless of the masques, is perhaps, in terms of its images and the connection between the Queen's Platonic love and her religion, the most significant, an optimistic assertion of the Catholic interests of the Queen.[7]

The case that Veevers makes for the masque as a demonstration of the queen consort's Catholicism is attractive, showing how neo-Platonism acted as both a vehicle for and a cover of a hidden religious meaning. Following her example, I want to examine the masque as a production that spoke to Henrietta Maria's own court and concerns while stressing that it was neither 'incoherent' nor 'meaningless'.

Enid Welsford has explored *Luminalia*'s debts to its continental sources, pointing out that it draws heavily upon Francesco Cini's *Notte D'Amore*, performed at the wedding of Cosimo de Medici in 1608, and that many of its anti-masque entries are borrowed from the French *Ballet du grand Demogorgon* (1633); it is also worth noting that Ben Jonson had previously made use of the Italian source in *The Vision of Delight* (1617), King James's Twelfth Night masque in which a series of fantastical characters (conceived along the lines of the entries of French *ballet de cour*) danced at the behest of Fant'sy.[8] In addition, Henrietta Maria herself had danced the role of Aurora in Anne of Austria's *Grand Ballet de la Reyne representant le Soleil* (1621) in a scene in which the Gods of Sleep, Dreams and Chimeras emerged from their caves and were driven away by Dawn. The influence of this French production on *Luminalia* is especially important because, seventeen years after she had uttered the prophetic lines, 'Parmy tant de clairté ie ne suis que l'Aurore, / Mais dedans peu de temps ie deuiendray Soleil' [Among so much brightness I am only the Dawn, / But in a little while I will become the Sun], Henrietta Maria appeared on the English stage in a mature manifestation of the imagery that had followed her from France.[9] Just as her wedding celebrations conflated the light of the sun with the light of faith, so the light evinced by neo-Platonism could be identified with the light of true religion. As Welsford's work shows, the idea of a masque of Night and Dreams dispelled by a glorious light was by no means novel, but in 1638, as Veevers suggests, it took on renewed significance.

Veevers's work on the main masque of *Luminalia* is comprehensive and impressive. She comments that *Luminalia* was conceived during a period of optimism for the Catholic party at court, following a series of high-profile conversions and the continuing presence in the country of George Conn.[10] In addition, she notes that, when the masque was in production, a controversy was raging both about the number of English converts around the queen, and about the festival of Candlemas. In 1637, Laud published a proclamation warning that the laws against English Catholics were to be strictly enforced.[11] Five days later, Henrietta Maria held a midnight mass in her chapel to which all recent converts were invited, after which she proclaimed triumphantly to Conn that 'now he might see the effect of the Proclamation'.[12] Veevers also suggests that the masque's subtitle, a 'Festival of Light', had contemporary religious significance, especially in relation to the Feasts of Mary. After the Reformation, she explains, 'Elizabeth's injunctions had condemned "all Candlesticks, Trendals, Rolls of Wax, and setting up of Tapers, for that they be things tending to Idolatry and Superstition"'.[13] The controversy surrounding this had recently been renewed by Anthony Stafford, who, in 1635, had published *The Female Glory, or The Life and Death of Our Blessed Lady, the Holy Virgin Mary*. This book, in its turn, was excoriated in Henry Burton's sermon *For God, and the King* in November 1636.

Stafford's text described the ceremony of Candlemas, explaining that

> the Church used to pray, that as the visible Lights chased away the darkenesse of the night: so the hearts of the Faithfull might be illuminated by the Invisible flames of the holy Spirit, & (being cured of their blindnesse brought upon them by vice) might with pure and cleare eyes discerne those things which are pleasing to God, and having pass'd through the sad, darke, and dismall accidents of this world might at length arrive at Heaven, where they shall behold a Light everlasting.[14]

Veevers suggests that the masque's all-pervasive theme of the triumph of light, combined with echoes of Marian imagery, 'seem to give religious significance to the whole masque, for which Stafford's exegesis on the significance of Candlemas might serve as a text'.[15] I am convinced of the validity of her argument, which is reinforced by her observation that Francis Lenton's companion-piece to the masque was entitled *Great Britain's Beauties, or The Female Glory*, and thus made explicit reference to Stafford's text.[16] The masque, like *Tempe Restored*, evokes a debased form of physicality which is overcome by beauty and light. Furthermore, and again like *Tempe Restored*, the light in question is internal; physical beauty is only a reflection of the beauty of the soul.

Veevers makes a convincing case for *Luminalia* as an expression of the queen consort's religion. I would also like to suggest that there is a political undercurrent in the masque. In 1637–8, a number of French exiles arrived in England, the most prestigious of whom was Marie de Médicis. She had been suing for asylum from Charles I for some time and her case was strengthened in April 1638 with the arrival in London of Henrietta Maria's old friend, Marie, duchesse de Chevreuse. Both Maries had pursued careers dogged with political intrigue and both were regarded in their own ways as troublemakers. Indeed, a brief review of their activities is not out of place here in order to contextualise their problematic presence in England.

Born in 1573, Marie de Médicis was raised by her uncle Ferdinand, Grand Duke of Tuscany, whose wife, Christine of Lorraine, was a granddaughter of Catherine de Médicis, the former queen regent of France. Relations between France and Tuscany were very close (not least because a succession of French kings had borrowed substantial sums of money from the Italians) and the prospect of marrying Marie into the Bourbon dynasty was attractive on both sides.[17] Her proxy wedding with the French king, Henri IV, took place on 5 October 1600, and that evening a banquet was held at the Palazzo Vecchio in the splendidly decorated *salone dei cinquecento*. The walls of the room were hung with paintings that celebrated the Médicis dynasty and which also evoked the marriage of Catherine de Médicis, Marie's famous ancestor.

A short theatrical performance also took place, in the form of a dialogue sung by the goddesses Juno and Minerva, written by Giovanni Battista Guarini (the author of *Il Pastor Fido*), and involving some spectacular changes of scenery designed by the architect Bernardo Buontalenti. The production was so magnificent that Peter Paul Rubens, who was one of the guests, would still be marvelling about it twenty-two years later.[18]

Indeed, Sara Mamone speculates that this entertainment greatly influenced the symbolism of the portrait cycle that he later painted for Marie's palais de Luxembourg. Mamone also notes that the image of Marie bringing peace, invoked in Guarini's dialogue, would become one of the driving images of the queen's regency.[19] When Marie left Florence, therefore, she took with her an iconography that located her within a powerful and culturally active family, and that promoted dynastic alliance as the key to harmony.

Once in France, Marie continued to demonstrate a love of ballet and theatrical spectacle, calling a succession of actors and artists to Paris from Italy. However, intrigue at the Bourbon court was rife and her position was constantly destabilised by her status as Henri's second wife. Eventually, in order to forestall any struggle over the royal succession, it was agreed that Marie should be crowned queen. The ceremony took place on 13 May 1610 at the basilica of Saint Denis. The following day, Henri IV was assassinated in his coach by Ravaillac, a Catholic zealot, and Marie became queen regent of France for the next four years. Indeed, even after 1614 when Louis XIII reached his majority, Marie found it difficult to give up her position of influence and continued to act as a policy maker, surrounding herself with her own servants and advisers. Frustrated by his lack of influence and abetted by his companion Charles d'Albert de Luynes, Louis rebelled against his mother in the spring of 1617 and took the government of the kingdom into his own hands. Marie was exiled from Paris and forced to reside at her château in Blois.

The ascendancy of Luynes was important, not only because it signalled the start of the intermittent wrangling between Louis and his mother that would end in the latter's permanent exile from France in 1631, but because it introduced his wife into the political frame. Marie de Montbazon was born into the powerful Rohan family in 1600 and was married to Luynes in 1617. Because of her husband's influence, she was given a prestigious post in Anne of Austria's household and established a close friendship with the queen. This association enabled her to wield significant political influence and also meant that she moved in the same circles as Henrietta Maria. Indeed, in 1625, and now married to the duc de Chevreuse, she acted as hostess to the English wooing ambassadors, lodging them at her Parisian home while they negotiated for the princess's hand in marriage. Although her own interests and those of Marie de Médicis often clashed at this time, not least because of her early connection with Luynes, the two women were soon to become united in their mutual antipathy for Louis's chief minister, Cardinal Richelieu.

By 1622, the queen mother had received a reprieve from Louis and had returned from Blois to take up a position on his council. Richelieu, though, was gaining in influence with the king in a manner detrimental to Marie's own concerns. She began to plot against him, and, in the autumn of 1630, succeeded in obtaining Louis's vague promise that he would expel the cardinal from Paris. However, as I noted in chapter 4, Richelieu was made aware of the plan and turned the tables on the queen mother by regaining the king's favour. Marie swore never to be reconciled with him and subsequently boycotted court functions and sessions of the king's council. Finally, in February 1631, an exasperated Louis decreed that his mother must be exiled from court. She was first banished to Compiègne, but, in July, hearing a rumour that Richelieu wished to repatriate her to Italy, she fled from France to the Infanta Isabella's court in the Spanish Netherlands where she remained for the next few years.

In April of 1638, Marie de Chevreuse arrived in England, seeking refuge, in her turn, from Louis XIII and Richelieu. During the previous year she had been involved in a conspiracy, later known as the Val-de-Grâce affair, with, among others, Anne of Austria, the duke of Lorraine and Anne's Spanish relations. Anne, childless and afraid of divorce, was corresponding with the Spanish (now at war with France) by means of one of the English ambassador's secretaries. Richelieu uncovered the correspondence, and Marie de Chevreuse, knowing that she would be implicated, fled from France to Spain, whence she made her way to England. Provisionally lodged at Greenwich, she quickly began to lobby for Marie de Médicis to be received in London, and, in October that same year, was rewarded for her efforts when the exiled queen mother arrived from Amsterdam. This arrival put the English king in a difficult position since it compromised his relationship with the Richelieu administration that had expelled both women from France. Richelieu's own opinion of the situation was that it had been conceived and put in motion by 'les femmes', and that it thus provided evidence of the weakness of Charles's method of government.[20] Furthermore, both Maries were looked upon in England as a severe drain on the crown's already over-stretched resources. Nonetheless, they were received with all honour by Henrietta Maria and, if they did nothing else, they had a profoundly influential effect upon the last masques of the Caroline reign.

Rumour had it that Henrietta Maria wanted to keep *Luminalia* in rehearsal for a second performance before Marie de Chevreuse, a sign both that she viewed the arrival of her friend with favour and that she did not, unlike modern commentators, perceive the masque to be unimportant. The production's religious overtones would obviously have pleased the duchess who, soon after her arrival, as the Venetian ambassador observed, set herself (unsuccessfully) to convert Henry Rich, earl of Holland.[21] Furthermore, *Luminalia* also spoke to Chevreuse's concern to see Marie de Médicis welcomed into England, not least because it already honoured a French exile. The young marquis de Vieuville, son of Charles, duc de Vieuville, one of Gaston d'Orléans's supporters, was in England in 1638 and took part in the queen's entertainment. He had already attended on Marie de Médicis in Brussels and had participated in the *Balet des princes indiens* (1634), a spectacle written by her poet, Jean Puget de la Serre, to celebrate and publicise her arrival in the city. Indeed, it is interesting to speculate whether Vieuville's presence in England was also connected with the queen mother's desire to settle in that country.

Puget de la Serre's production, in which the young Vieuville played several parts, was premised on the idea that the 'Princes indiens', nephews of the Sun, had renounced their former alliance the moment they saw the ladies of Marie de Médicis's entourage.[22] Preferring to be the ladies' slaves rather than the kinsmen of 'ce grand Dieu', they professed already to have forgotten their natal country, remembering nothing but their vow to live and die in the ladies' service.[23] The production took the form of a long series of burlesque entries, followed by an interlude depicting the Judgement of Paris, and concluded with a 'Grand Balet de Parade' of the Indian princes. From Fame's opening stanzas, which lauded Marie's reputation and declared that 'Nous qui faisons un tour plus grand que le Soleil / N'auons dans l'univers rien treuué de pareil' [We, who travel a circuit larger than the sun's, haven't found anything similar in the universe] (sig. A3v), the ballet made continual use of solar imagery. The ladies of Marie's court were persistently invoked as suns, and the ballet concluded with the Indian princes' declaration:

> Issus de ces superbes Roys
> Qui ont eu le Soleil pour Pere
> Et de qui les prudentes loix
> Gouuernent tout nostre hemisphere
> Nous venons icy dans ces lieux
> Pour recognoistre dans vos yeux
> Les vrays parens de nostre Ancestre
> Ou pour mieux dire ses pareils
> Car ayant tous eu un mesme estre
> Ils portent comme luy le beau nom de Soleils. (sig. D3r)

[Descendants of those great kings
Whose father was the Sun
And whose prudent laws
Govern all our hemisphere,
We come here to this place
To recognise in your eyes
The true kin of our ancestor
Or, to put it better, his equals,
Because having all had the same origin
They bear like him the lovely name of suns.]

When one considers that the 'princes indiens' of the ballet's title were performed by members of the nobility exiled from France, the ballet's topic begins to have a slight edge. Abandoning their homeland, the dancers prefer to exist in the orbit of the ex-queen regent who is somehow more famous and more noble than other masters. It seems likely that Puget de la Serre's ballet contained coded references to Marie de Médicis's exile, offering both compliment and consolation to the queen and her followers, excluded from their lands, their friends and their offices.

In the light of this, *Luminalia*'s choice of subject is interesting. Veevers has suggested that the references to flamens and arch-flamens in the masque refer to 'the Catholic priests who were dispersed from England, and who now return once more under the protection of the King and Queen'.[24] Given the masque's insistence that the flamens have been forced to 'live in disguises or hide their heads', her argument makes perfect sense. However, the Muses, too, we are told, have been forced to live a peripatetic existence, being continually moved on, even from '*the more civilised parts, where they hoped to have taken some rest*' (lines 23–4). While the association with Catholic priests is a particularly convincing one and entirely appropriate for the flamens, it must be remembered that a significant and militantly Catholic figure was also negotiating to come to England in the winter of 1637/8.

That autumn, the Spanish who, in the words of the Venetian ambassador, were suspicious that Marie de Médicis 'was carrying on secret intrigues with France', thoroughly searched her house in Brussels, 'using such insults and threats as to cause her the greatest agitation'.[25] Henrietta Maria, it was reported, was 'sensible of the affront and deeply sympathises with her mother'.[26] The queen mother's welcome in the Low Countries was obviously wearing thin and overtures were made to England about the possibility of receiving her there. In October, the Venetian ambassador reported that she had 'sent M. de Monsigot, her secretary, here, they say to make arrangements for her coming to this kingdom', but insisted that 'the king has always seemed to object strongly and he will stop it, unless he yields to his wife's prayers'.[27]

Luminalia, with its imagery of light and its tale of the Muses being welcomed into the Garden of the Britanides, seems to speak not only to the queen consort's Catholicism, but also to her desire to see her mother safely established in England. As such, it is an aspect of the 'prayers' she offers up to Charles. Following in the tradition of the *Balet des princes indiens*, Henrietta Maria, the goddess of brightness, takes the place of the Sun. Indeed, as Hesperus sings to Aurora, 'This earthly star, long since the boast of fame, / Is both become his envy and his shame' (lines 282–3). Although the epithet 'Sun-King' is most readily associated with Louis XIV, Henrietta Maria's nephew, the icon of the Sun is easily identifiable with early modern monarchs, and was used on several occasions in connection with Louis XIII.[28] The presence of Vieuville in the production, coupled with Henrietta Maria's evident concerns about her mother's situation, make the association of England with a safe haven a particularly poignant one.

POLITICAL ASYLUM AND THE LAST MASQUE

If *Luminalia* is perhaps more overtly religious than political, then *Salmacida Spolia*, written by Davenant and performed by Charles and Henrietta Maria at Whitehall in January 1640, certainly invokes the problematic figure of the French queen mother. The masque is usually read as a response to the domestic crisis of the Scottish rebellion and to Charles's recall of parliament after eleven years of personal rule: a critical approach that has ensured that discussions of the masque have focused primarily upon the king, seeing *Salmacida Spolia* as a production that spoke to the nation about national concerns. For example, Martin Butler observes that, although the masque's guest of honour and principal spectator was the queen consort's mother, 'it is tempting to suppose that the real audience was the political nation whom Charles needed to convince of his goodwill in the approach to the new parliament'.[29] While I am by no means suggesting that the masque did not engage with such domestic anxieties, a consideration of the largely overlooked presence of Marie de Médicis under the State opens up the production to additional readings which connect *Salmacida Spolia* to Europe, and which, as well as expressing the position of the king, draw attention to the role of his wife. I want to show how *Salmacida Spolia* drew upon imagery promoted of Marie de

Médicis which celebrated her as her husband's support and as an advocate of peace in Europe. However, I will also discuss how the masque registered disquiet about the queen mother's political intriguing, and about her potential for disruption within Charles's kingdom.

Writing in December 1639, Amerigo Salvetti, the Florentine agent in London, remarked that Henrietta Maria was rehearsing 'her' masque to entertain the queen mother at Christmas. In a subsequent letter, he observed:

> The queen's masque goes ahead, with the addition of the person of the king and nine other titled gentlemen who, together with the queen and nine of her ladies, will make up a total of twenty.[30]

These comments indicate that the production was probably first conceived as a queen's masque, and only later extended to include the participation of the king. The king's inclusion was, nonetheless, significant, making this the only occasion on which Charles and Henrietta Maria took to the stage together. Indeed, Butler interprets this dual participation as evidence of what he sees as the masque's reconciliatory agenda, remarking that 'the spectacle of the king and queen dancing among courtiers who favoured accommodation and a parliamentary way was . . . a gesture of royal willingness to build bridges to moderate opinion'.[31] Placing the production within the context of a new parliament and Charles's troubled relationship with the Scots, Butler interrogates *Salmacida Spolia*'s image of a unified 'Great Britain', showing it to be the masque's fantasy.

Nonetheless, despite this sensitivity to tensions within the masque, Butler reads Henrietta Maria's presence on stage as an Amazon and the chorus's address to Marie de Médicis as a fount of royal valour, as unproblematically subtending an image of Charles as a benevolent, but politically determined leader.[32] However, an investigation into the way that the masque made connections between the figures of mother and daughter shows that *Salmacida Spolia* did not just try to create a fantasy about a unified Britain (something which was, of course, an ideologically fraught concept at the time of the performance), but that it was also engaged in the production of a fantasy of genealogical and marital unity. This fantasy was, furthermore, just as problematic as that discussed by Butler. As I will show, the masque registered unmistakable anxieties about female collectivity and about the itinerant and controversial French queen mother.

Marie de Médicis's presence in England in 1640 was largely unwelcome, not least because of her ostentatious Catholicism and her well-publicised pro-Spanish sentiments. *Salmacida Spolia* was, therefore, a masque that had to negotiate a difficult problem. It was performed before and addressed a song directly to the queen mother, but was nonetheless a production which took place in a climate of unease about Marie's political intentions during her stay in England. Performed by both the king and queen, it had to address itself to national concerns. However, it also looked beyond the shores of England to the Europe of the Thirty Years' War, synthesising elements of Marie de Médicis's personal iconography with that of the English royal couple.

*

The masque's links to continental culture are made evident in its structure, and through its borrowings from French and Italian productions. The opening scene drew on a stock motif from French *ballet de cour* when the Fury, Discord, appeared on the stage stating her intention to put the whole of the world into disorder. She was followed by a series of anti-masque grotesques who danced in the manner of a French *ballet à entrées*, thus reinforcing the continental flavour of the production. These anti-masque figures cannot be regarded as a purely domestic phenomenon, yet Sharpe has described them as 'Politic Would-Bes', who are offering absurd proposals for the resolution of the problems of the realm.[33] Nevertheless, some of them, at least, must be seen as the figuration of discord conceived as an international disease that is endangering the nation.

For example, the name of Wolfgangus Vandergoose, the first of the grotesques, may be compared with that of Vangoose, the meddlesome Dutchman of Jonson's *Masque of Augurs* (1622), in a manner which demonstrates the dangerous effects that foreign borrowings can have upon English culture and, consequently, upon the strength of the nation.[34] Vangoose, in the earlier masque, while providing a satirical image of the Dutch, was not, in fact, a Dutchman, but 'a *Britaine* borne, [who had] learn'd to misuse his owne tongue in travell, and now speakes all languages in ill *English*'.[35] In *Salmacida Spolia*, Vandergoose's recipes, intended to cure the defects of nature and the diseases of the mind, actually encouraged the sort of imitative behaviour implicitly criticised in the figure of Vangoose.

To add to the anti-masque's continental connections, Enid Welsford has pointed out that some of Vandergoose's recipes were translated from the French *Ballet de la Foire Saint Germain*, danced in the presence of

Henri IV and Marie de Médicis in 1607.[36] It is interesting to speculate whether they found their way into *Salmacida Spolia* through the influence of the queen mother, or whether they were invoked by Davenant to appeal to her notorious love of burlesque. Whatever their genesis, they demonstrate a direct connection with French court spectacle, showing the masque to be deliberately invoking a continental precedent. However, what is even more intriguing is the fact that three new recipes were joined to those translated from the French *ballet*, all of which invoked aspects of European culture in a derogatory manner. The most striking of them recommended:

> *A gargarism of* Florio's First Fruits, Diana de Montemayor, *and the scraping of Spanish Romanzas distilled* in balneo, *to make a sufficient linguist without travelling or scarce knowing himself what he says.* (lines 206–9)

In keeping with the theme of the masque, which saw a foreign Discord breaching the defences of the realm, this recipe demonstrated that one no longer needed to travel to be infected with continental mannerisms. The masque articulated a view of foreign influence which harked back to Elizabethan anxieties about linguistic borrowing, characterised by worries about the weakening of the sinews of the English language through the use of foreign calques. The entries which followed that of Vandergoose further illustrated this contention about corruption, figuring the adulterous combination of another Dutchman, his wife and her Italian lover, as well as an over-dressed courtier and soldiers, plus the continental figures of pedants of Francolin, some Swiss, and a Spanish Cavallerizzo (lines 219–54). If the riotous confusion of anti-masques in *Salmacida Spolia* was to figure discord, then that discord was conceived as international, not narrowly confined to Britain. The entries were intricately linked to the message of the masque which represented popular rumour as contagiously malicious and evoked the image of Discord arriving from overseas.

As Graham Parry has noted, the Fury's arrival from the sea displaced the threat of disruption on to a foreign body, thus ensuring that there were 'naturally no internal grounds for discontent' within the masque.[37] France had renewed hostilities with Spain in 1635, and the image of the Fury arriving in a storm 'having already put most of the world into disorder' manifestly called to mind the warring factions of Europe. Inigo Jones adapted the masque's first scene from Alfonso Parigi's 'storm scene' in *La Flora* (1628), but added the image of a ship tossed around at sea. Coming soon after the naval battle of the Downs when a Spanish fleet was captured by the Dutch and the Thirty Years' War was brought close to

Britain's shores, this image could not help but evoke European conflict. The protective defences which Peace had charged the gods to provide for Albion at the end of *Albion's Triumph* were breached at the start of *Salmacida Spolia* and concord in England was threatened from outside, thus implicitly locating Charles as one of the last European leaders standing against the Fury's disruption.

Interestingly, Jones's costumes for the Fury were based upon a Nancy entertainment performed for the duchesse de Chevreuse during her exile from France in 1626. Charles IV of Lorraine, the duchess's host, took part in the production which was designed by Jacques Callot and which included the entry of a 'Garrison of Hell', dressed up in fire and flames. This Garrison was accompanied by 'three ladies forming the court of honour for the princess of Hell' whose heads were covered with hissing snakes, and who carried blazing torches and 'vipers and entwined serpents as frightening as their headgear'.[38] The close connection of *Salmacida Spolia*'s Fury with this entertainment is interesting, not only because it demonstrates Marie de Chevreuse's very probable contribution to *Salmacida Spolia*'s design, but also because it joins the masque with another entertainment performed for the exiled duchess. On one hand, it sets up an echo with Marie's honourable reception in Nancy, implicitly allying England with Lorraine against the Richelieu administration that had expelled her from France.[39] On the other, to an observer sceptical of Marie's political activity, it could also imply a connection between the Fury and the duchess herself.

Marie de Médicis, like Chevreuse, was also deeply embroiled in the European turmoil which the masque represented as threatening Charles's kingdom. Indeed, Anzolo Correr, the Venetian ambassador in Paris, reported that the French were convinced that Marie had left Flanders for Britain, 'on purpose to make trouble against this kingdom everywhere'.[40] *Salmacida Spolia*'s figure of Discord was a subversive feminised image, invoked in order to be contained by the king's intelligent, masculine control. However, to an observer of the masque unsympathetic to the predicament of the queen mother, it could not help but evoke the memory of Marie de Médicis's arrival on England's shores in a ship borne across the Channel in a storm. Caroline Hibbard has noted of Marie's entry into London that it was greeted by terrible gales that unsympathetic Londoners dubbed 'queen mother's weather'.[41] Furthermore, in 1638, Lord Feilding received a letter from a foreign correspondent which referred to Marie and her entourage as 'these monsters', while a political squib addressed to the Council in 1639 made a specific equation between

Marie's presence in London and popular discontent over ship money and religious reform.[42]

The image of Discord thus accumulated associations with the itinerant and exiled queen mother, whose presence under the State at the masque's performance, in this context, represented a real danger to the harmony of Charles's nation. Internal discontents were indeed displaced in the masque on to a foreign body arriving from outside, but that foreign body, through its accumulation of associations with Charles's mother-in-law, was also already inside, signalling a domestic threat at the very heart of the king's household. Marie de Médicis therefore posed a central problem for the masque which, constrained by the obligations of deference and hospitality, had to praise her, yet which registered an ambivalence about her influence over her daughter and her potential to destabilise Charles's, and thus Britain's, domestic harmony.

Nevertheless, it was precisely in the terms of domestic harmony that the masque lauded Marie, adopting and mirroring back to her the iconography she encouraged of herself. Writing an open letter in England in 1638 to explain her departure from the Netherlands, the queen mother reflected on her regency, employing concepts of union and concord very similar to those later made integral to the message of *Salmacida Spolia.* She remarked of the renewed hostilities between France and Spain:

> I have ever passionately longed for that Union and Concord between the two Crowns, whereof in former times I had laid the foundations by a double Alliance. And that beside I have alwayes endeavoured since the rupture, to contribute all I was able to the reestablishment of Peace.[43]

During her regency, Marie de Médicis tackled the difficult problem of maintaining peace in Europe by arranging the marriages of her eldest son with Anne of Austria, and her eldest daughter with the future Philip IV of Spain. To celebrate the betrothals she organised a massive Parisian pageant, which Sara Mamone describes as the explicit and spectacular result of her political policy.[44] The pageant's overwhelming design was a celebration of Marie as the bringer of peace and glory to France: she was addressed as the saviour of the French people and the bearer of a wisdom that had averted war.[45] In the years that followed, she promoted an image of herself as the mother of great monarchs and the broker of marriages, and was frequently referred to by court poets as Cybele or as Juno. These divine incarnations, while appropriate for a queen regent who was safeguarding the kingdom for her son, also accorded her a great deal of power, locating her as the source of a godlike race and the bearer of mystical authority. Indeed, as Deborah Marrow remarks, her iconology consistently 'took traditionally female subjects such as marriage and made them metaphors for power, successful rule, and political legitimacy'.[46]

Nowhere was this more evident than in the great project for the renovation of the palais de Luxembourg that Marie began in 1620. The palace was to be a symbol both of Marie's importance within France, and of her genealogical inheritance as a daughter of the Médicis. It was also, through its magnificence and its allegorical decorations, to be a means by which she could consolidate and increase both her cultural and her political influence within Paris. The decorative themes in the Luxembourg all conspired to glorify her success as a ruler, as well as the importance of her family connections. Central to the painted ceilings in her apartments were her coat of arms, or female allegorical figures whose attributes (the caduceus, cornucopia, gold and laurel crowns, steering oar, olive branch and globe) all indicated that they represented good government, peace, prosperity and glory.[47] The queen mother also commissioned two series of massive canvases from Rubens that were to provide a pictorial representation of both her own and her husband's biographies. Only the first series was completed, and included a painting placed above the fireplace in the gallery of the Luxembourg known as 'The Queen Triumphant', 'Minerva Victrix', or 'Marie as Minerva or Bellona'.[48] In it, a helmeted Marie surmounted a pile of armour, while a crown of laurel was held above her head by two cupids. The portrait unmistakably represented the queen as a woman renowned for good government, presenting her with the trappings of victory and immortality. In the fallen arms and armour, there was also, as Marrow observes, 'the strong reference to Maria as a peacemaker'.[49] As I have already noted, the queen's personal iconography situated her as central to the dynastic shape of a peaceful Europe, stressing her overwhelming importance as a mediator between monarchs who were also her relations. It was in precisely those terms that she presented herself in her English letter of 1638, and it was in precisely those terms that *Salmacida Spolia* praised her, locating her as the English queen's mother and the fount of peace.[50]

Salmacida Spolia was so named because its principal motif was the Salmacis spring at Halicarnassus whose pure taste had the ability to civilise barbarian natures. Marie and Henrietta Maria were connected in the masque to this motif, and were represented as spiritually beneficial influences and as the tender supports of their husbands. The masque's subject, its printed text declared, was that the king, 'out of his mercy and clemency' would seek, by all means, 'to reduce tempestuous and turbulent natures into a sweet calm of civil concord' (lines 91–2). This was precisely what the action of the masque proceeded to effect, with Wolfgangus Vandergoose and his riotous companions being 'stopped in their motion by a secret power whose wisdom they tremble[d] at' (lines 6–7). This 'secret power' was incarnated in the body of the king, or 'Philogenes', the 'Lover of his People' (line 12), whose presence mysteriously calmed discord. A chorus of Beloved People then assembled on the stage to sing the praises of both the monarch and his mother-in-law, and the production ended with the descent of Henrietta Maria from heaven in the costume of an Amazon as a reward from Pallas for Philogenes's prudence.

The pacific message of Davenant's masque was underscored by the use of many of the symbolic images favoured by Marie. For example, when the king made his entrance seated in the Throne of Honour, he was surrounded, in a manner reminiscent of Rubens's Luxembourg portrait, by 'captives bound in several postures, lying on trophies of armours, shields, and antique weapons' (lines 310–12). Butler has quite rightly pointed to the ambiguity of this image at a time when many were wondering whether the king was in fact promoting, not harmonious civilisation, but repression.[51] Nevertheless, the image belonged to an established iconological tradition which predominantly associated it with peace, and which had already found favour with the French queen regent. Similarly, *Salmacida Spolia*'s proscenium arch was decorated with icons such as the caduceus, cornucopia and ship's rudder, all of which were to be found in the decorative scheme of the palais de Luxembourg. I do not wish to imply that these images had an exclusive connection with Marie de Médicis since they were widely deployed in Europe as symbols of peace and good government. However, their presence in the masque showed *Salmacida Spolia* to be making use of a common European iconography. They bore witness to the interconnected nature of European monarchical display, recalling productions that had been sponsored both by Marie de Médicis in France and by her relations in Italy. Davenant's masque was not, therefore, a performance pointing ultimately to the 'frightening isolation' of the Stuart court or epitomising a dynasty on the edge of collapse, but was in dialogue with continental forms of monarchical representation, recirculating iconographical images in a manner which connected the English court to Bourbon spectacle in France and to the grand Florentine productions of the Médicis.

In a continuation of the imagery that celebrated Marie as an advocate of peace in Europe, *Salmacida Spolia* constructed her marriage to Henri IV as a blueprint for successful rule. The masque's chorus of Beloved People approached the State and addressed her directly in a song which claimed:

> You, in whose bosom ev'n the chief and best
> Of modern victors laid his weary head
> When he rewarded victories with rest;
> Your beauty kept his valour's flame alive,
> Your Tuscan wisdom taught it how to thrive. (lines 282–6)

The queen mother was located as the spring from which all Great Britain's blessings flowed because she was the mother of 'the fair partner of our monarch's throne' (line 271). Henrietta Maria, who was pregnant at the time of the masque, was the source of 'blessings' (line 270) and 'growing comforts' (line 273) in what was undoubtedly a reference to the royal children and the stability of continuance they represented for the Stuart monarchy. The imagery which presented Marie as the spring which bred Henrietta Maria harked back to the title and controlling adage of the masque. The waters of the fountain of Salmacis, at 'the top of the right horn of the hill which surrounds Halicarnassus', had the ability, we are told, to reduce the barbarous natures of the Carie and Lelegi 'of their own accord to the sweetness of the Grecian customs' (lines 69–77). While the masque explicitly engaged with national concerns, recognising the civil strife with which Charles was faced and the need to find a method for dealing with it, the text made a connection between Marie de Médicis, the fecund Henrietta Maria who was the source of Britain's future health, and the Salmacis fountain whose benefits were to spread peace. Henrietta Maria, in giving rise to the 'comforts' by whom Britain's hopes were 'longer lived' (lines 273–4), thus provided a source of future concord like that offered by the Salmacis spring. In addition, the masque's concluding scene depicted a bridge over a large river, figuring a reconciled nation and drawing the metaphorical water images to their promised conclusion. The masque deployed imagery which connected Marie and Henrietta Maria, promoting women as integral to the generation of national and international harmony. By emulating her mother's role as Henri IV's wife, Henrietta Maria strengthened her husband, who was seen to be striving to maintain England as the last bastion of tranquillity in a sea of European discord.

Furthermore, not only was Marie described in the song as providing comfort for Henri, she was also represented as providing counsel. Indeed, the song's evocation of Marie's Tuscan wisdom might perhaps have brought to mind Machiavelli, another famous Florentine political adviser, whose *Il principe* was written for the Médicis.[52] Marie was linked by implication to a family of leaders and statesmen, her relationship to Henri being represented in a manner reminiscent of the *discordia concors* image of Venus and Mars, figuring the reconciliation of peace with war. The image of the harmonious Stuart marriage was projected back on to the marriage of Henri and Marie, constructing this Bourbon union as a successful historical precedent for Charles's marriage and his method of government. Just as Marie was shown to keep the flame of her husband's valour alive (line 285), so Henrietta Maria was praised in a song which located her as the source from which the valiant took their fire (line 385). A connection was made between mother and daughter and their respective husbands. Through his wife's genealogical connections, Charles was represented as the political heir of Henri and, like that 'chief and best / Of modern victors' (lines 282–3), was imagined be able to produce concord out of chaos.

In an image reminiscent of Plato's divine hermaphrodite, the masque celebrated the king and queen as two parts of one whole, 'tuning [their] thoughts to either's will', until they found 'the good success / Of all [their] virtues in one happiness' (lines 421–38). This image was typical of masque representations of the Caroline couple during the 1630s; as I have said, they were invoked as the joint 'Mary-Charles' in Aurelian Townshend's *Albion's Triumph* (1632) and as 'Carlomaria' in Thomas Carew's *Coelum Britannicum* (1634). However, in *Salmacida Spolia*, the image had a further dimension, linking Henrietta Maria's position as a wife to that of Marie de Médicis. The queen consort, as her mother before her, was her husband's solace and the manifestation of his 'inward helps' (line 340) in an image of incorporation which saw the balancing influence of femininity as integral to good, masculine government. As well as finding a resonance with previous Caroline productions, this was an image that also found echoes in royal French iconography. As Orgel has shown, and as I have discussed, François I and Henri II often made use of this notion of balance, depicting themselves, not as gods, but as goddesses, with the cross-dressed image of François accompanied by the motto: 'the king is a Mars in war, a Minerva or Diana in peace'.[53] *Salmacida Spolia*'s representations of Marie de Médicis and Henrietta Maria located them within this tradition where they became synonymous with balanced and harmonious rule, acting as their husbands' feminised other selves and tempering confrontational masculine tendencies with feminine softness and the promise of peace.

Interestingly, Henrietta Maria's entry on to the masquing stage occurred during the chorus's recitation of a song to the king, which concluded with the lines:

> Since strength of virtues gained you Honour's throne,
> Accept our wonder and enjoy your praise!
> He's fit to govern there and rule alone
> Whom inward helps, not outward force, doth raise. (lines 337–40)

The queen consort's appearance in Amazonian dress positioned her, at this moment, almost as the incarnation of the king's 'inward helps'. In fact, the masque presented her as her husband's spiritual support in a manner similar to that exemplified in Lenton's *Great Britain's Beauties*, a series of anagrams and acrostics based on the names of *Luminalia*'s lady masquers, which played upon the women's 'natural' identities, locating them above all as chaste, religious and virtuous. Female heroism was conceived in this work to operate exclusively in the service of the women's husbands: the duchess of Lennox, for example, was represented as a 'trusty arme' who was to provide a 'safeguard, or defence' for her husband.[54] In other words, she was to be her husband's domestic and spiritual helpmate in the same way that Henrietta Maria, in Davenant's masque, was to be a reward for the king's heroic endeavours. Although Charles appeared on the masquing stage surrounded by the trappings of physical combat, his victories were represented primarily as spiritual ones: inspired by his virtuous wife, he was shown to reform malevolent discord through educative example.

The costumes for Henrietta Maria and her ladies in *Salmacida Spolia* reinforced the propriety of their Amazonian incarnations. Unlike the dresses designed for Queen Anna in the *Masque of Queens* which were diaphanous and revealed the dancers' ankles, Henrietta Maria's costumes reached to the floor, had excessively high collars and covered the masquers' arms to the wrists.[55] Their design was modelled on the fashion of the day, its only concessions to the Amazonian theme being the addition of a plumed helmet and a baldric slung diagonally across the breast. Paradoxically, though, this intense conservatism gave force to the Amazonian motif, focusing attention on the costumes' serious nature, rather than on the deliberate transgression of sartorial codes. The queen's relatively sober appearance befitted her status as the reward for Charles's virtue, yet it also imported the trappings of war on to the stage. Just as the image of the king surrounded by weapons in the Throne of Honour expressed a certain ambiguity of intent, so Henrietta Maria's Amazonian incarnation produced a moment in which the masque's ostensible pacific meanings confronted the reality of the royal couple's less-than-pacific agenda.

Salmacida Spolia's representation of the queen consort as an Amazon shadowed her active support of Charles's martial intentions. By 1640, under the influence of her mother and friends, Henrietta Maria had swung away from her previous Protestant affiliations and was endorsing a pro-Spanish and very Catholic policy. To bolster the king's straitened exchequer, she endorsed letters to English Catholics, exhorting them to contribute funds to the war effort. The masque's representation of her as a warrior maiden thus reflected her interest in her husband's martial intentions, while her relationship with the other lady masquers provided evidence of the Catholic bias of her group. The women who danced in the masque were faithful members of her circle, so much so that the earl of Northumberland, an anti-Spanish Protestant whose credit with the queen was on the wane, wrote sourly to his sister:

> A company of worse faces did I never see assembled than the Queen has got together upon this occasion; not one new woman amongst them. Lady Carnarvon conditioned, before she would promise to be of the mask, that it should not be danced upon a Sunday, for she is now grown so devout by conversing with Lord Powis and the doctor that now she will neither dance nor see a play upon the Sabbath.[56]

Butler implies that Lady Carnarvon's was a strongly Protestant outlook by suggesting that her religious affiliations probably mirrored the sympathies of her father, a future member of Cromwell's Council of State.[57] However, she was married to the son of an 'absolute recusant', Alice, daughter of Sir Richard Molyneux of Sefton, and her husband, Robert Dormer, figures in the list of Catholics who fell in Charles's cause. Most interestingly, Percy Herbert, the Lord Powis with whom Northumberland records her conversing, was, in 1639, one of the collectors of the Catholics' money for the war against the Scots.[58] There is, therefore, a connection between at least one of Henrietta Maria's lady masquers and her political associates. Among the other masquers, the countess of Portland, wife of Henrietta Maria's old opponent, Weston, had long supported Spanish Catholicism, while the countess of Newport created a scandal at court by converting from Protestantism in the mid 1630s. The duchess of Lennox and Lady Kinalmeaky were both members of the Villiers clan, whose allegiances with Protestantism were not at all clear: the duchess's grandmother, the duke of Buckingham's mother, had strongly Catholic predilections, while Buckingham's sister, Lady Kinalmeaky, converted to Catholicism while in exile in France with the queen. Henrietta Maria's Amazonian costume could, therefore, be read either as the visual representation of her role as Charles's spiritual support, or as a reference to her complicity in his attempts to finance a war.

The courtly Catholicism focused around the queen consort was precisely that to which many of Charles's opponents took exception, castigating it as foreign and dangerous. Although Henrietta Maria's presence in Davenant's masque did seem to confront and annul the threat of Discord, contrasting a civilised female figure with the Fury's uncontrollably wandering body, the potential parallels between the latter and the itinerant Marie de Médicis complicated this association, encoding a profound distrust of foreign influence, conceived as feminine. The subversive Fury dangerously oversignified in a manner which destabilised the symbolic roots of the masque text and which gestured to an anxiety about the failure of monarchical (and masculine) control. When Discord appeared on the masque's stage, she expressed an envious malice towards Britain's 'full body, overgrown with peace' (line 120), remarking that the country's 'long health' would never be altered except by its 'surfeits on felicity' (lines 117–18). The image of the country's full body was evocative of Henrietta Maria's pregnancy, while the masque's representation of the queen consort as the source of the country's 'growing comforts' (line 273) associated her with the felicity Discord declared would be the nation's downfall. Rather than being the means through which the masque contained the Fury's destabilising potential, *Salmacida Spolia* unconsciously suggested that Charles and Henrietta Maria's marriage contributed to the nation's disorder: the already problematic concept of a unified Great Britain was endangered precisely because of the unity of the royal couple. Certainly, the masque's articulation of the queen consort's neo-Platonic fashion located her as the helpmate of her husband, diffusing a civilised and ordered influence over the court and country. However, it also engaged with anxieties about women's place as central to generation, and gestured to a concern about female activity that saw it endangering, or usurping, man's control.

Salmacida Spolia's title and controlling adage were associated with not one, but two, mythological histories which invoked images of emasculation and the female appropriation of power. The masque made reference both to the Ovidian story of Salmacis and Hermaphroditus, and also, obliquely, to the myth of Artemisia and Mausolus. These references undercut the masque's spiritualised image of perfect marital unity, recalling Richelieu's comments about the weakness of Charles's method of government, and pre-empting civil-war polemic which represented the king as swayed by the malignant influence of his wife. The hermaphroditic image of the king and queen as complementary parts, effecting the concord expressed by the Salmacis fountain, could not help but invoke that fountain's mythological origins which were rooted in an anxiety about female sexuality and desire. In the Ovidian story, the nymph Salmacis fell in love with Hermaphroditus, embraced him while he was swimming in her spring and prayed that nothing would ever part them. Their bodies blended together and, as George Sandys translated in 1632, Hermaphroditus prayed in horror to his parents, 'May every man, that in this water swims, / Returne halfe-woman, with infeebled lims'.[59] *Salmacida Spolia*'s representation of the Salmacis fountain as a source of civil concord at once coincided with courtly neo-Platonism's insistence on women's civilising influence over men, yet also registered unease about feminine influence because of the emasculatory horror evinced by the myth's origins. Henrietta Maria, conceived as the spring giving rise to the nation's hopes, shared the spring's apparently beneficial attributes, yet her Amazonian appearance in the masque permeated *Salmacida Spolia*'s mythological unconscious and gave rise to an image of femininity which endangered masculine power.

Henrietta Maria's appearance as an Amazon also linked her to an iconological history of illustrious heroines, invoked poetically as paragons in order to celebrate powerful women. Jonson's *Masque of Queens* had conjured up such a gallery of women on the English court stage in 1609 when Anna and her ladies danced in the guises of, among others, Penthesilea, Thomyris and Artemisia.[60] Later, in France, Marie de Médicis commissioned a series of eight statues for the dome of the palais de Luxembourg which were to depict illustrious women, and was famously painted by Rubens in Amazonian costume as Minerva. Following in this tradition, Davenant, *Salmacida Spolia*'s poet, celebrated Henrietta Maria in a poem which imagined her to be attended by Thomyris, Penelope and Artemisia.[61]

This poem, entitled 'To The Queene', declared it would celebrate her 'Royall Lover' through a comparison with the Roman emperor 'Julius, who had thoughts so high / They humble seem'd when th'aimed at victorie' (line 64 and lines 57–8). Julius was represented as the archetypal philosopher king, 'In anger valiant, gently calme in love' (line 61), an image proleptic of the manner in which *Salmacida Spolia* represented Charles. However, interestingly, Orpheus, the narrator of the poem, told the queen he would have occasion to make the comparison between her royal lover and Julius 'when / The Destinies are so much vex'd with Men / That the just God-like Monarch of your brest / Is ripe, and fit to take eternall rest' (lines 49–52). The language here is reminiscent of the language used in *Salmacida Spolia* to figure the relationship between the widowed queen mother and Henri IV. Furthermore, the proximity in the poem of the image of Artemisia, 'whom Truths best Record / Declar'd a living Tomb unto her Lord' (line 48), to the imagined death of the queen's royal lover, invoked the possibility that a husband's spirit could be absorbed within the body of his wife.

Artemisia was a queen of Caria who married Mausolus, her brother, and was renowned for her valour in battle. One version of her story maintained that, after her husband's death, she dissolved his ashes and drank them. Thus, she became his living tomb and might also be said to have absorbed Mausolus's masculine qualities and martial courage in an image of consumption that saw her literally becoming one with her husband. She erected a magnificent monument to Mausolus's memory at Halicarnassus, which is, very significantly, the place *Salmacida Spolia* invokes as the site of the Salmacis spring.

Sheila ffolliot has investigated the powerful Artemisian iconography which was developed by Nicolas Houel in 1562 for the French queen regent, Catherine de Médicis, commenting that Artemisia proved the perfect prototype for Catherine 'in that she both dramatically mourned the loss of her husband – the rightful monarch – and stood as an authoritative ruler in his stead'.[62] Fifty-nine cartoons were designed for tapestries, but the queen's financial constraints probably forced her to spend her money elsewhere and there is no firm evidence to show the tapestries were ever woven. However, the cartoons made a sufficient impact on Marie de Médicis and Anne of Austria that these two French queens regent had tapestries made, attesting to the success of Artemisia as a prototype. However, the figure of Artemisia was explicitly excluded by Marie's advisers from the list of statues of illustrious women proposed in the 1620s for the palais de Luxembourg because of the fear that its inclusion might provoke adverse criticism. Artemisia's most laudable action was to provide a sepulchre for her husband, 'something which', as Rubens was informed, '[the Queen Regent] has never wished to think about'.[63] Marie, though (adopting the alternative version of the Artemisia story), liked to represent herself as Henri's living tomb, writing of her welcome into England in 1638 that 'those things, which were prepared for my delight . . . made me thinke, that the late King, my lord, appeared yet living in my person'.[64] Marrow has also noted contemporary French comments that observed Marie de Médicis 'embodied Henri's mausoleum'.[65] Marie adopted the idea of Artemisia's physical incorporation of her husband's body to legitimise her use of monarchical power in a state operating under Salic law. Perhaps Artemisia's exclusion from the plan for the Luxembourg sculptures can also be explained by the subversive connotations her story accrued when associated with the politically ambitious Florentine.

Salmacida Spolia's controlling device, the Salmacis fountain at Halicarnassus, was located in the region once presided over by the widowed Artemisia. Henrietta Maria's entry on to the masquing stage as an Amazon replicated the image invoked of her in Davenant's poem 'To The Queene', and situated her within a mythological history of warrior women and faithful wives. A reading of *Salmacida Spolia* undertaken with an awareness of the queen mother's presence reveals internal connections within the masque linking Marie de Médicis to her daughter through a replication of the imagery in which they were figured, and also uncovers a strand of images which have a connection with Marie's personal iconography and with the iconography adopted by a succession of French queens regent. While the masque overtly represented Henrietta Maria and Marie as the virtuous supports of their respective husbands, it also registered an anxiety about Henrietta Maria's connection to her mother, manifested in the masque's margins which were full of histories of the absorption and incorporation of the masculine.

Henrietta Maria's appearance on stage as an Amazon at once visibly located her as her husband's support in a synthesis of her neo-Platonic spirituality with Charles's British heroism. However, it also linked her to a history of powerful women and to the imagery promoted by Marie de Médicis of herself as queen regent. By comparing the Caroline marriage to the marriage of Henri IV and Marie, the masque had to confront the problem that Henri was dead, and that Marie ruled in his stead. The links between Marie and her daughter threatened to marginalise Charles and to divert from the king the loyalty owed to him by his wife. The image of Marie as a detested and disruptive mother-in-law, as well as an itinerant exile within Europe, haunted *Salmacida Spolia*, at the same time as the masque lauded the French queen mother for her familial connections with the Stuart court and replicated her ideas about the propagation of peace through marriage and generation.

CHAPTER 10

'Tyer'd, in her Banish'd dress': Henrietta Maria in exile

I began this book by discussing how critical interpretations of Henrietta Maria's cultural patronage have tended to marginalise the queen consort as a frivolous lightweight, rendering her contributions to Caroline court theatre virtually invisible. However, if her cultural influence is barely apparent in modern histories of the 1630s, then it is even less easy to detect in critical studies of the civil wars. Most notably, after 1644, when Henrietta Maria escaped to France, her presence in historical accounts becomes nearly indiscernible. While recent studies have begun to investigate her activities in England and Holland during the war, nobody has yet attempted an analysis of her years in exile. Veevers's study of her theatrical productions is concerned solely with the glamour years of the Caroline court, while Leslie Hotson's and Alfred Harbage's works touch only briefly upon the Stuart exiles, and then in the context of Prince Charles. Nevertheless, apart from two relatively short returns to London in 1660 and 1662, Henrietta Maria lived the last twenty-five years of her life in France. It is staggering that this time has been ignored by historians and critics, almost as if, as in *The Shepherds' Paradise*, a woman over the age of thirty is no longer worth considering. To conclude, then, I wish to begin an investigation into the years between the outbreak of war and Henrietta Maria's death in 1669.

PARLIAMENT AND THE AMAZONS

Lois Potter's work on the royalist literature of the interregnum proposes that the genre of pastoral romance, popular among courtiers in the 1630s, became politicised during the civil wars, remarking:

> In defending the role of women and of the private life, romance allows the major religious differences between the king and queen, and the hostility between their two countries, to be glossed over by the myth of a love which transcends conflict.

Those who attack romance want that conflict to be fought out openly, not transcended.[1]

Potter comments that the assumption of pastoral pseudonyms by royalist supporters like Sir John Berkenhead (Cratander) and Katherine Phillips (Orinda) was not just the collective indulgence of a fantasy, but the declaration of a serious political position.[2] Her work is important because it introduces a consideration of literary forms into historical discussions of the civil wars, making evident the cultural polarisation between a ruling élite that celebrated theatrical performance and a parliament that banned it.

Potter also makes the observation that Henrietta Maria's civil-war letters to Charles showed that she saw herself as an heroic female warrior like the Amazon she enacted in *Salmacida Spolia*, concluding that it 'was the visibility of women on the royalist side, as much as their actions, that inspired hostility from parliamentarians'.[3] Indeed, in 1642, the pro-parliamentarian news sheet, *The Scots Scouts Discoveries*, announced disparagingly that,

since the King's departure from *London, Whitehall* is become an *Amazonian Castle, St James* [Marie de Médicis's lodgings] an hospital for Strangers, *Somerset House* a Catholicke Colledge, *Westminster*, a receptacle for Seminary Priests and Jesuits.[4]

This comment makes evident the anxieties underlying *Salmacida Spolia* that would become increasingly apparent in parliamentarian rhetoric in the 1640s. The king's absence (whether through physical distance or psychological weakness) engenders a coalition that is female, foreign and Catholic, and which invades the English landscape much as, in 1628, Henrietta Maria's turreted tents surrounded Wellingborough with images of a French invasion. Just as then, the representation of the queen consort as an Amazon is paradoxical: for some, her actions and her links to international Catholicism provide a sign of Charles's uxorious weakness; for others, the king's martial wife could be interpreted as a sign of his heroic mastery through her position as (to co-opt Francis Lenton's phrase) his loving, 'trusty arme'.[5]

Sophie Tomlinson, expanding on Potter's ideas, has remarked that Henrietta Maria's actions at the start of the civil wars saw her 'drawing on a discourse of female performance that her acting helped to set in motion', noting that when the queen consort travelled into Holland like a lady-errant to pawn her jewels and raise money for the war effort, the letters she wrote to Charles showed that she was ironically aware of the role she was playing as a 'she-majesty generalissima'.[6] In part, this is certainly true. Madame de Motteville, one of the French Queen Anne's ladies in waiting and Henrietta Maria's confidante, later described her in even more resonant terms as a princess 'qui paroissoit plutôt une misérable héroïne de roman qu'une reine véritable' [who seemed more an unfortunate romance heroine than a true queen], demonstrating how Henrietta Maria's wartime activities were understood by some in the terms of romance.[7] As Tomlinson notes, this move provides women with a means of representing female military action. However, it also romanticises and contains the reality of conflict, distancing it and, perhaps, rendering its horrors more comprehensible.

Interestingly, Henrietta Maria's military activities were also invoked in 1669 by the prelate Jacques Bossuet in his funeral oration for the queen.[8] Speaking of her stormy sea crossing to England from Holland, he praised her steadfastness and the manner in which she encouraged all who accompanied her to trust in God, before describing how,

> Elle marche comme un général à la tête d'une armée royale, pour traverser des provinces que les rebelles tenaient presque toutes; elle assiege et prend d'assaut en passant une place considérable qui s'opposait à sa marche, elle triomphe, elle pardonne.[9]
>
> [She marched like a general at the head of a royal army to cross regions held almost entirely by the rebels; she besieged and took by force a substantial place that opposed her march. She was triumphant and she pardoned.]

In Bossuet's hands, Henrietta Maria's military actions take on the colour of a religious crusade in which the Catholic queen triumphs over apostate rebels before showing her magnanimity in pardoning them. Furthermore, he places responsibility for the royalists' defeat firmly at the feet of the king and his advisers when he notes that, had the queen's army marched directly upon London as she counselled, rather than being divided and sent to Hull and Gloucester, 'cette campagne eût fini la guerre' [this campaign would have finished the war].[10] Division breeds discord, Bossuet notes, remarking:

> Il est visible que, puisque la séparation et la révolte contre l'autorité de l'Eglise a été la source d'où sont dérivés tous les maux, on n'en trouvera jamais les remèdes que par le retour à l'unité et par la soumission ancienne.[11]
>
> [It is obvious that, since the separation from and the revolt against the authority of the Church was the source of all these ills, remedies will never be found except by the return to unity and by reversion to the old ways.]

Bossuet places unity at the centre of an harmonious state in a manner predicated upon the Caroline iconography of the royal union, locating Henrietta Maria as an Esther and invoking the conversionary hopes that accompanied her marriage in 1625.[12] She was right, he says, to judge that there was no way of removing the causes of the civil wars except through a return to the 'unité catholique'.[13] In the light of his oration, Henrietta Maria's civil-war letters do not just draw on the discourse of female performance made available by her dramatic activities, they also make use of a religious vocabulary to validate her intervention in the conflict.

This strategy finds its analogy in the neo-Platonic conceit of steadfast feminine constancy articulated in the queen consort's masques and pastorals, presenting her as an active agent and locating her as her husband's support and inspiration. For example, writing from the Hague in 1642, Henrietta Maria exhorted Charles to fight, declaring that if she pawned all her jewels and he did nothing both the cause and the jewels would be lost. She urged him not to hold back from action until parliament declared war, because by then he would have consumed ('aurés mangé') all the money she had raised.[14] This notion of consumption appears forcefully in her correspondence with Charles, serving at once to urge the king to war, to demonstrate her selfless devotion to her husband and to emphasise that she, at least, is aware of their straitened circumstances.[15] The letters represent her as a provider and Charles as a passive consumer in a manner which upturns conventional gendered hierarchies and which carries with it the ominous subtext that the king is no longer capable of looking after either his wife or his affairs: Charles is located in the letters as the devourer of his wife's jewels, of her actions, her writing and ultimately of her life force.

The king's perceived inadequacies lead, in the letters, to the repeated assertion that Henrietta Maria will be forced to put herself into a convent if he does not act appropriately.[16] Writing to him in May 1642, she asserted:

Je vois que je seray contrainte par mes malheurs de me retirer en un lieu, pour prier Dieu pour vous . . . [si vous avés passé le *bill de la milice*] il fault songer à s'en aller pour ce temps à couvert, car vous n'este plus capable de protéger personnne, pas mesme vous.[17]

[I see I shall be constrained by my misfortunes, to retire to some place where I can pray to God for you . . . [If you have passed the militia bill], I must think about retiring for the present, into a convent, for you are no longer capable of protecting any one, not even yourself.[18]]

The queen consort's projected flight lays down a challenge to her husband, denying him access to her body and implying that she needs the protection of a convent because the protection he offers is not sufficient. However, this is not just a functional solution to her financial problems and separation from Charles, but a rhetorical motif that draws on Catholic theology and on the neo-Platonic ideas developed in her pastorals. Both *Artenice* and *The Shepherds' Paradise* contained convent-like spaces which provided temporary sanctuaries for their heroines. By asserting her intention to put herself into a convent, Henrietta Maria acts like a troubled shepherdess fleeing to a chaste sanctuary in order to be protected from the vagaries of the world. Indeed, she makes this comparison explicit when she writes:

> Adieu, la royauté! Il n'y en a plus du tout pour moy: je suis résolue de tout souffrir et de vivre en lieu, où je me croiray une damoiselle des champs, et vous laisseray suivre les conseils de ceux qui sont plus sages que moy, comme ils croient; j'oserois dire, pour le moins, plus fins.[19]
>
> [Adieu royalty. There is no more of it at all for me; I am resolved to bear all, and to live in some place where I shall fancy myself a country girl, and leave you to follow the counsel of those who are wiser than I, as they think. I would venture at least to say, they are more cunning.[20]]

Motifs from the pastorals appear in Henrietta Maria's letters as metaphors which allow her to explore and express her situation. By recalling a pastoral idyll ('some place where I shall fancy myself a country girl'), she makes an appeal to a discourse which endowed her with influence, reminding her husband of her objectivity and social efficacy, both through the sardonic comment, 'as they think', and through her use of the pastoral metaphor itself. In addition, her comment that Charles's advisers are 'cunning' draws upon the idea (expressed in *The Shepherds' Paradise*) that men are more self-interested than women. Not only does the letter locate Henrietta Maria as her husband's most faithful adviser because of the love she bears him, it allows her to inhabit a position of selflessness and disinterested objectivity because of her gender.

This disinterested objectivity, while asserting that women are properly political, paradoxically dislocates them from the political world. In her letters, Henrietta Maria constantly insists that, without the presence of her husband, the world has no meaning or place for her. Worldly instability, therefore, becomes juxtaposed against the queen consort's resolution to enter a convent, yet this is less a declaration of feminine weakness than an assertion of spiritual strength. Just as Bossuet's funeral oration would locate strength in unity, her professed desire to enter a convent demonstrates that her faith is stronger than the schismatic beliefs of her husband: Charles is weak because the English have broken with the true Church; Henrietta Maria is constant because she submits to the only true religion. Her spiritual constancy enables her to know herself, to recognise evil and to remain strong. By following his wife's example (and her advice), the vacillating Charles will be strengthened and drawn to success.

It was precisely this vocabulary of active femininity to which parliamentarian polemicists took exception when the royal couple's correspondence was seized at Naseby in 1645. Charles and Henrietta Maria's letters were annotated and published in a tract entitled *The Kings Cabinet Opened* in a manner that condemned the emasculatory role the queen was believed to have had over her husband. Drawing attention to Henrietta Maria's religion, the tract announced:

> It is plain, here, first, that the King's Counsels are wholly governed by the queen; though she be of the weaker sex, born an alien, bred up in a contrary religion . . . He seems more zealous for bishops and papists (called his and the queen's friends) than the queen herself.[21]

Henrietta Maria's influence over Charles is not only deemed to be emasculating in itself, but leads him to support an emasculating religion. The annotation to *The Kings Cabinet Opened* becomes a religious exhortation, locating Protestantism and the parliamentary cause as the only true, uncorrupted and, indeed, masculine positions. The tract places itself beyond the false spectacle of Catholicism and laments the fact that the king has been corrupted by his wife's maleficent and theatrical faith. In a very specific example of the ideological conflict being played out, *The Kings Cabinet Opened* demonstrates how the vocabulary of the queen's pastorals and the possibilities for female action that they opened up were condemned by the Protestant opposition.

Diane Purkiss has proposed that the association of female power with emasculation, when applied to the relationship between Charles and Henrietta Maria, suggested that the queen's power in public affairs was a dubious by-product of Charles's failure to enact his proper role.[22] Parliamentary critics of Charles invoked just such a fear of the eclipse of the king by the seductive counsels of his wife. For example, a tract entitled, *The Great Eclipse of the Sun, or Charles His Waine Over-clouded* (1644), reappropriated the cosmological imagery of government propounded in court masques, comparing the commonwealth to the globe of the heavens whose sun was the king and whose bright stars were parliament.[23]

The tract presents Charles as a king eclipsed by the counsel of 'this Popish Plannet, the Queen', who, 'under the Royall Curtaines', has persuaded him 'to advance the Plots of the Catholickes'.[24] The queen, it is asserted, has persuaded Charles that darkness is light and that it is better to be a papist than a Protestant. Her influence is coloured by a subversive sexuality that binds Charles to her will, upsetting the natural flow of authority through the kingdom. The tract does not seek radically to depose the king, just to divorce him from the influence of evil counsellors and from his devotion to his Catholic wife.

Similarly, *Tyrannicall-Government Anatomized*, an anonymous pamphlet play authorised for publication by parliament in 1642, paints a picture of evil counsel and maleficent female influence that is particularly interesting if compared with Montagu's *The Shepherds' Paradise*. In the queen consort's play, the court lady Fidamira exerts a beneficent influence over the corrupt King of Castile, purifying him through her example and thus encouraging him to govern properly. However, although Fidamira is the vehicle of the king's salvation, she also initiates his fall. Castile has been contaminated by a physical desire for the young woman which affects his ability to govern himself and, implicitly, his ability to govern the nation. Fidamira's justification to herself for her flight from the king's corrupt court therefore encodes the possibility that feminine beauty can un-king a king, dislocating him from his reason and opening up the threat of irrationality and tyranny. She says:

> he spoke with such a degradation of himself, as if he meant to aske som what, which would not sute with the divine Image; and therefore did depose himselfe from being King to make himselfe all man for his pretention: such preposterous humility to me could imply no lesse, though yet his words have had no other guilt then his submission. And I am bound in sense of all his gracious care, to provide against the perversion of all this into his sin. And to secure his innocence even by my hazard.[25]

Fidamira's influence over the king causes the rupture of the concept of his two bodies as the temporal man's mortal desires divorce him from the transcendental notion of divine kingship. The king deposes himself and is thus a traitor to himself, the monarchy and the state. Although Fidamira risks herself and her own reputation to secure the king's, her words describe a process suspiciously reminiscent of the Fall. However unwittingly, she has provided a temptation too great for her master to resist and, paradoxically, stands both as a 'desexualised bestower of good' and as an Eve suborning Adam.[26]

Tyrannicall-Government Anatomized capitalises on this female threat: the similarities between its representation of women and the anxieties about Fidamira in *The Shepherds' Paradise* not only make evident Henrietta Maria's own dangerous potential in the eyes of Protestant polemicists, but also evince anxieties about her neo-Platonic fashion as a whole.[27] The play presents Herod as a well-intentioned king who is unhappily influenced by both his wife and his daughter. The women act in concert to gain John the Baptist's decapitation: Herod's daughter, advised by her mother, begging this boon from her father as a reward for her part in a dancing display. Female publicity therefore becomes equated with female unruliness, subverting the order of society and inspiring women to develop voracious political ambition. Herod, cornered into promoting the tyrannous desires of the women and thus no longer revered by his people, is toppled from his pre-eminent position. Indeed, the very structure of society is shown to be crumbling, as the Chorus concludes in its address to the city 'where King *David* reign'd':

> no Godly zeale perswades the Churchman to restraine his hand from horrible deceits, the people now forsake the Lord, that all things did create, and worship Idols for God, stone and wood . . . The barbarous foe, shall all thy Buildings, Farmes and Lands possess; The Vineyard Keeper shall repaire his fruit to an Out-landish Master . . . O therefore, while Gods favour to repent affords thee respit of thy ill-past life the sinnes forsaking, utterly amove those fruitless Images of forreigne Rites.[28]

When the king, as head of the Church, is corrupted, the Church itself becomes corrupt. This leads to the construction of false gods, which, for militant Protestants, was inevitably analogous with the worship of the 'wooden saints' of Catholicism.[29] Such idolatry then lays the nation open to invasion by 'Out-landish' masters who are alien in both their persons and their practices, diluting the identity of the realm and rendering it a vassal to foreign powers. In sum, in *Tyrannicall-Government Anatomized*, Herod's disastrous regime is directly equated with the maleficent influence wielded by his wife, and the king's selfish absolutism is, interestingly, displaced on to the queen in a manner that renders her, rather than her husband, the tyrant. Herod might be weak (a damning enough indictment), but he is not beyond salvation: he simply needs to benefit from the advice of judicious, rational, male counsellors in order to reaffirm his links with the political realm.

The play makes a specific equation between a queen, female dancing and false religion, the direct result of which is the realm's colonisation by an idolatrous faith. As I discussed in chapter 5, these connections were strongly present in the mid 1630s in the minds of Protestants like Nathaniel Richards and William Prynne, the latter of whom described actors as 'dissolute in their lives, which drawes them on to a dissolute Religion; the most of our present English Actors . . . being professed Papists'.[30] Henrietta Maria, as a Catholic, was always already a traitor to England because of the allegiance she owed to a foreign power; as a Catholic who wantonly displayed herself upon the court stage, she was doubly problematic because she ignored Biblical injunctions which located her as the inarticulate adjunct of her husband. Her theatrical articulacy was indelibly linked in the minds of her detractors with her religion and this, together with her neo-Platonic social fashion, became the prime image of her corruption in the hands of parliament.

Indeed, even in the 1650s, Andrew Marvell's 'Upon Appleton House', written while the poet was in the employ of the parliamentarian general Fairfax, represented Catholicism in suspiciously neo-Platonic terms. The '*Suttle Nunns*' of Nun Appleton weave tales to tempt the virgin Thwaites to join their community of '*Virgin-Amazons*', offering a vision of female power within which each woman is 'a *Spouse*, and each a *Queen*' (lines 106 and 118). Thwaites is wooed with a tale of the power her beauty would accord her in the exclusively feminine economy of the convent: 'so already consecrate', it should draw her to the service of religion, demanding honourable service from Fairfax as her '*Devoto*', not her '*Love*' (lines 146 and 152). Thwaites's beauty makes her the most fit person to draw the other nuns 'to perfection', and it is this, she is told, that will eventually establish her as abbess (lines 163–4). Like Bellessa's inauguration as queen of the Shepherds' Paradise, Thwaites will be elected by the consensus of her peers. Moreover, her beauty, able to inspire spirituality in others, should, for honour's sake, demand the chaste service of a male admirer just as Henrietta Maria's masques and plays exhorted men to adore the queen. 'Upon Appleton House' demonises the pre-Reformation nuns in terms which, whether consciously or unconsciously, also demonise the court culture associated with Henrietta Maria, demonstrating the apparently irreconcilable cultural differences between the royalist Amazons and those who sided with parliament in the 1640s and 50s.

SHARING IN HER DISEASE: THE QUEEN'S COURT IN EXILE

In 1644, Henrietta Maria fled from England back to the country that had nourished her taste for theatre and whose principal religion was her own. Arriving in Paris, she was lodged at the Louvre, a pension was accorded her by Louis XIV and she was given her childhood home of St Germain-en-Laye as a country residence. From the thirty furnished rooms made available to her, it would appear that she arrived in France with a significant number of her household officers, a fact corroborated by her niece, Mademoiselle de Montpensier, who commented of her arrival that 'Elle parut durant quelques mois en équipage de reine; elle avoit avec elle beaucoup de dames de qualité, des filles d'honneur, des carrosses, des gardes, des valets de pieds' [she appeared, for a little while, with the splendour of a royal equipage; she had a full number of ladies, of maids of honour, of running footmen, coaches and guards].[31] Nonetheless, as time went on, her entourage diminished, until, as Montpensier explained, 'rien ne fut plus éloigné de sa dignité que son train et son ordinaire' [at last nothing could be more mean than her train and appearance].[32]

Agnes Strickland has remarked that Henrietta Maria was generously provided for by her French relations until 'the civil war of the Fronde reduced them all to similar destitution'.[33] However, she notes that the queen sold everything she could and sent it 'to her suffering husband', thus exacerbating her financial position. Henrietta Maria was certainly awarded a pension by Louis XIV that amounted to 30,000 livres, or 10–12,000 écus a month.[34] This figure is borne out by the accounts of Sir Richard Forster, her treasurer, which contain receipts for payment of the monies. Forster's accounts also reveal that the queen periodically received other sums of money from the French government and was entitled to 72,000 livres a year from the entrance fees levied at the gates of villages around Paris, such as Melun and Meaux.[35] Nonetheless, she was already heavily in debt: a fact borne out by a memo prepared by Forster for the French financier Thomas Cantarini, which specified he was owed 350,000 livres by the English royal family.[36]

Although the accumulation of large debts was an occupational hazard for the crown even during peacetime, it is obvious that Henrietta Maria was trading precariously on her royal status and needed to remain credible in the face of her financiers. Appearances were paramount, not only for the queen, but for the courtiers who depended upon her. In 1646, for example, Endymion Porter famously lamented to Secretary Nicholas that he had been reduced to borrowing money from his barber, complaining: 'I am so retired into the streets of a suburb that I scarce know what they do at the Louvre, and I want Clothes for a Court, having but that poor riding suit I came out of England in.'[37] To be taken seriously, one had to look the part and, although some of his subsequent letters indicate that Porter did attend upon the queen, he found little favour with her and was finally forced to leave Paris when his credit dried up. Henrietta Maria was able to assist some of her faithful adherents, paying £2,000 to William Cavendish, earl of Newcastle, in partial return for a loan, but the poverty of the exiled English court was acute and is invoked in Thomas Killigrew's 1654 play, *Thomaso, or the Wanderer*, which describes the Louvre and the Palais Royal, to which Henrietta Maria moved in 1652, as 'sad enchanted castles' and 'a nest of poverty', where 'darkness' and 'leanness' reign.[38] The queen was surrounded, not only by her own household, but by many other English nobles, all exiled to France because of their adherence to the royalist cause and all consequently feeling that she owed them support. Indeed, it is just this situation that is invoked in a play written by Cosmo Manuche, a captain and major of foot in the royalist army, on the eve of Charles II's restoration. His manuscript pastoral, 'The Banished Shepherdess', very interestingly recycles elements from the court literature of the 1630s in the new context of the royalist exile, and, as such, seems a fitting vehicle through which to explore the ways in which court drama from the 1630s took on a new role during the interregnum.

*

'The Banished Shepherdess' overtly presents Henrietta Maria, 'tyer'd, in her Banish'd dress', as Corilliana, a shepherdess exiled to Thessaly because of her Arcadian subjects' rebellion.[39] Dale Randall has noted of the play that it 'is both a tribute to endurance in adversity and a fervent expression of royalist hope that a well-remembered near-paradise might soon be regained', while Nancy Klein Maguire comments that it showed Manuche's 'formal recovery of the masque and Fletcherian-Caroline tragicomedy'.[40] 'The Banished Shepherdess' certainly does strive to present masque-like moments, and in a manner that self-consciously evokes not just Fletcher, but, more specifically, Henry Killigrew's *The Conspiracy*, performed before the king and queen at York House during the 1635 wedding celebrations for the marriage of Mary Villiers and Charles Herbert.

The Conspiracy was republished in 1653 under the new title of *Pallantus and Eudora*, having been reworked to make its meanings more obviously political. In the 1653 edition, as in the original play, Cleander, the kingdom's rightful heir, experienced a prophetic dream, heralded by Morpheus, in which his good angel fetched down a vision of his coronation.[41] Manuche's play engages with this moment as it describes Corilliana and her ladies mutually experiencing a masque-like dream in which Morpheus appears 'with a leaden croune on his head', before an angel descends from the heavens to crown Charilaus, the shepherdess's son (sig. 15r). Just as in *Pallantus and Eudora*, the sleepers in 'The Banished Shepherdess' awake, 'thinking they have been in paradise' (sig. 15v), and the play eventually concludes with the promise that the prophetic coronation will be realised. In other words, Manuche positions his play alongside the dramatic products of the queen's own circle in a manner that again demonstrates how early Caroline drama became a political tool in the construction of a royalist identity. Furthermore, as I will show, he also uses his play to legitimise song and dance as valuable and efficacious to the royalist exiles.

In 'The Banished Shepherdess', Corilliana's attendants, both male and female, are marked by their constant battle against melancholy. On the first occasion we meet them, Pausanius, Corilliana's chief male servant (associated by Randall with Henry Jermyn), chides Urania, a waiting woman, for giving in to her passions.[42] The language used is decidedly neo-Platonic and it is some time before one realises that the passions in question are not those of love, but of despair. 'Consider, ffayre one', Pausanius exhorts,

> what atention those Godds gave
> When you: so Godd'ess-like, diswaded the matchlesse
> Corilliana: from nourishing the same disease,
> You to too greedily imbrace. (sig. 6v)

The hyperbolic vocabulary used of both Urania and Corilliana locates the women as neo-Platonic heroines and love-objects, while the imagery of embraces, greed and disease calls to mind the distrust of physical appetites evinced in masques such as *Tempe Restored*. Indeed, Urania's 'distemper' (sig. 6v) has every sign of resulting from the kind of erotic melancholy experienced by neo-Platonic lovers who are prevented from acknowledging or acting upon their love.[43]

Lesel Dawson has suggested that neo-Platonic chastity in plays of the 1630s could be 'constructed as a spiritual ideal, or conversely, as the cause of sterility and sickness'.[44] Arguing that the prolongation of the time of courtship in neo-Platonism inverted the traditional gender hierarchies of a 'husband's government', she also suggests that, for many, the philosophy constituted an 'emasculating force'.[45] In 'The Banished Shepherdess', lovesickness is recast in two ways pertinent to Dawson's argument. Firstly, the love that Corilliana's servants have for her infects them all with melancholy because, as Urania asserts, they feel they 'must share in her desease . . . Though to [their] certaine ruine' (sig. 6v). Just as a neo-Platonic lover is dependent on his mistress, so Corilliana's servants take their emotional lives directly from her. Her position as a queen who owes a responsibility of care towards her subjects is predicated upon a discourse of neo-Platonic love that placed women in dominant positions over their suitors during what Dawson has termed the 'liminal period' of courtship.[46] Without Corilliana's beneficent intervention, such contagious melancholy has the ability to undo and 'ruine' all her servants.

Secondly, this 'liminal period' of courtship is transformed in 'The Banished Shepherdess' into the time of exile in a manner that makes an equation between the emasculatory potential of amorous delay and exile's effeminising effects. Pausanius notes specifically that the 'stormes of fortune' suffered by Corilliana, 'Would haue made Greate Joue: Efeminate' (sig. 12v), while Prince Charilaus and his companions cast off 'malincholly, and all sad thoughts' (sig. 20r) by raising virile-sounding healths 'to our Noble / Masters Lady, who shall bring foorth Boyes' (sig. 20v). The disempowerment visited on the royalists by their continental exile is represented in 'The Banished Shepherdess' as engendering a melancholy lovesickness for queen and country that will be cured only by Charilaus's restoration, but which, interestingly, may be combatted by pursuits such as drinking, singing and dancing.

The state of exile in Manuche's play bears some comparison, then, with the Biblical Psalm 137's depiction of the Israelites' captivity in Babylon. Famously, the Israelites refused to sing for their captors, but the Psalm continues with the exhortations: 'If I forget thee, O Jerusalem, let my right hand forget her cunning'; and, 'If I do not remember thee, let my tongue cleave to the roof of my mouth'.[47] Forgetting leads to silence, while remembrance is couched in the terms of song and music. Corilliana's chief role in 'The Banished Shepherdess' is to prove to her followers that she has cast off her own melancholy and to persuade them to cast off theirs. She does this by encouraging them to sing songs which exhort 'sorrowes' to 'fly . . . hence' (sig. 9r) and 'long deiected speritts' to be roused (sig. 24r). Not only, therefore, is the promotion of festivity a political device that helps to constitute a royalist identity, it also builds community, combats melancholy and facilitates remembrance. Constituting exile as a place in which sickness and alienation reign, 'The Banished Shepherdess' proposes 'harmeles sporte' (sig. 24r) as a means of recovering 'light heartes' (sig. 30r), and shows Corilliana's continuing concern for her servants, her sons and her rebellious subjects to be the means through which such sickness will be cured. In other words, Manuche's play recycles a significant theatrical moment from the 1630s in order to facilitate remembrance of happier times, while it also posits leisured entertainment as entirely necessary to the furtherance of the royalist cause.

PLUM PORRIDGE AND CHRISTMAS PIES: HENRIETTA MARIA'S 1646 ENTERTAINMENT

Historically, there is little evidence of Henrietta Maria's promotion of such moments of efficacious festivity at her exiled court. Rather, as I will discuss, she chose to participate in the ceremonies of the Bourbon court that were managed, in the main, by her sister-in-law, the French queen regent. Nevertheless, one particularly significant occasion of English cultural patronage does stand out: a Christmas entertainment that shares certain similarities of imagery and intention with Manuche's representation of Prince Charilaus and his carousing companions.

On New Year's Eve 1646, Henrietta Maria's household produced a festive masque that involved a burlesque dance of the figures of Time, Janus and Christmas. This was not just a response to the Christmas season, but also a snub to the Puritan authorities in England who had tried to abolish Christmas as a popish festival.[48] By celebrating Christmas with masques and plays, Henrietta Maria's exiled court publicly kept the old traditions alive, providing a rallying point for expatriates and disaffected Englishmen. Moreover, in the autumn of 1646, Henrietta Maria had received the news that Prince Charles was on his way to Paris.[49] The Christmas of 1646/7 was therefore the first the prince spent alongside his mother in exile, and his presence at her court raised its profile. In order to be taken seriously by those who might provide financial assistance for his cause, the heir to the English throne had to appear with the trappings of monarchy and this prominent Christmas entertainment was probably undertaken with this in mind. Indeed, it was significant enough to be noticed by the popular news sheets in England, one of which reproduced a detailed account of the performance.[50]

First, we are informed, three 'grand old Seigniours', Janus, Christmas and Time enter, with Janus accompanied by the four seasons. Two 'conceited dances' then follow, the first undertaken by Shuffle, 'in the habit of an old sage Petiffogger', Cut, 'a factious Lady', and Trumpe, 'Madam Cuts own Chambermaid'. The second dance involves four Knaves: Spades, 'the country knave', with his wassail bowl; Clubs, 'the Camp-knave', with swords; Diamonds, 'the Citie-knave', with a cornucopia; and Hearts, 'the Court-knave', who performs a mumming. These are then robbed by four Aces, who, we are told, 'were Elder Brothers to the 4 Knaves'.[51] Both Lois Potter and Leah Marcus have explored the construction of royalist identities based on nostalgia for the Caroline past, while Marika Keblusek has recently investigated the imagery of drinking and wine as a signal of defiant royalism.[52] Henrietta Maria's entertainment draws explicitly on all these ideas, unapologetically promoting dancing, wassailing and gaming both in its subject matter and in its own status as a Christmas (rather than a Christ-tide) celebration.

As well as harking back to a happier royalist past, the production also marks a continuity between the personnel of the Caroline court and the queen's court in exile. In 1646/7, Davenant, the favoured Caroline masque writer, was in Paris in the service of the queen, and might well have been responsible for writing the Christmas entertainment. The playwright Thomas Killigrew had accompanied Prince Charles into exile that summer; and Abraham Cowley, who had recently introduced his friend, the poet Richard Crashaw, to the exiled court, was employed in Henry Jermyn's household as a secretary, encoding the queen's letters.[53] Several royal musicians were also near her at the time: Anthony Robert, one of her lutenists, is recorded as standing as a godfather in the parish of St Germain l'Auxerrois, near the Louvre, in June 1646; François Richard the elder died in Paris in 1650; Jean Prevost was in Paris by June 1645, living in the parish of St Paul; and Bocan, the royal dancing master, was also in the French capital that Christmas.[54] In addition, a group of English players who, at least according to parliamentary pamphlets, were affiliated to Prince Charles, had recently been disbanded in Paris so might feasibly have been available to play the more histrionic roles in the queen's production.[55]

Their company, as *The Kingdomes Weekly Intelligencer* sourly noted, was supported by William Cavendish, the earl of Newcastle, who is reported to have penned 'Prologues and Epilogues' for them.[56] His involvement in drama during the interregnum is borne out by manuscript evidence, and I would not be surprised to discover his hand in the 1646 production. In Antwerp, in 1658, he certainly collaborated with Nicholas Lanier in an entertainment that was intended for Charles II, and his Restoration play, 'a Debauschte Gallante', is of a similar flavour to the Christmas festivity. One of its songs is especially resonant, declaring:

Gallantts you shall haue maskes & Playes
Soe all the Commons hapye-Dayes,
Ande the People will no more Rise,
Hauing Plumm Porege Christmas Pise.[57]

This explicit evocation of Christmas in its association with feasting and theatre is extremely pertinent to Henrietta Maria's entertainment, and reveals it to have been more than just a pleasant way of celebrating the season.

Just as Manuche's pastoral proposed singing and dancing as cures for melancholy, positing such 'harmeles sporte' as a means of promoting social harmony, so Cavendish's song implies that public disorder will be overcome if people are allowed to celebrate Christmas with plays and traditional feasting. However, as I have noted, such celebration was frowned upon by the puritan clergy who denounced Christmas as a popish festival and abolished its observance by ordinance of parliament in June 1645.[58] Indeed, an explicit connection between the queen and the festival had been made in 1645/6 in a satirical pamphlet entitled *The Arraignment, Conviction, and Imprisoning of Christmas*, printed by 'Simon Minc'd Pye, for Cissely Plum-porridge' in London.[59] Although the tract does evince a certain sympathy for the loss of Christmas, it makes no bones about the fact that 'he crept from under the Romish Chaire, and was placed in the Kalendar only by a popish edict'.[60] In the queen's chapel, we are told, 'you might have found him standing against the wall, and the Papists weeping, and beating themselves before him, and kissing his hoary head with superstitious teares, in a theater exceeding all the playes of the red Bull, the Fortune, or the Cockpit'.[61] Idolatry, Catholicism, Christmas and the theatre are all condemned here as corrupting activities sanctioned by the queen.

The portrayal of traditional Christmas customs in the queen's entertainment, such as the wassail bowl and mumming, therefore constitutes an act of resistance against parliament at the same time as it harks back to a tradition that was sanctioned by King James in his *Book of Sports* (1618) and promoted in shows such as Ben Jonson's *Christmas His Masque* (1616). It demonstrates Henrietta Maria's disregard of parliamentary authority, while it also implicitly promises that if the king is reinstated all such pleasures will again be sanctioned.[62] Furthermore, in its portraits of the four knaves, and in the character of Madam Cut, 'Widow of an old Souldier of the Queen', it warns about the danger of faction, and promotes community in its audience who are drawn together in opposition to parliament and in remembrance of a happier past.[63]

Significantly, limiting the negative effects of faction was extremely important in the winter of 1646/7. Prince Charles had arrived in Paris after a bitter wrangle between the queen's party who were insistent that he would be safest in France and the principal members of his entourage who wished him to remain on English soil, even if that soil was in Jersey. The queen's party won, but Charles's arrival not only meant that there were more mouths to feed, but also that there was a proliferation of competing opinions about royalist policy. By mounting a play at this potentially fraught time, the queen promoted community and reminded the royalists of their common cause.

HENRIETTA MARIA AND FRENCH CEREMONIES (1645–8)

Charles's appearance in Paris not only exacerbated potential divisions among the English party, it also raised questions of precedence between the prince and his French relations. Strickland has noted that Anne of Austria expressed her favour to Henrietta Maria and her son 'by offering them precedence to herself and her sons on every occasion', and comments that, much against Henrietta Maria's natural instincts, 'time [was] tediously spent in ceremonials idle and absurd'.[64] It is evident, though, despite Strickland's assertion, that the queen consort placed great importance on hierarchy and visual display, much as her mother had in her own exile from France.

In the *Declaration* that she published to explain her departure from the Low Countries, Marie de Médicis wrote:

> By [the King of Great Britain's] extraordinary magnificence at my entrance into *London*, he hath published the esteem he had of my Person, by the cheerfulness appearing in his own Countenance, and in that of all his Subjects; he shewed how dear my presence was to him.[65]

The historical accuracy of her pronouncement is of little relevance to the exiled queen mother: what matters is that people believed she had been treated with respect, and that she was maintained in a good bargaining position with France. This puts a different complexion on the entertainments laid out for Henrietta Maria in the early years of her exile and, as I have noted, suggests that, while she was being ostentatiously fêted by her French relations, her creditors could be kept at bay. However, just as substantial political assistance had been unforthcoming for continental exiles in England, so, in France, Henrietta Maria received only a series of symbolic gestures. Nonetheless, these had their uses and their cessation can be shown to have had significant effects.

Like Henrietta Maria, Anne of Austria is reputed to have been a lover of the theatre. Indeed, Madame de Motteville, one of her ladies-in-waiting, reports that before the end of the official period of mourning for Louis XIII, she would attend plays incognito, protected by her women from the public gaze.[66] Once her mourning was over, and supported by Cardinal Mazarin, Anne began to wield a significant amount of cultural influence and was instrumental in encouraging the growth of Italian opera in France. An Italian acting troupe was assembled in Paris, and stage designers and composers were called to Paris from Italy. In February 1645, Henrietta Maria was invited to a very private entertainment at the Palais Royal, credited as France's first operatic spectacle.[67] It starred Atto Melani, a castrato who had recently been summoned from Italy, and was performed before the king, his mother and brother, the English queen, Gaston d'Orléans and Mademoiselle de Montpensier.[68] Despite its exclusive nature, it marked the beginning of a flourishing period of Italian theatre and music at the French court. The following December, Giulio Strozzi's play, *La Finta Pazza*, was performed at the Petit Bourbon 'par la grande Trouppe Royalle des Comediens Italiens'; then, in February 1646, Francesco Cavalli's opera, *Egistéo*, was presented before the queens of France and England.[69] In 1647, the long-awaited *Orphée*, with music by the Italian Luigi Rossi, was performed at the Palais Royal, with amazing scenic effects, machines and other inventions never before seen in France.[70]

On Shrove Tuesday 1647, Henrietta Maria was summoned to *Orphée*'s last performance before the Easter fast. Prior to the performance, she joined Anne, Gaston d'Orléans and Mademoiselle de Montpensier at a formal dinner given by the king in a gallery at the Palais Royal at which they were entertained by his famous band of twenty-four violins.[71] The performance itself consisted of a series of entries which depicted, among other things, the wedding of Orpheus and Eurydice; her death; the flames and smoke of the underworld; Orpheus's charming of wild animals and his eventual immortalisation at the hand of Jupiter.[72] The scenery and costumes were sumptuous and the whole affair appears to have lasted more than six hours.[73] After the performance, a number of courtiers danced in a ball which had been ordered by the queen regent, at which both Henrietta Maria and her brother were given the honour of being seated under the State.[74] In other words, just as Marie de Médicis was honoured in 1640 as the principal observer of *Salmacida Spolia*, so

Henrietta Maria and her brother were privileged by the French court and its regent as Bourbon princes and the offspring of the famous Henri le Grand.

Not only did this occasion provide visible proof of the esteem with which Henrietta Maria was held in France, it also provided her with an opportunity to assert her own agenda. Although she had no control over the arrangement of the formalities themselves, she was sufficiently aware of the workings of a court to be able to manipulate events to her advantage. The royalist cause was desperately lacking in funds and Mademoiselle de Montpensier, her niece, was one of the wealthiest women in France. The queen was keen to marry Prince Charles to this source of finance, and used the shrovetide celebrations to further her designs. Montpensier reports that Henrietta Maria expressed a desire around this time to help her to dress for an important ball, and lent her all her own jewels as well as those of the English crown. When this became general knowledge, it reinforced the rumours that had been circulating all winter about the queen's matrimonial policy.[75] By showing such extreme favour to her niece, Henrietta Maria therefore managed to co-opt a part of the shrovetide celebrations to her own designs. Nevertheless, although Anne of Austria was certainly going out of her way to demonstrate both her affection and respect for her exiled relation, behaviour such as this could be a problem, and it is obvious that a difficult juggling act was going on behind the scenes. Anne and Mazarin certainly did not support Henrietta Maria's desires for the marriage, and Anne had already intimated to Montpensier that she did not expect her to marry Charles. Mazarin, in his turn, was so far from wanting to help the exiles that he was spying on and obstructing their designs, and profiting from their misfortunes by buying up their libraries and works of art.[76] The English queen and her entourage presented a real dilemma to the French crown and accommodating them politely into the life of the court could cause irritating problems.[77]

Furthermore, the outbreak of the French civil wars of the Fronde meant that both the French crown's visible support and the queen's French pension stopped almost instantly, and Henrietta Maria found herself beset by her creditors and unable to pay them. In the July of 1648, Madame de Motteville and a friend went to visit her in the Carmelite convent to which she had retired and discovered her alone, writing dispatches she claimed were vitally important.[78] Secluded in a small, enclosed space in an institution whose prime tenets were female chastity and religious virtue, Henrietta Maria struggled to assert her influence over the course of the war to the benefit of her male relations. Bereft of money and servants, she was forced, at last, to pursue the line of action she had threatened in her earlier letters to Charles, retreating into a traditionally feminine world, impoverished and soon to be stripped even of her position as queen by the execution of her husband.

HENRIETTA MARIA AND FRENCH CEREMONIES (1648–61)

There is little evidence of Henrietta Maria's involvement in French court ceremony between 1648 and 1653, in part because of the Fronde, and in part because Charles I's death plunged the English court into mourning. In May 1648, she stood as godmother to the duc d'Anjou, her nephew, in a meagre ceremony attended by the princes Charles and Rupert. Henrietta Anne, her youngest daughter, was present in February 1651 at Louis XIV's debut as a dancer in the royal *Ballet de Cassandre*, and might well also have attended the *Ballet des Fêtes de Bacchus* in May.[79] However, in 1653, with the re-establishment of peace in France, the widowed queen's offspring began to be invited to participate with the French nobility in *ballets de cour*.

That February, the dukes of York and Buckingham took part in Louis's *Ballet Royal de la Nuict*, an extravagant entertainment composed of forty-five entries divided into four sections or 'watches' of the night. Buckingham took three roles in the entertainment: he danced first as a bandit, then as the Demon of Fire and then as a bashful lover. His many entries indicate that he was as accomplished a dancer as his famous father and, indeed, in his incarnation as Fire he recited verses which invoked his prestigious ancestry. However, the most significant aspect of the entertainment from a royalist perspective was the appearance of James Stuart, the duke of York, Henrietta Maria's second son, as the first of the bashful lovers to take the stage: 'La gloire seule est ma Maistresse', he declared, 'Déja mon ieune coeur paroist fier & terrible / Par dessus le débris horrible / Des Throsnes renuersez, & des Sceptres perdus' [Glory alone is my mistress . . . Already my young heart appears proud and terrible among the hideous debris of overturned thrones and lost sceptres].[80] His three stanzas are powerful and incongruous beside the heavily neo-Platonised laments of the other bashful lovers and constitute a veritable call to arms. 'Ie veux faire des coups dignes d'elle & de moy', he announced,

Vanger les Rois, & les Royaumes,
Au restablissement d'un Royaume & d'un Roy.
Il faut punir ce grand outrage
Par la force & par la courage.[81]

[I want to strike blows worthy of Glory and myself . . .
To avenge kings and kingdoms,
For the reestablishment of a kingdom and a king.
We must punish this great outrage
With strength and courage.]

If any doubt remains that court ballets could be used to promote a specific political agenda, then this outright declaration of a martial intent should be enough to dispel it.

The following year, the importance of spectacle to the royalist cause was again reinforced when the duke of York and his sister, Henrietta Anne, were both invited to take part in the extravagant Italian-influenced entertainment of *Les Noces de Pelée et de Thétis*.[82] News of the event was reported in the English *Weekly Intelligencer*, which noted that at 'the last acting of the Comedy at Paris . . . there was present the late Queen of England, the titular King of Scotland, and the titular Dukes of York, and Glocester'.[83] However, the news sheet significantly neglects to mention that the 'titular' duke of York and his sister took histrionic roles in the production and certainly does not expound upon the substance of their verses. Henrietta Anne played the part of the muse, Erato, and, like the duke of York previously, was given verses which made reference to her royal ancestry and which complained that people always came to her to lament the fall of crowns. In the hands of James Howell, who published an English translation of the entertainment in the same year, her words became:

My stemm is more then of a mortall race;
For to great Henries Granchild all give place:
My Innocent and young aspect,
Inspires both pitty and respect;
And he who loudly would complain
Of Princes falls and Peoples raign,
Of angry starrs, and destiny,
Let him but cast his eyes on me.[84]

Although this quite faithfully represents the spirit of the French, Howell's translation gives less space to the assertions about Henrietta Anne's noble ancestry that justified her inclusion in the ballet to the French audience, and spends proportionately more time on the subject of her dispossession. Indeed, his stanza's penultimate line is a complete innovation, introducing a notion of fatal intervention into the poem that blames the royalists' fall on the vagaries of destiny.

The same heightening of emphasis is evident in Howell's translation of the duke of York's verses. In the third entry of *Les Noces de Pelée et de Thétis*, James Stuart played a coral fisher, and declared:

> Loin de ne faire ici que pescher le coral,
> Il faut que d'un endroit malheureux et fatal,
> Que la vaste Mer environne,
> Je m'applique en homme expert,
> A pescher tout ce qui sert
> A refaire une Couronne.[85]

Howell rendered this as:

> Tis not for me to fish for Corrall here
> I to another Coast my course must steer,
>   A fatall ground
>   Which seas surround.
> There I must fish upon an angry Main,
> More then two Crowns and Sceptres to regain. (sig. B3v)

Although this is again a reasonably faithful translation, there are some singular differences in emphasis. The 'malheureux et fatal' place of the French original is effectively placed beyond France's concern, rendered small and distant by the notion of the 'vaste Mer'. However, in Howell's translation, the 'fatall ground' becomes more prominent, largely through the use of a dimetric middle couplet which emphasises the significance of the prince's destination. Furthermore, in its singular use of the adjective 'fatall', rather than the 'malheureux et fatal' of the French original, the translation moves away from a general representation of an unhappy land, to a more personal description which glances obliquely at the fatal end of James's father, executed by parliament five years before. In addition, it emphasises the loss of two crowns and sceptres, in the place of the French verse's single 'Couronne'.[86]

Marie-Claude Canova-Green has noted that this French entertainment, in contrast to that of the previous year, shifted the emphasis of the duke of York's verses from a collective vengeance to a more personal one. She explains this subtle but significant difference by noting that a change had occurred in the exiles' situation: France had begun to renew its diplomatic relations with England.[87] Indeed, a treaty of peace was signed with France in the following year which meant that Charles II's continued residence in the French capital was somewhat of an embarrassment and he subsequently left the country. However, by this time the royal family's ranks had been swelled by the addition of Elizabeth, the widowed princess of Orange, who arrived at the Louvre on 1 February 1655. She was just in time to attend Louis's *Ballet des Plaisirs* which took place on 4 February, and in which the duke of York danced the role of a courtier alongside his cousin, the young duc d'Orléans. His part in this entertainment was small and equivocal: 'Si la Vertu pouvoit, elle m'auroit donné / Tout ce que la Fortune m'oste' [If Virtue could, she would give me all that Fortune takes from me], his verses declared.[88] Canova-Green has noticed the alteration here from earlier ballets' present tenses to this use of the conditional.[89] The change expresses the precariousness of James's situation and denies him active support as it places him at the mercy of Virtue and Fortune. It is, as Canova-Green comments, indicative of France's new relationship with England and demonstrates that, although the Stuart princes were permitted, up to a point, to integrate their own concerns into the Bourbon entertainments, they had to consent to an image of themselves that was acceptable to the French.[90]

Henrietta Maria's children don't appear to have danced in any more French ballets until the eve of the Restoration, although they continued to attend them and took part in the balls afterwards. In February 1656, for example, the *Mercurius Politicus*, an English newsbook, noted that 'the Queen, the Princesse of Orange, her brother the Titular Duke of York . . . with many other great Lords and Ladies' attended *Psyche*, 'or the Power of Love', danced by Louis XIV to the music of Jean-Baptiste Lully.[91] Similarly, in the winter of 1659, John Reresby reported seeing Henrietta Anne dance alongside the French king after a 'great maske' at the Louvre, yet it was only after her marriage to the duc d'Orléans in 1661 that she again took up a position on the French court stage.[92]

Despite lack of finance and in the face of huge political obstacles, Henrietta Maria and her household nevertheless struggled to maintain a significant presence on the European stage, firstly to advance Charles I's war effort, and then to secure the English throne for his heir. If anything, the intersection between Henrietta Maria's cultural and political activities is clearer to see during this period than at any other time. Unerring in her attempts to help her son regain his throne, her political activity was intimately bound up with her social fashion, and seems to have been strongly influenced by her own mother's ideas about a European politics based both on display and on matrimonial ties. She tried hard to effect a financially advantageous marriage for her eldest son, and was also eager to promote the fortunes of her daughter, creating an attractive environment that drew the Parisian élite into her social circle.[93] Indeed, John Reresby reported in his memoirs that, during the winter of 1659/60,

> ther was a greater resort to the Palais Royall then to the French Court, the good humour and witt of the Queen Mother of England and the beauty of the Princesse her daughter giveing greater invitation then the more perticular humour of the French Queen, being a Spaniard.[94]

Despite her frequent religious retreats, it would appear that Henrietta Maria maintained a presence both at the French court and within noble Parisian society that was facilitated by the arts of conversation she had encouraged in England; arts of conversation, it must be remembered, that were rooted in the religious teachings of divines such as Cardinal Bérulle and St François de Sales.

Epilogue

In 2004, the BBC broadcast a mini series entitled *Charles II: The Power and the Passion*. The actress Diana Rigg, famous for her West End stage portrayal of Euripides' tragic princess, Medea, was cast as Henrietta Maria, in a costume that made her look like both Miss Havisham and Davros, lord of the Daleks.[1] The casting of an actress famous for playing a woman who murdered her own children was no accident: the serial gained some mileage out of Henrietta Maria's rejection of her youngest son, Henry, the duke of Gloucester, because of his refusal to convert to Catholicism, and concluded with a scene in which Catherine of Braganza, Charles II's queen, advised Louise de Keroualle, his erstwhile mistress, how to regain his affections. 'If you want him to love you again, be the woman he yearns for, but has never had', Catherine generously suggested, answering the simpering Keroualle's question, 'What woman?', with the portentously inflected: 'An aff*ect*ionate m*oth*er'.[2] Although Charles II was portrayed earlier in the drama rejecting Edward, Lord Hyde's attempts to take the place of his martyred dad, its conclusion implied that his inveterate womanising resulted from Henrietta Maria's maternal inadequacies and his desire to replace her with a surrogate.

This characterisation of the queen consort flies in the face of the Caroline iconography explored in the earlier chapters of this book which represented Charles I and Henrietta Maria's marriage as loving and fecund, and which consistently celebrated the offspring of their union. This imagery culminated, perhaps, in Cosmo Manuche's 'The Banished Shepherdess' which made a virtue out of the queen consort's love for her children and which represented her falling on the necks of her 'poore vnfortunate poore Boyes', kissing them and weeping for joy at their reunion.[3] It is interesting, in an age that struggles with anxieties about career women and working mothers, that Henrietta Maria's posthumous reputation is again undergoing transformation. From being represented patronisingly in the late nineteenth century as a frivolous and gay butterfly with no political understanding, she is now being portrayed as a callous, bloodthirsty and ambitious woman, who castigates her unfortunate son with the accusation: 'weak, you've always been weak'.[4]

These more recent personifications can, nevertheless, be traced back to the anti-royalist polemics discussed in the last chapter which demonised the queen consort for her love of theatrical display and for an ambitious influence over her uxorious husband. Both of these positions were, furthermore, linked indelibly in the minds of her detractors with her Catholicism. To conclude, then, in an attempt to qualify or to correct modern interpretations of the queen, I want briefly to look at the ways in which Henrietta Maria pursued her faith during her exile, and to examine the ways in which she was represented in the contemporary writings of her countrymen and women.

PIETY, POLITICS AND PLEASURE

After the execution of her husband, Henrietta Maria notoriously abandoned personal adornment and affected a black gown and a white, nun-like cap.[5] This act, which served as a continual reminder of her status as a widow and a Catholic, also constituted a moment of powerful self-construction, indicating that all her cares were now directed beyond the mortal world. In a culmination of the imagery promoted in her pastorals and civil-war letters, she is recorded in several texts as referring to herself as 'une Reine Malheureuse', whose history provided an example of the fact that 'tout passe en ce monde, et n'est que vanité'.[6] Fixing her eyes on heaven, she fended off her detractors by projecting a pious disregard for mortal frippery.

This adoption of a quasi-nun-like persona was accompanied by two significant developments. Firstly, Henrietta Maria's position as a proselytising Catholic became tougher, and concomitantly, she began the negotiations that would lead to her foundation of a convent. In 1651, increasingly oppressed by her debts, the queen threatened to dismiss her Protestant ladies unless they would 'come-over to the *Romish* Masse' and, under the dogmatic influence of Walter Montagu who had replaced Father Philip as her confessor, forbade the performance of Anglican services under her roof.[7] At the same time, in a public demonstration of her piety and desire to renounce the world, and thanks to funds raised by a group of Visitandine nuns, she became the *fondatrice* of a convent at Chaillot, just over the river from the modern-day site of the Eiffel Tower.

The Order of the Visitation had been created in 1610 by St François de Sales and the widow, Jane, baronne de Chantal. It was specifically conceived to admit, not only virgins, but widows who had divested themselves of their worldly responsibilities, most notably towards their children. In addition, to permit the entry of the aged and infirm, it suppressed such monastic austerities as sleeping on hard surfaces and rising at night, and forbade the nuns physically to punish themselves without orders from their mother superior.[8] Henrietta Maria's foundation was the third Visitandine convent in Paris and she was considered especially fit to be its benefactress because of her knowledge of Sales's *Introduction à la vie dévote* and her veneration for the mysteries it contained.[9] It was also fitting because of her situation as a widow, and may be seen as the culmination of the spiritual project that she pursued at the Caroline court. Père Cyprien de Gamache, her Capuchin biographer, writing an almost hagiographical account of her life, states that she spent many months of every year at the convent, adding that it was only her responsibilities as a mother that kept her from fully embracing the religious life.[10] This comment is significant for it makes evident a tension in all of the contemporary religious biographies of the queen which tried to reconcile her continued involvement in politics with a desire to present her as a woman who preferred to renounce the world.

Even in the nineteenth century, the biographer Henrietta Haynes remarked that the convent of Chaillot was a peaceful retreat for the queen after all her sorrows, 'for the world', she says, 'was strictly excluded, and the convent never became, like [Queen Anne's] Val-de-Grâce, a centre of political intrigue'.[11] It is significant, though, that the institution became a sanctuary not only for Henrietta Maria, but for many former *salonnières.* Its second abbess was Louise de la Fayette, a former *fille d'honneur* to Anne of Austria and one of the late Louis XIII's neo-Platonic loves. She was also the sister-in-law of the writer Madame de la Fayette, who paid frequent visits to the convent. Madame de Sévigné, the famous letter writer and denizen of the Rambouillet *salon*, also retreated to Chaillot after her beloved daughter's marriage, and Madame de Motteville's sister became one of its nuns. The convent became a truly femino-centric space into and out of which the queen could move at will. Not only was it a concrete manifestation of the desire for retreat expressed in her letters to her husband, it also fulfilled the fantasies of her pastorals, according her a place in a female community that provided a sanctuary from the inconstant world.

It is nonetheless interesting to speculate whether the widowed queen conducted social and political meetings at Chaillot, a place secure from prying eyes and vituperative critics. Indications of this can certainly be discerned in a series of memoirs, written by Soeur Marie-Henriette Revellois, one of the foundation's original nuns. Revellois's text eulogises Henrietta Maria as the convent's founder and is keen to represent her as an example of constant Catholicism. The vagaries of her fortune are used to demonstrate the mutability of the material world and, in a manner similar to that implicit in *Artenice* and *Tempe Restored*, show that true security is to be found only in heaven. Taking Ecclesiastes 1.2 as its subtext ('vanity of vanities; all is vanity'), the text seeks to demonstrate that 'tout passe en ce monde, et n'est que vanité', and asserts that God has given the queen the opportunity of demonstrating her faith through her submission to a series of divinely inflicted disasters.[12] The eulogy describes Henrietta Maria as a woman who had 'une fidélité pour Dieu admirable' and who thanked Him every day for rendering her 'une Reine Malheureuse'.[13] In a strategy very similar to that deployed by the queen consort in her letters, she is figured as an example of true Christian constancy, virtually a martyr for her religion. This strategy is entirely necessary because Henrietta Maria is the convent's figurehead: if her life is not shown to be exemplary, the foundation's very identity as a religious house is called into question. Nevertheless, one aspect of Revellois's eulogy strikes a strange note, encoding an anxiety about Henrietta Maria's presence at the convent that deserves further investigation.

Revellois is careful to emphasise that the queen's presence was not disruptive and did nothing to alter the convent's sanctity. However, right from the start of the narrative, questions are raised about the number of secular visitors her presence draws to Chaillot and the nuns become aware of rumours that they are being too much exposed to 'le grand monde'.[14] The convent's boundaries become so permeable that the nuns develop the habit of closing off their own bodies, attending mass with their eyes closed to avoid being contaminated by the outside world.[15] Eventually, they are forced to approach Henrietta Maria to ask her to curtail the visits. From this point on, Revellois's text is punctuated by references to moments when the doors to the queen's apartments were closed to the nuns because secular visitors were attending upon the queen. In 1651 and 1652, for example, during the French civil wars of the Fronde, the text makes reference to the arrival of several important dignitaries, one of whom was Gaston, duc d'Orléans, Henrietta Maria's brother.[16] A comparison of Revellois's text with the *Gazette de France*, with Madame de Motteville's

Mémoires and with the queen's own letters to her sister Christine in Savoy, shows that Henrietta Maria was involved at that time in negotiations with Orléans, the duc de Lorraine and Louis XIV, mainly concerned with managing the civil unrest. Revellois's text thus provides an indication that the queen did use Chaillot for informal political meetings, profiting from its seclusion.

Chaillot was also a place where Henrietta Maria could entertain her closest colleagues and to which she retreated with the faithful Catholic core of her household. She maintained an antechamber, an inner chamber, a 'cabinet' and a *prie-dieu*, whose serried formality is reminiscent of the hierarchy of rooms at her more public court. She ate in a room laid aside for Henrietta Anne, which gave into a parlour whose outer door permitted people to enter without troubling the convent. Above her apartment were the rooms of Lady Guildford, named as her 'dame d'honneur' or lady-in-waiting. Rooms were also provided for Madame Vantelet, her 'dame de lit'; for 'Madame la nourrice' (that is Françoise de Monbodeac, Madame Garnier); for Garnier's daughters, Madame Coignet and 'Madame Harpe' (Catowe Garnier, wife of Thomas Arpe); for Madame de Plansy; and the younger Madame Vantelet, the queen's chamberers.[17] The bulk of the women who went with the queen to this, her most intimate establishment, were, it would seem, French, and had, for the most part, been in her train since 1625. Henrietta Maria's confidante, Madame de Motteville, also maintained an apartment there and spent much time in the queen's company. Very often, in the evenings, the queen asked the nuns to visit her and kept them in conversation even after the bell had rung for the evening service.[18] She also continued to entertain 'des personnes de la première qualité' in her parlour.[19] While I am certain that Henrietta Maria's religious beliefs were strongly held, there is sufficient indication here that she used Chaillot as a social base as well as a religious retreat, entertaining her closest friends and her political allies away from the gossip and spies of her more formal court. Furthermore, she obviously continued to pursue the fashion for chaste conversation that she had promoted in England and which was fittingly sanctioned in the writings of St François de Sales.

Just as Henrietta Maria's letters used religious motifs to validate her entry into politics, so Revellois's narrative represented the queen as a model of devout Catholicism in order to deflect criticism of her more worldly activities. The foundation of the convent performed a strategic function, underlining both to the queen's compatriots and to her opponents in England that she was a Catholic and a princess of France. As well as being a site of religious retreat into whose relative obscurity she could retire, it also spoke loudly of her unfortunate situation and provided a location from which she could conduct political affairs under the aegis of chastity and propriety. However, most importantly, Revellois's text demonstrates how the figure of the queen was deployed for ideological ends, serving to guarantee the propriety of the Chaillot convent and its nuns.

*

The modes of social interaction promoted by the likes of Honoré d'Urfé and Sales burgeoned in Paris in the 1650s into the full-blown *salon* fashion satirised under the name of *préciosité* by Molière and his contemporaries. In 1659, Molière's *Les Précieuses ridicules* was performed in Paris to great acclaim, marking the emergence on to the public stage of this new, affected type of woman. During the previous year, Mademoiselle de Montpensier, Henrietta Maria's niece, had been the leading *salonnière* in Paris, in a manner that demonstrates that royalty and the *salons* were not inimical. In addition, her activities help to locate Henrietta Maria within this social nexus.

In the winter of 1651, during the ongoing Fronde, Montpensier began hosting a gathering that began around five or six in the evening, and continued until nine.[20] All the young people in Paris assembled there, she explained in her memoirs, because the queen regent and her court were not in the capital and there was nothing else to do. Henrietta Maria was often present, together with her two eldest sons, and they played cards, danced and listened to music, participating, in essence, in the same kind of refined social activities that the queen consort had promoted at the Caroline court. Montpensier's gathering grew into one of the most famous of all the Parisian *salons*, and was responsible for introducing the new literary fashion of the prose portrait into France. The vogue for complimentary descriptions of members of the social élite swept Paris in 1658, giving rise to a two-volume collection dedicated to Montpensier. The first volume contains a prose description of Henrietta Anne written by the comtesse de Bregis in a manner that indictates that Henrietta Maria's family were circulating within the fashionable Parisian world.[21] Although the collection does not contain a portrait of Henrietta Maria, Madame de Motteville's *Mémoires* – which begin with a complimentary portrait of Queen Anne – also include a portrait of the English queen, which suggests that she, too, was honoured by this new fashion for descriptions.[22]

The first volume of portraits understandably contains a series of eulogies to Montpensier, one of which represents her in terms familiar to anyone conversant with the young Henrietta Maria's iconography: 'Comme on voit la naissante Aurore / Semer sur l'Empire de Flore / Et la pourpre & l'azur dont elle peint les fleurs', the verses begin, 'Ainsi la jeune Iris vous donne des couleurs / Pour la peindre aussi belle, & plus brillante encore' [As we see the nascent Dawn spreading over the empire of Flora, and [see] the purple and blue with which she paints the flowers, so the young Iris gives you colours that paint her as beautiful and more brilliant still].[23] Thirty-five years after Henrietta Maria took to the stage as Iris in Anne of Austria's *Grand Ballet de la Reyne representant les Festes de Junon la Nopcière*, it was the turn of her niece, not her daughter, to be heralded as the fresh hope of the French court. In contrast, Bregis's portrait of Henrietta Anne presents her as 'douce & obligeante' [gentle and obliging], quietly learning the skills 'qui peut faire une Princesse parfaite' [that can make a perfect princess].[24] The young woman has 'une grace incomparable' and sings 'comme un Ange' in a cluster of imagery that lends a distinctly spiritual tone to the description. Most significantly, she is somehow obscured from the view of Fortune, who, if she would just lift up her blindfold to see, would not be able to refuse the princess 'toutes les grandeurs de la Terre'.[25] Just as in Louis XIV's *ballets*, Bregis's portrait locates the princess as the victim of an unfortunate political fate, while representing her as a virtuous and untroublesome addition to the Bourbon court.

Motteville's description of Henrietta Maria draws on this fashion for portraits, presenting the queen as someone who had 'infiniment de l'esprit, de cet esprit brillant qui plaît aux spectateurs' [enormous spirit, and that sparkling spirit which pleased onlookers].[26] In a manner that resounds with Manuche's 'The Banished Shepherdess', she describes how, despite her tears, Henrietta Maria would often divert her companions with pleasantries, and had exhausted her treasury 'à faire du bien à ceux qu'elle aimoit' [to do good for those she loved].[27] Furthermore, remarking on the queen's ruined appearance she notes with gentle humour that,

> comme sa beauté n'avoit duré que l'espace du matin et l'avoit quittée avant son midi, elle avoit accoutumé de maintenir que les femmes ne peuvent plus être belles passé vingt-deux ans.[28]

> [As her beauty had lasted only the space of a morning and had left her before midday, she was accustomed to maintain that women could no longer be beautiful after the age of twenty-two.]

Resounding with *The Shepherds' Paradise*'s injunction that no woman could become queen after the age of thirty, Motteville's comment locates the height of Henrietta Maria's beauty in 1631, the year in which she danced in *Chloridia*, surrounded by an imagery of natural health that had now devolved on to Mademoiselle de Montpensier.

Despite her frequent religious retreats, therefore, it would appear that Henrietta Maria maintained a presence both at the French court and within aristocratic Parisian society. Moreover, her connections with this world were not just social. As I discussed in chapter 10, she hoped to arrange the marriage of the wealthy Montpensier to Charles II in order to provide him with funds to regain the English throne and to increase France's obligations towards Britain. In her memoirs, Montpensier describes a pertinent conversation with Henrietta Maria which took place in 1656 during which the exiled queen reputedly informed her that she should marry Charles because she would then be mistress of her own desires and would be able to make use of anyone she pleased.[29] Montpensier attributes to Henrietta Maria a notion of marriage that accords women a great deal of power and which locates Charles as a neo-Platonic lover, helplessly devoted to the young woman's beauty.[30] Here again, the language of the pastorals is deployed in a political context, both to privilege women's agency and as a bid to win support for the royalist cause. However, Montpensier's version of Henrietta Maria's views on marriage is in striking contrast to Père Cyprien de Gamache's account of how, with the exiled queen's approval, he taught Henrietta Anne that a married woman's greatest duty was to submit to her husband.[31] These examples show how the queen consort's identity was applied rhetorically through discourse, reflecting the position of a text's author as much as that of its subject: existing within a range of stories, Henrietta Maria was both, and neither, of these women.

*

The queen consort's political activity was intimately bound up with her social fashion and, as I have shown, seems to have been strongly influenced by her mother's ideas about a European politics based on display and matrimonial ties. Her social and political activities also bear witness to the fact that noblewomen wielded a significant amount of influence within seventeenth-century society, acting as patrons and brokers, and facilitating meetings and treaties between influential men. Even at the end of her life, Henrietta Maria continued to assist in political negotiations, hosting a series of meetings at her country house at Colombes, outside Paris, to try to settle the recent Anglo-French conflict over Holland. As the daughter of Marie de Médicis, and later, as an important player on the European stage in her own right, she pursued a policy of piety, politics and pleasure to the end.

History might consider that Henrietta Maria's interests contributed to the downfall of the Caroline regime, but she nevertheless made important contributions to the theatrical culture of the Stuart court, not least in her promotion of women as actresses. As I have made clear, I do not subscribe to the view that her cultural patronage consisted simply in the facile reproduction of French fashions, nor that it was entirely apolitical. As the daughter of a French queen regent and as the wife, sister and sister-in-law of three monarchs, Henrietta Maria understood the role she had to play in both European culture and politics. Moreover, she exploited St François de Sales's religious teachings in order to promote women as the keystones of a devout and ordered society.

At times she might have been influenced by her advisers, acting, as instructed, to further the causes of both France and her religion. However, at others, she took up an oppositional position, aligning herself with English Protestants against Louis XIII's regime and against her husband's non-interventionist foreign policy. Most of all, her court entertainments reflect her political position, showing that she remained committed to her mother's cause throughout her life: in the early years, this meant forming an alliance with men like the earl of Holland; in the later, it meant promoting her religion more actively at court.

The queen consort's French heritage was exploited in her masques and plays to provide her with an iconography that, while compatible with her husband's, could be used to assert an independent political and cultural identity. It was this independence that caused her to be solicited by the likes of Cardinal Richelieu and which rendered her an important conduit to Charles, and it was this that caused foreign ambassadors continually to eye her activities at the English court. To conclude, despite Alison Plowden's assertion that she was 'simply not interested in affairs of state unless . . . one of her friends happened to be involved', I remain convinced that she was.

Appendix: An early entertainment by Aurelian Townshend

In 2003, Peter Beal uncovered a manuscript in the National Library of Wales written in the hand of Henry Herbert, master of the revels, and containing copies of three songs for a masque by Aurelian Townshend.[1] He surmised that the entertainment was intended for performance before King Charles by the Merchant Adventurers' Company and suggested that it was probably written 'when Townshend was actively engaged in court masques (1631–7)'.[2] It featured, he said, a 'Rabble' of mariners who danced and then, 'whether by verbal implication, actual display or symbolic representation', brought to the shore a cargo of rich merchandise.[3] References in two of the songs, firstly to 'the Merchant royall' and then to 'this bright & glorious sunn', allude, he suggested, to the king himself who was a spectator at the masque.[4] He also pointed out that the manuscript contains two additional notes in Herbert's hand, the second of which reads: '16. Marche. / The wine was frenche'.[5] He deduced from this that the production occurred on an otherwise unidentifiable 16 March and suggested that it was put on by the Merchant Adventurers as 'a propaganda exercise to secure or retain the King's support of their charter'.[6]

Beal's description of the first part of the entertainment is astute. The first song certainly describes a kind of anti-masque in which a 'Rabble' of mariners danced 'Leuoltoe's' to the sound of a kettle drum, after which, the singer promises, 'you shall perceiue this barke of mine containes / fraught, that deserues y^{r} purchase & my paines'.[7] In other words, after the disorderly dance, a ship appears to have come to the shore, filled with a precious cargo. However, rather than being the verbal, actual or symbolic representation of 'gold, diamonds, dye, silk, and sugar' that Beal associates with 'Merchants' who 'Venture', I suggest that this cargo comprised the main masquers and that, furthermore, these were women. The song represents these masquers through blazon, locating them as desirable commodities brought to the stage for the pleasure of an audience conceived as male. We are told the boat contains gold 'such as Colchos, & Arabia blest / Neuer in mine or farr fam'd Fleece possest' (lines 7–8) in a manner that resounds with blazonic representations of a beloved's hair, and which also introduces an image of conquest through its invocation of Jason and the golden fleece.[8] The diamonds the boat carries combine together 'fier & water' so they 'rather lightninge then alight begett' (lines 9–10) in the same manner that courtly love poetry would represent a woman's eyes, while the red of 'Cutcheneele' describes the women's lips and cheeks, and the 'smoothe', 'glossy' and 'white' texture of 'Rawsilke' their fair skins (lines 11–13). In all, the boat's wares are 'Sugars, so perfect as those lips that meete / But with a taste, itt makes their whole liues sweet' (lines 15–16) – an image of kissing if ever there was one. The verses conclude with a warning not to expect to see this cargo in 'Canes, in Ingats or in Bales', but in 'scarfes & vailes' (lines 17–18) – in other words, in female masquing costume.

The merchant's second song begins with an address to the 'Faire suretys of [his] truthe' (line 1) and concludes with the promise that others 'will growe as poore as I / As soone as they haue seen your eyes' (lines 11–12). This is not the kind of invocation that would herald the appearance of male masquers, but it certainly resounds with songs that call in a group of ladies. For example, in *Tempe Restored*, Townshend's 1632 masque for the queen, the lady masquers are heralded by the words: 'there are stars to rise, / That, far above our song / Are music to all eyes'.[9] Female beauty invariably has a transformatory impetus in Caroline masques and, just as here, inspires love and devotion in those that witness it. Moreover, the merchant's first song, here, ends with the promise to the audience that 'when this route is all disperst & gonn, / The tyme, the place, the goods arr all y^r owne' (lines 19–20). In other words, when the rabble of mariners leave, the audience will remain to take possession of the masquing hall and the ship's rich cargo. If this cargo is female, and if Beal is correct that the references to 'the Merchant royall' and 'this bright & glorious sunn' indicate the king, then these masquers can only be noble ladies, represented as the proper possessions of the monarch and his courtiers.

I would suggest, therefore, that this was not a production written by Townshend for the Merchant Adventurers, but that it was closely connected with the court. Indeed, if one were to disregard Beal's suggestion that the production took place on 16 March, then it might be associated with one of Henrietta Maria's lost productions. If one were to look for a suitable March, though, then that of 1627 might be appropriate for a performance involving merchant sailors. That year saw Buckingham's mobilisation of England's fleet for his ill-fated attempts to relieve the French Huguenots at La Rochelle, as well as the performance of his own naval masque before the court in May. Furthermore, Charles granted the earl of Warwick a liberal privateering commission in March that would enable him to attack the Spanish at sea.[10] On 13 March, Henrietta Maria dined at Blackwall aboard the *Neptune*, Warwick's ship, thus marking her support of his venture.[11] Her approbation of his intentions might well have been sealed with a short entertainment, performed either by the queen herself or by other noble ladies.

Kevin Sharpe has suggested that Townshend attached himself to the queen's circle in the late 1620s noting that, in 1629, he was granted custody of the estate of the widow Philippa Ivatt after submitting a petition to the king underwritten by the earl of Holland.[12] Holland, as I have noted, was one of Henrietta Maria's close associates, and was also Warwick's brother, thus putting the poet in a good position to be commissioned to write a masque to celebrate their maritime ambitions. Indeed, in 1629 Holland and Warwick joined together to found the Providence Island Company, whose purpose, in part, was to disrupt the passage of wealth to Spain from her American colonies. As Malcolm Smuts has observed, war with Spain would serve the Rich brothers' interests, not least because it would necessitate a recall of parliament, several sessions of which in the early 1620s had been managed by Warwick and his associates.[13] Henrietta Maria was, at this time, notoriously anti-Spanish, attending ceremonies related to the signing of the Anglo-Spanish peace accord in 1630 in her plainest clothes, and instructing her ladies to do likewise.[14] With all the sabre-rattling directed at her native France in the spring of 1627, it seems likely that she would be happy to lend her support to a venture that would divert attention towards Spain, at the same time as it contrasted her friends' interests with those of Buckingham.

Nevertheless, although Townshend's maritime entertainment might have been a queen's masque, it is still very conservative on the level of gender, representing its lady masquers as beautiful commodities and defining them in relation to their male partners. Patricia Parker has noted that the language of blazon, of 'opening up to the eye or gaze', is linked 'to the possibility of an eroticized, even potentially prurient and voyeuristic, looking'.[15] Just as Buckingham described Charles spying on his new wife's dancing on her first arrival in Dover, so the bodies and movements of Townshend's lady masquers were opened to the gaze of the court in a manner that rendered them the silent objects of male eroticism, valued for their status as goods that would display and increase the wealth of their possessors. In Parker's words, 'The "inventory" of parts becomes a way of taking possession by the very act of naming or accounting.'[16]

Martin Butler has argued that the masques of the 1630s were increasingly private and personal, and suggests that each presented Charles 'as a ruler in the act of taking possession of his empire, the masculine emperor stamping his identity on his feminized state'.[17] This notion of possession certainly maintains in Townshend's masque, not least in the evocative image of the lady masquers as the golden fleece desired and won by Jason, and, if performed in a production for the queen, might indicate an early date, before the maturation of her imagery in masques such as *Tempe Restored*. That said, if the admittedly tentative attribution of date and patron holds, Henrietta Maria perhaps emerges both from the masque and from the privateering enterprise associated with distinct policies, demonstrating that, although her entertainments might deploy an idiom compatible with the king's, they did not necessarily have to mimic his political concerns.

Notes

INTRODUCTION

1 Samuel R. Gardiner, *History of England from the Accession of James I to the Outbreak of the Civil War, 1603–1642*, 10 vols. (London, 1883–4), IX (1884), p. 228.
2 Ibid., pp. 227–8.
3 Alison Plowden, *Henrietta Maria: Charles I's Indomitable Queen* (Stroud, 2001), p. 86.
4 See ibid., p. 106.
5 Martin Butler, 'Reform or Reverence? The Politics of the Caroline Masque', in *Theatre and Government under the Early Stuarts*, ed. J. R. Mulryne and Margaret Shewring (Cambridge, 1993), pp. 118–56, p. 128.
6 See, especially, Henrietta Maria's letters to Christine in *Lettres de Henriette-Marie de France, Reine d'Angleterre à sa soeur Christine duchesse de Savoie*, ed. Hermann Ferrero (Rome, 1881), *passim.*
7 See Eliza, Viscountess Falkland, to Walter, Lord Aston, 19 December 1635: *CSPD, 1635*, p. 578.
8 Margaret M. McGowan, *L'Art du ballet de cour en France (1581–1643)* (Paris, 1963), p. 87; Françoise Kermina, *Marie de Médicis: reine, régente et rebelle* (Paris, 1979), p. 103.
9 Wendy Gibson, *Women in Seventeenth-Century France* (Basingstoke, 1989), pp. 172–3.
10 Gabriele Finaldi, 'Orazio Gentileschi at the Court of Charles I', in *Orazio Gentileschi at the Court of Charles I*, ed. Gabriele Finaldi (London, 1999), pp. 9–37, p. 11.
11 Ibid., p. 12 and p. 24.
12 Ibid., p. 29.
13 Deborah Marrow, *The Art Patronage of Maria de' Medici* (Michigan, 1978; repr. 1982), p. 28.
14 I use the term 'French design' with caution. John Peacock, discussing French art, points out that French culture synthesises Italian elements: Peacock, 'The French Element in Inigo Jones's Masque Designs', in *The Court Masque*, ed. David Lindley (Manchester, 1984), pp. 149–68.
15 See Peter Walls, *Music in the English Courtly Masque 1604–1640* (Oxford, 1996), p. 222.

16 Ibid., note 7.
17 See Eugène Griselle, *Etat de la maison du Roi Louis XIII* (Paris, 1912), p. 85.
18 Walls posits that the 1634 payment 'may indicate some involvement in *Coelum Britannicum*'. He also draws attention to entries in the Paris civic records between 1630 and 1640 relating to Bocan's family: Walls, *Music*, p. 223 and p. 222, note 7. These entries indicate that Bocan's family home remained in Paris, despite his frequent attendance at the English court.
19 Andrew Ashbee and David Lasocki, *A Biographical Dictionary of English Court Musicians 1485–1714*, 2 vols. (Aldershot, 1998), II, *sub.* La Pierre, Sebastian, and La Pierre, Guillaume.
20 See PRO, SP 16/3, no. 112 where he is called 'mr. a danser des filles d'h'.
21 Barbara Ravelhofer has undertaken a detailed study of dancing at the Stuart court: see Ravelhofer, 'The Stuart Masque: Dance, Costume, and Remembering' (unpublished doctoral thesis, University of Cambridge, 1999), *passim.*
22 See Ashbee and Lasocki, *Biographical Dictionary, sub.* Richard and *sub.* Flelle. It appears that there were two Louis Richards active in this period, one of whom served in England and one of whom remained in Paris to train boys to sing in Henrietta Maria's chapel.
23 See Walls, *Music*, p. 164.
24 Quoted in ibid., p. 220.
25 See Ashbee and Lasocki, *Biographical Dictionary, sub.* Prevost, Margaret.
26 Archives nationales, Paris, 'Instruction de la Reine Marie de medicis – a la Reine dangleterre sa fille marie-anriette de France', K 1303, numéro 1.
27 See Bibliothèque nationale, MS 22, 884, fol. 104ff; *Marie de Médicis à sa fille Henriette de France Reyne d'Angleterre*, ed. Abbé F. Duffo (Lourdes, 1936); and Charles Cotolendi, *Histoire de la Tres-Haute et Tres-Puissante Princesse Henriette-Marie de France, Reyne de la Grand' Bretagne* (Paris, 1694), pp. 15–19.
28 Archives nationales, 'Instruction de la Reine Marie de medicis'.
29 Duffo, ed., *Marie de Médicis*, p. 7.
30 Ibid., p. 8.
31 Alison Shell, *Catholicism, Controversy and the English Literary Imagination, 1558–1660* (Cambridge, 1999), pp. 155–6.
32 Ibid., p. 156.
33 Henrietta Maria was interested all her life in other Frenchwomen who had become English queens. For example, in 1628, François Garnier, identifying himself as the queen's 'Procureur General', dedicated to her his manuscript translation of John Stow's history of Isabelle, wife of Edward II, and the history of Bertha, wife of Ethelbert, King of Kent. See Brotherton Library, Special Collections, MS 97: Françoys Garnier de Blois, 'Histoire d'Ethelbert Roy de Kent et d'Edouard 2. Roy d'Angleterre'.
34 *Mercure François*, 11 (Paris, 1626), pp. 373–4.
35 Ibid., p. 380.
36 The other queens were: Judith, a Saxon queen; Marguerite[*sic*], wife of Henry II; Isabelle, wife of Edward II; Catherine, wife of Henry V: ibid., pp. 380–1.

37 See Erica Veevers, *Images of Love and Religion: Queen Henrietta Maria and Court Entertainments* (Cambridge, 1989), p. 143.
38 Ibid., p. 134 and p. 148.
39 Ibid., p. 19.
40 Ibid., p. 20.
41 Ibid., p. 21.
42 Ibid., p. 22. I am uncomfortable with the term 'Devout Humanism' which was coined by Henri Bremond in the twentieth century and homologises Bourbon court Catholicism in a way that is unhelpful.
43 Ibid., pp. 35–7.
44 Ibid., p. 37.
45 Ibid., pp. 20–1.
46 Domna Stanton, 'The Fiction of *Préciosité* and the Fear of Women', *Yale French Studies*, 62 (1981), pp. 107–34, p. 113. Stanton cites as examples the work of Molière, Scarron and Saint-Evremond.
47 Ibid., p. 126.
48 Veevers, *Images*, p. 35.
49 Ibid., pp. 38–9.
50 J. W. Ebsworth, ed., *Poems and Masque of Thomas Carew* (London, 1893), p. 218.
51 See, for example, Julie Sanders's otherwise excellent article, 'Caroline Salon Culture and Female Agency: The Countess of Carlisle, Henrietta Maria, and Public Theatre', *Theatre Journal*, 52 (2000), pp. 449–64, especially p. 453.
52 Veevers, *Images*, p. 39.
53 Ibid. and p. 214n. See also Carolyn C. Lougee, *Le Paradis des Femmes: Women, Salons and Social Stratification in Seventeenth-Century France* (Princeton, 1976), Appendix One, p. 216.
54 A. Baudeau de Somaize, *Le Grand Dictionnaire des Pretieuses* (Paris, 1661), reproduced as *Dictionnaire des Precieuses par le Sieur de Somaize*, ed. M. Ch. L. Livret, 2 vols. (Paris, 1856), II, p. 58.
55 Voiture's admiration for Lucy is evident in letters he wrote from Dover in 1633 to his London host, 'Monsieur Gourdon': see Vincent Voiture, *Les Oeuvres de Monsieur de Voiture* (Paris, 1650), pp. 174–6. Lucy did go to Spa in 1621, but there is no indication that she visited Paris. I can find no evidence that she accompanied her husband on his embassy in 1624.
56 Livret, ed., *Dictionnaire*, II, p. 34 and pp. 51–2.
57 Ibid., pp. 51–2.
58 Ibid., p. 80.
59 Mary M. Rowan, 'Between Salon and Convent: Madame de Rohan, a Precious Abbess', *Papers on French Seventeenth-Century Literature*, 12.22 (1985), pp. 191–207.
60 Ibid., p. 202.
61 Rambouillet had a well-known antipathy for both Marie de Médicis and Louis XIII – so much so that Julie Lucie, her daughter, worried this aversion might damn her: see Nicole Aronson, *Madame de Rambouillet ou la magicienne de la Chambre bleue* (Paris, 1988), pp. 62–8.

62 Ibid., pp. 91–2. In addition, she seems to have shown an interest in Henrietta Maria's cultural activities in England – see chapter 2 below.
63 See R. Malcolm Smuts, 'The Puritan Followers of Henrietta Maria in the 1630s', *The English Historical Review*, 93.366 (1978), pp. 26–45, p. 28; and Veevers, *Images*, pp. 84–5.
64 See Sophie Tomlinson, 'She That Plays the King: Henrietta Maria and the Threat of the Actress in Caroline Culture', in *The Politics of Tragicomedy*, ed. Gordon McMullan and Jonathan Hope (London, 1992), pp. 189–207.

1 SEX AND DANCING: HENRIETTA MARIA'S WEDDING BALLETS

1 Draft letter of George Villiers to the King of France, 13 June 1625: National Archives of Scotland, GD 24/1/825. Quoted in *Records of Early English Drama: Kent: Diocese of Canterbury*, ed. James M. Gibson, 3 vols. (London, 2002), II, pp. 519–20.
2 Ibid.
3 See John Drakakis, 'Shakerley Marmion and the Politics of Dancing' (unpublished seminar paper given at the University of Stirling, 12 April 2004).
4 Interestingly, this phrase is slightly ambiguous and can be translated as either 'which makes me hope she will feel better', or 'behave better'.
5 See James Knowles's new work, *Criticism and Consensus: Politics and Political Culture in the Masque* (forthcoming). See also Clare McManus's comments about Anna of Denmark's refusal of the Protestant sacrament at James I's coronation in London which was, McManus says, 'intended, despite the enclosed nature of an elite ceremony during a time of plague, to reach an aristocratic and diplomatic audience throughout Europe': McManus, *Women on the Renaissance Stage: Anna of Denmark and Female Masquing in the Stuart Court, 1590–1619* (Manchester, 2002), p. 92.
6 Joan B. Landes, *Women and the Public Sphere* (London, 1988), pp. 17–19.
7 See chapter 2 below for more serious examples of the queen consort's refusal to take part in the ceremonies of the Caroline court.
8 Karen Britland, 'A Fairy-tale Marriage: The Myth of the Caroline in Romance', in *The Spanish Match: Prince Charles' Journey to Madrid, 1623*, ed. Alexander Samson (Aldershot, forthcoming 2006).
9 The French *sarabande* was a processional dance, and not as energetic as the English version.
10 Martin Butler, 'Courtly Negotiations', in *The Politics of the Stuart Court*, ed. David Bevington and Peter Holbrook (Cambridge, 1998), pp. 20–40, p. 27.
11 Ibid., p. 27 and p. 28.
12 McManus, *Women*, p. 94.
13 Skiles Howard, *The Politics of Courtly Dancing in Early Modern England* (Amherst, 1998), p. 113.
14 Ibid.

15 Howard notes that dances like the *sarabande* and canary 'functioned as a mimetic synecdoche of the subjection of land and woman, since in colonialist discursive formations, the imprinted land was female': ibid., p. 114.
16 McManus, *Women*, p. 95.
17 See Marie-Claude Canova-Green, 'Le Mariage du lys et de la rose, ou les fêtes de l'alliance d'Angleterre (1625)' (unpublished conference paper). I am extremely grateful to Dr Canova-Green for her generosity in sharing her work.
18 See below.
19 Marie-Claude Canova-Green, *La Politique-spectacle au grand siècle: les rapports franco-anglais* (Paris, 1993), p. 27.
20 See Marc Antonio Morosini to the Doge and Senate, 9 December 1624: *CSPV, 1623–5*, p. 508.
21 See particularly, Pierre de La Porte, *Mémoires de M. De La Porte, premier valet de chambre de Louis XIV* (Paris, 1791), p. 3.
22 See *Mémoires du Cardinal de Richelieu*, ed. Michaud et Poujoulat (Paris, 1866), p. 328.
23 Marrow, *Art Patronage*, p. 20.
24 He was the great nephew of Mary Stuart and was, thus, distantly related to Charles I. Indeed, he acted as Charles's proxy when the Anglo-French marriage was celebrated in Paris.
25 Emile Magne, *Le Plaisant Abbé de Boisrobert, fondateur de l'Académie française 1592–1662*, 2nd edn (Paris, 1909), p. 85.
26 Claude Malleville, *Poesies du Sieur de Malleville* (Paris, 1649), p. 120.
27 Jean Jacquot, too, has commented that it is reasonable to suppose that Boisrobert's verses came from a ballet danced in France after the wedding: Jacquot, 'La Reine Henriette-Marie et l'influence française dans les spectacles à la cour de Charles Ier', *9e Cahier de l'Association Internationale des Etudes Françaises* (Paris, 1957), pp. 128–60, p. 154.
28 Canova-Green, *La Politique-spectacle*, pp. 38–9.
29 *Mercure François,* 11, p. 366.
30 Marie-Claude Canova-Green, 'Remarques sur la datation et l'attribution de ballets de cour sous le règne de Louis XIII', *Dix-septième Siècle* (1987), pp. 421–6, p. 423. Germain Habert was associated in Paris with the group of literary figures who, under the leadership of Valentin Conrart, became the first members of the Académie française in 1634. I am slightly uneasy about Canova-Green's attribution because Habert seems to have been born in 1615 and would therefore have been only about ten years old at the time of the ballet's composition: see Albert Pauphilet *et al.*, eds., *Dictionnaire des lettres françaises: le XVIIe siècle*, 2nd edn rev. Patrick Dandrey (Paris, 1996), *sub.* Habert (Germain).
31 Little is known about Mareschal. From 1630 onwards, he wrote tragicomedies for the Parisian theatre and, in 1632, might have become librarian to Gaston d'Orléans.
32 Anon., *Recueil des plus beaux vers* (Paris, 1627), pp. 793–5.

33 Ibid., p. 796.
34 See John Orrell, 'Amerigo Salvetti and the London Court Theatre, 1616–1640', *Theatre Survey*, 20.1 (1979), pp. 1–26, p. 12. See also Canova-Green, 'Le Mariage du lys et de la rose'.
35 Canova-Green, *La Politique-spectacle*, p. 17.
36 Anon., *Recueil des plus beaux vers*, p. 793.
37 Marie-Claude Canova-Green, 'L'Equivoque d'une célébration: les fêtes du mariage de Louis XIII et d'Anne d'Autriche à Bordeaux (1615)', *XVIIe Siècle*, 222 (2004), pp. 3–24, p. 19.
38 Anon., *Recueil des plus beaux vers*, p. 578.
39 Canova-Green, too, comments on France's superiority in these verses: see *La Politique-spectacle*, p. 329.
40 Anon., *Recueil des plus beaux vers*, p. 575.
41 Ibid., p. 579.
42 'O heavenly beauty / Who has given us this goddess / Who we see to be the living image of your virtues': ibid., p. 578.
43 See Marrow, *Art Patronage*, *passim.*
44 Malleville, *Poesies*, p. 117.
45 Philippa Berry, *Of Chastity and Power: Elizabethan Literature and the Unmarried Queen* (London, 1989), p. 38.
46 Ibid., p. 39.
47 Stephen Orgel, *Impersonations: The Performance of Gender in Shakespeare's England* (Cambridge, 1996), p. 94.
48 Marjorie Garber, *Vested Interests: Cross-Dressing and Cultural Anxiety* (London, 1993), p. 6.
49 M. C. Hippeau, ed., *Mémoires inédits du Comte Leveneur de Tillières* (Paris, 1862), pp. 52–3. See also Melinda Gough, 'A Newly Discovered Performance by Henrietta Maria', *Huntington Library Quarterly*, 65.3–4 (2002), pp. 435–47, p. 446.
50 Paul M. Lacroix, ed., *Ballets et mascarades de cour sous Henri IV et Louis XIII (de 1581 à 1652)*, 6 vols. (Geneva, 1868–70), II, p. 354.
51 Anon., *Recueil des plus beaux vers* (Paris, 1627), p. 576. See also Mareschal's Juno, in ibid., p. 794.
52 See also Bernard Cottret, 'Diplomatie et éthique de l'état: l'ambassade d'Effiat en Angleterre et le mariage de Charles Ier d'Angleterre et d'Henriette-Marie de France', in *L'Etat baroque: regards sur la pensée politique de la France du premier XVIIe siècle*, ed. Henry Méchoulan (Paris, 1985), pp. 221–42.
53 See Hippeau, ed., *Tillières*, p. xii.
54 Canova-Green, 'Le Mariage du lys et de la rose'.
55 Sir John Beaumont, *The Theater of Apollo*, ed. W. W. Greg (London, 1926), p. 9.
56 Ibid., p. 6.
57 Ibid., p. 7.
58 Ben Jonson, *The Fortunate Isles and Their Union*, in *Ben Jonson*, ed. C. H. Herford *et al.*, 11 vols. (Oxford, 1925–52), VII, p. 728, lines 624–76.
59 Canova-Green, 'L'Equivoque d'une célébration', p. 14.

60 Thomas Cogswell, *The Blessed Revolution: English Politics and the Coming of War, 1621–1624* (Cambridge, 1989), pp. 10–12, and p. 107.
61 Ibid., p. 121.
62 Jean Puget de la Serre, *Les Amours du Roy et de la Reine* (Paris, 1625), p. 440.
63 Malleville, *Poesies*, p. 119.
64 Boisrobert, 'Ode, Présentée à la Reine d'Angleterre, par Monsieur le Comte de Carlisle, de la part du Roy son Espous', lines 122–4, in Anon., *Recueil des plus beaux vers*, pp. 536–41.
65 Katherine Gorges was the widow of Edward Haselwood, and the daughter of Sir Robert Osborne and his wife Margaret. She was married to Sir Edward Gorges, son of Sir Thomas Gorges of Longford Castle, Wiltshire. Sir Hugh Smyth, her correspondent, was the husband of Elizabeth, sister to Sir Edward Gorges.
66 Katherine Gorges to her brother-in-law from Longford in Wiltshire, 7 December 1625, Bristol Record Office, Ashton Court Muniments, AC/C/47–3. I am very grateful to James Knowles for drawing my attention to this letter.
67 St François de Sales, *Introduction à la vie dévote*, ed. Etienne-Marie Lajeunie (Paris, 1962), p. 160.
68 See Pierre de Bérulle, *Elévation sur sainte Madeleine*, ed. Joseph Beaude (Grenoble, 1998), p. 30.
69 Katherine Gorges to her brother-in-law from Longford in Wiltshire, 7 December 1625, Bristol Record Office, Ashton Court Muniments, AC/C/47-3.
70 McGowan, *Ballet de cour*, pp. 133–47.
71 Ibid., pp. 134–5.
72 In August 1628, the queen consort ordered costumes for a masque that should have been performed at Wellingborough (see chapter 3 below). Similarly, in the autumn of 1632, she danced an impromptu masque with her maids to celebrate the birth of her nephew, the prince of Savoy.
73 Chamberlain to Carleton, 25 June 1625: Thomas Birch, ed., *The Court and Times of Charles the First*, 2 vols. (London, 1848), I, p. 35.
74 For an excellent discussion of the politics of Henrietta Maria's circle in the early 1630s and its difference from the policies being propounded by Charles and his government, see Smuts, 'Puritan Followers', pp. 26–45.
75 Several of the daughters of Henrietta Maria's French ladies did go on to marry English gentlemen: see National Library of Wales, Wynnstay 181, fols. 14r–v. See also chapter 8 below.
76 One of the first contentious issues on Henrietta Maria's arrival was the presence of Madame de Saint Georges in the queen's coach. Charles would not allow Saint Georges to ride with the queen, although Henrietta Maria requested it. The dispute raised issues of precedence and also signalled an anxiety that the familiarity between Henrietta Maria and some of her female attendants blocked English courtiers' access to preferment and patronage through their wives. See *CSPV, 1625–6*, p. 129 and p. 144.
77 Pory to Mead, 1 July 1626: Birch, *Court and Times*, I, p. 119.

2 *ARTENICE*: A NEW FRENCH FASHION AT THE ENGLISH COURT

1 Honorat de Bueil, sieur de Racan, *Les Bergeries*, ed. Louis Arnould (Paris, 1937), pp. v–vii.
2 See Graham Parry, *The Golden Age Restor'd: The Culture of the Stuart Court, 1603–42* (Manchester, 1981), p. 189. Stephen Orgel and Roy Strong also subscribe to this view: see Orgel and Strong, *Inigo Jones: The Theatre of the Stuart Court*, 2 vols. (Berkeley, 1973), I, p. 25. Although Racan's identity as author of the pastoral was established in 1937, Marion Wynne-Davies follows Alfred Harbage in assuming that Henrietta Maria wrote the play herself: see Wynne-Davies, 'The Queen's Masque: Renaissance Women and the Seventeenth-Century Court Masque', in *Gloriana's Face: Women, Public and Private, in the English Renaissance*, ed. S. P. Cerasano and Marion Wynne-Davies (Detroit, 1992), pp. 79–104, p. 81; and Harbage, *Cavalier Drama: An Historical and Critical Supplement to the Study of the Elizabethan and Restoration Stage* (London, 1936), p. 12.
3 Veevers, *Images*, pp. 33–4.
4 Ibid., p. 34.
5 '[I]t is wonderful to see the revival of the hostility between the two nations at the time of this alliance': Zuane Pesaro, Venetian ambassador in England, 21/31 July 1625, *CSPV, 1625–6*, p. 129; 'Apparently discords and disputes have arisen between the two nations from the marriage instead of true friendship': Marc Antonio Morosini, Venetian ambassador in France, 12/22 August 1625, *CSPV, 1625–6*, p. 144; '[T]here is every prospect of the creation of a permanent bad feeling between the two nations': Salvetti, 5/15 September 1625, HMC, *The Manuscripts of Henry Duncan Skrine, Esq.: Salvetti Correspondence, Eleventh Report*, Appendix, Part I (London, 1887), p. 37.
6 Sir Nathaniel Bacon, to Jane, Lady Bacon, 16 February 1626: Richard Griffin, Baron Braybrooke, ed., *The Private Correspondence of Jane, Lady Cornwallis, 1613–1644* (London, 1842), p. 143.
7 John Finet, *Finetti Philoxenis: som choice observations of Sr John Finett Knight, and Master of the Ceremonies to the two last kings* (London, 1656), p. 171.
8 See Sir John Chamberlain to Sir Dudley Carleton, 19 January 1626 and Sir Benjamin Rudyerd to [Sir Francis Nethersole], 3 February 1626: *CSPD, 1625–6*, p. 225 and p. 246.
9 Shell, *Catholicism*, p. 153.
10 Zuane Pesaro to the Doge and Senate, 26 January/5 February 1626: *CSPV, 1625–6*, p. 309. In 1621, the French crown had become involved in a war with the Huguenot princes, Henri, duc de Rohan, and Benjamin, prince de Soubise. An initial peace was signed in 1622, but the war flared up again in 1625, drawing the English into the conflict in support of the La Rochelle Protestants. Richelieu besieged La Rochelle in the summer of 1627, and Charles I's fleet, led by the duke of Buckingham, sailed to the aid of the French Protestants. However, the presence of the English did not alter the

balance of the conflict, and on 28 October 1628, La Rochelle capitulated to Richelieu.

11 Dispatch of the Tuscan Resident to the Grand Duke of Florence, 24 February/6 March 1626: Orrell, 'Amerigo Salvetti', pp. 10–11.
12 Louis Arnould, *Racan (1589–1670): histoire critique de sa vie et de ses oeuvres* (Paris, 1896), p. 204 and p. 218.
13 See Bernard Yon, 'La Conversation dans *L'Astrée*, texte littéraire et art de vivre', *Dix-septième siècle*, 179.2 (1993), pp. 273–89, p. 287; see also Pauphilet *et al.*, eds., *Dictionnaire*, *sub.* Urfé.
14 Francis de Sales, *Introduction to the Devout Life*, trans. Michael Day (London, 1962), p. 2.
15 Arnould, *Racan*, pp. 175–6.
16 The play obviously proved popular as it went through twelve editions before 1635; see Jean Parrish and William A. Jackson, 'Racan's *L'Artenice*, an Addition to the English Canon', *Harvard Library Bulletin*, 14 (1960), pp. 183–90, p. 185.
17 HMC, *Salvetti Correspondence*, p. 41.
18 Parrish and Jackson, '*Artenice*', pp. 186–7.
19 Ibid., p. 190.
20 Ibid., p. 188.
21 See ibid., pp. 184–5. The poem is in a private collection and I have been unable to trace it.
22 See Magne, *Boisrobert*, p. 89.
23 H. M. Colvin, ed., *The History of the King's Works*, 6 vols. (London, 1982), IV, 2, p. 261.
24 See Orgel and Strong, *Inigo Jones*, I, p. 385.
25 See ibid.
26 Ibid.
27 Ibid., p. 25.
28 John Peacock, *The Stage Designs of Inigo Jones* (Cambridge, 1995), pp. 87–8.
29 Ibid.
30 Ibid., pp. 178–9. It is worth, nonetheless, observing with John Orrell that, although these settings are the first recorded designs of their type, 'their style may have been set earlier' in other scenes that Jones provided for Anna of Denmark's productions at Somerset House: Orrell, *The Theatres of Inigo Jones and John Webb* (Cambridge, 1985), p. 80.
31 Orrell, *Jones and Webb*, p. 88.
32 Ibid., pp. 88–9.
33 For a summary of the architectural style that Jones developed for Henrietta Maria, see John Harris and Gordon Higgot, *Inigo Jones: Complete Architectural Drawings* (New York, 1989), especially pp. 190–2. (As I noted above, I use the term 'French' with caution: see Peacock, 'French Element'.)
34 More than £2,000 was spent on the costumes alone and the carpentry and other works amounted to more than £168: see Parrish and Jackson, '*Artenice*', p. 183, note 1.

35 On 14 February 1626, a week before the performance of *Artenice*, a warrant had been issued granting Somerset House and all its furnishings to Henrietta Maria as part of her jointure: *CSPD, 1625–6*, p. 561.
36 Orrell, *Jones and Webb*, p. 82.
37 This was particularly important in Jacques Du Bosc's *L'Honneste Femme*, translated as *The Accomplish'd Woman* by Walter Montagu in 1655. See, for example, Du Bosc, *L'Honneste Femme*, 3rd edn (Paris, 1635), p. 309.
38 Sales, *Introduction à la vie dévote*, p. 139.
39 Sales, *Introduction to the Devout Life*, pp. 108–9.
40 Racan, *Les Bergeries*, p. 47.
41 Ibid., p. 48.
42 'On appelle la chasteté honnêteté, et la profession d'icelle honneur': Sales, *Introduction à la vie dévote*, p. 154. I am using Day's translation, p. 121.
43 'Lisez souvent aux choses sacrées, car *la parole de Dieu est chaste* et rend ceux qui s'y plaisent chastes': Sales, *Introduction à la vie dévote*, p. 160. Day's translation, p. 126.
44 Sophie Tomlinson has explored this paradox in the context of Henrietta Maria's *The Shepherds' Paradise* (1633) which, she says, 'struggles with the doubts and dilemmas of female subjectivity in a wholly new theatrical context'; see her essay, 'Theatrical Vibrancy on the Caroline Court Stage', in *Women and Culture at the Courts of the Stuart Queens*, ed. Clare McManus (Basingstoke, 2003), pp. 186–203, p. 192.
45 Marie Laporte, the first professional French actress, had taken on the role of Artenice in Valleran Lecomte's troupe's 1619 production of *Les Bergeries*. Racan's pastoral had also enjoyed great popularity among French amateur theatrical circles where again women played speaking roles: Arnould, *Racan*, p. 228 and p. 280.
46 Rev. Joseph Mead to Sir Martin Stuteville, 4 March 1626: Birch, ed., *Court and Times*, I, p. 85.
47 Chamberlain to Carleton, 7 March 1626, in *The Letters of John Chamberlain*, ed. Norman Egbert McClure, 2 vols. (Philadelphia, 1939), II, p. 630. The works accounts for the production bear out Chamberlain's statement. Orgel and Strong print the following: 'Item to John Walker for Lawrell wreaths heire and beards iiij li iij s iiij d': Orgel and Strong, *Inigo Jones*, II, p. 384. *Tempora mutantur et nos* ['the times change and we change with them'] is a famous, anonymous Latin phrase that was, for a long time, wrongly attributed to Ovid.
48 The Venetian ambassador reported home that 'the pastoral did not give complete satisfaction, because the English objected to the first part being declaimed by the Queen': *CSPV, 1625–6*, p. 346.
49 Orgel, *Impersonations*, p. 4 and p. 11.
50 Sir Ralph Winwood, *Memorials of State*, 3 vols. (London, 1725), II, p. 44.
51 See a letter to the Rev. Joseph Mead, dated 3 December 1626: Birch, ed., *Court and Times*, I, p. 180. It is also worth noting that Lady Alice Egerton took a vocal role in Milton's *Masque at Ludlow* in 1634 without apparent criticism.

52 Will Fisher, 'The Renaissance Beard: Masculinity in Early Modern England', *Renaissance Quarterly*, 54 (2001), pp. 155–87, p. 150 and p. 166.
53 Fisher also makes the important observation that, while beardless men could be regarded as effeminate, bearded women were looked on as monstrous (ibid., pp. 169–70). This point is upheld by A. R. Braunmuller's discussion of the witches in *Macbeth* which invokes the early modern theory that non-menstruating women grew beards: see Braunmuller, ed., *Macbeth* (Cambridge, 1997; repr. 2001), pp. 34–5. In the light of this, the sight of Henrietta Maria's women dressed in beards upon the stage was troubling, not only because it constituted a transgression of gender norms, but because it provided an image of femininity that was sterile and therefore of no material use to the family or state.
54 *Letters of John Chamberlain*, ed. McClure, II, p. 625.
55 Landes, *Women*, p. 24.
56 Ibid., p. 22.
57 Ibid., p. 24 and p. 22.
58 'Certes le seul bien à quoi ie veus pretendre, / Est qu'avant mon trespas vous me donniez un gendre': (Racan), *L'Artenice* (London, (1626)), p. 14.
59 Ibid., p. 63.
60 Duffo, ed., *Marie de Médicis*, p. 8.
61 Ibid., p. 9.
62 Gisèle Mathieu-Castellani, 'La Poétique du fleuve dans les *Bergeries* de Racan', in *Le Genre pastoral en Europe du XVe au XVIIe siècle: Actes du colloque international tenu à Saint-Etienne du 28 septembre au 1er octobre 1978* (Saint-Etienne, 1980), pp. 223–32, p. 227.
63 Duffo, ed., *Marie de Médicis*, p. 9.
64 (Racan), *L'Artenice*, p. 38.
65 Racan, *Les Bergeries*, p. 103.
66 (Racan), *L'Artenice*, p. 38.
67 Ibid., p. 48.
68 Ibid.
69 Sales, *Introduction à la vie dévote*, p. 11.
70 Duffo, ed., *Marie de Médicis*, p. 9. Bertha was the French princess who married Ethelbert, King of Kent, in the year 566. She managed to convert her husband and several of his noblemen to Christianity and encouraged the king to found churches in London and Rochester.
71 See Cottret, 'Diplomatie', p. 234.

3 FOREIGN BODIES: CONFLICT AND CO-OPERATION IN THE EARLY MASQUES

1 For a discussion of the diplomatic negotiations over the Anglo-French marriage, see Cottret, 'Diplomatie', *passim.*
2 Plowden, *Henrietta Maria*, p. 24.
3 For a discussion of this plot, see chapter 6 below.

4 After joining her husband and the new English queen consort at Boulogne, the duchess of Buckingham sent Anne of Austria the gift of an expensive fan of feathers. This gesture seems more the consolidation of an alliance of friendship than the response of a jealous wife. See La Porte, *Mémoires*, pp. 7–8.
5 Hippeau, ed., *Tillières*, p. 254.
6 Caroline Hibbard, 'The Role of a Queen Consort: The Household and Court of Henrietta Maria, 1625–1642', in *Princes, Patronage and the Nobility: The Court at the Beginning of the Modern Age, c. 1450–1650*, ed. Ronald G. Asch and Adolf M. Birke (Oxford, 1991), pp. 393–417, p. 405.
7 The countess of Tillières to her husband at court, 9 August 1626: Hippeau, ed., *Tillières*, p. 252.
8 Ibid.
9 Ibid., p. 249.
10 National Library of Wales, Wynnstay 161: 'Receipts of Sir Richard Wynn, Treasurer and Receiver-General to Henrietta Maria, 1629–42', sig. 157v. The Parish Records at Bolsover in Derbyshire record the birth of a son to the couple in September 1636: Bolsover Parish Records, 1603–1746 (M46, I).
11 Christian Vantelet was married at court in 1636 to William Shelley, son of Sir John Shelley, and subsequently took up a position as a 'chamberer' alongside her mother in the queen consort's household. See chapter 8 below.
12 Archives du Ministère des Affaires Etrangères, Paris: Fonds de la Correspondance Politique – Angleterre (origines–1871), XLII, fol. 207v.
13 See *CSPV*, 8 October 1634.
14 Martin Butler, *Courtly Negotiations: The Early Stuart Masque and Political Culture* (forthcoming), chapter 9.
15 See ibid. See also *CSPV, 1625–6*, p. 574.
16 Maréchal [François] de Bassompierre, *Journal de ma vie: mémoires du maréchal de Bassompierre*, 3 vols. (Paris, 1875), III, p. 274.
17 Orrell, 'Amerigo Salvetti', p. 12.
18 On the *Theater of Apollo*, see Canova-Green, 'Le Mariage du lys et de la rose'; see also chapter 1 above.
19 John Holles noted that the production was to be 'composed of english and frenche': see P. R. Seddon, ed., *Letters of John Holles 1587–1637*, 3 vols. (Nottingham, 1983), II, p. 339.
20 Maréchal [François] de Bassompierre, *Négociation du Maréchal de Bassompierre envoyé Ambassadeur Extraordinaire, en Angleterre de la part du Roy très-Chrestien, l'an 1626* (Cologne, 1668), p. 259.
21 Seddon, ed., *Letters of John Holles*, II, pp. 337–8.
22 Birch, ed., *Court and Times*, I, p. 180. This letter misrepresents the family relationships between Gargantua, Pantagruel and Gargamella. In Rabelais's text, Gargamelle is the mother of Gargantua who, in turn, is the father of Pantagruel. It is difficult to assess whether the entertainment itself confused these characters, or whether this was the fault of Mead's correspondent. However, as Margaret McGowan has noted, even French ballet writers did

not always read Rabelais with proper attention: see McGowan, *Ballet de cour*, p. 147.

23 See Malone Society, *Collections*, II, 3 (Oxford, 1931), pp. 332–3.

24 Anne Lake Prescott, 'The Stuart Masque and Pantagruel's Dreams', *ELH*, 51.3 (1984), pp. 407–30.

25 I see no reason to suppose that the performers in the anti-masque did not recite short verses themselves, before beginning to dance. Mead's correspondent does, after all, use the word 'acted' and observes that Buckingham's role was 'histrionical'.

26 See Bibliothèque nationale de France, MS Fonds français 12491, fol. 117r. The costume accounts for the English production make it clear that it included a vaulting master, a dancing master, a schoolmaster, two nurses and Gargamella: see Malone Society, *Collections*, II, 3, pp. 332–4. Orgel and Strong have tentatively associated some of Jones's sketches with this masque: see Orgel and Strong, *Inigo Jones*, I, pp. 390–1.

27 Françoise Gourier, *Etude des oeuvres poétiques de Saint-Amant* (Paris, 1961), p. 20. Bassompierre had been implicated in Gaston d'Orléans's rebellion after the Day of Dupes and was imprisoned by Richelieu in the Bastille in 1631.

28 See Bibliothèque nationale de France, MS Fonds français 12491, fol. 117r.

29 'quand ma Phylis sommeille / ie faict du bruict si doucement / que chaque nuict ie la resueille / au doux son de mon instrument': ibid.

30 'un autre en scait plus ie croy / mais tout le monde menuironne / pour scauoir un coup que perssonne / ne scait que ma maistresse et moy': ibid.

31 See Archives du Ministère des Affaires Etrangères, Paris: Fonds de la Correspondance Politique – Angleterre (origines–1871), XLII, fol. 15v.

32 See Birch, ed., *Court and Times*, I, p. 185.

33 See Finet, *Finetti Philoxenis*, p. 198.

34 Birch, ed., *Court and Times*, I, p. 185.

35 *Huntingdon Papers (The Archives of the Noble Family of Hastings)*, 2 vols. (London, 1926), II, p. 26. This edition incorrectly dates the letter to 18 January 1633, two days before the countess died. As the letter also mentions the Forced Loan and England's bad relations with France, it dates better to 1627.

36 Gordon McMullan, *The Politics of Unease in the Plays of John Fletcher* (Amherst, 1994), pp. 22–4.

37 See Thomas Cogswell, *Home Divisions: Aristocracy, the State and Provincial Conflict* (Manchester, 1998), pp. 144–5.

38 Ibid., p. 145.

39 See James Knowles, 'Stanley, Elizabeth, countess of Huntingdon', in *ODNB* (Oxford, 2004); http://www.oxforddnb.com, accessed 9 November 2004.

40 See PRO LR5/63.

41 See, for example, *CSPD, 1625–6*, p. 411 and p. 499; *CSPD, 1628–9*, p. 162, p. 190 and p. 585; *CSPD, 1629–31*, p. 185; *CSPD, 1631–3*, p. 126 and p. 369.

42 See Archives du Ministère des Affaires Etrangères, Paris: Fonds de la Correspondance Politique – Angleterre (origines–1871), XLII, fol. 61v.

43 See Roy E. Schreiber, *The First Carlisle: Sir James Hay, First Earl of Carlisle as Courtier, Diplomat and Entrepreneur, 1580–1636* (Philadelphia, 1984), p. 100.

44 Archives du Ministère des Affaires Etrangères, Paris: Fonds de la Correspondance Politique – Angleterre (origines–1871), XLII, fol. 45v.

45 Ibid., fol. 46r.

46 One of his letters, dated 20 April 1627, contains details about the massing of Charles's troops and was entrusted into the care of 'le s[r] du Val l'un de la Musique de la Reyne de la Grande Bretagne laquelle luy a donné congé d'aller veoir ses amys en France': ibid., fol. 52v.

47 Ibid., fol. 88r.

48 Smuts, 'Puritan Followers', pp. 27–8. Interestingly, though, Monsieur Aubert, her personal surgeon, was temporarily dismissed from England for spying in January 1628: see Birch, ed., *Court and Times*, I, p. 310.

49 Butler, *Courtly Negotiations*, chapter 9. See also, Malone Society, *Collections*, X: *Dramatic Records in the Declared Accounts of the Office of Works, 1560–1640*, ed. F. P. Wilson and R. F. Hill (Oxford, 1975; repr. 1977), pp. 38–9; Birch, ed., *Court and Times*, I, p. 312; C. E. McGee and J. C. Meagher, 'Preliminary Checklist of Tudor and Stuart Entertainments: 1625–1634', *Research Opportunities in Renaissance Drama*, 36 (1997), pp. 23–85, pp. 43–4.

50 The portrait is untraced, but see Susan A. Sykes, 'Henrietta Maria, Queen of Scotland and England', in *Grove Dictionary of Art Online* (Oxford, 2004), accessed August 2004 (http://www.groveart.com). On the Wellingborough masque, see PRO LR5/65: 'A bille of those thinges that weare Maide by Hughe Pope for a Maske that should haue beene p*er*formed at Wellingeborow the 12th of August 1628'.

51 John H. Astington, *English Court Theatre 1558–1642* (Cambridge, 1999), p. 132. See also PRO E351/2947 and PRO E351/2948.

52 Astington, *English Court Theatre*, p. 132.

53 Ibid.

54 'A bille of those thinges that weare Maide by Hughe Pope for a Maske that should haue beene p*er*formed at Wellingeborow the 12th of August 1628': PRO, LR5/65.

55 It is tempting to associate Buckingham's assassination with the cancellation of this production. However, that did not take place until the end of August. Instead, it is possible that the cancellation resulted from the smallpox contracted by Lucy, Lady Carlisle, Henrietta Maria's close companion at this time.

56 William Davenant, *Salmacida Spolia*, in David Lindley, ed., *Court Masques: Jacobean and Caroline Entertainments 1605–1640* (Oxford, 1995), p. 209, line 340. Amazonian imagery was also present in the queen's lost masque of March 1633. See the costume accounts in the queen's debenture books: PRO LR5/65. See also, Barbara Ravelhofer, 'Bureaucrats and Courtly Cross-Dressers in the *Shrovetide Masque* and *The Shepherd's Paradise*', *ELR*, 29.1 (1999), pp. 75–96.

57 Shell, *Catholicism*, p. 155.

58 Page duBois, *Centaurs and Amazons: Women and the Pre-History of the Great Chain of Being* (Michigan, 1982; repr. 1991), p. 5.
59 Butler, *Courtly Negotiations*, chapter 9.
60 Ibid.
61 Ben Jonson and Inigo Jones, *Love's Triumph Through Callipolis*, in *Ben Jonson*, ed. Herford *et al.*, VII, pp. 735–43, lines 16–17 and 22–4. All subsequent line references will be taken from this edition.
62 Orgel and Strong note that Jones's designs for the depraved lovers did not bear out the text's instructions and did not depict the 'habits of the four prime European nations'. Most of the costumes were Italianate and drawn from *commedia dell'arte*, although there were a few north European costumes: Orgel and Strong, *Inigo Jones*, I, p. 409. Martin Butler has commented that the 'ostensible occasion of *Love's Triumph* was the Treaty of Madrid, which put an end to five years' war with Spain': Butler, *Courtly Negotiations*, chapter 9.
63 This motif of amorous reciprocity is more fully expounded in Jonson's *Love's Welcome at Bolsover*, performed before the king and queen consort in 1634.
64 Soon after its completion, Van Dyck was asked to repaint various portions of Mytens's canvas, notably the representation of Henrietta Maria.
65 All subsequent line references to this text are taken from Orgel and Strong, *Inigo Jones*, II, pp. 453–8.
66 Graham Parry notes that 'The name Albanactus is taken from Geoffrey of Monmouth's *History of the Kings of Britain*, where he is named as the son of the founder of Britain, Brutus, and the first king of Scotland. The name, therefore, is a tribute to Charles's Scottish birth and ancestry': Parry, *Golden Age*, p. 228, note 7.
67 Kevin Sharpe, *Criticism and Compliment: The Politics of Literature in the England of Charles I* (Cambridge, 1987), p. 190.
68 Ibid., p. 225.
69 Parry, *Golden Age*, p. 191.
70 Sharpe, *Criticism and Compliment*, p. 226.
71 See Birch, ed., *Court and Times*, I, p. 23. She was initially to be called 'Queen Henry', but this was quickly changed to 'Queen Mary'. Henrietta Maria's sister, in contrast, adopted the name Isabella (in place of Elizabeth) after marrying Philip of Spain.

4 FAMILY AFFAIRS: HENRIETTA MARIA AND CONTINENTAL POLITICS IN 1631

1 For discussions of the quarrel, see Herford *et al.*, eds., *Ben Jonson*, X, pp. 681–2; D. J. Gordon, 'Poet and Architect: The Intellectual Setting of the Quarrel Between Ben Jonson and Inigo Jones', *Journal of the Warburg and Courtauld Institutes*, 12 (1949), pp. 152–78. See also Jonson's poems, 'An Expostulation with Inigo Jones', 'To Inigo, Marquis Would-Be: A Corollary' and 'To a Friend: An Epigram of Him', in *Ben Jonson: Poems*, ed. Ian Donaldson (Oxford, 1975), pp. 319–26.

2 *Court Masques*, ed. Lindley, p. 259.
3 Butler, 'Reform or Reverence?', p. 128.
4 Ibid.
5 Ben Jonson and Inigo Jones, *Chloridia*, in *Ben Jonson*, ed. Herford *et al.*, VII, pp. 749–50, lines 1–12. All subsequent line references will be to this edition.
6 Jonson and Jones, *Love's Triumph*, in *Ben Jonson*, ed. Herford *et al.*, VII, p. 736, line 13.
7 Orgel and Strong, *Inigo Jones*, I, p. 56.
8 Veevers, *Images*, p. 176.
9 Ibid.
10 Ovid, *Fasti*, trans. James George Frazer (Cambridge, Mass., 1931; repr. 1996), p. 275.
11 Veevers, *Images*, p. 130.
12 Edmund Spenser, *The Faerie Queene*, ed. Thomas P. Roche (London, 1978; repr. 1987), pp. 464–8.
13 See D. J. Gordon, 'Ben Jonson's *Haddington Masque*: The Story and the Fable (1947)', in *The Renaissance Imagination: Essays and Lectures by D. J. Gordon*, ed. Stephen Orgel (Berkeley, 1975), pp. 185–93, pp. 185–6.
14 Veevers, *Images*, p. 176.
15 See A. M. Nagler, *Theatre Festivals of the Medici, 1539–1637* (New Haven, 1964), p. 139. The discussion of *La Flora* that follows is strongly indebted to Nagler.
16 Ibid., p. 140.
17 René Bordier, *Grand Ballet de la Reyne representant le Soleil, dancé en la Salle du petit Bourbon, en l'annee mil six cens vingt & un* (Paris, 1621), p. 3.
18 Canova-Green, *La Politique-spectacle*, p. 223. The word was later used in descriptions of *Britannia Triumphans*, *Luminalia* and *Salmacida Spolia*.
19 See Thomas Campion, *The Lords' Masque*, lines 1–2, in *Campion's Works*, ed. Percival Vivian (Oxford, 1909), pp. 89–100; Ben Jonson, *Lovers Made Men*, line 154, in *Ben Jonson*, ed. Herford *et al.*, VII, pp. 449–60. Jonson also uses the term in *Pan's Anniversary* (1621), line 190, *The Masque of Augurs* (1622), lines 364–5, *Time Vindicated* (1623), lines 332–3, *Neptune's Triumph* (1624), line 453, and *The Fortunate Isles* (1625), line 567. Martin Butler suggests that the first time Jonson actually used successive entries was in *The Vision of Delight* (1617): see Martin Butler, ed., *The Vision of Delight*, in *The Cambridge Edition of the Works of Ben Jonson*, ed. David Bevington, Martin Butler and Ian Donaldson, 6 vols. (Cambridge, forthcoming 2007).
20 For Jones's various designs for the costume of Chloris, see Orgel and Strong, *Inigo Jones*, I, pp. 441–8. For comments on Henrietta Maria's control over the final design, see Susan Alexandra Sykes, 'Henrietta Maria's "House of Delight": French Influence and Iconography in the Queen's House, Greenwich', *Apollo*, 133 (1991), pp. 332–6, p. 333.
21 Orgel and Strong, *Inigo Jones*, I, pp. 56–7.
22 Veevers, *Images*, p. 127.
23 In 1621, the French crown became involved in a war with the Huguenot princes, Henri, duc de Rohan, and Benjamin, prince de Soubise. An initial

peace was signed in 1622, but the war flared up again in 1625. The Huguenot navy was defeated that September, and a peace treaty was signed in February 1626. Nonetheless, the conflict began again, and Richelieu besieged La Rochelle in the summer of 1627, while the duc de Condé fought Rohan in Languedoc. The duc de Soubise sought refuge in England and was one of the men who sailed to the aid of the French Protestants in the fleet led by Buckingham. On 28 October 1628, La Rochelle capitulated. In April 1629, the treaty of Susa was signed. That July, Rohan retired to Venice and the town of Montauban was defeated by Richelieu, thus ending the war. In November 1629, Richelieu was made Louis XIII's *principal ministre.*

24 Claude Malleville, 'Vers presentez par Diane à la Reyne Mere du Roy, pour le Balet de la Reyne d'Angleterre', in Malleville, *Poésies*, p. 119.

25 Louis XIII to Marie de Médicis, April 1624; in Philippe Delorme, *Histoire des reines de France: Marie de Médicis* (Paris, 1998), p. 236.

26 See La Porte, *Mémoires*, pp. 34–5.

27 Under England's pre-1753 Julian calendar, the Day of Dupes occurred on 31 October 1630. In French history, the Gregorian date of 10 November 1630 is infamous. I have, therefore, preferred to keep the French date in this instance.

28 For a detailed discussion of the Day of Dupes, see Georges Mongrédien, *La Journée des Dupes, 10 novembre 1630* (Paris, 1961). See also Delorme, *Marie de Médicis*, pp. 264–70.

29 *Les Papiers de Richelieu: section politique intérieure*, ed. Pierre Grillon, 6 vols. (Paris, 1975–85), V (1982), pp. 637–8. The editor of Richelieu's correspondence is confused by the date of this letter which he believes to pre-date the Day of Dupes. He also admits that he can't identify its author. Goring (who had helped negotiate Charles and Henrietta Maria's marriage, and was therefore known to the cardinal) was writing from England whose Julian calendar was ten days behind that in use in France. The letter should therefore be dated 19 November according to the Gregorian calendar.

30 Nagler, *Theatre Festivals*, p. 141.

31 Veevers, *Images*, p. 127. Interestingly, in *La Flora*, Cupid goes to hell to seek only Jealousy, who then helps him to set Zephyrus and Chloris against each other: see Nagler, *Theatre Festivals*, p. 141.

32 See ibid., pp. 140–2.

33 Suzanne Gossett, '"Man-maid, Begone!" Women in Masques', in *Women in the Renaissance*, ed. Kirby Farrell, Elizabeth H. Hageman and Arthur F. Kinney (Amherst, 1990), pp. 118–35, p. 127.

34 Ibid. During the previous reign, compliments to Anne of Austria were also characterised by their emphasis upon her status as the wife of the king. For example, Jonson's contribution to 'The King's Entertainment in passing to his Coronation' (1604), referred to her as 'You daughter, sister, wife of seuerall kings': Herford *et al.*, eds., *Ben Jonson*, VII, p. 94.

35 François le Metel, sieur de Boisrobert, *Le Grand Ballet de la Reyne representant les Festes de Junon la Nopcière*, in *Ballets et mascarades*, ed. Lacroix, II, p. 354.

36 Ibid.
37 Delorme, *Marie de Médicis*, p. 271.
38 Salvetti to Sacchetti, 25 February/7 March 1631: Orrell, 'Amerigo Salvetti', pp. 15–16.
39 PRO, SP 16/185. Sir John Ashburnham to Elizabeth of Bohemia, 26 February 1631, fol. 75. I am grateful to Dr Katharine Craik for this reference.
40 Orrell, 'Amerigo Salvetti', p. 15.
41 Ibid., p. 14.
42 John Orrell notes that there was an intention to restage *Chloridia* after Easter (which, in 1631, fell at the beginning of April), and identifies a payment on 2 May in the Revels Accounts for 'ye practice of ye Masque': ibid., p. 16. However, this payment is more an indication of a rehearsal than of a repeat performance and does not provide sufficient evidence that the masque was ever restaged. If *Chloridia* shadowed a reconciliation between Richelieu and Marie, by April 1631 this possibility was no longer viable and the masque's meanings were therefore redundant. Marie de Médicis fled from France to the Spanish Netherlands in July 1631, and was never to return.
43 John Finet, *Ceremonies of Charles I: The Notebooks of John Finet, 1628–1641*, ed. Albert J. Loomie (New York, 1987), p. 106.
44 For a good discussion of this plot, see Smuts, 'Puritan Followers'.
45 Jonson, 'An Expostulation with Inigo Jones', line 50, line 59 and lines 63–5, in Donaldson, ed., *Ben Jonson: Poems*, p. 322.

5 *TEMPE RESTORED*: EXILE/DISPOSSESSION/ RESTITUTION

1 See National Library of Wales, Wynnstay 174, where Jonson was paid £40; see National Library of Wales, Wynnstay 175, where Townshend was paid £50.
2 See Sharpe, *Criticism and Compliment*, pp. 154–5.
3 See ibid., p. 154.
4 For Lord Herbert of Cherbury's connections with French court culture and with Marguerite de Valois, Henri IV's first wife, see McGowan, *Ballet de cour*, p. 66.
5 See Peter Beal, 'Songs by Aurelian Townshend, in the hand of Sir Henry Herbert, for an Unrecorded Masque by the Merchant Adventurers', *Medieval and Renaissance Drama in England*, 15 (2003), pp. 243–60. See Appendix for my alternative interpretation of this entertainment and for further possible links between Holland and Townshend.
6 Shell, *Catholicism*, p. 155.
7 See Baltasar de Beaujoyeulx, *Balet Comique de la Royne, faict aux nopces de Monsieur le Duc de Joyeuse et madamoyselle de Vaudemont sa soeur* (Paris, 1582).
8 Tomlinson, 'Theatrical Vibrancy', p. 189.
9 Ibid.; Melinda J. Gough, '"Not as Myself": The Queen's Voice in *Tempe Restored*', *Modern Philology*, 101.1 (2003), pp. 48–67, p. 52.

10 James Knowles, '"Can Ye Not Tell a Man from a Marmoset?" Apes and Others on the Early Modern Stage', in *Renaissance Beasts: Of Animals, Humans, and Other Wonderful Creatures*, ed. Erica Fudge (Urbana, 2004), pp. 138–63, p. 149. Knowles cites William Prynne when he refers to 'whorishly impudent' women actors.
11 Ibid., pp. 148–9.
12 Roy Booth, 'The First Female Professional Singers: Madam Coniack', *Notes and Queries*, 242 (1997), p. 533. See also *The Poems of Thomas Randolph*, ed. G. Thorn Drury (London, 1929), pp. 115–17.
13 Booth, 'Professional Singers', p. 533.
14 That is, unless one counts the payments to Margaret Prevost for unspecified musical activities from 1637 to 1640. She was the wife of Camille Prevost, and these payments could simply be interpreted as a widow's pension. See Introduction above.
15 Nathaniel Richards, 'The Vicious Courtier', in *The Celestiall Publican* (London, 1630/1), sig. G8r.
16 Ibid., sig. H1v.
17 Gough, 'Not as Myself', p. 64.
18 Ibid., p. 65.
19 Ibid., p. 64.
20 Ibid., pp. 55–6.
21 Ibid., p. 55.
22 Aurelian Townshend, *Tempe Restored*, in Orgel and Strong, *Inigo Jones*, II, p. 481, lines 151–2.
23 Tomlinson, 'Theatrical Vibrancy', p. 188.
24 See Lindley, ed., *Court Masques*, for convenient short biographies of the children.
25 Interestingly, the playwright William Davenant's mother was a Sheppard. Thomas, her eldest brother, was a professional colleague of Shakespeare, and, as a member of the royal household, attended Elizabeth I's funeral in 1603. It is likely that Anne Sheppard was a member of this family. See Mary Edmond, 'Davenant [D'Avenant], Sir William (1606–1668)', in *ODNB* (Oxford, 2004); http://www.oxforddnb.com, accessed 8 February 2005.
26 See Oliver Millar, *Sir Peter Lely 1618–80* (London, 1978), p. 44; Sidney, Sixteenth Earl of Pembroke, *A Catalogue of the Paintings and Drawings in the Collection at Wilton House, Salisbury, Wiltshire* (London, 1968), p. 63 and plate 56.
27 J. Murdoch and V. J. Murrell, 'The Monogrammist, DG: Dwarf Gibson and his Patrons', *Burlington Magazine*, 123 (1981), pp. 282–9, p. 284.
28 See Herford *et al.*, eds., *Ben Jonson*, VII, p. 753, line 123.
29 See Lucy Munro, *Children of the Queen's Revels: A Jacobean Theatre Repertory* (Cambridge, forthcoming 2005).
30 They were: mistresses Jacamote Brussels, Mary Arls, Ann Tindall, Oungelo, Mary Cranfield, Elizabeth Jeffs, Susan Harvey and Lea Wadson.
31 McManus, *Women*, p. 185.

32 Ibid., p. 186.
33 The comment is Gough's: see 'Not as Myself', p. 61.
34 Veevers, *Images*, pp. 130–3.
35 In the autumn of 1631, Louis confiscated the lands of the dukes of Elbeuf, Bellegarde and Rohannez, and those of the count of Moret and the marquess of Vieuville: see *Mercure François*, 17 (Paris, 1633), pp. 372–3 and table.
36 Thomas M. Greene, 'The King's One Body in the *Balet Comique de la Royne*', *Yale French Studies*, 86 (1994), pp. 75–93, p. 77.
37 See Tomlinson, 'Theatrical Vibrancy', p. 190.
38 For a more extended discussion of Circe's objection, see Gossett's excellent 'Man-maid, Begone!'
39 Among the designs that Orgel and Strong associate with *The Shepherds' Paradise* is a sketch of a garden based on Callot's *Le Grand Parterre de Nancy* (1625). In line with *Tempe Restored*'s description of Circe's garden, it includes a great staircase and walls lined with cyprus trees, and would make a direct visual link between the masque and the duchy of Lorraine. It does not, however, obviously include '*a sumptuous palace*' (line 100) and therefore cannot be unequivocally associated with the masque. See Orgel and Strong, *Inigo Jones*, II, pp. 518–19.
40 Gourier, *Saint-Amant*, p. 20. Saint-Amant received much honour from the royal couple, but his efforts were obviously unsuccessful as Bassompierre remained imprisoned until Richelieu's death.
41 Finet, *Ceremonies*, p. 114.
42 Ibid., p. 115.
43 Pory suggests that the duke detested the queen mother 'because she was the author of his seven years' imprisonment': see Birch, ed., *Court and Times*, II, p. 153.
44 See *Recueil des Gazettes Nouvelles 1632* (Paris, 1633), *sub.* De Londres, le 19 février 1632.
45 See Finet, *Ceremonies*, p. 121.
46 Smuts, 'Puritan Followers', pp. 27–34.
47 This was eventually postponed for financial reasons.
48 See Veevers, *Images*, pp. 86–7.
49 Katherine Manners, Susan Feilding and the countess of Buckingham all eventually converted to Catholicism.
50 See Smuts, 'Puritan Followers', p. 27.
51 See Barbara Donagan, 'A Courtier's Progress: Greed and Consistency in the Life of the Earl of Holland', *The Historical Journal*, 19 (1976), pp. 317–53, p. 342.
52 See David L. Smith, 'Herbert, Philip, first earl of Montgomery and fourth earl of Pembroke (1584–1650)', in *ODNB* (Oxford, 2004); http://www.oxforddnb.com, accessed 24 May 2005.
53 See Schreiber, *The First Carlisle*, p. 122.
54 See David L. Smith, 'Herbert, Philip, first earl of Montgomery and fourth earl of Pembroke (1584–1650)', in *ODNB* (Oxford, 2004); http://www.oxforddnb.com, accessed 24 May 2005.

55 Salisbury's father, Sir Robert Cecil, had been Aurelian Townshend's first major patron: see Sharpe, *Criticism and Compliment*, pp. 152–4.

56 Barbara Ravelhofer, '"Virgin Wax" and "Hairy Men-Monsters": Unstable Movement Codes in the Stuart Masque', in *The Politics of the Stuart Court Masque*, ed. David Bevington and Peter Holbrook (Cambridge, 1998), pp. 244–72, p. 267.

57 Anne Cecil (born *c.* 1603) was the second cousin of Elizabeth Cecil (born *c.* 1620), daughter of the second earl of Salisbury. This latter danced in *Tempe Restored* alongside Thomas and Elizabeth Grey of Stamford.

58 See Louis A. Knafla, 'Egerton, John, first earl of Bridgewater (1579–1649)', in *ODNB* (Oxford, 2004); http://www.oxforddnb.com, accessed 9 November 2004.

59 Ibid.

60 For an indication of Henrietta Maria's sympathies towards Sweden, note her grace towards the visiting baron of Oxenstern in February 1633: see Finet, *Ceremonies*, p. 137.

61 Kevin Sharpe, *The Personal Rule of Charles I* (New Haven, 1992), p. 83. See also Finet, *Ceremonies*, pp. 127–8.

62 See Sharpe, *Personal Rule*, p. 83. See also, Robin Briggs, *Early Modern France 1560–1715* (Oxford, 1977, repr. 1979), pp. 108–9.

63 In the summer of 1631, the Infanta Isabella provided 400,000 écus towards an army for Marie de Médicis: see Delorme, *Marie de Médicis*, p. 284.

64 John Pory to Sir Thomas Puckering, 14 December 1631: Birch, ed., *Court and Times*, II, p. 153.

65 Veevers, *Images*, pp. 130–3.

66 *Recueil des Gazettes de l'année 1631* (Paris, 1632), *sub.* De Londres, le dernier novembre 1631.

67 *Recueil des Gazettes Nouvelles 1632* (Paris, 1633), *sub.* De Londres, le 30 aoust 1632.

68 Bérulle, *Elévation*, p. 30.

69 Ibid., p. 77.

70 Ibid., p. 103.

71 Ibid., p. 153.

72 Ibid., p. 67.

73 Ibid., p. 63.

74 On the erasure of Magdalen's self, see Bérulle's comments: 'Elle sort hors de son palais et plus encore d'elle-même'; and '[son] esprit fait une entière effusion de soi-même aux pieds de Jésus'; ibid., p. 46 and pp. 146–7.

75 'Et comme la solitude de cette âme était l'occupation de votre solitude, aussi l'obscurité de sa grotte était à votre esprit une lumière claire et brillante qui allumait en vous un feu céleste dans vos saints exercises'; ibid., p. 31.

76 In a comparison between painting and poetry in *Discoveries*, Jonson finds poetry more noble because the pen can 'speak to the understanding; the other, but to the sense': *Timber: or, Discoveries*, in *Ben Jonson*, ed. Herford *et al.*, VIII, p. 610.

77 On this subject, see, for example, J. B. Bossuet, 'Traité de la Concupiscence', in Bossuet, *Discours sur la vie cachée en Dieu. Traité de la Concupiscence. Opuscules. Maximes et réflexions sur la Comédie* (Paris, 1821), pp. 26–110, especially pp. 81–98.
78 Shell, *Catholicism*, p. 155.
79 See PRO, LR5/65 ('Charles Gentie imbrothere his bill'). See also Veevers, *Images*, p. 133.
80 Smuts, 'Puritan Followers', pp. 33–4.

6 'IT IS MY VOYCE': THE FASHIONING OF A SELF IN *THE SHEPHERDS' PARADISE*

1 The Somerset House theatre is described in the works accounts as 76 feet long, by 36 feet wide and 25 feet high: Malone Society, *Collections* X: *Dramatic Records*, p. xviii. For information on the audience, see John Pory to Sir Thomas Puckering in Gerald Eades Bentley, *The Jacobean and Caroline Stage*, 7 vols. (Oxford, 1941–68), IV, p. 918.
2 Abraham Rémy, *La Galatée et les adventures du Prince Astiagés* (Paris, 1625), sig. A4v and sig. B4r. See also Racan, *Les Bergeries*, pp. 34–7, pp. 146–7.
3 Other early dedications to her of pastoral works include Gervais de Bazire d'Amblainville's *La Princesse ou l'heureuse bergère* (Rouen, 1627) and I. D. B.'s *Eclogue, ou Chant Pastoral sur les nopces des serenissimes princes Charles . . . & de Henriette Marie* (London, 1627).
4 See Magne, *Boisrobert*, p. 112.
5 See ibid., p. 170, note 1. See also Pauphilet *et al.*, *Dictionnaire*, *sub.* Corneille.
6 Sarah Poynting, 'A Critical Edition of Walter Montagu's *The Shepherds' Paradise*, Acts 1–3' (unpublished doctoral thesis, University of Oxford, 2000), p. 158.
7 Ibid.
8 Poynting lists as its most important textual influences, '*Cymbeline*, Honoré d'Urfé's *L'Astrée*, and Barclay's *Argenis* (of which Charles I commissioned a translation in 1628)': see ibid., p. 106.
9 Munro, *Queen's Revels*, chapter 3.
10 Annabel Patterson, *Pastoral and Ideology: Virgil to Valéry* (Oxford, 1988), p. 147.
11 Ibid., p. 151.
12 For a discussion of Fidamira's criticism, see chapter 10 below.
13 Sophie Tomlinson, 'Theatrical Vibrancy on the Female Court Stage? *Tempe Restored* and *The Shepherds' Paradise*' (unpublished conference paper given at 'The Queen's Court: Elite Female Cultural Production and the Cultures of the Early Stuarts (1603–42)', Centre for the Study of the Renaissance, University of Warwick, 18–19 April 1998).
14 William Prynne, *Histriomastix: The Players Scourge or Actors Tragaedie* (London, 1633), index.
15 James Shirley, *The Bird in a Cage* (London, 1633), sig. A2r–v.
16 John Marston, *The Workes of Mr. Iohn Marston, Being Tragedies and Comedies, Collected into One Volume* (London, 1633), sigs. A3r–A4v. Shirley's

verses before Ford's *Love's Sacrifice* also alluded to Prynne, while Thomas Heywood castigated him on three occasions. The prologue to William Cartwright's *The Royal Slave* also mentioned the dispute.

17 Harbage, *Cavalier Drama*, p. 14. See also Orgel and Strong who assert that 'Beside Montagu's pastoral, *Parsifal* is a romp': Orgel and Strong, *Inigo Jones*, I, p. 63.

18 Walter Montagu, *The Shepherds' Paradise*, ed. Sarah Poynting (Oxford, 1997), p. vii. Unless otherwise stated, all subsequent references to *The Shepherds' Paradise* will be from this edition.

19 Veevers, *Images*, p. 39.

20 Duffo, ed., *Marie de Médicis*, p. 8.

21 See, for example, Montagu, *The Shepherds' Paradise*, 1.2.101–9, where Basilino terms Fidamira an angel and describes his thoughts as carried up to heaven.

22 Walter Montagu, *The Shepheard's Paradise: A Comedy Privately Acted before the Late king Charls by the Queen consort's Majesty, and Ladies of Honour* (London, 1659), sig. M2v.

23 The name has a classical precedent. Agenor was the father of Europa and of Cadmus, founder of Thebes. After its appearance in *The Shepherds' Paradise*, the name was recycled by Lodowick Carlell, one of Henrietta Maria's servants, appearing in *The Passionate Lovers* (produced in 1638 and published in 1655) and in *The Fool Would Be A Favourite* (published in 1657).

24 Diane Purkiss, 'Gender, Power and the Body: Some Figurations of Femininity in Milton and Seventeenth-Century Women's Writing' (unpublished doctoral thesis, University of Oxford, 1991), p. 366 and p. 372.

25 Since first writing this section, I have become aware of Sophie Tomlinson's work on this episode. Her conclusions differ slightly from my own. See Tomlinson, *Women on Stage in Stuart Drama* (Cambridge, forthcoming 2006). I am very grateful to Dr Tomlinson for sharing her work.

26 Ibid.

27 Ibid.

28 See Gayatri Chakravorty Spivak, 'Echo', *New Literary History*, 24 (1993), pp. 17–43, pp. 27–30.

29 Clare Nouvet, 'An Impossible Response: The Disaster of Narcissus', *Yale French Studies*, 79 (1991), pp. 103–34, p. 105. Nouvet's text proceeds to locate Echo not as a body, but as the embodiment of language which has ceased to be Narcissus's own.

30 Poynting observes that this passage is an adaptation of Juliet's speech after the balcony scene in *Romeo and Juliet*: Poynting, 'A Critical Edition', p. 105.

31 This connection may be extended further by reference to William Prynne who was violently punished by the power structure which patronised and guaranteed Henrietta Maria's performance.

32 See Sharpe, *Criticism and Compliment*, pp. 39–44; Orgel and Strong, *Inigo Jones*, II, p. 522; Veevers, *Images*, pp. 42–3.

33 Orgel and Strong, *Inigo Jones*, II, p. 522.

34 Veevers, *Images*, p. 42.

35 Ibid., pp. 39–40.
36 Poynting, 'A Critical Edition', p. 106 and p. 135.
37 Ibid., pp. 135–6.
38 For a more detailed discussion of the romanticisation of the match and for the evidence that this was a portrait of the infanta, see my essay: Britland, 'A Fairy-tale Marriage'.
39 Poynting, 'A Critical Edition', p. 136.
40 Rémy, *La Galatée*, sig. A4v.
41 See also Smuts, 'Puritan Followers', *passim.*
42 Denis Tillinac, *L'Ange du désordre: Marie de Rohan, duchesse de Chevreuse* (Paris, 1985), p. 153.
43 Paris, 13/23 April 1632; *Recueil des Gazettes Nouvelles 1632* (Paris, 1633).
44 See Smuts, 'Puritan Followers', p. 29.
45 See ibid., pp. 33–4.
46 See Ferrero, ed., *Lettres de Henriette-Marie*, especially pp. 39–45.
47 See Tillinac, *L'Ange du désordre*, pp. 161–2.
48 Poynting, 'A Critical Edition', p. 138.
49 Ibid., p. 141.
50 On these productions, see Martin Butler, 'Entertaining the Palatine Prince: Plays on Foreign Affairs, 1635–1637', *ELR*, 13 (1983), pp. 319–44, *passim.*
51 Malcolm Smuts, *Court Culture and the Origins of the Royalist Tradition in Early Stuart England* (Philadelphia, 1987), p. 251.
52 Veevers, *Images*, pp. 43–4.
53 Poynting, 'A Critical Edition', pp. 156–7.
54 St François de Sales, *Regles de Sainct Augustin et Constitutions pour les Soeurs Religieuses de la Visitation saincte Marie* (Lyon, 1645), p. 242 and p. 312. Sales's text is based on St Augustine's rules for the Carmelite sisters. The Order of the Visitation was conceived in 1607. Sales died in 1622.
55 Poynting, 'A Critical Edition', p. 157.
56 Ibid.
57 Orgel and Strong, *Inigo Jones*, II, p. 522.
58 Poynting, 'A Critical Edition', p. 156.
59 François Rabelais, *Gargantua – Pantagruel: les cinq livres. Version intégrale en français moderne*, 2 vols. (Paris, 1988), I, p. 189.
60 Ibid., I, p. 190.
61 Poynting, 'A Critical Edition', p. 133.
62 Ibid.
63 See chapter 3 above.

7 'FATE HATH MADE THY REIGN HER CHOICE': *THE TEMPLE OF LOVE* (1635)

1 Kenneth Richards, 'Queen Henrietta Maria as a Patron of the Drama', *Studia Neophilologica*, 42 (1970), pp. 9–24, p. 20.
2 Martin Butler, *Theatre and Crisis 1632–1642* (Cambridge, 1984), pp. 84–5.

3 *Recueil des Gazettes Nouuelles 1634* (Paris, 1635), *sub.* De Londres, le 19 mars 1634.
4 Richard Dutton, '"Discourse in the Players, though no Disobedience": Sir Henry Herbert's Problems with the Players and Archbishop Laud, 1632–34', *Ben Jonson Journal*, 5 (1998), pp. 37–61, p. 38 and p. 40.
5 Ibid., pp. 44–5.
6 David R. Como, 'Predestination and Political Conflict in Laud's London', *The Historical Journal*, 46.2 (2003), pp. 263–94, p. 265.
7 Meg Powers Livingston, 'The Reinvention of John Fletcher as Caroline Court Playwright' (unpublished paper given at the 1999 Group for Early Modern Cultural Studies conference).
8 On the St James's theatrical space, see Astington, *English Court Theatre*, pp. 67–9 and p. 209. See also *Recueil des Gazettes Nouuelles 1633* (Paris, 1634), *sub.* le 11 decembre 1633.
9 John Pory to Sir Thomas Puckering, 20 September 1632: Bentley, *Jacobean and Caroline Stage*, II, p. 176. Nevertheless, Henrietta Maria seems stubbornly to have clung to French. For example, in 1634, Henry Herbert recorded her approbation of the costumes for *Coelum Britannicum*: 'The Q. was pleased to tell mee before the king, "pour les habits, elle n'avoit jamais rien vue de si brave"': Joseph Quincy Adams, ed., *The Dramatic Records of Sir Henry Herbert, Master of the Revels, 1623–1673* (New Haven, 1917), p. 55.
10 In Thomas Heywood's *Apology for Actors* (London, 1612), the author notes, 'plays have . . . taught the unlearned the knowledge of many famous histories, instructed such as cannot read in the discovery of all our English chronicles' (sig. F3r). Ben Jonson, though, was sceptical about Shakespeare's accuracy in his history plays: see *Every Man In His Humour*, Prologue, lines 9–12.
11 On this, see Rebecca Bailey, 'Queen Henrietta Maria, the "Old Faith" and "Her Majesties Servants": Roman Catholicism and the Caroline Stage' (unpublished PhD thesis, Birkbeck College, University of London, 2003), p. 62.
12 See Claude Kurt Abraham, *Gaston d'Orléans et sa cour: étude littéraire* (Chapel Hill, (1963)), pp. 54–5.
13 Part of the plan was to encourage the marquis of Hamilton to leave his English wife and to marry Huntly's eldest daughter, thus encouraging Hamilton to convert to Catholicism and allying him with Huntly, a person who was already 'engagé à la France': see Hippeau, ed., *Tillières*, pp. 207–13.
14 *Recueil des Gazettes Nouuelles 1633* (Paris, 1634), *sub.* De Paris, le 5 mars 1633. I suspect that this 'marquis' was actually the younger George Gordon, Huntly's son. The first marquis was seventy-one years old at the time and unlikely to have been able to captain a group of horse. In contrast, the future second marquis is known to have served for the French in Lorraine and Alsace.
15 Notably, in October 1634, Gaston abandoned his mother and new wife, and defected back to Paris, having reached an accommodation with the cardinal.

16 *The Young Admiral* was based on the Spanish play, *Don Lope de Cordona*, by Lope de Vega: see John Loftis, 'English Renaissance Plays from the Spanish *Comedia*', *ELR*, 14 (1984), pp. 230–48, pp. 240–1.
17 Bailey, 'Queen Henrietta Maria', p. 26.
18 Ibid., p. 148 and p. 26.
19 James Shirley, *The Young Admirall* (London, 1637), sig. E4r.
20 Bailey, 'Queen Henrietta Maria', p. 151.
21 Ibid., pp. 152–3.
22 Ibid., p. 153.
23 Ira Clark, *Professional Playwrights: Massinger, Ford, Shirley, and Brome* (Lexington, 1992), p. 114. See also Adams, ed., *The Dramatic Records of Sir Henry Herbert*, p. 19. Herbert's note is dated 3 July 1633.
24 N. W. Bawcutt, *The Control and Censorship of Caroline Drama: The Records of Sir Henry Herbert, Master of the Revels, 1623–73* (Oxford, 1996), p. 75.
25 Dutton, 'Discourse', p. 44.
26 Ibid., pp. 42–5.
27 Ibid., p. 54.
28 In 1633, Charles I was considering refilling the vacant position of lord high admiral which had been empty since the assassination of Buckingham in 1628. The play's subject was therefore a topical one. See Vicenzo Gussoni to the Doge and Senate, 15/25 March 1633 in *CSPV, 1632–6*, p. 87.
29 *The Gamester* was licensed in November 1633, and was performed at court on 6 February 1634, so was probably written by Shirley the previous summer; that is, *before* the November performance of *The Young Admiral*.
30 Astington, *English Court Theatre*, pp. 224–7.
31 Ibid., pp. 254–6.
32 See Dutton's persuasive reading of *The Women's Prize* controversy as an instance of religious censorship: Dutton, 'Discourse', pp. 45–58.
33 Livingston, 'The Reinvention of John Fletcher'.
34 John Fletcher, *The Faithful Shepherdess*, ed. Cyrus Hoy, in *The Dramatic Works in the Beaumont and Fletcher Canon*, ed. Fredson Bowers, 10 vols. (1966–96), III (1976), p. 497, 'To the Reader', lines 4–8. All subsequent line references to this play will be taken from this edition.
35 Cécile Istria, '*The Faithful Shepherdess*, une pastorale protestante' (unpublished paper given at the Epistémè seminar, Université de Paris 3, February 2001).
36 Martin Butler, 'Ben Jonson's *Pan's Anniversary* and the Politics of Early Stuart Pastoral', *ELR*, 22.3 (1992), pp. 369–404, p. 376. For Butler's convincing redating of the pastoral, see especially pp. 397–404.
37 Davenant's prologue in Fletcher, *The Faithful Shepherdess*, p. 499, lines 1–4 and lines 9–10.
38 Interestingly, Henrietta Maria appears to have intervened to soften the severity of Prynne's punishment: see Sharpe, *Personal Rule*, p. 680.
39 In a chapter which interestingly investigates the relationship between Thomas Heywood and James Shirley as dramatists for the Queen's Company,

A. M. Clark notes that the character of Midas, in *Love's Mistress*, might well have been a satirical representation of William Prynne: an attribution that would help to explain the play's popularity at court. See Clark, *Thomas Heywood: Playwright and Miscellanist* (Oxford, 1931), p. 138.

40 Orrell, *Jones and Webb*, p. 88.

41 Thomas Heywood, *Loves Mistresse: or the Queenes Masque* (London, 1640), sig. A3r.

42 Orgel and Strong refute Simpson and Bell's suggestion that this drawing was prepared for Davenant's *Triumphs of the Prince d'Amour* (1636) on the grounds that the scenery for the latter was the work of James Corsellis: Orgel and Strong, *Inigo Jones*, II, p. 796.

43 Ibid., I, p. 329.

44 It is often surmised that the masque was performed again on 14 February. However, the *Gazette de France* makes clear that the performance on that date was of a 'comédie Françoise'. See *Recueil des Gazettes Nouvelles 1635* (Paris, 1636), *sub.* De Londres, le 28 février 1635.

45 National Library of Wales, Wynnstay 178, fol. 25r. The warrant for Davenant's payment is accompanied by 'an acquittance of Mr Henry Jerman authorised to receaue the same'.

46 See Mary Edmond, 'Davenant [D'Avenant], Sir William', in *ODNB* (Oxford, 2004); http://www.oxforddnb.com, accessed 8 February 2005.

47 Sharpe, *Criticism and Compliment*, pp. 244–7. The winter of 1634/5 was so cold one could drive across the Thames in a coach. Many of the images of sterility and freezing in the masque can, therefore, be related to this seasonal peculiarity, and are less a reference to the writer's dislike of neo-Platonism than a clever use of a topical event.

48 Kathleen McLuskie, 'The Plays and the Playwrights: 1613–42', in *The Revels History of Drama in English IV, 1613–1660*, ed. Philip Edwards (London, 1981; repr. 1996), pp. 129–258, p. 146.

49 To these misdemeanours can be added the 1632 prosecution of the laird of Lusse for incest, the rape trial of the earl of Castlehaven, the imprisonment of the earl of Arundel for complicity in his son's ill-advised marriage, and the disapproval directed at the marquis of Hamilton for his refusal to cohabit with his wife.

50 Butler, *Theatre and Crisis*, p. 29.

51 Veevers, *Images*, pp. 135–42.

52 Ibid., pp. 141–2.

53 Bailey, 'Queen Henrietta Maria', pp. 190–1.

54 See, for example, the anonymous sonnet on the queen's embarkation printed in the *Mercure François*, 11 (Paris, 1626), p. 395.

55 William Davenant, *The Temple of Love*, in Orgel and Strong, *Inigo Jones*, II, pp. 598–629, line 186 and line 122. All subsequent line references will be taken from this edition.

56 See Anon., *Les Royales Ceremonies faites en l'edification d'une Chapelle de Capucins à Londres en Angleterre, dans le Palais de la Roine* (Paris, 1632), *passim.*

57 Barberini to Mazarin, 10/20 October 1635: *The Memoirs of Gregorio Panzani*, ed. Joseph Berington (London, 1793), p. 195; Barberini to Panzani, 30 November/10 December 1635: ibid., p. 203.
58 See E. Cobham Brewer, *The Dictionary of Phrase and Fable* (London, 1894; repr. 1993), *sub.* Isabelle.
59 See Veevers, *Images*, p. 122.
60 See Sharpe, *Criticism and Compliment*, pp. 252–5; Bailey, 'Queen Henrietta Maria', p. 13 and p. 28.
61 Elias Ashmole, *The History of the Most Noble Order of the Garter* (London, 1715), p. 148.
62 Roy Strong, *Van Dyck: Charles I on Horseback* (London, 1972), pp. 59–60.
63 J. S. A. Adamson, 'Chivalry and Political Culture in Caroline England', in *Culture and Politics in Early Modern England*, ed. Kevin Sharpe and Peter Lake (Basingstoke, 1994), pp. 161–97, pp. 171–2.
64 Thomas Carew, *Coelum Britannicum*, in Orgel and Strong, *Inigo Jones*, II, pp. 566–97, lines 1,024–7.
65 Shell, *Catholicism*, pp. 149–50.
66 Ibid.
67 Veevers, *Images*, p. 200. In part, their inclusion in the masque engages with the Huguenot Rabelais's satiric representation of the abbaye de Thélème, the behaviour of whose inhabitants, living by the motto 'do what you will', both secularised and denigrated the doctrine of free will.
68 Orgel and Strong, *Inigo Jones*, II, p. 604.
69 W. B. Patterson, *King James VI and I and the Reunion of Christendom* (Cambridge, 1997; repr. 2000), p. 340.
70 See Como, 'Predestination', p. 264, note 2.
71 Ibid., pp. 286–7.
72 See ibid., p. 270.
73 See Gordon Albion, *Charles I and the Court of Rome* (London, 1935), especially p. 221.
74 Ibid., p. 218.

8 *FLORIMÈNE*: THE AUTHOR AND THE OCCASION

1 See Allardyce Nicoll, *Stuart Masques and the Renaissance Stage* (London, 1937), p. 34, pp. 79–80, pp. 112–13; Stephen Orgel, *The Illusion of Power* (Berkeley, 1975; 1991), pp. 27–36.
2 Veevers, *Images*, p. 111 and p. 162.
3 Ibid., p. 49.
4 Harbage, *Cavalier Drama*, p. 18.
5 Stephen Orgel, '*Florimène* and the Ante-Masques', *Renaissance Drama*, 4 (1971), pp. 135–53, *passim.*
6 Henry Herbert, *The Argument of the Pastorall of Florimène* (London, 1635), p. 10.
7 Ibid., pp. 8–9.

8 Ibid., p. 9.

9 Suzanne Trill, '"The Glass that Mends the Looker's Eyes": The Mirror, the Text and the Gaze in *Salve Deus Rex Judaeorum*' (unpublished conference paper given at 'The Queen's Court: Elite Female Cultural Production and the Cultures of the Early Stuarts (1603–42)', Centre for the Study of the Renaissance, University of Warwick, 18–19 April 1998).

10 Herbert, *Florimène*, p. 11.

11 Ibid., p. 17.

12 See Mirella Levi D'Ancona, *The Garden of the Renaissance: Botanical Symbolism in Italian Painting* (Florence, 1977), pp. 272–5. See also Van Dyck's painting of Elena Grimaldi, Marquise Cattaneo (1623) which uses similar imagery: National Gallery of Art, Washington.

13 Pierre Dinet, *Cinq livres des hieroglyphiques*, ed. Stephen Orgel (New York, 1979), p. 352 and pp. 486–8. James Knowles has independently reached similar conclusions about this painting. See Knowles, 'Apes and Others'.

14 Interestingly, a copy of the painting at Petworth House in Surrey, made in 1633 or shortly thereafter, does not include the image of the orange tree. The house belonged to the Protestant Percy family, several of whose members (most notably Henry Percy) were close associates of the queen. The omission of the tree from this version of the painting seems to underline the image's Catholic resonances.

15 In Marie de Médicis's 1625 letter to her daughter, she made the point that Henrietta Maria was named after the Virgin: Archives nationales, 'Instruction de la Reine Marie de medicis'.

16 See chapter 7 above.

17 Orrell, 'Amerigo Salvetti', p. 22; *CSPV, 1632–6*, p. 499.

18 Boisrobert's connection with this pastoral has previously been noted by Marie-Claude Canova-Green: see *La Politique-spectacle*, p. 208. See also McGowan, *Ballet de cour*, pp. 243–4, note 86.

19 *Gazette de France*, ed. Théophraste Renaudot (Lyon, 1636), p. 59.

20 A warrant was issued on 23 February 1635/6 to pay Sir John Shelley (the father of William) a sum of money 'which her Matie was gratiously pleased to bestowe upon Christian Vantlett her ma^{tes} Goddaughter towards her Marriage': National Library of Wales, Wynnstay 181, fol. 14r.

21 Archives du monastère de la Visitation, Paris: MS G-2: Soeur Marie-Henriette Revellois, 'Mémoires', 9 vols. (*c.* 1673–97), I, p. 21.

22 See National Library of Wales, Wynnstay 181, fol. 14v.

23 For the following biographical details, I have relied heavily upon Magne, *Boisrobert*.

24 *Recueil de Lettres Nouvelles*, ed. Nicolas Faret, 2 vols. (Paris, 1634), I, pp. 270–3.

25 Anon., *Recueil des plus beaux vers* (Paris, 1627), p. 447; Jacquot, 'La Reine Henriette-Marie', p. 156.

26 Magne, *Boisrobert*, p. 97.

27 Smuts, 'Puritan Followers', p. 35.

28 Sharpe, *Personal Rule*, pp. 510–17.
29 Ferrero, ed., *Lettres de Henriette-Marie*, p. 43.
30 On this embassy see Finet, *Ceremonies*, pp. 163–7, p. 182.
31 Ibid., p. 167.
32 Correr to Doge and Senate, 12 October 1635: *CSPV, 1632–6*, p. 464.
33 It should be noted that, while Marie de Médicis had recently sent a representative to Charles I, her activities in the Spanish Netherlands were far from creating the impression that she was at all pro-French or inclined towards a reconciliation with Richelieu.
34 Finet commented with a certain amount of reserve that, the day after Senneterre's arrival, the king being at Theobalds, the queen had a three-hour private conference with the ambassador. He added, 'whether this were done with communication of [the queen's] intention to the King before his departure out of town, or her own motion for satisfaction of her desire (impatient perhaps to attend the knowledge how matters stood in France till the uncertain time of his audience) appeared not to me': Finet, *Ceremonies*, p. 174.
35 See Butler, 'Entertaining the Palatine Prince', pp. 319–44.
36 In 1634–5, at the conception of the Académie française, Boisrobert was considered to be 'en sa plus haute faveur auprès du Cardinal de Richelieu' [in his greatest favour with Cardinal Richelieu]: Paul Pellisson-Fontanier, *Relation Contenant l'Histoire de l'Académie Françoise* (Paris, 1672), p. 9.
37 Georges Couton, *Richelieu et le théâtre* (Lyon, 1986), p. 7. Couton also made the important observation that, after Richelieu's death, Louis XIII cancelled the gratuities to men of letters with the words, 'nous n'avons plus affaire de cela': ibid.
38 '[L]a Comédie, depuis qu'on a banni des théâtres tout ce qui pouvait souiller les oreilles les plus délicates, est l'un des plus innocents divertissements et le plus agréable à [la] bonne ville de Paris' [The Comedy, since all that could soil the most delicate ears has been banished from the theatres, is one of the most innocent diversions, and the most pleasant in the good town of Paris]: *Gazette de France*, ed. Renaudot, 6 janvier 1635.
39 Pellisson-Fontanier, *Relation*, pp. 23–4.
40 In 1635, the Académie produced four laudatory volumes of poetry, two dedicated to Louis (*Le Parnasse Royal* and *Les Palmae Regiae*) and two to Richelieu (*Le Sacrifice des Muses* and *Epicina Musarum*). As Couton has observed, the quality of the editions left no doubt that they had been officially financed: Couton, *Richelieu*, p. 8.
41 Ibid., pp. 25–6.
42 Although the play opened and closed at Diana's Temple, the scenic designs differed. It was the play's boast that 'no Scoene but that of the Pastoral was twice seene': Herbert, *Florimène*, sig. C1r.
43 Couton, *Richelieu*, p. 55.
44 Peacock, 'French Element'.
45 See Erica Veevers, 'A Masque Fragment by Aurelian Townshend', *Notes and Queries*, 210 (1965), p. 343.

46 Orgel, '*Florimène*', p. 137.
47 Cedric C. Brown, ed., *The Poems and Masques of Aurelian Townshend with Music by Henry Lawes and William Webb* (Reading, 1983), p. 109.
48 For my previous reservations about this attribution, see Karen Britland, 'Neoplatonic Identities: Literary Representation and the Politics of Queen Henrietta Maria's Court Circle' (unpublished PhD thesis, University of Leeds, 2000), pp. 208–15. I have since become more certain that Townshend's fragment should be associated with *Florimène.*
49 Aurelian Townshend, *The Ante-Masques* (?1635), sigs. *2r–*2v.
50 See Joel H. Caplan, 'A Man of Canada 1635', *Canadian Literature*, 110 (1986), pp. 191–2.
51 Townshend, *Ante-Masques*, sig. *2r.
52 Brown, *Aurelian Townshend*, p. 113.
53 Charles I had initially ceded English interests in Canada to the French in 1629 in the wake of the Ile de Rhé conflict. In 1632, the *Mercure François* reported that French and English deputies had met at Saint-Germain 'pour la restitution des choses prises par les subjets des uns des autres depuis le Traicté fait à Suze entre les deux Couronnes': *Mercure François*, 18 (Paris, 1633), p. 56.
54 Townshend, *Ante-Masques*, sig. *3v.
55 Lindley, ed., *Court Masques*, p. 33, lines 560–1.
56 Townshend, *Ante-Masques*, sig. *4r.
57 Ibid., sig. *3v.
58 National Library of Wales, Wynnstay 181, sig. 14r–v.
59 She married Thomas Arpe, Esq. He was probably the Mr Arpe who danced in *Salmacida Spolia* (1640).
60 Interestingly, a date of 'the last of December' was originally ascribed to the gift to Christian Vantelet in the queen's accounts. This has been corrected to 'xxiiith of February' in line with the gift to Mademoiselle Garnier. It is possible that this was a simple error of transcription, yet it could indicate a postponement of the wedding. Henrietta Maria gave birth to her daughter, Elizabeth, on 28 December 1635, making it unlikely that she would be able to attend a wedding three days later.
61 Veevers, *Images*, p. 135.
62 William Shelley's great grandmother was the maternal granddaughter of Sir Richard Sackville. It should be noted that Edward Sackville, earl of Dorset, was not Catholic.
63 Bailey, 'Queen Henrietta Maria', p. 27.
64 See Smuts, 'Puritan Followers', pp. 26–45.
65 Veevers, *Images*, p. 142.

9 MARIE DE MÉDICIS AND THE LAST MASQUES

1 Veevers, *Images*, pp. 134–49.
2 Parry, *Golden Age*, p. 199; Bentley, *Jacobean and Caroline Stage*, III, p. 214.
3 See Orgel and Strong, *Inigo Jones*, I, p. 72; Parry, *Golden Age*, pp. 199–203.

4 The masque is thought to be by Davenant, although it was excluded from his posthumous *Works* (1673). It is possible that it was such a collaborative effort he did not claim it.
5 William Davenant, *Britannia Triumphans*, in Orgel and Strong, *Inigo Jones*, II, pp. 660–703, lines 627–44.
6 William Davenant, *Luminalia*, in ibid., pp. 704–23, lines 89–90.
7 Veevers, *Images*, pp. 148–9.
8 Enid Welsford, *The Court Masque* (New York, 1927). Martin Butler has noted this was the first time that Jonson made use of the French structural model in one of his masques. See Bevington *et al.*, eds., *Works of Ben Jonson*.
9 Bordier, *Soleil*, p. 10.
10 Veevers, *Images*, p. 142.
11 See ibid.
12 Ibid., p. 143.
13 Ibid.
14 Anthony Stafford, *The Female Glory, or The Life and Death of Our Blessed Lady, the Holy Virgin Mary* (London, 1635), sigs. L5v–L6r. See also Veevers, *Images*, p. 144.
15 Veevers, *Images*, p. 145.
16 Ibid., p. 146.
17 In the words of Louis Battifol, 'Henri IV's debt to Florence was already greater than he could pay': Battifol, *Marie de Médicis and her Court*, trans. Mary King (London, 1908), p. 11.
18 See Sara Mamone, *Paris et Florence: deux capitales du spectacle pour une reine – Marie de Médicis*, trans. Sophie Bajard (Paris, 1990), pp. 53–4.
19 Ibid., p. 64.
20 Richelieu to Monsieur de Chavigni, 29 August 1638: in M. Avenel, ed., *Lettres, instructions et papiers d'état du Cardinal Richelieu*, 8 vols. (Paris, 1967), VI, p. 121.
21 *CSPV, 1636–9*, p. 417.
22 The princess of Faltzbourg is singled out in the ballet for particular mention.
23 (Jean Puget de la Serre), *Balet des princes indiens, dansé a l'arrivée de son A. R.* (Brussels, 1634), sig. D3v.
24 Veevers, *Images*, p. 148.
25 Anzolo Correr to the Doge and Senate, 4 September 1637: *CSPV, 1636–9*.
26 Ibid.
27 Ibid.
28 On Louis's entry into Lyon in 1622, the city took on the character of 'Heliopolis', saluting the young king with the inscription: 'Au Soleil de la France, à Louis XIII destructeur de la Guerre, le plus grand des Rois, la merveille de son siècle'. Léonard Gaultier's engraving of Louis XIII showed him in the guise of Apollo alongside Henri IV as Hercules on the title page of Jean Leclerc, *Théâtre géographique du Royaume de France* (Paris, 1620), while in 1621 he danced before the French court as Apollo.

29 Martin Butler, 'Politics and the Masque: *Salmacida Spolia*', in *Literature and the English Civil War*, ed. Thomas Healy and Jonathan Sawday (Cambridge, 1990), pp. 59–74, p. 66.
30 Orrell, 'Amerigo Salvetti', p. 25.
31 Butler, 'Politics and the Masque', p. 66.
32 Ibid., p. 67 and p. 69.
33 Sharpe, *Criticism and Compliment*, p. 253.
34 Davenant, *Salmacida Spolia*, in Lindley, ed., *Court Masques*, lines 179–80. All subsequent line references to *Salmacida Spolia* will be taken from this edition.
35 Ben Jonson, *The Masque of Augurs*, in *Ben Jonson*, ed. Herford *et al.*, VII, p. 633, lines 111–13.
36 Welsford, *The Court Masque*, p. 203.
37 Parry, *Golden Age*, p. 200.
38 See Gerald Kahan, *Jacques Callot: Artist of the Theatre* (Athens, Ga., 1976), pp. 54–9.
39 Interestingly, the *Balet des princes indiens* also contained the figure of 'la Deesse Discorde', danced, significantly, by 'un des Gentilhommes de Monsieur le Marquis de la Vieuville': (Puget de la Serre), *Balet des princes indiens*, sig. C4v.
40 Anzolo Correr to the Doge and Senate, 30 November 1638: *CSPV, 1636–9*, p. 475.
41 Caroline Hibbard, *Charles I and the Popish Plot* (Chapel Hill, 1983), p. 87.
42 B. Gerbier to Lord Feilding, 11/21 August 1638, HMC *Denbigh*, part V (London, 1911), p. 59; Anonymous squib addressed to the council, 'Reasons that ship and conduct money ought to be paid': *CSPD, 1639–40*, p. 246.
43 Mary de' Medici, *A Declaration of the Queene, mother of the most Christian King, Containing the reasons of her departure out of the Low-Countreys, and disavowing a manifest set out in her name upon the same argument* (London, 1639), p. 9. (A French version of this document bears the date 1638.)
44 Mamone, *Paris et Florence*, p. 237.
45 Ibid., p. 242.
46 Marrow, *Art Patronage*, p. 72.
47 Ibid., p. 29.
48 Ibid., pp. 68–9; Francis H. Dowley, 'French Portraits of Ladies as Minerva', *Gazette des Beaux-Arts*, 45 (1955), pp. 261–86, p. 264.
49 Marrow, *Art Patronage*, p. 69.
50 Marie's role as a peacekeeper had already found currency in English cultural production; Buckingham's 1626 entertainment saw her waving the kings of Europe together, and Waller's poem 'To the Queen Mother of France upon her Landing' hailed her as 'Great Queen of Europe! where thy offspring wears / All the chief crowns': see Orrell, 'Amerigo Salvetti', pp. 11–12; Edmund Waller, 'To the Queen Mother of France upon her Landing', in *The Poems of Edmund Waller*, ed. G. Thorn Drury, 2 vols. (London, 1901), I, p. 35, lines 1–2.
51 Butler, 'Politics and the Masque', p. 69.

52 Machiavelli's *Il principe* (1513) was dedicated to Lorenzo de Médicis (1492–1519), the father of Catherine de Médicis: see *The Prince*, ed. George Bull (London, 1961; repr. 1981), p. 29.
53 Orgel, *Impersonations*, p. 94. See chapter 1 above.
54 Francis Lenton, *Great Britain's Beauties: or, the female glory epitomized* (London, 1638), p. 4.
55 Compare Orgel and Strong, *Inigo Jones*, I, pp. 140–4 with II, p. 785.
56 Algernon Percy, earl of Northumberland, to his sister, the countess of Leicester, 5 December 1639: Bentley, *Jacobean and Caroline Stage*, III, p. 213. The countess of Carlisle, too, was sister to the earl: a fact that perhaps helps to explain her allegiances.
57 Butler, 'Politics and the Masque', p. 66 and p. 74, note 32.
58 Furthermore, during Charles II's reign, Percy Herbert's son, William, duke of Powis, was generally regarded as the chief of the Roman Catholic aristocracy: *DNB*, *sub.* Robert Dormer; *sub.* Percy Herbert; and *sub.* William Herbert. Veevers also registers Lady Carnarvon's Catholic connections: see Veevers, *Images*, p. 87.
59 G[eorge] S[andys], *Ouids Metamorphosis Englished* (Oxford and London, 1632), p. 122.
60 Ben Jonson, *The Masque of Queens*, in *Ben Jonson*, ed. Herford *et al.*, VII, pp. 306–13.
61 William Davenant, 'To the Queene, presented with a suit, in the behalfe of F.S. directed, from Orpheus Prince of Poets, To the Queene of Light; In favour of a young listner to his Harpe', in A. M. Gibbs, ed., *Sir William Davenant: The Shorter Poems, and Songs from the Plays and Masques* (Oxford, 1972), pp. 32–4. All subsequent line references to this poem will be taken from this edition.
62 Sheila ffolliott, 'Catherine de' Medici as Artemisia: Figuring the Powerful Widow', in *Rewriting the Renaissance: The Discourses of Sexual Difference in Early Modern Europe*, ed. Margaret W. Ferguson *et al.* (Chicago, 1986; repr. 1987), pp. 227–41, p. 230.
63 Quoted in Marrow, *Art Patronage*, p. 10.
64 Medici, *Declaration*, p. 7.
65 Marrow, *Art Patronage*, p. 56.

10 'TYER'D, IN HER BANISH'D DRESS': HENRIETTA MARIA IN EXILE

1 Lois Potter, *Secret Rites and Secret Writing: Royalist Literature 1641–1660* (Cambridge, 1989), p. 80.
2 Ibid., pp. 72–3.
3 Ibid., p. 79.
4 D. L., *The Scots Scovts Discoveries: by Their London Intelligencer* (London, 1642), sig. E1r.
5 See Lenton, *Great Britain's Beauties*, p. 4. This phrase was used by Lenton in connection with the duchess of Lennox. See chapter 9 above.

6 Tomlinson, 'She That Plays the King', pp. 201–2.
7 Madame [Françoise] de Motteville, *Mémoires de Madame de Motteville*, ed. Michaud et Poujoulat (Paris, 1838), p. 81.
8 Henrietta Maria's official state funeral at Saint Denis was conducted by the bishop of Amiens. However, Bossuet presided over a more intimate ceremony at Henrietta Maria's Chaillot convent where her heart was interred. See François Faure, *Oraison funèbre de Henriette-Marie de France* (Paris, 1670); Jacques Bossuet, *Oraison funèbre de Henriette-Marie de France, Reine d'Angleterre* (Paris, 1905).
9 Bossuet, *Oraison*, p. 24.
10 Ibid., p. 25.
11 Ibid., p. 19.
12 Ibid., p. 6.
13 Ibid., p. 19.
14 Charles, comte de Baillon, *Henriette-Marie de France, Reine d'Angleterre: étude historique suivie de ses lettres inédites* (Paris, 1877), p. 373.
15 Henrietta Maria writes, variously, 'si nous mettions toutes nos pierreries en gage, pour les manger sans rien faire, elles seroient perdues et nous aussy' [if we pawn all our jewels, in order to eat them without doing anything, they will be lost and us as well]; 'je mourray de faim devant que vous manquiés' [I will die of hunger before you go without]; 'je m'en vais souper, et, quand il couste de l'argent, il ne fault pas laisser gaster' [I am going to supper, and, because it costs money, it mustn't be wasted]; ibid., p. 377, p. 407 and p. 451.
16 For selected examples of this assertion, see ibid., pp. 369, 408, 434, 446, 467 and 480.
17 Ibid., pp. 381–2.
18 Mary Anne Everett Green, ed., *Letters of Queen Henrietta Maria, Including her Private Correspondence with Charles I* (London, 1857), p. 69.
19 Baillon, *Henriette-Marie*, p. 427.
20 Green, *Letters*, p. 120.
21 Anon., *The Kings Cabinet Opened* (London, 1645), sigs. G2r–G3v.
22 Purkiss, 'Gender, Power and the Body', p. 376.
23 G. B., *The Great Eclipse of the Sun, or Charles His Waine Over-clouded, by the evill Influence of the Moon, the malignancie of Ill-aspected Planets, and the Constellations of Retrograde and Irregular Starres* (London, 1644).
24 Ibid., p. 3.
25 Montagu, *The Shepheard's Paradise*, p. 38.
26 The phrase is Domna Stanton's, used, in her essay, to describe the women who nurtured seventeenth-century male *honnêteté*. See Stanton, '*Préciosité*', p. 126.
27 The pamphlet play is an adapted translation, perhaps by John Milton, of George Buchanan's *Baptistes Sive Calumnia* (1541).
28 Anon., *Tyrannicall-Government Anatomized: or, a discourse concerning evil-counsellors, being the life and death of John the Baptist and presented to the kings most excellent majesty by the Author* (London, 1642), p. 26.

29 See Andrew Marvell, 'Upon Appleton House', in *Andrew Marvell: Complete Poetry*, ed. George deF. Lord (London, 1984), p. 70, line 250. All subsequent line references to this poem will be taken from this edition.
30 Prynne, *Histriomastix*, p. 142.
31 [Anne Marie Louise d'Orléans], Mademoiselle de Montpensier, *Mémoires de Mademoiselle de Montpensier, fille de Gaston d'Orléans, frère de Louis XIII*, ed. Michaud et Poujoulat (Paris, 1838), p. 26. The translation is adapted from Agnes Strickland, *The Queens of England*, 6 vols. (London, 1901–4), IV, p. 240.
32 Montpensier, *Mémoires*, p. 26. The translation is from Strickland, *Queens*, IV, p. 240.
33 Strickland, *Queens*, IV, p. 240.
34 Abbé Fr. Duffo notes that the pension was 30,000 livres a month: see Duffo, *Henriette-Marie, Reine d'Angleterre (1609–1669)* (Paris, 1935), p. 24. Madame de Motteville records that it was 'dix ou douze mille écus par mois': Motteville, *Mémoires*, p. 84. A livre was valued at about one-third of an écu so these figures approximate each other.
35 Archives départementales de Val d'Oise, 68.H.8, troisième liasse, 'Papiers de Richard Foster, trésorier de la reine d'Angleterre'.
36 Cantarini inherited the rights to loans made by the banker Philip Burlamachi after the latter's death. The memo dates from the late 1640s.
37 Quoted in Mary Edmond, *Rare Sir William Davenant* (Manchester, 1987), p. 97.
38 On Newcastle, see Katie Whitaker, *Mad Madge: Margaret Cavendish, Duchess of Newcastle, Royalist, Writer and Romantic* (London, 2003), p. 101. See also Thomas Killigrew, *Thomaso: or, The Wanderer: A Comedy in two parts*, in Thomas Killigrew, *Comedies and Tragedies* (London, 1664), Part 1, Act 3, scene 1 (sig. Vv4r).
39 See British Library: Cosmo Manuche, 'The Banished Shepherdess', BL Add. 60273 (Castle Ashby Manuscripts, I), sig. 3r. Two copies of the play exist: one in the Huntington Library, and one in the British Library that is dedicated to Manuche's patron, James Compton, earl of Northampton.
40 See Dale B. J. Randall, *Winter Fruit: English Drama 1642–1660* (Lexington, 1995), p. 205; Nancy Klein Maguire, *Regicide and Restoration: English Tragicomedy, 1660–1671* (Cambridge, 1992), p. 46.
41 See Henry Killigrew, *The Conspiracy* (London, 1638), sig. E1v; and Henry Killigrew, *Pallantus and Eudora: a Tragoedie* (London, 1653), sig. E4v. The only substantial change to the scene in the 1653 edition comes in the song sung by Cleander's good angel where the word '*Clouds*' in line 9 is changed to '*Heavens*', and the phrase '*holy vision*' in line 10 is changed to '*lively Vision*'.
42 See Randall, *Winter Fruit*, p. 203.
43 Compare, for example, Alcidor's lament at the start of *Les Bergeries* in which he complains that, since the first time he laid eyes on Artenice, 'Je n'ay fait en tous lieux que plaindre mon tourment, / Sans espoir d'y trouver aucun soulagement' [I have done nothing but lament my torment everywhere, without hope of finding any relief]: Racan, *Les Bergeries*, 1.1.99–100.

44 Lesel Dawson, '"New Sects of Love": Neoplatonism and Constructions of Gender in Davenant's *The Temple of Love* and *The Platonick Lovers*', *Early Modern Literary Studies*, 8.1 (2002), paragraphs 1–36, paragraph 4 (http://www.shu.ac.uk/emls, accessed September 2003).
45 Ibid., paragraphs 1–3.
46 Ibid., paragraph 2.
47 Psalm 137, verses 5 and 6.
48 See Leslie Hotson, *The Commonwealth and Restoration Stage* (Cambridge, Mass., 1928), p. 23.
49 See her letter to Christine of Savoy [September 1646]: Ferrero, ed., *Lettres de Henriette-Marie*, p. 67.
50 See Hotson, *Commonwealth*, pp. 22–3. See also *Mercurius Candidus*, no. 1 (London, 20–28 January 1646/7).
51 *Mercurius Candidus*, sig. A4v.
52 See Leah S. Marcus, *The Politics of Mirth: Jonson, Herrick, Milton, Marvell, and the Defense of Old Holiday Pastimes* (Chicago, 1986), especially the discussion of Lovelace in chapter 6; Potter, *Secret Rites*; Marika Keblusek, 'Wine for Comfort: Drinking and the Royalist Exile Experience, 1642–1660', in *A Pleasing Sinne: Drink and Conviviality in Seventeenth Century England*, ed. Adam Smyth (Cambridge, 2004), pp. 55–68.
53 The poet Edmund Waller was also on the continent, as was John Denham.
54 See Ashbee and Lasocki, *English Court Musicians*. Edward Fremin, Simon de la Garde and William le Grand were all also paid both before and after the interregnum and might well have continued to serve the queen in exile. Notably, the harpist La Flelle passed much of the 1650s at the court of Christine of Savoy because Henrietta Maria felt she must forego music.
55 Hotson, *Commonwealth*, p. 21. They were disbanded in November 1646.
56 *The Kingdomes Weekly Intelligencer* (London, 23 February–2 March 1647); quoted in Hotson, *Commonwealth*, pp. 21–2.
57 Lynn Hulse, *Dramatic Works by William Cavendish* (Oxford, 1996), p. 100.
58 The debate on the observance of holy days was begun by the Westminster Assembly of Divines in the summer of 1643. In 1644, Christmas day fell on the last Wednesday of the month which, since 1641, had been nominated a fast day. However, it was not until 1645 that parliament abolished the observance of Christmas, Easter and Whitsuntide.
59 Dated 1646, but George Thomason annotates as 1645.
60 Anon., *The Arraignment, Conviction, and Imprisoning of Christmas* (London, 1646), p. 4.
61 Ibid., p. 3.
62 I am grateful to Stacey Jocoy Houck for many of the ideas about Christmas and royalists expressed here. These were outlined in her paper, 'Drive the Cold Winter Away: Christmas Songs as Royalist Propaganda', Richard Murphy Colloquium (2003), Oberlin College, Ohio.
63 There is also the possibility here that Madam Cut was a satirical portrait of a known 'factious' widow (Lady Carlisle?), a characterisation that would

increase the humour of the entertainment for those who recognised the connection.

64 Strickland, *Queens*, IV, p. 248.

65 Medici, *Declaration*, p. 6.

66 Motteville, *Mémoires*, p. 69.

67 Marie-Françoise Christout, *Le Ballet de cour de Louis XIV, 1643–72* (Paris, 1967), p. 39.

68 Although it is hard to prove, this production might well have been the pastoral *Nicandre e Fileno*, designed for six voices and set to music by Marco Marazzoli: see ibid.; Henry Prunières, *L'Opéra italien en France avant Lulli* (Paris, 1913), pp. 59–64.

69 See the comments of the Tuscan resident, quoted in Prunières, *L'Opéra*, pp. 81–2. Madame de Motteville remarked of this evening that it was cold and boring: Motteville, *Mémoires*, p. 98.

70 Christout, *Ballet de cour*, pp. 47–8, p. 258.

71 Archives du Ministère des Affaires Etrangères, Paris: 'Mémoires et Documents – France/Ceremonial' (numéro 1832); 'Le Roi donné a Diner a la Royne sa mere' (1647), sig. 173r–v.

72 Christout, *Ballet de cour*, pp. 50–1.

73 Ibid., p. 51.

74 The king, his mother and Mazarin watched from a gallery. See Archives du Ministère des Affaires Etrangères, Paris: 'Mémoires et Documents – France/Ceremonial' (numéro 1832), sig. 173r–v.

75 Montpensier, *Mémoires*, p. 35.

76 See especially the Archives du Ministère des Affaires Etrangères, Paris: Fonds de la Correspondance Politique – Angleterre (origines–1871), LI: dispatch to Mazarin, 14/24 August 1645, fol. 540r–541r; LII: dispatch to Mazarin, 21 May 1646, fols. 260r–261r; dispatch to Mazarin, 4 August 1646, fols. 475v–476v.

77 For example, see the problems surrounding the procession for the wedding of the duchess of Nevers to the King of Poland in 1645. Henrietta Maria eventually did not take part in this event: Archives du Ministère des Affaires Etrangères, Paris: 'Mémoires et Documents – France/Ceremonial' (numéro 1835); 'Mémoires et relations de Mr de Colosan' (1601–45), sig. 275v. See also Archives du Ministère des Affaires Etrangères, Paris: 'Mémoires et Documents – France/Ceremonial' (numéro 1827); 'Ceremonie du mariage de la Princesse Marie Louise de Gonzague', sigs. 29v–30r; and Bibliothèque nationale de France: 'Mémoires de M. de Sainctot', 4 vols., MS Fonds français 14120, IV, sigs. 36v–38r.

78 Motteville, *Mémoires*, p. 174.

79 Canova-Green, *La Politique-spectacle*, p. 67. John Evelyn attended the *Ballet des Fêtes de Bacchus* twice that May, once with Sir Richard Brown, the English resident in Paris: Evelyn, *Diary*, ed. E. S. de Beer, 6 vols. (Oxford, 1955), III, pp. 31–2.

80 Isaac de Benserade, *Ballet Royal de la Nuict*, in *Les Oeuvres de Monsieur de Benserade*, 2 vols. (Paris, 1698), II, p. 58.

81 Ibid., pp. 58–9.
82 Henrietta Anne's ballet dress might well be the 'robe de ballet qui avait servi à Mme' donated by the queen to her newly founded convent at Chaillot in 1654; see Archives du monastère de la Visitation: I, p. 63.
83 *The Weekly Intelligencer* (London, 16–23 May 1654); also quoted in Hotson, *Commonwealth*, pp. 136–7.
84 James Howell, *The Nuptials of Peleus and Thetis* (London, 1654), sig. A4v. The French original reads: 'Ma race est du plus pur sang / Des Dieux, et sur nos Montagnes, / On me voit tenir un rang / Tout autre que mes Compagnes; / Mon jeune et Royal aspect / Inspire avec le respect / La veritable Tendresse / Et c'est à moi qu'on s'adresse, / Quand on veut plaindre tout haut / Le sort des grandes Personnes, / Et dire tout ce qu'il faut / Sur la chute des Couronnes': Benserade, *Oeuvres*, II, p. 67.
85 Benserade, *Oeuvres*, II, p. 74. Literally translated, the stanza reads: 'Far from only fishing for coral here, in an unhappy and deadly place surrounded by the vast sea, I must apply myself like an expert to fish for everything that helps to regain a crown.'
86 Howell's translation went through two editions in 1654, demonstrating the reading public's continued interest in royal spectacle.
87 Canova-Green, *La Politique-spectacle*, p. 106.
88 Benserade, *Oeuvres*, II, p. 123.
89 Canova-Green, *La Politique-spectacle*, p. 107.
90 Ibid., p. 109.
91 *Mercurius Politicus* (London, 14–21 February 1656); also quoted in Hotson, *Commonwealth*, p. 137.
92 John Reresby, *Memoirs of Sir John Reresby*, ed. Andrew Browning (Glasgow, 1936), p. 30. Henrietta Maria continued to be honoured by the king who performed masquerades in her apartments and made a point of dancing his latest ballet for her in 1661: see Canova-Green, *La Politique-spectacle*, p. 69.
93 Henrietta Anne was betrothed to her cousin, the duc d'Orléans, in August 1660.
94 Reresby, *Memoirs*, p. 30.

EPILOGUE

1 Rigg played Medea in 1993. She has since been acclaimed for, among others, her roles in *Mother Courage* and *Who's Afraid of Virginia Woolf.*
2 See *Charles II: The Power and the Passion*, directed by Joe Wright for the BBC (London, 2004), episode 4.
3 British Library: Manuche, 'The Banished Shepherdess', BL Add. 60273, sig. 40v.
4 *Charles II: The Power and the Passion*, episode 1. See also Gardiner, *History*, IX (1884), p. 228.
5 See Baillon, *Henriette-Marie*, pp. 309–10.

6 See Archives du monastère de la Visitation, I, pp. 65–6; III, p. 16. See also Motteville, *Mémoires*, p. 285; Bossuet, *Oraison*, p. 31.
7 See Evelyn, *Diary*, III, p. 44.
8 Sales, *Regles*, pp. 38–40.
9 Archives du monastère de la Visitation, I, p. 314.
10 Father Cyprien de Gamache, 'Memoirs of the Mission in England of the Capuchin Friars of the Province of Paris from the year 1630 to 1669', in Birch, ed., *Court and Times*, II, p. 470.
11 Henrietta Haynes, *Henrietta Maria* (London, 1912), p. 296.
12 Archives du monastère de la Visitation, I, pp. 65–6; III, p. 16.
13 Ibid., III, p. 16.
14 Ibid., I, p. 21.
15 Ibid., II, p. 27.
16 Ibid., I, p. 29.
17 Ibid., p. 21.
18 Eventually, Mère L'Huillier, the mother superior, had to ask the queen not to do this so often: ibid., p. 29.
19 Ibid.
20 Montpensier, *Mémoires*, p. 83.
21 Anon., *Recueil des Portraits et Eloges en vers et en prose dedié à son altesse royalle Mademoiselle*, 2 vols. (Paris, 1659), I, pp. 54–7.
22 See Motteville, *Mémoires*, pp. 84–5.
23 Anon., *Recueil des Portraits*, I, p. 40.
24 Ibid., p. 56.
25 Ibid., p. 57.
26 Motteville, *Mémoires*, p. 85.
27 Ibid.
28 Ibid.
29 'Songez que si vous l'eussiez épousé . . . vous seriez maîtresse de vos volontés; vous vous serviriez de qui il vous plairoit': Montpensier, *Mémoires*, p. 211.
30 Ibid.
31 Gamache, 'Memoirs', in Birch, ed., *Court and Times*, II, pp. 424–5.

APPENDIX: AN EARLY ENTERTAINMENT BY AURELIAN TOWNSHEND

1 See Beal, 'Songs by Aurelian Townshend', pp. 243–60.
2 Ibid., p. 257.
3 Ibid., p. 248.
4 Ibid.
5 Ibid., pp. 255–6. The other note reads 'Troye 165/114 – waight' which Beal interprets as possibly referring to a sizeable piece of treasure weighing over ten pounds (p. 256).
6 Ibid., pp. 256–7.

7 Ibid., p. 246, lines 5–6. All subsequent line references will be taken from Beal's transcription.
8 The image of the golden fleece was often used in French panegyric at the time of royal weddings. See Canova-Green, 'L'Equivoque d'une célébration', pp. 20–2. See also Henrietta Maria's own wedding celebrations, during which she was likened to the golden fleece, and Charles to Jason: *Mercure François,* 11, p. 377.
9 Aurelian Townshend, *Tempe Restored,* in Orgel and Strong, *Inigo Jones,* II, p. 481, lines 169–71.
10 *DNB, sub.* Robert Rich.
11 Birch, ed., *Court and Times,* I, p. 206. The 13th March 1627 was a Tuesday, the 16th a Friday.
12 Sharpe, *Criticism and Compliment,* pp. 154–5.
13 Smuts, 'Puritan Followers', p. 37.
14 Ibid., p. 34.
15 Patricia Parker, *Literary Fat Ladies: Rhetoric, Gender, Property* (London, 1987), p. 129.
16 Ibid., p. 131.
17 See Butler, *Courtly Negotiations,* chapter 9. I am grateful to Professor Butler for his generosity in sharing his unpublished work.

Bibliography

ABBREVIATIONS

CSPD *Calendar of State Papers, Domestic Series*
CSPV *Calendar of State Papers, Venetian Series*
DNB *Dictionary of National Biography*
ELH *English Literary History*
ELR *English Literary Renaissance*
HMC Historical Manuscripts Commission
ODNB *Oxford Dictionary of National Biography*
PRO Public Record Office

MANUSCRIPTS

Archives départementales de Val d'Oise, 68.H.8, troisième liasse, 'Papiers de Richard Foster, trésorier de la reine d'Angleterre'

Archives du Ministère des Affaires Etrangères, Paris: Fonds de la Correspondance Politique – Angleterre (origines–1871), XLII, LI and LII

Archives du Ministère des Affaires Etrangères, Paris: 'Mémoires et Documents – France/Cérémonial' (numéro 1827); 'Cérémonie du mariage de la Princesse Marie Louise de Gonzague'

Archives du Ministère des Affaires Etrangères, Paris: 'Mémoires et Documents – France/Cérémonial' (numéro 1835); 'Mémoires et relations de Mr de Colosan' (1601–45)

Archives du Ministère des Affaires Etrangères, Paris: 'Mémoires et Documents – France/Cérémonial' (numéro 1836); 'Mémoires et relations de Mr de Colosan' (1644–97)

Archives du Ministère des Affaires Etrangères, Paris: 'Mémoires et Documents – France/Cérémonial' (numéro 1832); 'Le Roi donné a Diner a la Royne sa mere' (1647)

Archives du monastère de la Visitation, Paris: MS G-2: Soeur Marie-Henriette Revellois, 'Mémoires', 9 vols. (*c.* 1673–97)

Archives nationales, Paris, 'Instruction de la Reine Marie de medicis – a la Reine dangleterre sa fille marie-anriette de France', K 1303, numéro 1

Bibliothèque nationale de France, MS 22, 884
Bibliothèque nationale de France, MS Fonds français 12491
Bibliothèque nationale de France, MS Fonds français 14120, 'Mémoires de M. de Sainctot', 4 vols.
Bolsover Parish Records, Births 1603–1746 (M46, I)
Bristol Record Office, Ashton Court Muniments, AC/C/47-3
British Library, BL Add. 60273 (Castle Ashby Manuscripts, I): Cosmo Manuche, 'The Banished Shepherdess'
Brotherton Library, Special Collections, MS 97; Françoys Garnier de Blois, 'Histoire d'Ethelbert Roy de Kent et d'Edouard 2. Roy d'Angleterre'
National Library of Wales, Wynnstay 161
National Library of Wales, Wynnstay 174
National Library of Wales, Wynnstay 175
National Library of Wales, Wynnstay 178
National Library of Wales, Wynnstay 181
National Library of Wales, Wynnstay 182
PRO E351/2947
PRO E351/2948
PRO LR5/63
PRO LR5/64
PRO LR5/65
PRO SP 16/3, no. 112
PRO SP 16/185

WORKS PUBLISHED BEFORE 1700

Anon., *The Arraignment, Conviction, and Imprisoning of Christmas* (London, 1646)
Anon., *The Kings Cabinet Opened* (London, 1645)
Anon., *Recueil des plus beaux vers* (Paris, 1627)
Anon., *Recueil des Portraits et Eloges en vers et en prose dedié à son altesse royalle Mademoiselle*, 2 vols. (Paris, 1659)
Anon., *Les Royales Ceremonies faites en l'edification d'une Chapelle de Capucins à Londres en Angleterre, dans le Palais de la Roine* (Paris, 1632)
Anon., *The true relation of the Queenes departure from Falmouth* (London, 22 July 1644)
Anon., *Tyrannicall-Government Anatomized: or, a discourse concerning evil-counsellors, being the life and death of John the Baptist and presented to the kings most excellent majesty by the Author* (London, 1642)
B., G., *The Great Eclipse of the Sun, or Charles His Waine Over-clouded, by the evill Influences of the Moon, the malignancie of Ill-aspected Planets, and the Constellations of Retrograde and Irregular Starres* (London, 1644)
B., I. D., *Eclogue, ou Chant Pastoral sur les nopces des serenissimes princes Charles . . . & de Henriette Marie* (London, 1627)

Bassompierre, Maréchal [François] de, *Négociation du Maréchal de Bassompierre envoyé Ambassadeur Extraordinaire, en Angleterre de la part du Roy très-Chrestien, l'an 1626* (Cologne, 1668)
Bazire d'Amblainville, Gervais de, *Lycoris, ou l'heureuse bergère* (Rouen, 1604)
Bazire d'Amblainville, Gervais de, *La Princesse ou l'heureuse bergère* (Rouen, 1627)
Beaujoyeulx, Baltasar de, *Balet Comique de la Royne, faict aux nopces de Monsieur le Duc de Joyeuse et madamoyselle de Vaudemont sa soeur* (Paris, 1582)
Benserade, Isaac de, *Les Oeuvres de Monsieur de Benserade*, 2 vols. (Paris, 1698)
Bordier, René, *Grand Ballet de la Reyne representant le Soleil, dancé en la Salle du petit Bourbon, en l'annee mil six cens vingt & un* (Paris, 1621)
Bosc, Jacques du, *L'Honneste Femme*, 3rd edn (Paris, 1635)
Cotolendi, Charles, *Histoire de la Tres-Haute et Tres-Puissante Princesse Henriette-Marie de France, Reyne de la Grand' Bretagne* (Paris, 1694)
Faret, Nicolas, ed., *Recueil de Lettres Nouvelles*, 2 vols. (Paris, 1634)
Faure, François, *Oraison funèbre de Henriette-Marie de France* (Paris, 1670)
Finet, John, *Finetti Philoxenis: som choice observations of Sr John Finett Knight, and Master of the Ceremonies to the two last kings* (London, 1656)
Guarini, Giovanni Battista, *Il Pastor Fido*, trans. (John Dymoke) (London, 1633)
Herbert, Henry, *The Argument of the Pastorall of Florimène* (London, 1635)
Heywood, Thomas, *Apology for Actors* (London, 1612)
Heywood, Thomas, *Loves Mistresse: or the Queenes Masque* (London, 1640)
Howell, James, *The Nuptials of Peleus and Thetis* (London, 1654)
Killigrew, Henry, *The Conspiracy* (London, 1638)
Killigrew, Henry, *Pallantus and Eudora: a Tragoedie* (London, 1653)
Killigrew, Thomas, *Comedies and Tragedies* (London, 1664)
The Kingdomes Weekly Intelligencer (London, 23 February–2 March 1647)
L., D., *The Scots Scovts Discoveries: by Their London Intelligencer* (London, 1642)
Leclerc, Jean, *Théâtre géographique du Royaume de France* (Paris, 1620)
Lenton, Francis, *Great Britain's Beauties: or, the female glory epitomized* (London, 1638)
Malleville, Claude, *Poesies du Sieur de Malleville* (Paris, 1649)
Marston, John, *The Workes of Mr Iohn Marston, Being Tragedies and Comedies, Collected into One Volume* (London, 1633)
Medici, Mary de', *A Declaration of the Queene, mother of the most Christian King, Containing the reasons of her departure out of the Low-Countreys, and disavowing a manifest set out in her name upon the same argument* (London, 1639)
Mercure François, 11 (Paris, 1626)
Mercure François, 17 (Paris, 1633)
Mercure François, 18 (Paris, 1633)
Mercure François, 25 (Paris, 1644)
Mercurius Candidus, no. 1 (London, 20–28 January 1646/7)
Mercurius Politicus (London, 14–21 February 1656)

Montagu, Walter, *The Shepheard's Paradise: A Comedy Privately Acted before the Late king Charls by the Queen consort's Majesty, and Ladies of Honour* (London, 1659)
Pellisson-Fontanier, Paul, *Relation Contenant l'Histoire de l'Académie Françoise* (Paris, 1672)
Prynne, William, *Histriomastix: The Players Scourge or Actors Tragaedie* (London, 1633)
Puget de la Serre, Jean, *Les Amours du Roy et de la Reine* (Paris, 1625)
(Puget de la Serre, Jean), *Balet des princes indiens, dansé a l'arrivée de son A. R.* (Brussels, 1634)
(Racan), *L'Artenice* (London, (1626))
Recueil des Gazettes de l'année 1631 (Paris, 1632)
Recueil des Gazettes Nouvelles 1632 (Paris, 1633)
Recueil des Gazettes Nouuelles 1633 (Paris, 1634)
Recueil des Gazettes Nouuelles 1634 (Paris, 1635)
Recueil des Gazettes Nouvelles 1635 (Paris, 1636)
Rémy, Abraham, *La Galatée et les adventures du Prince Astiagés* (Paris, 1625)
Renaudot, Théophraste, ed., *Gazette de France* (Lyon, 1636)
Richards, Nathaniel, *The Celestiall Publican* (London, 1630/1)
Sales, St François de, *Regles de Sainct Augustin et Constitutions pour les Soeurs Religieuses de la Visitation saincte Marie* (Lyon, 1645)
S[andys], G[eorge], *Ouids Metamorphosis Englished* (Oxford and London, 1632)
Shirley, James, *The Bird in a Cage* (London, 1633)
Shirley, James, *The Young Admirall* (London, 1637)
Somaize, A. Baudeau de, *Le Grand Dictionnaire des Pretieuses* (Paris, 1661)
Stafford, Anthony, *The Female Glory, or The Life and Death of Our Blessed Lady, the Holy Virgin Mary* (London, 1635)
Townshend, Aurelian, *The Ante-Masques* (?1635)
Voiture, Vincent, *Les Oeuvres de Monsieur de Voiture* (Paris, 1650)
The Weekly Intelligencer (London, 16–23 May 1654)

WORKS AND EDITIONS OF WORKS PUBLISHED AFTER 1700

Ashmole, Elias, *The History of the Most Noble Order of the Garter* (London, 1715)
Avenel, M., ed., *Lettres, instructions et papiers d'état du Cardinal Richelieu*, 8 vols. (Paris, 1967)
Bailbé, Jacques, ed., *Saint-Amant: oeuvres*, 2 vols. (Paris, 1971)
Baillon, Charles, comte de, *Henriette-Marie de France, Reine d'Angleterre: étude historique suivie de ses lettres inédites* (Paris, 1877)
Bassompierre, Maréchal [François] de, *Journal de ma vie: mémoires du maréchal de Bassompierre*, 3 vols. (Paris, 1875)
Beaumont, Sir John, *The Theater of Apollo*, ed. W. W. Greg (London, 1926)
Berington, Joseph, ed., *The Memoirs of Gregorio Panzani* (London, 1793)

Bérulle, Pierre de, *Elévation sur sainte Madeleine*, ed. Joseph Beaude (Grenoble, 1998)

Bevington, David, Martin Butler and Ian Donaldson, eds., *The Cambridge Edition of the Works of Ben Jonson*, 6 vols. (Cambridge, forthcoming 2007)

Bossuet, J. B., *Discours sur la vie cachée en Dieu. Traité de la Concupiscence. Opuscules. Maximes et réflexions sur la Comédie* (Paris, 1821)

Bossuet, Jacques Bénigne, *Oraison funèbre de Henriette-Marie de France, Reine d'Angleterre* (Paris, 1905)

Bowers, Fredson, ed., *The Dramatic Works in the Beaumont and Fletcher Canon*, 10 vols. (1966–96)

Braunmuller, A. R., ed., *Macbeth* (Cambridge, 1997; repr. 2001)

Brown, Cedric C., ed., *The Poems and Masques of Aurelian Townshend with Music by Henry Lawes and William Webb* (Reading, 1983)

Dinet, Pierre, *Cinq livres des hieroglyphiques*, ed. Stephen Orgel (New York, 1979)

Donaldson, Ian, ed., *Ben Jonson: Poems* (Oxford, 1975)

Drury, G. Thorn, ed., *The Poems of Edmund Waller*, 2 vols. (London, 1901)

Drury, G. Thorn, ed., *The Poems of Thomas Randolph* (London, 1929)

Duffo, Abbé F., ed., *Marie de Médicis à sa fille Henriette de France Reyne d'Angleterre* (Lourdes, 1936)

Ebsworth, J. W., ed., *Poems and Masque of Thomas Carew* (London, 1893)

Evelyn, John, *Diary*, ed. E. S. de Beer, 6 vols. (Oxford, 1955)

Faugère, A. P., ed., *Journal d'un voyage à Paris en 1657–1658* (Paris, 1862)

Ferrero, Hermann, ed., *Lettres de Henriette-Marie de France, Reine d'Angleterre à sa soeur Christine duchesse de Savoie* (Rome, 1881)

Finet, John, *Ceremonies of Charles I: The Notebooks of John Finet, 1628–1641*, ed. Albert J. Loomie (New York, 1987)

Fletcher, John, *The Faithful Shepherdess*, ed. Cyrus Hoy, in *The Dramatic Works in the Beaumont and Fletcher Canon*, ed. Fredson Bowers, 10 vols. (1966–96), III (1976)

Gibbs, A. M., ed., *Sir William Davenant: The Shorter Poems, and Songs from the Plays and Masques* (Oxford, 1972)

Gibson, James M., ed., *Records of Early English Drama: Kent: Diocese of Canterbury*, 3 vols. (London, 2002)

Green, Mary Anne Everett, ed., *Letters of Queen Henrietta Maria, Including her Private Correspondence with Charles I* (London, 1857)

Griffin, Richard, Baron Braybrooke, ed., *The Private Correspondence of Jane, Lady Cornwallis, 1613–1644* (London, 1842)

Grillon, Pierre, ed., *Les Papiers de Richelieu: section politique intérieure*, 6 vols. (Paris, 1975–85)

Herford, C. H., Percy Simpson and Evelyn Simpson, eds., *Ben Jonson*, 11 vols. (Oxford, 1925–52)

Hippeau, M. C., ed., *Mémoires inédits du Comte Leveneur de Tillières* (Paris, 1862)

HMC, *The Manuscripts of the Earl of Denbigh*, part V (London, 1911)

HMC, *The Manuscripts of Henry Duncan Skrine, Esq.: Salvetti Correspondence, Eleventh Report*, Appendix, part I (London, 1887)
Hulse, Lynn, *Dramatic Works by William Cavendish* (Oxford, 1996)
Huntingdon Papers (The Archives of the Noble Family of Hastings), 2 vols. (London, 1926)
La Porte, Pierre de, *Mémoires de M. De La Porte, premier valet de chambre de Louis XIV* (Paris, 1791)
Lacroix, Paul M., ed., *Ballets et mascarades de cour sous Henri IV et Louis XIII (de 1581 à 1652)*, 6 vols. (Geneva, 1868–70)
Lindley, David, ed., *Court Masques: Jacobean and Caroline Entertainments 1605–1640* (Oxford, 1995)
Livret, M. Ch. L., ed., *Dictionnaire des Precieuses par le Sieur de Somaize*, 2 vols. (Paris, 1856)
Lord, George deF., ed., *Andrew Marvell: Complete Poetry* (London, 1984)
McClure, Norman Egbert, ed., *The Letters of John Chamberlain*, 2 vols. (Philadelphia, 1939)
Machiavelli, Niccolò, *The Prince*, ed. George Bull (London, 1961; repr. 1981)
Malone Society, *Collections*, II, 3 (Oxford, 1931)
Malone Society, *Collections*, X: *Dramatic Records in the Declared Accounts of the Office of Works, 1560–1640*, ed. F. P. Wilson and R. F. Hill (Oxford, 1975; repr. 1977)
Michaud J. F., et J. J. F. Poujoulat, eds., *Mémoires du Cardinal de Richelieu* (Paris, 1866)
Montagu, Walter, *The Shepherds' Paradise*, ed. Sarah Poynting (Oxford, 1997)
Montpensier, [Anne Marie Louise d'Orléans] Mademoiselle de, *Mémoires de Mademoiselle de Montpensier, fille de Gaston d'Orléans, frère de Louis XIII*, ed. J. F. Michaud et J. J. F. Poujoulat (Paris, 1838)
Motteville, Madame [Françoise] de, *Mémoires de Madame de Motteville*, ed. J. F. Michaud et J. J. F. Poujoulat (Paris, 1838)
Ovid, *Fasti*, trans. James George Frazer (Cambridge, Mass., 1931; repr. 1996)
Plato, *Symposium*, trans. Walter Hamilton (London, 1951)
Plato, *Timaeus and Critias*, trans. Desmond Lee (London, 1965; repr. 1977)
Poynting, Sarah, 'A Critical Edition of Walter Montagu's *The Shepherds' Paradise*, Acts 1–3' (unpublished doctoral thesis, University of Oxford, 2000)
Rabelais, François, *Gargantua – Pantagruel: les cinq livres. Version intégrale en français moderne*, 2 vols. (Paris, 1988)
Racan, Honorat de Bueil, sieur de, *Les Bergeries*, ed. Louis Arnould (Paris, 1937)
Reresby, John, *Memoirs of Sir John Reresby*, ed. Andrew Browning (Glasgow, 1936)
Sales, Francis de, *Introduction to the Devout Life*, trans. Michael Day (London, 1962)
Sales, St François de, *Introduction à la vie dévote*, ed. Etienne-Marie Lajeunie (Paris, 1962)
Seddon, P. R., ed., *Letters of John Holles 1587–1637*, 3 vols. (Nottingham, 1983)

Spenser, Edmund, *The Faerie Queene*, ed. Thomas P. Roche (London, 1978; repr. 1987)
Vivian, Percival, ed., *Campion's Works* (Oxford, 1909)
Winwood, Sir Ralph, *Memorials of State*, 3 vols. (London, 1725)

SECONDARY SOURCES

Abraham, Claude Kurt, *Gaston d'Orléans et sa cour: étude littéraire* (Chapel Hill, (1963))
Adams, Joseph Quincy, ed., *The Dramatic Records of Sir Henry Herbert, Master of the Revels, 1623–1673* (New Haven, 1917)
Adamson, J. S. A., 'Chivalry and Political Culture in Caroline England', in *Culture and Politics in Early Modern England*, ed. Kevin Sharpe and Peter Lake (Basingstoke, 1994), pp. 161–97
Albion, Gordon, *Charles I and the Court of Rome* (London, 1935)
Alneau, Joseph, *Les Grandes Dames du Palais-Royal (1635–1870)* (Paris, 1943)
Angelier, François, *St François de Sales* (Paris, 1997)
Arnould, Louis, *Racan (1589–1670): histoire critique de sa vie et de ses oeuvres* (Paris, 1896)
Aronson, Nicole, *Madame de Rambouillet ou la magicienne de la Chambre bleue* (Paris, 1988)
Ashbee, Andrew, and David Lasocki, *A Biographical Dictionary of English Court Musicians 1485–1714*, 2 vols. (Aldershot, 1998)
Astington, John H., *English Court Theatre 1558–1642* (Cambridge, 1999)
Bailey, Rebecca, 'Queen Henrietta Maria, the "Old Faith" and "Her Majesties Servants": Roman Catholicism and the Caroline Stage' (unpublished PhD thesis, Birkbeck College, University of London, 2003)
Barkan, Leonard, 'The Imperialist Arts of Inigo Jones', *Renaissance Drama*, 7 (1976), pp. 257–85
Battifol, Louis, *Marie de Médicis and her Court*, trans. Mary King (London, 1908)
Bawcutt, N. W., *The Control and Censorship of Caroline Drama: The Records of Sir Henry Herbert, Master of the Revels, 1623–73* (Oxford, 1996)
Beal, Peter, 'Songs by Aurelian Townshend, in the hand of Sir Henry Herbert, for an Unrecorded Masque by the Merchant Adventurers', *Medieval and Renaissance Drama in England*, 15 (2003), pp. 243–60
Bentley, Gerald Eades, *The Jacobean and Caroline Stage*, 7 vols. (Oxford, 1941–68)
Berry, Philippa, *Of Chastity and Power: Elizabethan Literature and the Unmarried Queen* (London, 1989)
Birch, Thomas, ed., *The Court and Times of Charles the First*, 2 vols. (London, 1848)
Booth, Roy, 'The First Female Professional Singers: Madam Coniack', *Notes and Queries*, 242 (1997)
Brewer, E. Cobham, *The Dictionary of Phrase and Fable* (London, 1894; repr. 1993)

Briggs, Robin, *Early Modern France 1560–1715* (Oxford, 1977; repr. 1979)
Britland, Karen, 'A Fairy-tale Marriage: The Myth of the Caroline Romance', in *The Spanish Match: Prince Charles' Journey to Madrid, 1623*, ed. Alexander Samson (Aldershot, forthcoming 2006)
Britland, Karen, 'Neoplatonic Identities: Literary Representation and the Politics of Queen Henrietta Maria's Court Circle' (unpublished PhD thesis, University of Leeds, 2000)
Butler, Judith, *Bodies that Matter: On the Discursive Limits of Sex* (London, 1993)
Butler, Martin, 'Ben Jonson's *Pan's Anniversary* and the Politics of Early Stuart Pastoral', *ELR*, 22.3 (1992), pp. 369–404
Butler, Martin, 'Courtly Negotiations', in *The Politics of the Stuart Court*, ed. David Bevington and Peter Holbrook (Cambridge, 1998), pp. 20–40
Butler, Martin, *Courtly Negotiations: The Early Stuart Masque and Political Culture* (forthcoming)
Butler, Martin, 'Entertaining the Palatine Prince: Plays on Foreign Affairs, 1635–1637', *ELR*, 13 (1983), pp. 319–44
Butler, Martin, 'Politics and the Masque: *Salmacida Spolia*', in *Literature and the English Civil War*, ed. Thomas Healy and Jonathan Sawday (Cambridge, 1990)
Butler, Martin, 'Reform or Reverence? The Politics of the Caroline Masque', in *Theatre and Government under the Early Stuarts*, ed. J. R. Mulryne and Margaret Shewring (Cambridge, 1993), pp. 118–56
Butler, Martin, *Theatre and Crisis 1632–1642* (Cambridge, 1984)
Canova-Green, Marie-Claude, 'L'Equivoque d'une célébration: les fêtes du mariage de Louis XIII et d'Anne d'Autriche à Bordeaux (1615)', *XVIIe Siècle*, 222 (2004), pp. 3–24
Canova-Green, Marie-Claude, 'Le Mariage du lys et de la rose, ou les fêtes de l'alliance d'Angleterre (1625)' (unpublished conference paper)
Canova-Green, Marie-Claude, *La Politique-spectacle au grand siècle: les rapports franco-anglais* (Paris, 1993)
Canova-Green, Marie-Claude, 'Remarques sur la datation et l'attribution de ballets de cour sous le règne de Louis XIII', *Dix-septième Siècle* (1987), pp. 421–6
Caplan, Joel H., 'A Man of Canada 1635', *Canadian Literature*, 110 (1986), pp. 191–2
Christout, Marie-Françoise, *Le Ballet de cour de Louis XIV, 1643–72* (Paris, 1967)
Clark, A. M., *Thomas Heywood: Playwright and Miscellanist* (Oxford, 1931)
Clark, Ira, *Professional Playwrights: Massinger, Ford, Shirley, and Brome* (Lexington, 1992)
Cogswell, Thomas, *The Blessed Revolution: English Politics and the Coming of War, 1621–1624* (Cambridge, 1989)
Cogswell, Thomas, *Home Divisions: Aristocracy, the State and Provincial Conflict* (Manchester, 1998)
Colvin, H. M., ed., *The History of the King's Works*, 6 vols. (London, 1982), IV, 2
Como, David R., 'Predestination and Political Conflict in Laud's London', *The Historical Journal*, 46.2 (2003), pp. 263–94

Cottret, Bernard, 'Diplomatie et éthique de l'état: l'ambassade d'Effiat en Angleterre et le mariage de Charles Ier d'Angleterre et d'Henriette-Marie de France', in *L'Etat baroque: regards sur la pensée politique de la France du premier XVIIe siècle*, ed. Henry Méchoulan (Paris, 1985), pp. 221–42

Couton, Georges, *Richelieu et le théâtre* (Lyon, 1986)

D'Ancona, Mirella Levi, *The Garden of the Renaissance: Botanical Symbolism in Italian Painting* (Florence, 1977)

d'Anthenaise, Claude, Michel Richard and Philippe Martial, *Palais du Luxembourg* (Paris, 1992)

Dawson, Lesel, '"New Sects of Love": Neoplatonism and Constructions of Gender in Davenant's *The Temple of Love* and *The Platonick Lovers*', *Early Modern Literary Studies*, 8.1 (2002), paragraphs 1–36 (http://www.shu.ac.uk/emls, accessed September 2003)

Delorme, Philippe, *Histoire des reines de France: Marie de Médicis* (Paris, 1998)

Donagan, Barbara, 'A Courtier's Progress: Greed and Consistency in the Life of the Earl of Holland', *The Historical Journal*, 19 (1976), pp. 317–53

Dowley, Francis H., 'French Portraits of Ladies as Minerva', *Gazette des Beaux-Arts*, 45 (1955), pp. 261–86

Drakakis, John, 'Shakerley Marmion and the Politics of Dancing', unpublished seminar paper given at the University of Stirling, 12 April 2004

duBois, Page, *Centaurs and Amazons: Women and the Pre-History of the Great Chain of Being* (Michigan, 1982; repr. 1991)

Duffo, Abbé Fr., *Henriette-Marie, Reine d'Angleterre (1609–1669)* (Paris, 1935)

Dutton, Richard, '"Discourse in the Players, Though no Disobedience": Sir Henry Herbert's Problems with the Players and Archbishop Laud, 1632–34', *Ben Jonson Journal*, 5 (1998), pp. 37–61

Edmond, Mary, *Rare Sir William Davenant* (Manchester, 1987)

Feil, J. P., 'Dramatic References from the Scudamore Papers', *Shakespeare Survey* (1958), pp. 107–16

ffolliott, Sheila, 'Catherine de' Medici as Artemisia: Figuring the Powerful Widow', in *Rewriting the Renaissance: The Discourses of Sexual Difference in Early Modern Europe*, ed. Margaret W. Ferguson, Maureen Quilligan and Nancy J. Vickers (Chicago, 1986; repr. 1987), pp. 227–41

Finaldi, Gabriele, 'Orazio Gentileschi at the Court of Charles I', in *Orazio Gentileschi at the Court of Charles I*, ed. Gabriele Finaldi (London, 1999), pp. 9–37

Fisher, Will, 'The Renaissance Beard: Masculinity in Early Modern England', *Renaissance Quarterly*, 54 (2001), pp. 155–87

Foster, Leonard, 'Two Drafts by Weckherlin of a Masque for the Queen of England', *German Life & Letters*, 18 (1964–5), pp. 258–63

Garber, Marjorie, *Vested Interests: Cross-Dressing and Cultural Anxiety* (London, 1993)

Gardiner, Samuel R., *History of England from the Accession of James I to the Outbreak of the Civil War, 1603–1642*, 10 vols. (London, 1883–4)

Gibson, Wendy, *Women in Seventeenth-Century France* (Basingstoke, 1989)

Gordon, D. J., 'Ben Jonson's *Haddington Masque*: The Story and the Fable (1947)', in *The Renaissance Imagination: Essays and Lectures by D J. Gordon*, ed. Stephen Orgel (Berkeley, 1975), pp. 185–93

Gordon, D. J., 'Poet and Architect: The Intellectual Setting of the Quarrel Between Ben Jonson and Inigo Jones', *Journal of the Warburg and Courtauld Institutes*, 12 (1949), pp. 152–78

Gordon, D. J., 'Rubens and the Whitehall Ceiling', in *The Renaissance Imagination: Essays and Lectures by D.J. Gordon*, ed. Stephen Orgel (Berkeley, 1975; repr. 1980), pp. 24–50

Gossett, Suzanne, '"Man-maid, Begone!" Women in Masques', in *Women in the Renaissance*, ed. Kirby Farrell, Elizabeth H. Hageman and Arthur F. Kinney (Amherst, 1990), pp. 118–35

Gough, Melinda, 'A Newly Discovered Performance by Henrietta Maria', *Huntington Library Quarterly*, 65.3–4 (2002), pp. 435–47

Gough, Melinda J., '"Not as Myself": The Queen's Voice in *Tempe Restored*', *Modern Philology*, 101.1 (2003), pp. 48–67

Gourier, Françoise, *Etude des oeuvres poétiques de Saint-Amant* (Paris, 1961)

Greene, Thomas M., 'The King's One Body in the *Balet Comique de la Royne*', *Yale French Studies*, 86 (1994), pp. 75–93

Gregory, John, *The Neoplatonists: A Reader*, 2nd edn (London, 1999)

Griselle, Eugène, *Etat de la maison du Roi Louis XIII* (Paris, 1912)

Hackett, Helen, 'Yet Tell Me Some Such Fiction: Lady Mary Wroth's *Urania* and the "Femininity" of Romance', in *Women, Texts and Histories 1575–1760*, ed. Clare Brant and Diane Purkiss (London, 1992), pp. 39–68

Harbage, Alfred, *Cavalier Drama: An Historical and Critical Supplement to the Study of the Elizabethan and Restoration Stage* (London, 1936)

Harris, John, and Gordon Higgot, *Inigo Jones: Complete Architectural Drawings* (New York, 1989)

Haynes, Henrietta, *Henrietta Maria* (London, 1912)

Hibbard, Caroline, *Charles I and the Popish Plot* (Chapel Hill, 1983)

Hibbard, Caroline, 'The Role of a Queen Consort: The Household and Court of Henrietta Maria, 1625–1642', in *Princes, Patronage and the Nobility: The Court at the Beginning of the Modern Age, c. 1450–1650*, ed. Ronald G. Asch and Adolf M. Birke (Oxford, 1991), pp. 393–414

Hodgson-Wright, Stephanie, 'Beauty, Chastity and Wit: Feminising the Centre-stage', *Women and Dramatic Production 1550–1700*, ed. Alison Findlay and Stephanie Hodgson-Wright (Harlow, 2000), pp. 42–67

Hotson, Leslie, *The Commonwealth and Restoration Stage* (Cambridge, Mass., 1928)

Howard, Skiles, *The Politics of Courtly Dancing in Early Modern England* (Amherst, 1998)

Irigaray, Luce, *Speculum of the Other Woman* (Ithaca, 1985; repr. 1992)

Istria, Cécile, '*The Faithful Shepherdess*, une pastorale protestante' (unpublished paper given at the Epistémè seminar, Université de Paris 3, February 2001)

Jacquot, Jean, 'La Reine Henriette-Marie et l'influence française dans les spectacles à la cour de Charles Ier', *9e Cahier de l'Association Internationale des Etudes Françaises* (Paris, 1957), pp. 128–60

Jocoy Houck, Stacey, 'Drive the Cold Winter Away: Christmas Songs as Royalist Propaganda', unpublished paper from the Richard Murphy Colloquium (2003), Oberlin College, Ohio

Kahan, Gerald, *Jacques Callot: Artist of the Theatre* (Athens, Ga., 1976)

Keblusek, Marika, 'Wine for Comfort: Drinking and the Royalist Exile Experience, 1642–1660', in *A Pleasing Sinne: Drink and Conviviality in Seventeenth Century England*, ed. Adam Smyth (Cambridge, 2004), pp. 55–68

Kermina, Françoise, *Marie de Médicis: reine, régente et rebelle* (Paris, 1979)

Kleinbaum, Abby Wettan, *The War Against the Amazons* (New York, 1983)

Knowles, James, '"Can Ye Not Tell a Man from a Marmoset?" Apes and Others on the Early Modern Stage', in *Renaissance Beasts: Of Animals, Humans, and Other Wonderful Creatures*, ed. Erica Fudge (Urbana, 2004), pp. 138–63

Knowles, James, *Criticism and Consensus: Politics and Political Culture in the Masque* (forthcoming)

Knowles, James, '"The Faction of the Flesh": Orientalism and the Caroline Masque', in *The 1630s: Interdisciplinary Approaches*, ed. Julie Sanders and Ian Atherton (Manchester, forthcoming 2005)

Landes, Joan B., *Women and the Public Sphere* (London, 1988)

Livingston, Meg Powers, 'Herbert's Censorship of Female Power in Fletcher's *The Woman's Prize*' (unpublished paper given at the 1998 Group for Early Modern Cultural Studies conference)

Livingston, Meg Powers, 'The Reinvention of John Fletcher as Caroline Court Playwright' (unpublished paper given at the 1999 Group for Early Modern Cultural Studies conference)

Loftis, John, 'English Renaissance Plays from the Spanish *Comedia*', *ELR*, 14 (1984), pp. 230–48

Lougee, Carolyn C., *Le Paradis des Femmes: Women, Salons and Social Stratification in Seventeenth-Century France* (Princeton, 1976)

Loxley, James, *Royalism and Poetry in the English Civil Wars: The Drawn Sword* (Basingstoke, 1997)

McGee, C. E., and J. C. Meagher, 'Preliminary Checklist of Tudor and Stuart Entertainments: 1625–1634', *Research Opportunities in Renaissance Drama*, 36 (1997), pp. 23–85

McGowan, Margaret M., *L'Art du ballet de cour en France (1581–1643)* (Paris, 1963)

McKerrow, Ronald B., 'Edward Allde as a Typical Trade Printer', in *Ronald Brunlees McKerrow: A Selection of His Essays*, ed. John P. Immroth (Metuchen, 1974), pp. 94–131

McLuskie, Kathleen, 'The Plays and the Playwrights: 1613–42', in *The Revels History of Drama in English IV, 1613–1660*, ed. Philip Edwards (London, 1981; repr. 1996), pp. 129–258

McManus, Clare, *Women on the Renaissance Stage: Anna of Denmark and Female Masquing in the Stuart Court, 1590–1619* (Manchester, 2002)

McMullan, Gordon, *The Politics of Unease in the Plays of John Fletcher* (Amherst, 1994)

Magne, Emile, *Le Plaisant Abbé de Boisrobert, fondateur de l'Académie française 1592–1662*, 2nd edn (Paris, 1909)

Maguire, Nancy Klein, *Regicide and Restoration: English Tragicomedy, 1660–1671* (Cambridge, 1992)

Mamone, Sara, *Paris et Florence: deux capitales du spectacle pour une reine – Marie de Médicis*, trans. Sophie Bajard (Paris, 1990)

Marcus, Leah S., *The Politics of Mirth: Jonson, Herrick, Milton, Marvell, and the Defense of Old Holiday Pastimes* (Chicago, 1986)

Marrow, Deborah, *The Art Patronage of Maria de' Medici* (Michigan, 1978; repr. 1982)

Marshal, Rosalind K., *Henrietta Maria: The Intrepid Queen* (London, 1990)

Mathieu-Castellani, Gisèle, 'La Poétique du fleuve dans les *Bergeries* de Racan', in *Le Genre pastoral en Europe du XVe au XVIIe siècle: Actes du colloque international tenu à Saint-Etienne du 28 septembre au 1er octobre 1978* (Saint-Etienne, 1980), pp. 223–32

Millar, Oliver, *Sir Peter Lely 1618–80* (London, 1978)

Mongrédien, Georges, *La Journée des Dupes, 10 novembre 1630* (Paris, 1961)

Munro, Lucy, *Children of the Queen's Revels: A Jacobean Theatre Repertory* (Cambridge, forthcoming 2005)

Murdoch, J., and V. J. Murrell, 'The Monogrammist, DG: Dwarf Gibson and his Patrons', *Burlington Magazine*, 123 (1981), pp. 282–9

Nagler, A. M., *Theatre Festivals of the Medici, 1539–1637* (New Haven, 1964)

Nicoll, Allardyce, *Stuart Masques and the Renaissance Stage* (London, 1937)

Nouvet, Clare, 'An Impossible Response: The Disaster of Narcissus', *Yale French Studies*, 79 (1991), pp. 103–34

Orgel, Stephen, '*Florimène* and the Ante-Masques', *Renaissance Drama*, 4 (1971), pp. 135–53

Orgel, Stephen, *The Illusion of Power* (Berkeley, 1975; 1991)

Orgel, Stephen, *Impersonations: The Performance of Gender in Shakespeare's England* (Cambridge, 1996)

Orgel, Stephen, 'Plato, the Magi, and Caroline Politics: A Reading of *The Temple of Love*', *Word and Image*, 4.3–4 (1988), pp. 663–77

Orgel, Stephen, and Roy Strong, *Inigo Jones: The Theatre of the Stuart Court*, 2 vols. (Berkeley, 1973)

Orrell, John, 'Amerigo Salvetti and the London Court Theatre, 1616–1640', *Theatre Survey*, 20.1 (1979), pp. 1–26

Orrell, John, 'The Paved Court Theatre at Somerset House', *British Library Journal*, 3.1 (1977), pp. 13–19

Orrell, John, *The Theatres of Inigo Jones and John Webb* (Cambridge, 1985)

Parker, Patricia, *Literary Fat Ladies: Rhetoric, Gender, Property* (London, 1987)

Parrish, Jean, and William A. Jackson, 'Racan's *L'Artenice*, an Addition to the English Canon', *Harvard Library Bulletin*, 14 (1960), pp. 183–90
Parry, Graham, *The Golden Age Restor'd: The Culture of the Stuart Court, 1603–42* (Manchester, 1981)
Patterson, Annabel, *Pastoral and Ideology: Virgil to Valéry* (Oxford, 1988)
Patterson, W. B., *King James VI and I and the Reunion of Christendom* (Cambridge, 1997; repr. 2000)
Pauphilet, Albert, Louis Pichard and Robert Barroux, eds., *Dictionnaire des lettres françaises: le XVIIe siècle*, 2nd edn, rev. Patrick Dandrey (Paris, 1996)
Peacock, John, 'The French Element in Inigo Jones's Masque Designs', in *The Court Masque*, ed. David Lindley (Manchester, 1984), pp. 149–68
The Stage Designs of Inigo Jones (Cambridge, 1995)
Pembroke, Sidney, Sixteenth Earl of, *A Catalogue of the Paintings and Drawings in the Collection at Wilton House, Salisbury, Wiltshire* (London, 1968)
Plowden, Alison, *Henrietta Maria: Charles I's Indomitable Queen* (Stroud, 2001)
Potter, Lois, *Secret Rites and Secret Writing: Royalist Literature 1641–1660* (Cambridge, 1989)
Prescott, Anne Lake, 'The Stuart Masque and Pantagruel's Dreams', *ELH*, 51.3 (1984), pp. 407–30
Prunières, Henry, *L'Opéra italien en France avant Lulli* (Paris, 1913)
Purkiss, Diane, 'Gender, Power and the Body: Some Figurations of Femininity in Milton and Seventeenth-Century Women's Writing' (unpublished doctoral thesis, University of Oxford, 1991)
Randall, Dale B. J., *Winter Fruit: English Drama 1642–1660* (Lexington, 1995)
Ravelhofer, Barbara, 'Bureaucrats and Courtly Cross-Dressers in the *Shrovetide Masque* and *The Shepherd's Paradise*', *ELR*, 29.1 (1999), pp. 75–96
Ravelhofer, Barbara, 'The Stuart Masque: Dance, Costume, and Remembering' (unpublished doctoral thesis, University of Cambridge, 1999)
Ravelhofer, Barbara, '"Virgin Wax" and "Hairy Men-Monsters": Unstable Movement Codes in the Stuart Masque', in *The Politics of the Stuart Court Masque*, ed. David Bevington and Peter Holbrook (Cambridge, 1998), pp. 244–72
Richards, Kenneth, 'Queen Henrietta Maria as a Patron of the Drama', *Studia Neophilologica*, 42 (1970), pp. 9–24
Rowan, Mary M., 'Between Salon and Convent: Madame de Rohan, a Precious Abbess', *Papers on French Seventeenth-Century Literature*, 12.22 (1985), pp. 191–207
Sanders, Julie, 'Caroline Salon Culture and Female Agency: The Countess of Carlisle, Henrietta Maria, and Public Theatre', *Theatre Journal*, 52 (2000), pp. 449–64
Schreiber, Roy E., *The First Carlisle: Sir James Hay, First Earl of Carlisle as Courtier, Diplomat and Entrepreneur, 1580–1636* (Philadelphia, 1984)
Sharpe, Kevin, *Criticism and Compliment: The Politics of Literature in the England of Charles I* (Cambridge, 1987)
Sharpe, Kevin, *The Personal Rule of Charles I* (New Haven, 1992)

Shell, Alison, *Catholicism, Controversy and the English Literary Imagination, 1558–1660* (Cambridge, 1999)

Smuts, Malcolm, *Court Culture and the Origins of the Royalist Tradition in Early Stuart England* (Philadelphia, 1987)

Smuts, R. Malcolm, 'The Puritan Followers of Henrietta Maria in the 1630s', *The English Historical Review*, 93.366 (1978), pp. 26–45

Spivak, Gayatri Chakravorty, 'Echo', *New Literary History*, 24 (1993), pp. 17–43

Stähler, Axel, 'Inigo Jones's *Tempe Restored* and Alessandro Piccolomini's *Della Institutione morale*', *The Seventeenth Century*, 18.2 (2003), pp. 180–210

Stanton, Domna, 'The Fiction of *Préciosité* and the Fear of Women', *Yale French Studies*, 62 (1981), pp. 107–34

Strickland, Agnes, *The Queens of England*, 6 vols. (London, 1901–4)

Strong, Roy, *Van Dyck: Charles I on Horseback* (London, 1972)

Sykes, Susan A., 'Henrietta Maria, Queen of Scotland and England', in *Grove Dictionary of Art Online* (Oxford, 2004), accessed August 2004 (http://www.groveart.com)

Sykes, Susan Alexandra, 'Henrietta Maria's "House of Delight": French Influence and Iconography in the Queen's House, Greenwich', *Apollo*, 133 (1991), pp. 332–6

Tillinac, Denis, *L'Ange du désordre: Marie de Rohan, duchesse de Chevreuse* (Paris, 1985)

Tomlinson, Sophie, 'She That Plays the King: Henrietta Maria and the Threat of the Actress in Caroline Culture', in *The Politics of Tragicomedy*, ed. Gordon McMullan and Jonathan Hope (London, 1992), pp. 189–207

Tomlinson, Sophie, 'Theatrical Vibrancy on the Caroline Court Stage', in *Women and Culture at the Courts of the Stuart Queens*, ed. Clare McManus (Basingstoke, 2003), pp. 186–203

Tomlinson, Sophie, 'Theatrical Vibrancy on the Female Court Stage? *Tempe Restored* and *The Shepherds' Paradise*' (unpublished conference paper given at 'The Queen's Court: Elite Female Cultural Production and the Cultures of the Early Stuarts (1603–42)', Centre for the Study of the Renaissance, University of Warwick, 18–19 April 1998)

Tomlinson, Sophie, 'Theatrical Women: The Female Actor in English Theatre and Drama 1603–1670' (unpublished doctoral thesis, University of Cambridge, 1995)

Tomlinson, Sophie, 'Too Theatrical? Female Subjectivity in Caroline and Interregnum Drama', *Women's Writing*, 6.1 (1999), pp. 65–79

Tomlinson, Sophie, *Women on Stage in Stuart Drama* (Cambridge, forthcoming 2006)

Trill, Suzanne, '"The Glass that Mends the Looker's Eyes": The Mirror, the Text and the Gaze in *Salve Deus Rex Judaeorum*' (unpublished conference paper given at 'The Queen's Court: Elite Female Cultural Production and the Cultures of the Early Stuarts (1603–42)', Centre for the Study of the Renaissance, University of Warwick, 18–19 April 1998)

Veevers, Erica, *Images of Love and Religion: Queen Henrietta Maria and Court Entertainments* (Cambridge, 1989)

Veevers, Erica, 'A Masque Fragment by Aurelian Townshend', *Notes and Queries*, 210 (1965), p. 343

Walls, Peter, *Music in the English Courtly Masque 1604–1640* (Oxford, 1996)

Wedgwood, C. V., *Truth and Opinion* (London, 1960)

Welsford, Enid, *The Court Masque* (New York, 1927)

Whitaker, Katie, *Mad Madge: Margaret Cavendish, Duchess of Newcastle, Royalist, Writer and Romantic* (London, 2003)

Wynne-Davies, Marion, 'The Queen's Masque: Renaissance Women and the Seventeenth-Century Court Masque', in *Gloriana's Face: Women, Public and Private, in the English Renaissance*, ed. S. P. Cerasano and Marion Wynne-Davies (Detroit, 1992), pp. 79–104

Yarnall, Judith, *Transformations of Circe: The History of an Enchantress* (Urbana, 1994)

Yon, Bernard, 'La Conversation dans *L'Astrée*, texte littéraire et art de vivre', *Dix-septième Siècle*, 179.2 (1993), pp. 273–89

Index

Note: literary works can be found under authors' names, except ballets de cour *which, for ease of referencing, are listed under* 'French ballets'.